LECTURES ON
REVIVALS OF RELIGION

WILLIAM B. SPRAGUE

LECTURES

ON

REVIVALS OF RELIGION

WILLIAM B. SPRAGUE

THE BANNER OF TRUTH TRUST

THE BANNER OF TRUTH TRUST
3 Murrayfield Road, Edinburgh EH12 6EL
P O Box 621, Carlisle, Pennsylvania 17013, USA

*

First published 1832
First Banner of Truth Trust edition 1958
Reprinted 1978

ISBN 0 85151 276 3

PRINTED IN GREAT BRITAIN BY OFFSET LITHOGRAPHY BY
BILLING AND SONS LTD, GUILDFORD AND LONDON

FOREWORD

This work was first published in 1832 by Dr. Sprague, who was a minister in the Presbyterian Church in the U.S.A. It was introduced to this country by two eminent ministers, one of whom was John Angell James, the great predecessor of Dr. R. W. Dale at Carr's Lane, Birmingham and well-known author of " The Anxious Enquirer," a book greatly used in the conviction and conversion of sinners in the nineteenth century.

I am glad to commend such a book at the present time for the following reasons.

The first and most important reason is that I am profoundly convinced that the greatest need in the world today is revival in the Church of God. Yet alas! the whole idea of revival seems to have become strange to so many good Christian people. There are some who even seem to resent the very idea and actually speak and write against it. Such an attitude is due both to a serious misunderstanding of the scriptures, and to a woeful ignorance of the history of the Church. Anything therefore that can instruct God's people in this matter is very welcome.

My second reason is that this particular book gives this instruction in an exceptionally fine manner. Dr.

Sprague's own treatment of the subject is scriptural, theological and balanced. Then to supplement that there is an Appendix of twenty letters by such great, saintly and scholarly men of God as Archibald Alexander, Samuel Miller, Ashbel Green and the seraphic Edward Payson dealing with their own experience in revivals. The result is a volume of outstanding merit and exceptional worth.

My third reason for commending it is that I do not know of any better preparation for the meetings that are to be held in 1959 in various places to recall the great revival of 1857-59, than the careful and prayerful study of this book.

My prayer is that as we read it and are reminded of " Our glorious God," and of His mighty deeds in times past among His people, a great sense of our own un-worthiness and inadequacy, and a corresponding longing for the manifestation of His glory and His power will be created within us. His " arm is not shortened." May this book stir us all to plead with Him to make bare that arm and to stretch it forth again, that His enemies may be confounded and scattered, and His people's hearts be filled with glad-ness and rejoicing.

D. M. LLOYD-JONES.

Westminster Chapel
December 1958.

PUBLISHERS' NOTE

In seeking to make available again this once famous work the Publishers' experienced considerable difficulty in obtaining a copy which could be reprinted by Photo-Litho Offset. It was found that the British edition of Sprague's Lectures was inferior to the original American edition, but the latter was never circulated in this country and consequently unobtainable. *The Evangelical Library*, however, informed us that there was in their possession a copy of the American first edition (1832). This particular copy had been sent by the author to the English Evangelical Leader, Charles Simeon of Cambridge, and is inscribed on the fly-leaf "The Rev. C. Simeon, with great regard from W. B. Sprague." Underneath this inscription Simeon recorded his impression of the volume:

"A most valuable book. I recommend my executor to keep it, as there are few, if any, others in this kingdom. I love the good sense of Dr. Sprague. C.S."

Through the generosity of the Evangelical Library the book now in the reader's hands is a reproduction of Charles Simeon's own copy. Naturally Simeon's copy, now one hundred and twenty-six years old, bears some marks of its age and it may be that some of these will reappear in this reprint. It is hoped that the unusual circumstances will enable the reader to overlook this imperfection.

The Rev. C. Simeon,
with good regard from
W.B. Sprague.

A Most valuable book
I recommend My Executor
to keep it; as there are
few, if any, others in this kingdom.
I love the good sense of Dr Sprague
C.S.

CONTENTS.

Page

LECTURE I.
NATURE OF A REVIVAL.
ISAIAH XLV. 8.

Drop down, ye heavens, from above, and let the skies pour down
righteousness: let the earth open, and let them bring forth
salvation, and let righteousness spring up together   1

LECTURE II.
DEFENCE OF REVIVALS.
ACTS II. 13.

Others mocking, said, these men are full of new wine   25

LECTURE III.
OBSTACLES TO REVIVALS.
1 CORINTHIANS IX. 12.

—Lest we should hinder the gospel of Christ.   61

LECTURE IV.
DIVINE AGENCY IN REVIVALS.
HABAKKUK III. 2.

O Lord, revive thy work   89

LECTURE V.
GENERAL MEANS OF PRODUCING AND PROMOTING REVIVALS.
PHILIPPIANS I, 27.

—Striving together for the faith of the gospel   115

Page

LECTURE VI.
TREATMENT DUE TO AWAKENED SINNERS.
ACTS III. 19.

Repent ye therefore, and be converted 153

LECTURE VII.
TREATMENT DUE TO YOUNG CONVERTS.
2 CORINTHIANS XIII. 5.

Prove your own selves 185

LECTURE VIII.
EVILS TO BE AVOIDED IN CONNECTION WITH REVIVALS.
ROMANS XIV. 16.

Let not then your good be evil spoken of 215

LECTURE IX.
RESULTS OF REVIVALS.
REVELATION V. 13.

Blessing, and honor, and glory, and power, be unto him that sitteth upon the throne, and unto the Lamb, forever and ever 259

APPENDIX.

LETTER I.
From the Reverend Archibald Alexander, D. D. 1

LETTER II.
From the Reverend Francis Wayland, D. D. 9

LETTER III.
From the Reverend Daniel Dana, D. D. 16

LETTER IV.
From the Reverend Samuel Miller, D. D...................... 22

LETTER V.
From the Reverend Alvan Hyde, D. D........................ 45

Page

LETTER VI.
From the Reverend Joel Hawes, D. D. 56

LETTER VII.
From the Reverend John M'Dowell, D. D. 61

LETTER VIII.
From the Reverend Noah Porter, D. D. 68

LETTER IX.
From the late Reverend Edward Payson, D. D. 78

LETTER X.
From the Reverend Alexander Proudfit, D. D. 80

LETTER XI.
From the Reverend Charles P. McIlvaine 87

LETTER XII.
From the Reverend William Neill, D. D. 99

LETTER XIII.
From the Reverend Philip Milledoler, D. D. 103

LETTER XIV.
From the Reverend Henry Davis, D. D. 108

LETTER XV.
From the Reverend Natban Lord, D. D. 111

LETTER XVI.
From the Reverend Heman Humphrey, D. D. 115

LETTER XVII.
From the Reverend Jeremiah Day, D. D. 121

LETTER XVIII.
From the Reverend Ashbel Green, D. D. 124

LETTER XIX.
From the Reverend Moses Waddel, D. D. 146

LETTER XX.
From the Reverend Edward D. Griffin, D. D. 151

PREFACE.

The following Lectures were delivered during the preceding autumn and winter, to the congregation with which the author is connected, in the ordinary course of his public ministrations. The grand object at which he has aimed has been to vindicate and advance the cause of *genuine* revivals of religion; and in doing this, he has endeavored to distinguish between a genuine revival and a spurious excitement; to defend revivals against the cavils of their opposers; to show the causes which operate to prevent or retard them; to exhibit the agency of God, and the instrumentality of men, by which they are produced and sustained; to guide the inquiring sinner and establish the young convert; to guard against the abuses to which revivals are liable, and to anticipate the glorious results to which they must lead. In the hope that the Lectures may prove a seasonable offering to the American church, at an interesting and critical period, the author has concluded to send them forth through the press; and in doing this it is a pleasure to him that he is complying with a request from the session and trustees of the church of which he is pastor, as well as acting in accordance with the wishes of several respected and beloved brethren in the ministry with whom he is more immediately associated.

In the Appendix the reader will find a series of letters on the same subject, from a number of the most distinguished clergymen of our country, and from six different religious denominations. The object in requesting these letters has been twofold—First, to obtain authentic history of our revivals, in which unhappily we have hitherto been greatly deficient ; and, Second, to ascertain the manner in which revivals have been conducted by men whose wisdom, experience, and standing in the church must at least entitle their opinion to great consideration. It was originally the author's intention to have republished the well known letters of Doctor Beecher and Mr. Nettleton written several years ago, in which the same general views which this volume inculcates, are defended with great zeal and ability. But upon examination he finds they are so much identified with the occasion in which they originated, that he thinks it best to omit them. He allows himself to hope that whatever the decision of the public may be in respect to the Lectures, they will find in the Letters which follow, much authentic and important information; and he doubts not that the testimony on this momentous subject of such a representation from our American church, will not only be gratefully received, but considerately and earnestly pondered. If the volume should, by the blessing of God, be instrumental, even in a humble degree, of promoting such revivals as those for which Edwards, and Dwight, and Nettleton, and a host of others both among the living and the dead, have counted it an honor to labor, the best wish of the author of the Lectures, and no doubt of the writers of the Letters also, will be answered.

Albany, May 1, 1832.

LECTURE I.

NATURE OF A REVIVAL.

ISAIAH XLV. 8.

Drop down, ye heavens, from above, and let the skies pour down righteousness; let the earth open, and let them bring forth salvation, and let righteousness spring up together.

The final and complete triumph of the church was a theme at which the mind of this prophet was always ready to kindle. So infinitely superior did he regard it to any thing that respects merely the present world, that when his predictions relate immediately to temporal mercies, they often look farther to spiritual blessings; and sometimes we find him apparently forgetting himself for a moment, and passing abruptly, and almost imperceptibly, from some national deliverance to the salvation of the gospel. In the verses immediately preceding our text, there is a manifest reference to the deliverance of the Jews from their captivity in Babylon; but in the text itself, there is a sudden transition to a subject of far higher import, even the blessings of Christ's salvation; and this latter subject continues to engross the prophet's mind to the close of the chapter. "Drop down, ye heavens, from above, and let the skies pour down righteousness: let the earth open, and let them bring forth salvation, and let righteousness spring up together."

There was some partial fulfilment of this prediction in the revival of true piety which attended the return of the Jews from Babylon; though it is evidently to be considered as referring principally to the more extensive prevalence of religion under the gospel dispensation. It may be regarded, in a general sense, as denoting the abundant grace by which the gospel would be attended, casting into the shade all previous measures of divine influence which had been enjoyed by the church; or it may be considered more particularly—as referring to special occasions, on which the agency of the Spirit would be signally manifest. In this latter sense, it may be applied to the wonderful effusions of the Holy Ghost which attended the preaching of Peter on the day of Pentecost; and to what in these latter days we are accustomed to denominate *revivals of religion*. It is in its application to revivals that I purpose to consider it at the present time.

I here commence a series of discourses, in which it will be my object to present before you, in its various bearings, the subject of REVIVALS OF RELIGION. The reasons which have determined me to this course, and the grounds on which I beg leave to commend this subject to your special attention, are the following:

1. It is a subject in which the church, especially in this country, is, *at this moment*, more deeply and practically interested than almost any other. You cannot look back upon the history of our American church, and compare the past with the present, without perceiving that within the last half century a wonderful change has taken place in the order of God's providence towards it. It is true, indeed, that through the ministry of Whitfield and others, there was a revival of considerable extent in this country, a little before the middle of the last century; but owing to various causes, which I shall not now stop to specify, the fruits of it were, in no small degree, blasted; and from that period till near the beginning of the present century, the church was only enlarged by very gradual additions. But at the period last mentioned, a different state of things seemed to commence, in the more copious and sudden effusions of the Holy Spirit; and now it has come to pass in these days in which we live, that far the greater number of those who are turned from darkness to light, so far as we can judge, experience this change, during revivals of religion. It is for revivals that the church is continually praying; and to them that she is looking for accessions both to her numbers and her strength. The praise of revivals is upon her lips, and upon the lips of her sons and daughters, who come crowding to her solemn feasts. Such being the fact, no one can doubt that this is a subject which she ought well to understand;—

which all should understand, who care for Zion's prosperity.

2. This is a subject in which the church is not only deeply interested at the present time, but is likely to be more and more interested *for a long time to come.* The cause of revivals has hitherto been gradually and yet constantly gaining ground. The last year has been, in this respect, unparalleled in the annals of the church; and there is much in prophecy to warrant the conviction that, as the millenial day draws near, these effusions of the Holy Spirit will be yet more frequent and powerful. Every thing decides that this is to be a practical subject, not with the present generation only, but with many generations to come. It is desirable, therefore, that we should form correct views of it, not merely for our own sake, but for the sake of those who come after us; for our views no doubt will, to a great extent, be propagated to future generations.

3. The views which we form on this subject, and the course we adopt in respect to it, must determine, in a great measure, *the actual effect* of revivals upon the interests of the church. This is a matter in relation to which God is pleased to leave much to human instrumentality. It is possible that his people may co-operate with him in carrying forward a revival, by such means that there may be many sound and scriptural conversions, and that his cause may thereby be greatly advanced; and it is possible that, by the neglect of duty, or by the adoption

of mistaken and unscriptural measures, they may grieve away the Holy Spirit, or confirm multitudes in fatal self-deception. It is not to be questioned that what commonly passes under the name of a revival of religion is an engine of prodigious power in the church. God intends it only for good: nevertheless it is capable of being perverted to evil. As so much, then, in respect to the influence of revivals is dependant on the human agency that is employed in them, and as our conduct on this subject will take its complexion from our views, you perceive that it is a matter of great moment that our views should be correct.

4. Every member of the church, whatever may be his standing in society, *has a part to act* in relation to this subject, and therefore ought to be enlightened concerning it. In days that have gone by, this may have been thought a matter almost exclusively for ministers and other officers of the church; while private Christians may have imagined, that out of their closets they had little to do in relation to it, but to look on and behold the wonderful work of God. But happily this mistake has, to a great extent, been corrected; and it seems now to be almost universally admitted, that this is a field in which even the obscurest Christian may find a place to labor. In a community in which there prevails a spirit of deep religious anxiety, and many are just forming the purpose to set their faces toward heaven, and many others are beginning to hope that they have yielded themselves to God, there must

needs be much occasion for private counsel and instruction; and the persons most likely to be applied to are often those with whom the individuals concerned happen to be most intimately associated. Every one, therefore, ought to be competent to give at least some general directions. One right direction, in certain circumstances, may be the means of saving the soul. One wrong direction, in similar circumstances, of ruining it forever. If all Christians, then, are so deeply and practically interested in this subject, there is good reason why it should be brought before you as a distinct theme for contemplation and instruction.

Having now stated some reasons for bringing this subject before you at this time, I proceed to the main design of the discourse, which is to exhibit the NATURE of a revival of religion. And that we may do this intelligently, it will be necessary previously to answer the question, in a single word, what is the nature of *religion*?

Religion consists in a conformity of heart and life to the will of God. It consists in a principle of obedience implanted in the soul, and in the operation of that principle in the conduct. Religion is substantially the same in all worlds; though the religion of a sinner is modified, in some respects, by his peculiar character and condition. In common with the religion of the angels, it consists in love to God—to his law, to his government, to his service; but in distinction from that, it consists in repentance of sin; faith in the merits of a crucified

Saviour; resignation under trials; opposition to spiritual enemies. Moreover, religion in the angels is an inherent principle; it begins with their existence; but in the human heart it is something superinduced by the operation of the Spirit of God. Wherever there exists a cordial belief of God's truth, and submission of the will to his authority, and the graces of the heart shine forth in the virtues of the life, there is true religion; whether it be in the palace or the cottage; whether it appear in a single individual, or be diffused over a whole community.

Now if such be the nature of religion, you will readily perceive in what consists a *revival* of religion. It is a revival of scriptural knowledge; of vital piety; of practical obedience. The term *revival of religion* has sometimes been objected to, on the ground that a revival of any thing supposes its previous existence; whereas in the renovation of sinners, there is a principle implanted which is entirely new. But though the fact implied in this objection is admitted, the objection itself has no force; because the term is intended to be applied in a general sense, to denote the improved religious state of a congregation, or of some other community. And it is moreover applicable, in a strict sense, to the condition of Christians, who, at such a season, are in a greater or less degree revived; and whose increased zeal is usually rendered instrumental of the conversion of sinners. Wherever then you see religion rising up from a state of

comparative depression to a tone of increased vigor
and strength; wherever you see professing Christians becoming more faithful to their obligations,
and behold the strength of the church increased by
fresh accessions of piety from the world; *there* is a
state of things which you need not hesitate to denominate a revival of religion.

Such a state of things may be advantageously
represented under several distinct particulars.

1. The first step usually is an *increase of zeal and
devotedness on the part of God's people.* They wake
up to a sense of neglected obligations; and resolve
to return to the faithful discharge of duty. They
betake themselves with increased earnestness to the
throne of grace; confessing their delinquencies with
deep humility, and supplicating the aids of God's
Spirit to enable them to execute their pious resolutions, and to discharge faithfully the various duties
which devolve upon them. There too they impor-
tunately ask for the descent of the Holy Ghost on
those around them; on the church with which they
are connected; on their friends who are living at a
distance from God; on all who are out of the ark
of safety. Their conversation becomes proportion-
ally more spiritual and edifying. They endeavor to
stir up one another's minds by putting each other in
remembrance of their covenant vows, and impressing each other with their individual and mutual re-
sponsibilities. When they meet in the common intercourse of life, their conversation shows that the
world is with them but a subordinate matter; and

that their controlling desire is, that God may be glorified in the salvation of sinners. They find it no difficult matter to be faithful in pressing the obligations of religion upon those who are indifferent to it; in warning them of their danger; and in beseeching them with the earnestness of Christian affection to be reconciled to God. It is a case of no uncommon occurrence at such a season that a professor of religion, under a deep sense of his wanderings, comes to regard his own Christian character with the utmost distrust; and sometimes wanders many days in darkness, before the joys of salvation are restored to his soul. There are indeed some professors who sleep through such a scene; and probably some who join with the wicked, so far as they dare, in opposing it; but many at least are awake; are humble; are active; and come up to the help of the Lord with renewed zeal and strength.

2. Another prominent feature in the state of things which I am describing, is *the alarm and conviction of those who have hitherto been careless.* Sometimes the change in this respect is very gradual; and for a considerable time nothing more can be said than that there is a more listening ear, and a more serious aspect, than usual, under the preaching of the word; and this increased attention is gradually matured into deep solemnity and pungent conviction. In other cases, the reigning lethargy is suddenly broken up, as if there had come a thunderbolt from eternity; and multitudes are heard simultaneously inquiring what they shall do to be saved. The young

man, and the old man, and the middle aged man;
the exemplary and orthodox moralist, the haughty
pharisee, the downright infidel, the profane scoffer,
the dissipated sensualist, may sometimes all be seen
collected with the same spirit in their hearts—a
spirit of deep anxiety; and the same question upon their lips—how they shall escape the threatening woes of perdition? In some cases, the conviction which is felt prompts to silence, and you are left
to learn it from downcast looks, or as the case may
be, from half-stifled sobs. In other cases, there is
no effect at concealment, and the deep anguish of
the heart comes out in expressions of the most painful solicitude. Those who once would have dis-
dained any thing which should indicate the least
concern for their salvation, hesitate not to ask and
to receive instruction even from the obscurest Christian, or to place themselves in circumstances which
are a virtual acknowledgement to all that they feel
their danger and desire to escape from it. All the
shame which they once felt on this subject they have
given to the winds; and their commanding desire
now is, that they may find that peace which passeth
understanding; that hope which is full of immortality.

There are others who are partially awakened;
whose attention is in some measure excited, but not
enough to prompt to any decided and vigorous effort. They look on and see what is passing; and
acknowledge God's agency in it; and at times manifest some feeling in respect to their own condition,

and express a wish that they may have more. They attend regularly not only upon the ordinary but upon some of the extraordinary means of grace, and treat the whole subject not only with great respect, but with decided seriousness; but after all do not advance to the decisive point of repentance, or even of true conviction of sin. In this state they often remain for a considerable time; until they return to their accustomed carelessness; or by some new impulse from on high they are carried forward and become the subjects of a genuine conversion; or else they are taken away in the midst of their half formed resolutions to a world where they will learn, to their eternal cost, that it was was most dangerous to trifle with the Spirit of God.

There are still others belonging to the same general class of awakened sinners, who struggle against their convictions; whose consciences proclaim to them that their all is in jeopardy, but who try to discredit the testimony. These persons sometimes rush with unaccustomed avidity into the haunts of business or the haunts of pleasure. They throw themselves into vain company, or engage in reading idle or infidel books; and in some instances even venture to deny what is passing within them, and to jeer at what is passing around them. Wherever you hear scoffing, and witness violent opposition in a revival of religion, it is scarcely possible that you should mistake, if you should put down those by whom it is exhibited on the list of awakened sinners. The true account of it is, that there is a war between the conscience and the passions. Conscience is awake and doing its office, and the heart is in rebellion against its dictates.

3. It also belongs essentially to a revival of religion, that there are those, from time to time, *who are indulging a hope that they are reconciled to God, and are born of the Spirit.* In some cases the change of feeling is exceedingly gradual, insomuch that the individual, though he is sensible of having experienced a change within a given period, is yet utterly unable to refer it to any particular time. Sometimes the soul suddenly emerges from darkness into light, and perceives a mighty change in its exercises, almost in the twinkling of an eye. Sometimes there is a state of mind which is only peaceful; sometimes it mounts up to joy and ecstacy. In some cases there is from the beginning much self distrust; in others much—too much, confidence. But with a great variety of experience, there are many who are brought, or who believe themselves brought, into the kingdom of Christ. They give reason to hope they have taken the new song upon their lips. Children sing their young hosannas to the Lamb that was slain. The aged tell with gratitude of what God has done for them while on the margin of the grave. Saints on earth rejoice, and in proportion as the work is genuine, so also do saints and angels in heaven. The church receives a fresh and often a rich accession both to her numbers and her strength; an accession which, in some cases, raises her from

the dust, and causes her to look forth in health and
beauty.

Such are the more prominent features of what
we commonly call a revival of religion. But revivals, like every thing else that is good, have their
counterfeits ; and not unfrequently there is a spurious admixture in those which, on the whole, must
be considered genuine. It becomes therefore a matter of great importance that we discriminate accurately between the precious and the vile ; that we
do not mistake a gust of animal passion for the
awakening or converting operations of God's Holy
Spirit. We will inquire briefly what *are not*, and
what *are*, the indications of a genuine revival.

1. It is no certain indication of a genuine revival, that there is *great excitement*. It is admitted
indeed that great excitement may attend a true revival ; but it is not the necessary accompaniment of
one, and it may exist where the work is wholly spurious. It may be an excitement produced not by
the power of divine truth, but by artificial stimulus
applied to the imagination and the passions, for the
very purpose of producing commotion both within
and without. Instances have occurred in which
Jehovah who has declared himself a God of order,
has been professedly worshipped in scenes of utter
confusion ; and impiety has been substituted for
prayer; and the wildest reveries of fanaticism have
been dealt out, instead of the sober and awful truths
of God's word. Here is the highest excitement ;
but it surely does not prove that the scene in which

it exists is a genuine revival. It does not stamp
confusion and irreverence, and impiety, with the seal
of God's Spirit. On the other hand, there may be
a true revival where all is calm and noiseless; and
multitudes of hearts may be broken in contrition
and yielded up to God, which have never been agitated by any violent, much less convulsive emotions,
nor even breathed forth a single sob, unless in the
silence of the closet, and into the ear of mercy.

2. It is no certain evidence of a genuine revival
that *great numbers profess to be converted*. We are
too much inclined, if I mistake not, to estimate the
character of a revival by the number of professed
converts; whereas there is scarcely a more uncertain test than this. For who does not know that
doctrines may be preached, or measures adopted,
or standards of religious character set up, which
shall lead multitudes, especially of the uninstructed,
to misapprehend the nature of conversion, and to
imagine themselves subjects of it, while they are yet
in their sins? We admit that there may be genuine
revivals of great extent; in which multitudes may
be almost simultaneously made the subjects of God's
grace; but we confidently maintain that the mere
fact that many *profess* to be converted does not
prove a revival genuine. For suppose that every
one of these individuals, or far the larger part of
them, should finally fall away, this surely we should
say, would prove the work spurious. If then, their
having originally professed to be Christians proved
it genuine, the same work is proved to be both genu-

LECTURE I.   15

ine and spurious. Does the fact that an *individual* imagines himself to be converted convey any certain evidence of his conversion? But if this is not true of an individual, it certainly cannot be true of any number of individuals; for if one may be self deceived, so may many. It follows that the genuineness of a revival is to be judged of, in a great measure, independently of the number of its professed subjects.

3. Nor yet, thirdly, is *the existence of an extensive and violent opposition*, any evidence that a revival is genuine. There are those who will have it, that God's Spirit cannot be poured out upon a community, but that all who are unrenewed, if their hearts are not at once broken in godly sorrow, will be excited to wrath and railing. Now I admit fully that the carnal mind is enmity against God; and I am willing to admit moreover that, in most cases, perhaps in all, in which revivals of any considerable extent exist, there are some who act out this enmity in the way of direct opposition;—some who revile God's people and ministers, and who ridicule even the operations of his Holy Spirit. But in an orderly and well instructed community, I hesitate not to say that we are not to look for any such general exhibition as this. Facts prove that there are multitudes who pass through a revival without becoming personally interested in it, who still never utter a word against it, and who say, and doubtless say honestly, that they feel no sensible hostility towards it. They have indeed a heart at enmity with

God; but that enmity may operate in some different way; or it may be to a certain extent controlled
and neutralized by constitutional qualities or habits
of education; and they may never feel a disposition to rail at God's work on the one hand, and may
be as little inclined to yield themselves to his service on the other. While I admit therefore that the
natural enmity of the heart does. sometimes assume
the form of direct opposition against revivals, where
there is nothing censurable in the manner in which
they are conducted, I am constrained to believe that
the opposition which is often complained of, or rather gloried in, is opposition to harsh expressions
which are fitted to irritate, but not to enlighten, to
convince, or in any way to profit. And then how
natural is it that the odium should be transferred,
or rather extended, from the severe language and
questionable measures, to the revival with which they
are connected; and so it comes to pass that a violent prejudice really grows up in the mind against
the whole subject of revivals, which originated in the
imprudent and mistaken zeal of some of their friends.
There are those, I know, who court opposition on
these occasions, and who seem to think that nothing
can be done to purpose, until the voice of railing is
heard from without. Such persons are sure to find
the opposition they seek; and in encountering it,
instead of suffering for righteousness' sake, they are
buffetted for their own faults. I repeat then, a genuine work of God's grace may be extensively op-

posed; but the existence of such opposition does not evince it to be genuine.

What then *are* some of the indications of a genuine revival of religion?

1. The fact that any thing which claims to be a revival has been effected *by scriptural means*, is an evidence in favor of its genuineness.

God has given us his word not only as a rule of faith but of practice; and in the same proportion that we adhere to it, we have a right to expect his blessing; in the same proportion that we depart from it, we have reason to expect his frown. His own institutions he will honor; and the institutions of men, so far as they are conformed to the spirit of his word, he will also honor; but whenever the latter are put in place of the former, or exalted above them, or assume a shape which God's word does not warrant, we cannot suppose that he can regard them with favor; and even if, for a time, there should seem to be a blessing, there is reason to believe that the event will show that in that apparent blessing were bound up the elements of a curse.

Now apply this to the subject of revivals. Suppose there were to be a powerful excitement on the subject of religion produced by means which are at war with the spirit of the gospel;—suppose doctrines were to be preached which the gospel does not recognize, and doctines omitted which the gospel regards fundamental;—suppose that for the simple, and honest, and faithful use of the sword of the

Spirit, there should be substituted a mass of machinery designed to produce its effect on the animal passions;—suppose the substance of religion, instead of being made to consist in repentance, and faith, and holiness, should consist of falling, and groaning, and shouting;—we should say unhesitatingly that that could not be a genuine work of divine grace; or if there were some pure wheat, there must be a vast amount of chaff and stubble. It may be safe to admit even in the wildest scenes, the possibility of some genuine conversions; because there may be some truth preached, and some believing prayer offered, which God may regard and honor, notwithstanding all the error and delusion with which it may be mingled. But in general it is perfectly fair to conclude that when men become dissatisfied with plain Bible truth, and simple Bible measures, and undertake to substitute doctrines or devices of their own, any excitement which may be produced, however extensive, however powerful, is of an exceedingly dubious character. If the effect partake of the same character with the cause, it must be of the earth, earthy.

On the other hand, where there is an attention to religion excited by the plain and faithful preaching of God's truth in all its length and breadth, and by the use of those simple and honest means which God's word either directly prescribes or fairly sanctions, we cannot reasonably doubt that here is a genuine work of the Holy Spirit. The means used may be in some respects feeble; that is, there may be the entire absence of an eloquent and powerful ministry; nevertheless if God's truth is dispensed fairly, and fully, and with godly sincerity, and other corresponding means used in a corresponding manner, the effect which is produced may reasonably be attributed to the operation of divine grace; and it is a fact which does great honor to the sovereignty of God, that the humblest instrumentality, when well directed, has often been honored by a multitude of conversions, which a course of holy living has proved sound and genuine.

If then we have a right to say that God honors his own word and his own institutions, the means employed in producing and carrying forward a revival furnish a good criterion by which to determine its character. It may not always be easy accurately to apply this rule in given cases, because there is often a strange mixture of good and bad; but without deciding how far any particular revival is genuine or spurious, we may safely decide that it is so in the same proportion that it is sustained by scriptural or unscriptural instrumentality.

2. A genuine revival is characterized by *a due proportion of reflection and feeling*.

I will not undertake to decide what amount of scriptural knowledge is necessary to conversion in any given case, or to question the fact that men under certain circumstances may be renewed where their knowledge is very limited; nevertheless it is certain that religious reflection precedes religious feeling in the order of nature. Before men can feel remorse, much more contrition, for their sins, they must have held strongly to their minds the fact that they are sinners. They must have reflected upon what it is to be a sinner; on the character of God, not only as a Father, but a Lawgiver; on the reasonableness of their obligations to Him, and on the guilt of violating those obligations. Before they can exercise faith in the Lord Jesus Christ, they must have reflected on the character of Christ, on the fulness of his atonement, and on the freeness and sincerity of the gospel offer. The Holy Spirit employs the truth not only in the work of sanctification, but even in the work of conversion; and the truth can never find its way to the heart, except through the understanding. If then the great truths of God's word are steadily held up before the mind as subjects of reflection; and if the feeling which is manifested by sinners, whether of anxiety and distress, or of peace and joy, be the effect of such reflection, there is good reason to believe that God's Spirit is really at work, and that that which claims to be a revival is really one. But if, in such a scene, the mind be kept in a great degree passive, if there be a great deal of feeling with very little thought— burning heat with only dim and doubtful light; if the sensibilities of the soul be wrought into a storm, none can tell how or why; then rely on it, it is not a work which God owns; or if there are some true conversions, far the greater number may be expected to prove spurious.

3. That on which we are principally to rely as evidence of the genuineness of a revival, is *its substantial and abiding fruit.* Precisely the same rule is to be applied to a revival as to individual cases of hopeful conversion. Those who have been most conversant with the subject of religious experience, do not rely chiefly for evidence of piety on the pungency of one's convictions, or the transports by which they may be succeeded, or the professions which may be made of devotedness to Christ; for they have learned that all this is equivocal; and that delusion and self-deception are consistent with the most promising appearances which are ever exhibited. While, therefore, they may hope favorably from what they see at the beginning, before they form a decisive opinion they wait to see whether the individual can endure temptation; whether he is faithful in the discharge of all duty; whether he is a good soldier of Jesus Christ. And if they see the fruits of holiness abounding in the life, whether the appearance at the beginning were more or less favorable, they infer with confidence that a principle of holiness has been implanted in the heart. In the same manner are we to test the character of revivals. If an excitement on the subject of religion (no matter how great it may have been) passes away, and leaves behind little or no substantial and enduring good; if most of those who profess to have been converted return speedily or gradually to the world, living a careless life, and exhibiting an unedifying example; or if they manifest a spirit of

pride, and uncharitableness, and a disposition to condemn all who do not exactly come to their standard, then rely on it, though that may be *called* a revival of religion, it has little more than the name. But if, after the excitement has gone by, the fruits of holiness remain and become more and more mature, if those who have been professedly converted hold on a course of humble, self denied, devoted obedience, exemplifying the spirit of Christ as well as professing his name, then you may take knowledge of them that they have come out of a true revival of religion. Religion acted out in the life is the best evidence that religion has its dwelling in the heart. Let the virtues and graces of the Christian adorn the lives of those who have professed to be converted during a revival, and you need ask for no better evidence that *there* has been the agency of the Spirit of God.

Such, as it seems to me, are the characteristics of a genuine revival of religion. I shall not stop here to prove that such a state of things has every thing in it to interest the best feelings of the Christian. If you have ever felt the power of God's grace, and especially if your hearts are now awake to the interests of his kingdom, and the salvation of your fellow men, it cannot be a matter of indifference with you whether or not God's work is to be revived in the midst of us. Let me entreat you then, as this subject is for several successive weeks to occupy your attention, to be fellow helpers together, in humble dependence on God's grace, to procure for ourselves those rich blessings on which your meditations will turn. While we are endeavoring to form correct views of this important subject, may we get our hearts thoroughly imbued with its spirit; and be able to point with devout joy to what is passing in the midst of us, as an example of a genuine, scriptural revival of religion.

LECTURE II.

DEFENCE OF REVIVALS.

––––

ACTS II. 13.

Others mocking, said, these men are full of new wine.

The occasion on which these words were spoken, marked a memorable era in the history of the church. The disciples of Jesus, a few days after his ascension, being assembled for devotional exercises in a certain room, in the city of Jerusalem, where they had been accustomed to meet, were surprised by a marvellous exhibition of the mighty power of God. There came suddenly a sound from heaven, as of a violent rushing wind ; and, at the same time, there appeared unto them a number of divided tongues, made as it were of fire ; and it was so ordered that one of these tongues rested upon each of them. And at the moment that these tongues, or lambent flames touched them, they were filled, in an extraordinary degree, with the Holy Spirit ; and began to speak a variety of languages which they had never before understood, with a fluency and fervor which were beyond measure astonishing. It is hardly necessary to add that this was a most signal attestation to the divinity of the gospel, and a glorious pledge of the Redeemer's final and complete triumph.

It is not strange that so wonderful an event as this should have been instantly noised abroad, or that it should have excited much curiosity and speculation. Accordingly, we are informed that the multitude came together, and were amazed to find that the fact was as had been represented ; that these ignorant Gallileans had suddenly become masters of a great variety of languages ; and were talking with men of different nations as fluently as if they had been speaking in their own mother tongue. The true way of accounting for this—that is, referring it to miraculous agency—they all seem to have overlooked ; nevertheless, as it was manifestly an effect of something, they could not but inquire in respect to the cause ; and we have one specimen of the wisdom that was exercised on the occasion in the words of our text—" Others mocking, said, these men are full of new wine ;"—as if they soberly believed that a state of intoxication, which often deprives a man of the power of speaking his own language, had strangely given to them the power of speaking languages not their own, and which they had never learned. All will admit that this was the very infatuation of prejudice.

The reason why this absurd and ridiculous account was given of this miraculous occurrence was, that the individuals were at war with that system of truth of which this was pre-eminently the seal; they could not admit that it was an evidence of the triumph of the crucified Jesus; and rather than even seem to admit it, they would sacrifice all claims to reason and common sense. Now I would not say that *all* objections that are made against revivals of religion, are made in the same spirit which prompted this foolish declaration of these early opposers of the gospel; but I am constrained to express my conviction that *many* of them are; and hence I have chosen the passage now read as introductory to a consideration of OBJECTIONS AGAINST REVIVALS. It was actually an effusion of the Holy Spirit, which drew forth the objection contained in the text; the commencement of a scene, which terminated, as revivals now do, in the conversion of many souls, and an important addition to the Christian church.

The sole object of this discourse then, will be to consider, and so far as I can, to meet, some of the most popular objections which are urged against revivals of religion. And I wish it distinctly borne in mind that the defence which I am to make relates, not to mere spurious excitements, but to genuine revivals;—such revivals as I have attempted to describe in the preceding discourse.

I. The first of these objections which I shall notice is, that revivals of religion, as we use the phrase, are *unscriptural*. It is proper that this objection should be noticed first, because if it can be sustained, it is of itself a sufficient reason not only for indifference towards revivals, but for positive opposi-

tion to them; and in that case, as it would be unnecessary that we should proceed, so it would be only
fair that, at the outset, we should surrender the
whole ground. No matter what else may be said
in favor of revivals; no matter how important they
may have been regarded, or how much we may
have been accustomed to identify them with the
prosperity of Christ's cause; if it can be fairly
shown that they are unscriptural, we are bound unhesitatingly to conclude that we have mistaken their
true character. God's word is to be our standard
in every thing; and wherever we suffer considerations of expediency in reference to this or any other
subject, to prevail against that standard, we set up
our own wisdom against the wisdom of the Highest;
and we are sure thereby to incur his displeasure.
To the law and the testimony then be our appeal.

In order to denominate any thing that is connected with the subject of religion unscriptural, it is not
enough that we should be able to show that it is not
expressly commanded; but we should also make
it appear that it is either expressly or implicitly forbidden. There are many things which all admit to
be right among Christians, and which are even regarded as important parts of duty, for which there
is no *express* warrant in the Bible; though no doubt
they judge rightly when they suppose that they find
a *sufficient* warrant for these things in the general spirit of the Bible. For instance the Bible has said
nothing about the monthly concert of prayer for the
conversion of the world, which is now so generally

observed throughout evangelical Protestant Christendom; and of course this is not to be regarded as
a divine institution; but so long as God has commanded his people to pray for the prosperity of Jerusalem, and so long as the Saviour has promised to
bless them where only two or three are met together
in his name, it would be folly for any one to contend
that the monthly concert is an antiscriptural institution. The spirit of the Bible manifestly justifies it,
though the letter of the Bible may not require it. In
like manner, even if we were to admit that what we
call a revival of religion, so far as human agency and
influence are concerned, were not directly required
by God's word, nevertheless, if it can be shown that
it is consistent with the spirit of God's word, no
man has a right to gainsay it, on the ground that it
is unscriptural.

Now we claim for revivals, (and it is the least
that we claim for them on the score of divine authority) that there is nothing in the general spirit of
the Bible that is unfavorable to them, but much of
an opposite character. It is the tendency of all the
instructions of God's word to form men to a habit
of serious reflection; to abstract their affections
from the world; to lead them to commune with
their hearts, and to commune with God, and to seek
with greater earnestness than any thing else the salvation of the soul. Now this is precisely what is
accomplished in a revival of religion. In such a
scene, if any where, is fulfilled the great design of
God's word in bringing men to serious considera-

tion; to self communion; to a right estimate of
the comparative value of the things which are seen
and are temporal, and the things which are not seen
and are eternal. We say nothing here of the means
employed, but simply speak of the effect produced;
and we are sure that no one who admits that the
effect is as we have stated, will doubt that it is in
keeping with the general tenor of God's word.

But we need not stop here: for the Bible has
given a more direct sanction to revivals; and in various ways. Look for instance at many of the
prayers which it records, as having been offered for
the spiritual prosperity of Zion, when she was in a
state of deep depression. Says the Psalmist, "Turn
us O God of our salvation, and cause thine anger
towards us to cease. Wilt thou be angry with us
forever? Wilt thou draw out thine anger unto all
generations? Wilt thou not revive us again, that
thy people may rejoice in thee? Shew us thy mercy, O Lord, and grant us thy salvation." And again,
"Return we beseech thee O God of Hosts; look
down from heaven, and behold and visit this vine;
and the vineyard which thy right hand hath planted,
and the branch that thou madest strong for thyself."
And again, the prophet Habakkuk prays—"O Lord
revive thy work; in the midst of the years make
known; in wrath remember mercy." These prayers
were offered in behalf of the church, when she was
in a state of temporal bondage, as well as of spiritual affliction; nevertheless, they relate especially
to spiritual blessings; and what was meant by a re-

vival then, was substantially the same thing as what
is intended by a revival now. Accordingly, we find
that these very prayers are constantly used by the
church at this day; and that from a regard to them,
as we cannot doubt, God often appears to lengthen
her cords and strengthen her stakes; the blessings
of divine grace descend upon her in such profusion,
that she puts on her beautiful garments, and looks
forth fair as the morning.

There are also recorded in the scriptures many signal *instances* in which God has poured out his spirit,
and effected a sudden and general reformation. If
you go back to the Jewish dispensation, you will
find this remark strikingly verified in the reigns of
David and Solomon, of Asa and Jehosaphat, of He-
zekiah and Josiah. After the church had languished during the long and gloomy period of the Baby-
lonish captivity, her interests were signally revived
under the ministry of Ezra. A similar state of
things existed in the days of John the Baptist, when
the kingdom of heaven is said to have suffered violence, and many of the most profligate part of the
community became impressed with religious truth,
and were baptized unto repentance. On the occasion referred to in our text, no less than three
thousand, and on the day following two thousand
more, were subdued to the obedience of the truth,
and were added to the Lord. Shortly after this,
multitudes in Samaria experienced the regenerating
power of the gospel; and upon the dispersion of
the disciples after the martyrdom of Stephen, they

were instrumental of exciting a general attention to
religion in the remote parts of Judea, and even as
far as the territories of Greece.   Here then are facts
recorded by the unerring finger of inspiration, precisely analagous to those which the objection we
are considering declares to be unscriptural.

But in addition to this, there is much in the *prophe-
cies* which might fairly lead us to expect the very
scenes which we denominate revivals of religion.
If you read the prophetical parts of scripture attentively, you cannot, I think, but be struck with
the evidence that, as the millenial day approaches,
the operations of divine grace are to be increasing-
ly rapid and powerful.   Many of these predictions
respecting the state of religion under the Christian
dispensation, it is manifest, have not yet had their
complete fulfilment; and they not only justify the
belief that these glorious scenes which we see
passing really are of divine origin, as they claim to
be, but that similar scenes still more glorious, still
more wonderful, are to be expected, as the Messiah travels in the greatness of his strength towards
a universal triumph.   I cannot but think that many
of the inspired predictions in respect to the progress of religion, appear overstrained, unless we admit that the church is to see greater things than she
has yet seen; and that they fairly warrant the conclusion that succeeding generations rejoicing in the
brighter light of God's truth, and the richer manifestations of his grace, may look back even upon this

blessed era of revivals, as a period of comparative darkness.

If then the general spirit of the Bible be in favor of revivals; if the prayers which holy and inspired men have offered for them are here recorded; if there be many instances here mentioned of their actual occurrence; and if the spirit of prophecy has been exercised in describing and predicting them; then we may consider the objection that they are unscriptural as fairly set aside; nay, we may regard them as having the sanction of divine authority in the highest and clearest possible manner.

II. It is objected, again, that revivals of religion are *unnecessary*. In the mouth of an infidel, this objection would doubtless imply that religion itself is unnecessary; and so, of course, must be all the means used for its promotion. But in this view it does not fall within our present design to consider it. There are those who profess to regard religion, who maintain that revivals are modern innovations; and that they are unnecessary on the ground that the cause of Christ may be sustained and advanced, as it has been in other days, without them. This is the only form of the objection which it concerns us at present to notice.

The first thing to be said in reply, is, that the objection supposes what is not true—viz. that revivals are of modern origin. The truth is that if, as the objection asserts, the cause of religion in preceding ages has been sustained and carried forward without them, so also it has been sustained and carried

forward with them ; and during the periods in which
they have prevailed, the church has seen her greatest prosperity. You have already seen that, instead
of being of recent origin, they go back to an early
period in the Jewish dispensation. And passing
from the records of inspiration, we find that revivals have existed, with a greater or less degree of
power, especially in the later periods of the Christian church. This was emphatically true during the
period of the Reformation in the sixteenth century :
Germany, France, Switzerland, Holland, Denmark,
the Low countries, and Britain, were severally visited by copious showers of divine influence. During
the season of the plague in London in 1665, there
was a very general awakening ; in which many thousands are said to have been hopefully born of the
Spirit. In the early part of the seventeenth century, various parts of Scotland and the North of Ire-
land, were blessed, at different periods, with signal
effusions of divine grace, in which great multitudes
gave evidence of being brought out of darkness
into marvellous light. During the first half of the
last century, under the ministrations of Whitfield,
Brainard, Edwards, Davies, the Tennents, and many other of the holiest and greatest men whose
labors have blessed the church, there was a succession of revivals in this country, which caused the
wilderness to blossom as the rose, and the desert to
put on the appearance of the garden of the Lord.
And when these revivals declined, and the church
settled back into the sluggish state from which she

had been raised, then commenced her decline in purity, in discipline, in doctrine, in all with which her prosperity is most intimately connected. And this state of things continued, only becoming worse and worse, until, a little before the beginning of the present century, the spirit of revivals again burst forth, and has since that period richly blessed especially our American church. The fact then, most unfortunately for the objection we are considering, turns out to be, that if the church has been sustained at some periods without these signal effusions of the Holy Spirit, she has barely been sustained; and that the brightest periods of her history have been those, in which they have prevailed with the greatest power. To object to revivals then on the ground that they are modern, or that they are unnecessary to the best interests of the church, betrays an utter ignorance of their history.

But let us inquire a little further why the old and quiet way, as it is often represented, of becoming religious, is the best. If you mean that you prefer that state of religion in which the dews of divine grace continually descend, and Christians are always consistent and active, and there is a constant succession of conversions from among the impenitent, to the more sudden and rapid operations of God's Spirit—be it so; there is as truly a revival in the one case as the other. But the state of things which this objection contemplates is that in which religion is kept in the back ground, and only here and there one at distant periods, comes forward to confess Christ, and the church is habitually in a languishing state. And is such a state of things to be preferred above that in which the salvation of the soul becomes the all engrossing object, and even hundreds within a little period, come and own themselves on the Lord's side? Is it not desirable that sinners should be converted immediately? Are they liable every hour to die, and thus be beyond the reach of mercy and of hope; and is it not right that they should be pressed with the obligations of immediate repentance; and is it not necessary that they should exert themselves to escape the tremendous doom by which they are threatened? Is it more desirable that the mass of sinners should be sleeping on in guilty security, liable every hour to fall into the hands of a sin-avenging God, or that they should be escaping by multitudes from the coming wrath, and gaining an interest in the salvation of the gospel? He, and only he, who will dare to say that the former is most desirable, can consistently object to revivals on the ground that the church had better revert to the quiet uniformity of other days.

Still farther: Before you decide that revivals are unnecessary, you must either settle it that they are not the work of God, or else you must assume the responsibility of deciding that he is not doing his work in the best way. Will you take the former side of the alternative, and maintain that this is not God's work? If you say this, then I challenge you to prove that God ever works in the renovation of men;

for the only evidence of the existence of a principle of religion in the heart, is the operation of that principle in the life ; and I hesitate not to say that I can show you as unequivocal fruits of holiness produced from a revival of religion, as you can show me in any other circumstances. Unless then you will assume the responsibility of saying that all the apparent faith, and love, and zeal, and holiness, which are produced from a revival, and which, so far as we can judge, have every characteristic of genuineness, are spurious, it were rash to decide that this is not a work effected by the agency of the Holy Spirit.

But if you admit that this is God's work, you surely will not dare to say that his way of accomplishing his purpose is not the best. Suppose that nothing *appeared* to render this course of procedure especially desirable, yet the point being established that it is the course which God hath chosen, the reflection that God's ways are not as our ways, ought to silence every doubt. But who, after all, will say that it even appears inconsistent with infinite wisdom and goodness, as the cause of God is advancing towards a complete triumph, that he should operate more powerfully, more suddenly, than in some other periods; in short, precisely as he does in a revival of religion ? Has God bound himself that he will convert men only by small numbers, or by a very gradual influence; or does he not rather, in this respect, claim the right of absolute sovereignty ? I ask again in view of the bearing which this objection has upon the character of God, who will dare say that revivals are unnecessary?

III. Another objection against revivals is, that they are *the nurseries of enthusiasm.*

If by enthusiasm you mean a heated imagination that prompts to excesses in conduct, then you meet with it in other departments beside that of revivals. You will see as much enthusiasm in a political cabal, or in an election of civil officers, or in a commercial speculation, or even in the pursuits of science, as you will find in a revival of religion. Yes, believe me, there is a worldly as well as a religious enthusiasm: and let me inquire how it comes to pass that you can tolerate the former, nay perhaps that you can exemplify and cherish it, and yet can regard the latter with so much disapprobation and abhorrence? Does it not look a little as if your objection lay rather against religion—the subject in respect to which the enthusiasm is exercised, than against the enthusiasm itself?

But are you sure that in passing judgment on the enthusiasm connected with revivals, you always call things by their right names? Is it not more than possible that much of what you call by this name, may be the fervor of true love to God, and of genuine Christian zeal? Suppose you were to go into a meeting composed entirely of persons of the same religious character with Isaiah, or David, or Paul; and suppose they were to utter themselves in expressions not more fervent than these holy men have actually used, do you not believe that you would think there was some enthusiasm in that meeting, and that the exercises would be better if they partook a little more of the earthly and a little less of the heavenly? Between enthusiasm on the one hand, and conviction of sin and love to God, and zeal in religion on the other, there is really no affinity; they are as unlike each other as any genuine quality is unlike its counterfeit; but is there not some danger that they who have a heart opposed to religion, and who are willing to find excuses for the neglect of it, will brand some of the Christian graces when they shine with unusual brightness, with the opprobrious epithet of enthusiasm?

But suppose there is some real enthusiasm mingled with revivals, (and to a certain extent, this no doubt must be admitted) shall we on this ground reject them altogether? Because some few individuals in such a scene may act the part of enthusiasts, is all the true Christian feeling, and Christian conduct, which is exemplified by many others to be considered of no account? Or suppose, if you will, that a small degree of enthusiasm may pertain to all, does this nullify all the exercises of genuine and perhaps elevated piety with which it may happen to be connected? Where is the man who adopts the same principle in respect to his worldly affairs? If you should import the productions of some foreign clime, and should discover that a small part of the quantity had been injured by the voyage, and that the rest had not suffered at all, would you cast the whole of it from you, or would you not rather make a careful separation between the good and the bad, retaining the one, and rejecting the other? Or if you should hear a lecture on science, or politics, or religion, or any other subject, in which you should discover a few mistakes, while nearly the whole of it was sound, and practical, and in a high degree instructive, would you condemn the whole for these trifling errors, and say it was all a mass of absurdity, or would you not rather treasure it up in your memory as in the main excellent, though you felt that, like every thing human it was marred by imperfection? And why should not the same principle be admitted in respect to revivals? Is it right, is it honest, because there may be in them a small admixture of enthusiasm, to treat them as if they were made up of enthusiasm and nothing else? Would it not be more equitable, would it not be more candid, to separate the precious from the vile, and to let the sentence of condemnation fall only where it is deserved?

But perhaps I shall be met here with the declaration that there are scenes which pass for revivals of religion, in which there is nothing but enthusiasm and its kindred evils; scenes which outrage the decorum of religious worship, and exert no other influence upon religion than to bring it into contempt. Be it so. If there be such scenes, whatever name they may assume, they are not what we plead for under the name of revivals; on the contrary, every friend of true revivals must, if he be consistent, set his face against them. And I maintain further, that

it is gross injustice to the cause of revivals, to confound those scenes in which there is nothing but
the wild fire of human passion, with those in which
there is the manifest operation of the Holy Spirit.
Suppose you should see a man practising the extreme of avarice, and calling it by the honest name
of economy; or suppose you should see a man in-
flexibly obstinate in an evil course, and calling his
obstinacy virtuous independence; would this justify
you in setting at naught a habit of economy and independence, as if a virtue could be turned into a
vice by the misapplication of a name? And suppose that any man, or any number of men, choose
to yield themselves up to gross fanaticism, and to
attempt to pass it off under the name of religion,
or of a revival of religion, who is there that does
not perceive that the existence of the counterfeit
contributes in no way to debase the genuine quality? Prove to me that any thing that takes the name
of a revival is really spurious, and I pledge myself
as a friend of true revivals, to be found on the list
of its opposers. Names are nothing. Things, facts,
realities, are every thing.

IV. Another objection to revivals closely allied
to the preceding is, that *the subjects of them often
fall into a state of mental derangement, and even commit suicide.*

The fact implied in this objection is, to a certain
extent, acknowledged; that is, it is acknowledged
that instances of the kind mentioned do *sometimes*
occur. But is it fair, after all, to consider revivals

as responsible for them? Every one who has any
knowledge of the human constitution, must be aware
that the mind is liable to derangement from any
cause that operates in the way of great excitement;
and whether this effect in any given case, is to be
produced or not, depends partly on the peculiar
character of the mind which is the subject of the
operation, and partly on the degree of self-control
which the individual is enabled to exercise. Hence
we find on the list of maniacs, and of those who
have committed suicide, many in respect to whom
this awful calamity is to be traced to the love of the
world. Their plans for accumulating wealth have
been blasted, and when they expected to be rich
they have suddenly found themselves in poverty and
perhaps obscurity; and instead of sustaining themselves against the shock, they have yielded to it;
and the consequence has been the wreck of their
intellect, and the sacrifice of their life. You who
are men of business well know that the case to
which I have here referred is one of no uncommon
occurrence; but who of you ever thought that these
cases reflected at all upon the fair and honorable
pursuit of the world? Where is the merchant who,
on hearing that some commercial adventurer had
become deranged in consequence of some miserable speculation, and had been found dead with a
halter about his neck, ever said, "I will close my
accounts and shut up my store, and abandon this
business of buying and selling, which leads to such
fatal results?" Is there one of you who ever made

such an inference from such a fact; or who ever relaxed at all in your worldly occupation, on the ground that some individuals had perverted the same occupation to their ruin? Here you are careful enough to distinguish between the thing, and the abuse of it; and why not be equally candid in respect to revivals of religion? When you hear of instances of suicide in revivals, remember that such instances occur in other scenes of life, and other departments of action; and if you are not prepared to make commerce, and learning, and politics, and virtuous attachment, responsible for this awful calamity, because it is sometimes connected with them, then do not attempt to cast this responsibility upon religion, or revivals of religion, because here too individuals are sometimes left to this most fearful visitation.

I have said that *some* such cases as the objection supposes occur; but I maintain that the number is, by the enemies of revivals, greatly overrated. Twenty men may become insane, and may actually commit suicide from any other cause, and the fact will barely be noticed; but let one come to this awful end in consequence of religious excitement, and it will be blazoned upon the house top, with an air of melancholy boding and yet with a feeling of real triumph; and many a gazette will introduce it with some sneering comments on religious fanaticism; and the result will be that it will become a subject of general notoriety and conversation. In this way, the number of these melancholy cases comes to be imagined much larger than it really is ; and in the common estimate of the opposers of revivals, it is no doubt multiplied many fold.

But admitting that the number of these cases were as great as its enemies would represent—admit that in every extensive revival there were one person who actually became deranged, and fell a victim to that derangement, are you prepared to say, even then, upon an honest estimate of the comparative good and evil that is accomplished, that that revival had better not have taken place? On the one side, estimate fairly the evil; and we have no wish to make it less than it really is. There is the premature death of an individual;—death in the most unnatural and shocking form; and fitted to harrow the feelings of friends to the utmost. There may be a temporary loss of usefulness to the world; and as the case may be, a loss of counsel, and aid, and effort, in some of the tenderest earthly relations. Yet it is not certain but that the soul may be saved: for though, at the time the awful act is committed, there may be thick darkness hanging about it, and even the phrenzy of despair may have seized hold of it, yet no mortal can decide that God's Spirit may not after all have performed its effectual work; and that the soul, liberated from the body by the most dreadful act which man can commit, may not find its way to heaven, to be forever with the Lord. But suppose the very worst—suppose this sinner who falls in a fit of religious insanity, by the violence of his own hand, to be unrenewed—why in this case he rushes prematurely upon the wrath of God; he cuts short the period of his probation; which, had it been protracted, he might or might not, have improved to the salvation of his soul. Look now at the other side. In the revival in which this unhappy case has occurred, besides the general quickening impulse that has been given to the people of God, perhaps one hundred individuals have had their character renovated, and their doom reversed. Each one of these was hastening forward perhaps to a death bed of horror, certainly to an eternity of wailing; but in consequence of the change that has passed upon them, they can now anticipate the close of life with peace, and the ages of eternity with unutterable joy. There is no longer any condemnation to them, because they are in Christ Jesus. And besides, they are prepared to live usefully in the world;—each of them to glorify God by devoting himself, according to his ability, to the advancement of his cause. Now far be it from us to speak lightly of such a heart-rending event as the death of a fellow-mortal, in the circumstances we have supposed; but if any will weigh this against the advantages of a revival, we have a right to weigh the advantages of a revival against this; and to call upon you to decide for yourselves which preponderates? Is the salvation of one hundred immortal souls (supposing that number to be converted) a light matter, when put into the scale against the premature and awful death of a single individual; or to suppose the very worst of the case—his cutting short his space for repentance, and rushing unprepared into the presence of his Judge?

V. It is further objected against revivals, that *they occasion a sort of religious dissipation;* leading men to neglect their worldly concerns for too many religious exercises; exercises too, protracted, not unfrequently, to an unseasonable hour.

No doubt it is possible for men to devote themselves more to social religious services than is best for their spiritual interests; because a constant attendance on these services would interfere with the more private means of grace, which all must admit are of primary importance. But who are the persons by whom this objection is most frequently urged, and who seem to feel the weight of it most strongly? Are they those who actually spend most time in their closets, and who come forth into the world with their hearts deeply imbued with a religious influence, and who perform their secular duties from the most conscientious regard to God's authority? Or are they not rather those who rarely, if ever, retire to commune with God, and who engage in the business of life from mere selfish considerations;—who, in short, are thorough going worldlings? If a multitude of religious meetings are to be censured on the ground of their interference with other duties, I submit it to you whether this censure comes with a better grace from him who performs these duties, or from him who neglects them? I submit it to you, whether the man who is

conscious of living in the entire neglect of religion,
ought to be very lavish in his censures upon those
who are yielding their thoughts to it in any way, or
to any extent? Would it not be more consistent at
least for him to take care of the beam, before he
troubles himself about the mote?

Far be it from me to deny that the evil which
this objection contemplates does sometimes exist;—
that men, and especially women, do neglect private
and domestic duties for the sake of mingling continually in social religious exercises: nevertheless,
I am constrained to say that the objection, as it is
directed against the mass of Christians, during a
well regulated revival, is utterly unfounded. For I
ask who are the persons who have ordinarily the
best regulated families, who are most faithful to
their children, most faithful in their closets, most
faithful and conscientious in their relative duties,
and even in their worldly engagements? If I may
be permitted to answer, I should say unhesitatingly,
they are generally the very persons, who love the
social prayer meeting, and the meeting for Christian instruction and exhortation; those in short who
are often referred to by the enemies of revivals, as
exemplifying the evil which this objection contemplates. God requires us to do every duty, whether
secular or religious, in its right place; and this the
Christian is bound to keep in view in all his conduct. But there is too much reason to fear that
the spirit which ordinarily objects against many religious exercises, is a spirit, which, if the whole

LECTURE II.

placency in any.

But it is alleged that, during revivals, religious
meetings are not only multiplied to an improper extent, but are protracted to an unseasonable hour.
That instances of this kind exist admits not of question; and it is equally certain that the case here
contemplated is an evil which every sober, judicious
Christian must discourage. We do not believe that
in an enlightened community, it is an evil of very
frequent occurrence ; but wherever it exists, it is to
be reprobated as an abuse, and not to be regarded
as any part of a genuine revival; or as any thing
for which a true revival is responsible. But here
again, it may be worth while to inquire how far many of the individuals who offer this objection are
consistent with themselves. They can be present
at a political cabal, or at a convivial meeting, which
lasts the whole night, and these occasions may be of
very frequent occurrence, and yet it may never occur
to them that they are keeping unseasonable hours.
Or their children may return at the dawn of day,
from a scene of vain amusement, in which they
have brought on an entire prostration both of mind
and body, and unfitted themselves for any useful exertion during the day ; and yet all this is not only
connived at as excusable, but smiled upon as commendable. I do not say that it is right to keep up
a religious meeting during the hours that Providence
has allotted to repose : I believe fully that in ordinary cases it is wrong; but sure I am that I could

not hold up my head to say this, if I were accustomed to look with indulgence on those other scenes of the night of which I have spoken. It is best to spend the night as God designed it should be spent, in refreshing our faculties by sleep ; but if any other way is to be chosen, judge ye whether they are wisest, who deprive themselves of repose in an idle round of diversion, or they who subject themselves to the same sacrifice in exercises of devotion and piety.

VI. It is objected against revivals that *they often introduce discord into families, and disturb the general peace of society.*

It must be conceded that rash and intemperate measures have sometimes been adopted in connection with revivals, or at least what have passed under the name of revivals, which have been deservedly the subject of censure, and which were adapted, by stirring up the worst passions of the heart, to introduce a spirit of fierce contention and discord. But I must be permitted to say that, whatever evil such measures may bring in their train, is not to be charged upon genuine revivals of religion. The revivals for which we plead are characterized, not by a spirit of rash and unhallowed attack on the part of their friends, which might be supposed to have come up from the world below, but by that wisdom which cometh down from above ; which is pure, peaceable, gentle, and easy to be entreated. For all the discord and mischief that result from measures designed to awaken opposition and provoke the bad passions, they only are to be held responsible by whom those measures are devised or adopted. We hesitate not to say that there is no communion between the spirit that dictates them, and the spirit of true revivals.

Nevertheless, it must be acknowledged that there are instances, in which a revival of religion conducted in a prudent and scriptural manner, awakens bitter hostility, and sometimes occasions, for the time, much domestic unhappiness. There are cases in which the enmity of the heart is so deep and bitter, that a bare knowledge of the fact that sinners around are beginning to inquire, will draw forth a torrent of reproach and railing; and there are cases too in which the fact that an individual in a family becomes professedly pious, will throw that family into a violent commotion, and waken up against the individual bitter prejudices, and possibly be instrumental of exiling a child, or a wife, or a sister, from the affections of those most dear to them. But you surely will not make religion, or a revival of religion, responsible for cases of this kind. Did not the benevolent Jesus himself say that he came not to send peace on the earth but a sword;—meaning by it this very thing—that in prosecuting the object of his mission into the world, he should necessarily provoke the enmity of the human heart, and thus that enmity would act itself out in the persecution of himself and his followers? The Saviour, by his perfect innocence, his divine holiness, his uncompromising faithfulness, provoked the Jews to imbrue their hands in his blood; but who ever supposed that the responsibility of their murderous act rested upon him? In like manner, ministers and Christians, by laboring for the promotion of a revival of religion, may be the occasion of fierce opposition to the cause of truth and holiness; but if they labor only in the manner which God has prescribed, they are in no way accountable for that opposition. It will always be right for individuals to secure the salvation of their own souls, let it involve whatever domestic inconvenience, or whatever worldly sacrifice it may. And so too, it will be always right for Christians to labor in God's appointed way for the salvation of others; though in doing so, they should kindle up against them the fiercest opposition. Where such opposition is excited, the opposers of religion may set it to the account of revivals; but God the righteous Judge will take care that it is charged where it fairly belongs.

VII. It is objected, again, to revivals that *the supposed conversions that occur in them are usually too sudden to be genuine; and that the excitement which prevails at such a time, must be a fruitful source of self-deception.*

That revivals are often perverted to minister to self-deception cannot be questioned; and this is always to be expected, when there is much of human machinery introduced. Men often suppose themselves converted, and actually pass as converts, merely from some impulse of the imagination, when they have not even been the subjects of true conviction. But notwithstanding this abuse, who will say that the Bible does not warrant us to expect sudden conversions ? What say you of the three thousand who were converted on the day of pentecost? Shall I be told that there was a miraculous agency concerned in producing that wonderful result? I answer there was indeed a miracle wrought in connection with that occasion; but there was no greater miracle in the actual conversion of those sinners than there is in the conversion of any other sinners; for conversion is in all cases the same work ; and accomplished by the same agency—viz. the special agency of the Holy Spirit. This instance then is entirely to our purpose ; and proves at least the possibility that a conversion may be sound, though it be sudden.

Nor is there any thing in the nature of the case that should lead us to a different conclusion. For what is conversion ? It is a turning from sin to holiness. The truth of God is presented before the mind, and this truth is cordially and practically believed ; it is received into the understanding, and through that reaches the heart and life. Suppose the truth to be held up before the mind already awake to its importance, and in a sense prepared for its reception, what hinders but that it should be received immediately? But this would be all that is intended by a sudden conversion. Indeed we all admit that the *act* of conversion, whenever it takes place, is sudden ; and why may not the preparation for it, in many instances, be so also? Where is the absurdi-

ty of supposing that a sinner may, within a very
short period, be brought practically to believe both
the truth that awakens the conscience, and that
which converts the soul;—in other words may pass
from a state of absolute carelessness to reconciliation with God? The *evidence* of conversion must
indeed be gradual, and must develope itself in a subsequent course of exercises and acts; so that it
were rash to *pronounce* any individual in such circumstances a true convert; but not only the *act* of
conversion but the *immediate preparation* for it, may
be sudden; and we may reasonably hope, in any giv-
en case of apparent conversion, that the change is
genuine.

I may add that the general spirit of the Bible is,
by no means, unfavorable to sudden conversions.
The Bible calls upon men to repent; to believe; to
turn to the Lord *now ;* it does not direct them to put
themselves on a course of preparation for doing
this at some future time; but it allows no delay;
it proclaims that now is the accepted time, now the
day of salvation. When men are converted suddenly, is there any thing more than an immediate
compliance with these divine requisitions which
are scattered throughout the Bible?

But what is the testimony of facts on this subject? It were in vain to deny that some who seem
to be converted during the most genuine revivals
fall away; and it were equally vain to deny that
some who profess to have become reconciled to God,
when there is no revival, fall away. But that any

considerable proportion of the professed subjects of
well regulated revivals apostatize, especially after
having made a public profession, is a position which
I am persuaded cannot be sustained. I know there
are individual exceptions from this remark; exceptions which have occurred under peculiar circumstances; but if I mistake not, those ministers who
have had the most experience on this subject, will
testify that a very large proportion of those whom
they have known professedly beginning the Christian life during a revival, have held on their way
stronger and stronger. It has even been remarked
by a minister who has probably been more conversant with genuine revivals than any other of the
age, that his experience has justified the remark,
that there is a smaller proportion of apostacies
among the professed subjects of revivals than among
those who make a profession when there is no unusual attention to religion.

After all, we are willing to admit that the excitement attending a revival may be the means of self-
deception. But we maintain that this is not, at least
to any great extent, a necessary evil, and that it may
ordinarily be prevented by suitable watchfulness and
caution on the part of those who are active in conducting the work. To accomplish this requires an
intimate knowledge of the heart, and of God's
word, and of the whole subject of experimental religion. But with these qualifications, whether in a
minister or in private Christians; and with the diligent and faithful discharge of duty, we believe that

little more is to be apprehended in respect to self-deception during a revival, than might reasonably be in ordinary circumstances.

VIII. It is objected that *revivals are followed by seasons of corresponding declension; and that, therefore, nothing is gained, on the whole, to the cause of religion.*

This remark must of course be limited in its application to those who were before Christians;— for it surely cannot mean that those who are really converted during a revival, lose the principle of religion from their hearts, after it has passed away. Suppose then it be admitted that Christians, on the whole, gain no advantage from revivals, on account of the reaction that takes place in their experience; still there is the gain of a great number of genuine conversions; and this is clear gain from the world. Is it not immense gain to the church, immense gain to the Saviour, that a multitude of souls should yield up their rebellion, and become the subjects of renewing grace? And if this is an effect of revivals (and who can deny it?) what becomes of the objection that, on the whole, they bring no gain to the cause?

But it is not true that revivals are of no advantage to Christians. It is confidently believed, if you could hear the experience of those who have labored in them most faithfully and most successfully, you would learn that these were the seasons in which they made their brightest and largest attainments in religion. And these seasons they have not

failed subsequently to connect with special praise
and thanksgiving to God. That there are cases in
which Christians, during a revival, have had so
much to do with the hearts of others, that they have
neglected their own ; and that there is danger, from
the very constitution of the human mind, that an
enlivened and elevated state of Christian affections
will be followed by spiritual languor and listlessness,
I admit ; but I maintain that these are not necessary evils ; and that the Christian, by suitable watchfulness and effort, may avoid them.   It is not in human nature always to be in a state of strong excitement ; but it is possible for any Christian to maintain habitually that spirit of deep and earnest piety,
which a revival is so well fitted to awaken and
cherish.

IX. The last objection against revivals which I
shall notice is, that *they cherish the spirit of secta-
rism, and furnish opportunities and inducements to different denominations to make proselytes.*

I own, Brethren, with grief and shame for our
common imperfections, that the evil contemplated
in this objection frequently does occur ; and though,
for a time, different sects may seem to co-operate
with each other for the advancement of the common cause, yet they are exceedingly apt, sooner or
later, to direct their efforts mainly to the promotion
of their own particular cause ; and sometimes it
must be confessed the greater has seemed to be almost forgotten in the less.   Wherever this state of
things exists, it is certainly fraught with evil ; and

the only remedy to be found for it is an increased degree of intelligence, piety, and charity, in the church.

But here again, let me remind you that, let this evil be as great as it may, the most that you can say of its connexion with revivals is, that they are the innocent occasion of it—not the faulty cause. Suppose an individual, or any number of individuals, were to take occasion from the fact that we are assembled here for religious worship, to come in, in violation of the laws of the land, and by boisterous and menacing conduct, to disturb our public service; and suppose they should find themselves forthwith within the walls of a jail;—the fact of our being here engaged in the worship of God might be the occasion of the evil which they had brought upon themselves; but surely no man in the possession of his reason would dream that it was the responsible cause. In like manner, a revival may furnish an opportunity, and suggest an inducement, to different religious sects to bring as many into their particular communion as they can; and they may sometimes do this in the exercise of an unhallowed party spirit; but the evil is to be charged, not upon the revival, but upon the imperfections of Christians and ministers, which have taken occasion from this state of things, thus to come into exercise. The revival is from above : the proselyting spirit is from beneath.

But the fallacy of this objection may best be seen by a comparison of the evil complained of, with the good that is achieved. You and I are Presbyterians : but we profess to believe that our neighbors of many of the different denominations around us, hold the fundamental truths of the gospel, and are walking in the way to heaven. As Presbyterians we have a right, and it is our duty to take special heed to the interests of our own church ; but much as we may venerate her order or her institutions, who among us is there that does not regard *Christian* as a much more hallowed name? In other words, where is the man who would not consider it comparatively a light matter whether an individual should join our particular communion or some other, provided he gave evidence of being a real disciple of Christ? Now apply this remark to revivals. The evil complained of is, that different sects manifest an undue zeal to gather as many of the hopeful subjects of revivals as they can into their respective communions. Suppose it be so—and what is the result? Why that they are training up—not as we should say, perhaps, under the best form of church government, or possibly the most unexceptionable views of Christian doctrine—but still in the bosom of the church of God, under the dispensation of his word, and in the enjoyment of his ordinances, and in communion with his people—are training up to become members of that communion in which every other epithet will be merged in that of sons and daughters of the Lord Almighty. Place then, on the one side, the fact that these individuals are to remain in their sins, supposing there is no revi-

val of religion, and on the other, the fact that they
are to be proselyted, if you please, to some other
Christian sect, provided there is one; and then tell
me whether the objection which I am considering
does not dwindle to nothing. I would not deem it
uncharitable to say that the man who could maintain this objection in this view, that is, the man who
could feel more complacency in seeing his fellow
men remain in his own denomination dead in trespasses and sins, than in seeing them join other denominations giving evidence of being the followers
of the Lord Jesus, whatever other sect he may belong to, does not belong to the sect of true disciples. Whatever may be his shibboleth, rely on it,
he has not learned to talk in the dialect of heaven.

I have presented this subject before you, my
friends, at considerable length, not because I have
considered myself as addressing a congregation hostile to revivals—for I bear you testimony that it is
not so—but because most of the objections which
have been noticed are more or less current in the
community, and I have wished to guard you against
the influence of these objections on the one hand,
and to assist you to be always ready to give an answer to any one that asketh a reason of your views
of this subject on the other. I hope that what has
been said may confirm your conviction that the
cause of revivals is emphatically the Saviour's cause;
and that you may be disposed, each one to labor in
it with increased diligence and zeal. And may your
labors be characterized by such Christian prudence,

and tenderness, and fidelity, that while you shall see
a rich blessing resting upon them, they may have a
tendency to silence the voice of opposition, and increase the number of those who shall co-operate
with you in sustaining and advancing this glorious
cause.

LECTURE III.

OBSTACLES TO REVIVALS.

I. Corinthians, ix. 12.

—Lest we should hinder the gospel of Christ.

It is impossible to contemplate either the life or
writings of the Apostle Paul, without perceiving
that the ruling passion of his renewed nature was
a desire to glorify God in the salvation of men.—
For the accomplishment of this end there was no
service which he would not perform; no earthly
comfort which he would not surrender; no suffering which he would not endure. A charming illustration of his disinterestedness in the cause of his
Master, occurs in the chapter which contains our
text. He maintains, both from scripture and from
general equity, the right which a minister of the gospel has to be supported by those among whom he
labors; and then shows how he had waived that
right in favor of the Corinthians, that the purpose
of his ministry might be more effectually gained.—
" *If others be partakers of this power over you,*" says
he, that is, " if it is the privilege of ministers in general to receive their support from those for whose

benefit they labor, *are not we rather* entitled to this privilege—we who have been instrumental not only of instructing and comforting you, but of leading you to the profession of christianity? *Nevertheless we have not used this power, but suffer all things, lest we should hinder the gospel of Christ:* we cheerfully submit to many inconveniences and deprivations, that our success in winning souls to Christ through the gospel, may not be in any degree hindered by the cavils of those who are always on the alert to misrepresent and censure us."

The text takes for granted that there may exist certain hindrances to the influence of the gospel. As every genuine revival of religion is effected through the instrumentality of the gospel, it will be no misapplication of the passage to consider it as suggesting some of the OBSTACLES which often exist in the way of a revival; and in this manner I purpose to consider it at the present time.

What then are some of the most common hindrances to a scriptural revival of religion?

I. *Ignorance or misapprehension of the nature of true revivals.*

It is not to be concealed or denied that much has passed at various periods under the name of revivals, which a sound and intelligent piety could not fail to reprobate. There have been scenes in which the decorum due to christian worship has been entirely forgotten; in which the fervor of passion has been mistaken for the fervor of piety; in which the awful name of God has been invoked not only with irreverence but with disgusting familiarity; in which scores and even hundreds have mingled together in a revel of fanaticism. Now unhappily there are those, and I doubt not good men too, who have formed their opinion of revivals from these most unfavorable specimens. These perhaps, and no others, may have fallen under their observation; and hence they conclude that whatever is reported to them under the name of a revival, partakes of the same general character with what they have witnessed; and hence too they look with suspicion on any rising religious excitement, lest it should run beyond bounds, and terminate in a scene of religious phrenzy.

There are others, (I here speak particularly of ministers of the gospel—for their influence is of course most extensively felt on this subject) who are led to look with distrust on revivals, merely from constitutional temperament, or from habits of education, or from the peculiar character of their own religious experience; and while they are hearty well wishers to the cause of Christ, they are perhaps too sensitive to the least appearance of animal feeling. Besides, they not improbably have never witnessed a revival, and as the case may be, have been placed in circumstances least favorable to understanding its nature or appreciating its importance. What is true of one individual in this case, may be true of many; and if the person concerned be a minister of the gospel, or even a very efficient and influential layman, he may contribute in no small degree to form the opinion that prevails on this subject through a congregation, or even a more extensive community.

Now you will readily perceive that such a state of things as I have here supposed, must constitute a serious obstacle to the introduction of a revival. There are cases indeed in which God is pleased to glorify his sovereignty, by marvellously pouring down his Spirit for the awakening and conversion of sinners, where there is no special effort on the part of his people to obtain such a blessing; but it is the common order of his providence to lead them earnestly to desire, and diligently to seek, the blessing, before he bestows it. But if, instead of seeking these special effusions of divine grace, they have an unreasonable dread of the excitement by which such a scene may be attended; if the apprehension that God may be dishonored by irreverence and confusion, should lead them unintentionally to check the genuine aspirations of pious zeal, or even the workings of religious anxiety, there is certainly little reason to expect in such circumstances a revival of religion. I doubt not that a case precisely such as I have supposed has sometimes existed; and that an honest, but inexcusably ignorant conscience on the part of a minister or of a church, has prevailed to prevent a gracious visit from the Spirit of God.

II. Another obstacle to a revival of religion is found in *a spirit of worldliness among professed christians.* The evil to which I here refer assumes a great variety of forms, according to the ruling passion of each individual, and the circumstances in which he may be placed. There are some of the professed disciples of Christ, who seem to think of little else than the acquisition of wealth ; who are not only actively engaged, as they have a right to be, to increase their worldly possessions, but who seem to allow all their affections to be engrossed by the pursuit; who are willing to rise up early, and sit up late, and eat the bread of carefulness, to become rich; and whose wealth, after it is acquired, serves only to gratify a spirit of avarice, or possibly a passion for splendor, but never ministers to the cause of charity. There is another class of professors whose hearts are set upon worldly promotion ; who seem to act as if the ultimate object were to reach some high post of honor; who often yield to a spirit of unhallowed rivalry, and sometimes employ means to accomplish their purposes which christian integrity scarcely knows how to sanction. And there is another class still, not less numerous than either of the preceding, who must be set down in a modified sense at least, as the lovers of pleasure: far enough are they from encouraging or tolerating any thing gross or offensive to a cultivated worldly taste; but they mingle unhesitatingly in scenes of amusement, from which they know before hand that every thing connected with religion must be excluded; and they talk afterwards with enthusiasm of the enjoyment they have experienced in such scenes ; and if the consistency of their mingling in them with christian obligations happens to be called in question, not improbably they will defend themselves with spirit against what they are pleased to call a whimsical or superstitious prejudice. There are professors of religion among those who take the lead in fashionable life : they seem to breathe freely only when they are in circles of gaiety; and if they were taken out of the ranks of pleasure, the language of their hearts, if not of their lips, would doubtless be, "ye have taken away my gods, and what have I more?" I am willing to hope that the number to whom this can apply, in all its extent, is, at this day, comparatively small—certainly it is becoming smaller; but there are many who are ready to make a partial compromise with conscience on this subject; and who, in keeping aloof from the extreme of too great strictness, slide too near, to say the least, to the confines of the opposite error. All these different classes, if their conduct is a fair basis for an opinion, have the world, in some form or other, uppermost. They are quite absorbed with the things which are seen and are temporal. Their conversation is not in heaven. It breathes not the spirit of heaven. It does not relate to the enjoyments of heaven, or the means of reaching those enjoyments. The world take knowledge of them, not that they have been with Jesus, but that like themselves, they love to grovel amidst the things below.

That the evil which I have here described existing in a church, must be a formidable obstacle to a revival of religion, none of us probably will doubt. Let us see for a moment, *how* it is so.

The individuals concerned constitute the church, or a portion of the church—the very body in which, according to the common course of God's providence, we are to expect a revival to begin.— But the prevalence of this worldly spirit of which I have spoken, is the very opposite of the spirit of a revival; and can have no more communion with it than light with darkness. So long as it exists then, it must keep out that general spirituality and active devotedness to the cause of Christ in which a revival, as it respects Christians, especially consists; and of course must prevent all that good influence, which a revival in the church would be fitted to exert upon the world.

But suppose there be in the church those who are actually revived, and who have a right estimate of their obligations to labor and pray for the special effusion of divine influences, how manifest is it that this spirit of worldliness must, to a great extent, paralyze their efforts? How painfully discouraging to them must it be, to behold those who have pledged themselves to co-operate with them in the great cause, turning away to the world, and virtually giving their sanction to courses of conduct directly adapted to thwart their benevolent efforts! And how naturally will careless sinners, when they are pressed by the tender and earnest expostulations of the faithful to flee from the wrath to come, shelter themselves in the reflection that there is another class of professors who estimate this matter differently, and whose whole conduct proclaims that they consider all this talk about religion as unnecessary—not to say fanatical. I know that a few Christians, have, in some instances, been enabled by God's special blessing, to stem such a current as this; and have been permitted to witness the most glorious results from their persevering labors; but I know too that nothing is more disheartening to a few devoted disciples of Christ—nothing more directly fitted to render their exertions of no effect, than for the mass of professors around them to be buried up in the world; to be found with them at the communion table commemorating the *death* of Christ, but never to go with them in any effort for the advancement of his *cause*.

But while this spirit of worldliness mocks in a great degree the efforts of the faithful, it exerts a direct and most powerful influence upon those who are glad to find apologies to quiet themselves in sin. I know that it is a miserable fallacy that the inconsistent lives of professed christians constitute any just ground of reproach against the gospel; nevertheless, it is a fact of which no one can be ignorant, that there are multitudes who look at the gospel only as it is reflected in the character of its professors; and especially in their imperfections and backslidings. These are all strangely looked at, as if religion were responsible for them; and whether it be a particular act of gross transgression, or a general course of devotedness to the world, it will be almost sure to be turned to account in support of the comfortable doctrine that religion does not make men the better, and therefore it is safe to let it alone altogether : or else it is inferred that, if religion be any thing, it may be safely delayed ; for it is so small a matter that it may be taken up at any time: or possibly the individual referring his own character to the low standard which he may observe among professors, may charitably conclude that he is already a Christian ; and thus by playing off upon himself the arts of self-deception, may lull himself into a lethargy, out of which he will never awake, until he is roused by the light of eternity both to conviction and despair.   None surely will question that whatever exerts such an influence as this on the careless and ungodly, must constitute a powerful barrier to a revival of religion.

But this worldly spirit is to be looked at moreover in the relation which it bears to the Spirit of God ; for God's Spirit, let it always be remembered, is the grand agent in every revival.   What then do professing Christians virtually say to the Holy Spirit, when they lose sight of their obligations, and open their hearts and their arms to the objects and interests of the world ?   Do they thereby invite him to come, and be with them, and dwell with them, and to diffuse his convincing and converting influences all around ?   Or do they not rather proclaim their indifference, to say the least, to his gracious operations ; and sometimes even virtually beseech him to depart out of their coasts ?   But it is the manner of our God to bestow his Spirit in unison with the desires and in answer to the prayers of his people—

can we suppose then, that where the spirit of the
world has taken the place of the spirit of prayer,
and the enjoyments of the world are more thought
of than the operations of the Holy Ghost—can we
suppose, I say, that He who is jealous of his honor,
will send down those gracious influences which are
essential to a revival of religion ?

Whether, therefore, we consider a worldly spirit
among professed Christians, in its relation to themselves, to their fellow professors who are faithful, to
the careless world, or to the Spirit of God, we cannot fail to perceive that it must stand greatly in the
way of the blessing we are contemplating.

III. *The want of a proper sense of personal responsibility among professed Christians*, constitutes another
obstacle to a revival of religion.	You all know how
essential it is to the success of any worldly enterprize, that those who engage in it should feel person-
ally responsible in respect to its results.	Bring to-
gether a body of men for the accomplishment of
any object, no matter how important, and there is
always danger that personal obligation will be lost
sight of ; that each individual will find it far easier
to do nothing, or even to do wrong, than if, instead
of dividing the responsibility with many, he was
obliged literally to bear his own burden.	And just
in proportion as this spirit pervades any public body,
it may reasonably be expected either that they will
accomplish nothing, or nothing to any good purpose.

Now let this same spirit pervade a church, or any community of professed Christians, and you can look for nothing better than a similar result. True it is, as we have already had occasion to remark, that, in a revival of religion, there is much of divine agency and of divine sovereignty too; but there is human instrumentality also; and much of what God does is done through his people; and if they remain with their arms folded, it were unreasonable to expect that God's work should be revived. Let each professor regard his own personal responsibility as merged in the general responsibility of the church, and the certain consequence will be that the church as a body will accomplish nothing. Each member may be ready to deplore the prevalence of irreligion and spiritual lethargy, and to acknowledge that something ought to be done in the way of reform; but if, at the same time, he cast his eye around upon his fellow professors, and reflect that there are many to share with him the responsibility of inaction, and that, as his individual exertions could effect but little, so his individual neglect would incur but a small proportion of the whole blame—if he reason in this way, I say, to what purpose will be all his acknowledgments and all his lamentations? In order that God's work may be revived, there must be earnest prayer; but where is the pledge for this, unless his people realize their individual obligations? There must also be diligent, and persevering, and self-denied effort; but where are the persons who are ready for this, provided each one feels that he has no personal responsibility? Who will warn the wicked of his wicked way, and exhort him to turn and live? Who will stretch out his hand to reclaim the wandering Christian, or open his lips to stir up the sluggish one? Who, in short, will do any thing that God requires to be done in order to the revival of his work, if the responsibility of the whole church is not regarded as the responsibility of the several individuals who compose it? Wherever you see a church in which this mistaken view of obligation generally prevails, you may expect to see that church asleep; and sinners around asleep; and you need not look for the breaking up of that slumber, until Christians have come to be weighed down under a sense of personal obligation.

Moreover, let it be remembered that the evil of which I am speaking, is fitted to prevent the revival of God's work, inasmuch as it has within itself all the elements of a grievous backsliding. Wherever you find professors of religion who have little or no sense of their own obligations apart from the general responsibility of the church, there you may look with confidence for that wretched inconsistency, that careless and unedifying deportment that is fitted to arm sinners with a plea against the claims of religion, which they are always sure to use to the best advantage. And on the other hand, wherever you see professing Christians realizing that arduous duties devolve upon them as individuals, and that the indifference of others can be no apology for their own, there you will see a spirit of self-denial, and humility, and active devotedness to the service of Christ, which will be a most impressive exemplification of the excellence of the gospel, and which will be fitted at once to awaken sinners to a conviction of its importance, and to attract them to a compliance with its conditions. In short, you will see precisely that kind of agency on the part of Christians which is most likely to lead to a revival, whether you consider it as bearing directly on the minds of sinners, or as securing the influence of the Spirit of God.

IV. *The toleration of gross offences in the church,* is another serious hindrance to a revival of religion. We cannot suppose that the Saviour expected that the visible church on earth would ever be entirely pure; or that there would not be in it those who were destitute of every scriptural qualification for its communion; or even those whose lives would be a constant contradiction of their profession, and a standing reproach upon his cause. He himself hath said that "it must needs be that offences come;" though he has added with awful emphasis, "wo unto that man by whom they come." And the whole tenor of God's word goes to show that it is required of the church—of the whole body, and of each particular member—that they keep themselves unspotted from the world; that they have no fellowship with the unfruitful works of darkness; that they exhibit, in all respects, that character which becomes " a chosen generation, a royal priesthood,

an holy nation, a peculiar people." And inasmuch
as there was danger from the imperfection and depravity of man, that the church would embody a
greater or less amount of hypocrisy and corruption,
it pleased the great Master to prescribe rules for the
maintenance of her purity. Hence Christians are
exhorted to stir up one another by putting each other
in remembrance ; to reprove and admonish each
other with fidelity as occasion may require ; and in
case of scandalous offences persisted in or not re-
pented of, the church as a body is bound to cut off
the offender from her communion. In performing
this last and highest act of discipline, as well as in
all the steps by which she is led to it, she acts, not
according to any arbitrary rules of her own, but under the authority, and agreeably to the directions
of her Head.

Now it is impossible to look at the state of many
churches, without perceiving that there is a sad disregard to the directions of the Lord Jesus Christ,
in respect to offending members. It sometimes
happens that professors of religion are detected in
grossly fraudulent transactions ; that they grind the
face of the widow and orphan ; that they take upon
their lips the language of cursing, and even profanely
use the awful name of God ; not to speak of what has
been more common in other days—their reeling under the influence of the intoxicating draught—I say it
sometimes happens that Christian professors exemplify some or other of these vices, and still retain a
regular standing in the church, and perhaps never

even hear the voice of reproof; especially if the individuals concerned happen to possess great worldly influence, and the church, as it respects temporal interests, is in some measure dependent upon them.   But rely on it, Brethren, this is an evil which is fitted to reach vitally the spiritual interests of the church; and wherever it exists, it will in all probability constitute an effectual obstacle to a revival of religion.

For its influence will be felt, in the first place, by the church itself.   The fact that it can tolerate gross offences in its members, proves that its character for spirituality is already low ; but the act of tolerating them must necessarily serve to depress it still more.   It results from our very constitution and from the laws of habit, that to be conversant with open vice, especially where there is any temptation to apologize for it, is fitted to lessen our estimate of its odiousness, and to impair our sense of moral and Christian obligation.   If a church tolerates in its members scandalous sins, it must know as a body that it is in the wrong ; nevertheless each individual will reconcile it to his own conscience as well as he can; and one way will be by endeavoring to find out extenuating circumstances, and possibly to lower a little the standard of Christian character.   Thus it will almost of course come to pass, that that deep and awful sense of the evil of sin which the Christian ought always to cultivate, and which is essential to a high degree of spirituality, will no longer be found ; and in place of it there will be, if not

an exhibition of open vice, yet a disposition to regard iniquity in the heart, and a readiness to partake of other men's sins.

Besides, the neglect of one duty always renders
the neglect of others more easy; not merely from
the fact that there is an intimate connection between
many of the duties which devolve upon Christians,
but because every known deviation from the path of
rectitude has a tendency to lower the tone of religious sensibility, and to give strength to the general
propensity to evil. Let the members of a church
do wrong in the particular of which I am speaking,
and it will make it more easy for them to do wrong
in other particulars. A disregard to their covenant
obligations in this respect, will render them less sensible of the solemnity and weight of their obliga-
gations generally: in short it will lead by almost
certain consequence to that state of things, which
is characterized by spiritual insensibility and death,
and which is the exact opposite of all that belongs
to a revival of religion.

But the evil to which I refer is not less to be deprecated in its direct influence upon the world, than
upon the church. For here is presented a professing Christian, not only practising vices, which, it
may be, would scarcely be tolerated in those who
were professedly mere worldly men, but practising
these vices, for aught that appears, under the sanction of the church. Wherever this flagrant inconsistency is exhibited, the scoffer looks on and
laughs us to scorn. The decent man of the world

concludes, that if the church can tolerate such gross evils, whatever other light she may diffuse around her, it cannot be the light of evangelical purity. And even those who feel the weight of Christian obligation, and who desire to join in the commemoration of the Redeemer's death, will sometimes hesitate whether they can become members of a community in which the solemn vows of God are so much disregarded. Need I say that there is every thing here to lead sinners to sleep on in carnal security to their dying day?

But observe still farther, that this neglect to purify the church of scandalous offences, is an act of gross disobedience to her Head; to him who has purchased for her all good gifts; and whose prerogative it is to dispense the influences of the Spirit. Suppose ye then that he will sanction a virtual contempt of his authority by pouring down the blessings of his grace? Suppose ye that, if a church set at naught the rules which he has prescribed, and not only suffer sin, but the grossest sin, in her members, to go unreproved, he will crown all this dishonor done to his word, all this inconsistency and flagrant covenant-breaking, with a revival of religion? No, Brethren, this is not the manner of Him who rules King in Zion. He never loses sight of the infallible directory, which he has given to his church; and if any portion of his church lose sight of it, it is at the peril of his displeasure. Disobedience to his commandments may be expected always to incur his frown; and that frown will be manifested at least by withholding the influences of his grace.

V. Another powerful hindrance to a revival of religion, is found in *the absence of a spirit of brotherly love among the professed followers of Christ.*

Christianity never shines forth with more attractive loveliness, or addresses itself to the heart with more subduing energy, than when it is seen binding the disciples of Jesus together in the endearing bonds of a sanctified friendship. Let it be said of Christians as it was in other days, " Behold how they love one another;" let them evince a strong regard to each other's interests, and a tender sympathy in each other's wo, and a ready condescension to each other's infirmities, and a willingness to bear each other's burdens; and, rely on it, this kindly spirit will diffuse a grateful influence all around; and even the enemies of religion will not be able to withhold from it at least the homage of their respect and approbation; and there is good reason to hope that it may be instrumental of subduing many to the obedience of the truth. But on the other hand, let the professed followers of the Saviour manifest towards each other a jealous or contentious spirit; let them appear more intent on the advancement of their own personal, or selfish, or party ends, than upon the promotion of each other's edification and benefit; and those who see them, instead of taking knowledge of them that they have been with Jesus, will take knowledge of them that they have imbibed the very spirit of the world.

The influence of such an example upon the careless, must be to lower their estimate of the importance of religion, and furnish them an excuse for neglecting to seek an interest in it. Oh how often has it been said by infidels and the enemies of godliness, to the reproach of the cause of Christ, that when Christians would leave off contending with each other, it would be time enough for *them* to think of embracing their religion!

But the want of brotherly love operates to prevent a revival of religion, still farther, as it prevents that union of Christian energy, in connection with which God ordinarily dispenses his gracious influences. It prevents a union of counsel. As the Saviour has committed his cause in a sense into the hands of his people, so he has left much as respects the advancement of it, to their discretion. And they are bound to consult together with reference to this end; and to bring their concentrated wisdom to its promotion. But if there be a spirit of alienation and discord among them, either they will never come together at all, or else their counsels will be divided, and they will do little else than defeat each-other's purposes. The same spirit will prevent a union in prayer. This is the grand means by which men prevail with God; and the prospect of their success is always much in proportion to the strength of their mutual Christian affection;—for this is a Christian grace; and if it is in lively exercise, other Christian graces which are more immediately brought into exercise in prayer, such as faith,

repentance and humility, will not be asleep: and as
concentrated effort is the most powerful in all other
cases, so it is in this—let the united prayers of many hearts go up to heaven for the revival of God's
work, and they may be expected to exert an influence
which will tell gloriously on the destinies perhaps
of many sinners. But on the other hand, if there
be not this feeling of brotherly kindness among professed Christians, even if they come together to
pray for the out-pouring of the Spirit, their prayers
will at best be feeble and inefficient, and their
thoughts will not improbably be wandering, and unchristian feelings towards each other kindling, at
the very time they are professedly interceding for
the salvation of sinners. And the same spirit is
equally inconsistent with a union of Christian effort;
for if they cannot take counsel together, if they
cannot pray together, they surely cannot act together. Who does not perceive that a spirit of
mutual unkindness among the professed followers
of Christ, thus carried out into action, must, if any
thing, oppose a powerful obstacle to the revival of
God's work?

But suppose some whom you should regard as
Christians should adopt measures in relation to revivals, unauthorized by God's word, and to say the
least, of very doubtful tendency, and you should
decline to co-operate in such measures, and your
conduct in this respect should be considered as
evincing the want of brotherly love—where, in this
case, would the blame really rest? Most unques-

tionably not on you, but on those who accused you.
There is nothing in the obligation of good will which
Christians owe to each other, to set aside the paramount obligation which they owe to their Master,
to take his word as the rule of their practice. Whatever you conscientiously believe to be unscriptural,
you are bound to decline at any hazard; and if
you do it kindly, (no matter how firmly) and the
charge of being wanting in brotherly love is preferred against you, you have a right to repel it as
an unchristian accusation. If, in such a case, evil
result from the want of concentrated action, and the
measures adopted are really unscriptural, the responsibility rests upon those who, by the adoption
of such measures, (however honestly they may do
it) compel you to stand aloof from them. You may
indeed, in other ways, give evidence of not possess-
ing the right spirit towards them; and it becomes
you to take heed that you do *not* give such evidence;
but the mere fact of refusing your co-operation certainly does not constitute it. And it would be well
if they should inquire whether they are not at as
great a distance from you as you are from them;
and whether their departure from you does not indicate as great a want of brotherly love as is indicated by the fact of your refusing to follow them?
   But it may be asked whether a spirit of brotherly
love may not exist between Christians whose views
on points not fundamental may differ? I answer,
yes undoubtedly; it may and ought to exist among
all who trust in a common Saviour. We may ex-

ercise this spirit even towards those whom we regard as holding errors, either of faith or practice, provided we can discover in them the faintest outline of the image of Christ. They may adopt opinions in which we cannot harmonize, and measures in which we cannot co-operate, and the consequence of this may be a loss of good influence to the cause of Christ, and perhaps positive evil resulting from disunion in effort; nevertheless we may still recognize them as Christians, and love them as Christians, and cordially co-operate with them, wherever our views and theirs may be in harmony. The right spirit among Christians would lead them to make as little of their points of difference, and as much of their common ground, as they can; and where they *must* separate, to do it with kindness and good will, not with bitterness and railing.

I must not dismiss this article without saying that the Spirit of God who is active in awakening and renewing sinners, is the Spirit of peace; he dwells not in scenes of contention; and we cannot reasonably expect his presence or agency, where Christians, instead of being fellow workers together unto the kingdom of God, are alienated from each other, and sell themselves to the service of a party. In accordance with this sentiment, it has often been found in actual experience that the Spirit of God has fled before the spirit of strife; and a revival of religion which promised a glorious result, has been suddenly arrested by some unimpor-

tant circumstance, which the imperfections of good
men have magnified, till they have made it an occasion of controversy. While they are yet scarcely
aware of it, their thoughts which had been engrossed by the salvation of their fellow men and the interests of Christ's kingdom, are intensely fastened
upon another object; and they wake up, when it is
too late, to the appalling fact, that the work of grace
among them has declined, and that sinners around
are sinking back into the deep slumber of spiritual
death.

VI. The last hindrance to a revival which I shall
notice, *is an erroneous or defective exhibition of Christian truth.*

As it is through the instrumentality of the truth
that God performs his work upon the hearts of men,
it is fair to conclude that just in proportion as any
part of it is kept back, or is dispensed in a different
manner from that which he has prescribed, it will
fail of its legitimate effect. It is not at the option
of God's ministers to select one truth from the Bible
and omit another; but they are required to preach
the whole counsel of God; and where they neglect
to do this, it were unreasonable to expect a blessing.
In the exercise of their own judgment on this subject, they may come to the conclusion that particular parts of divine truth are of little importance;
and that even some of the peculiar doctrines of the
gospel may well enough be lightly passed over; but
this is an insult to the author of the Bible which

they have good reason to expect he will punish by sending them a barren ministry.

There is a way of preaching certain doctrines out of their proper connection, which is exceedingly unfriendly to revivals of religion. Suppose, for instance, the doctrine of God's sovereignty be exhibited in such a partial or insulated manner as to leave the sinner to infer that it is but another name for tyranny;—or suppose the doctrine of a divine influence be preached in such a way as to authorize the inference that man has nothing to do in respect to his salvation, but wait to be operated upon like a mere machine; or suppose the doctrine of man's apostacy be so exhibited as to lead sinners to deny their responsibility for their transgressions, and to take refuge from the accusations of conscience in the relation which they bear to the father of our race;—in either of these cases, there is little probability that they will be converted or even awakened. It is natural for them to find excuses for remaining in a state of sinful security as long as they can; and so long as they are furnished with such excuses as these, and by the ministers of the gospel, there is not the least ground for expecting that their consciences will be disturbed. The evil to which I refer, has, I have no doubt, often existed in all its extent, where the minister has actually believed all the truths of God's word; and yet he has exhibited some in such a manner as to neutralize the power of others, and even to prevent the legitimate effect of those he has attempted to enforce.

There is also an unnatural mixing up of human wisdom with God's word, which, so far as it has any effect, must be unfriendly to the influence of divine truth. Let the naked sword of the Spirit be brought home to the consciences of men, and the effect of it must and will be felt, and the anxious inquiry will be heard, and sinners, in all probability, will be renewed. But let the wire-drawn theories of metaphysicians be substituted in place of the simple truth; or even let the genuine doctrines of the gospel be customarily exhibited in connection with the refined speculations of human philosophy; and though I dare not say that God in his sovereignty may not bless the truth which is actually preached, yet I may say with confidence that but little effect can be reasonably expected from such a dispensation of the word. And the reasons are obvious; for God has promised to bless nothing but his own truth; and the refinements of philosophy are to the mass of hearers quite unintelligible.

I may add that a want of directness in the manner of preaching the gospel, may prevent it from taking effect on the consciences and hearts of men. It is only when men are made to feel that the gospel comes home to their individual case, that they are themselves the sinners whom it describes, and that they need the blessings which it offers,—it is only then, I say, that they hear it to any important purpose. Suppose that its doctrines, instead of being exhibited in their practical bearings, and enforced by strong appeals to the conscience, are discussed merely as abstract propositions, and with no direct application, the consequence will be that, though the great truths of the Bible may be presented before the mind, yet they will rarely, if ever, sink into the heart. Sinners will hear them, and instead of realizing that they involve their immortal interests, will probably be as indifferent, as if they were matters of idle speculation. So it has been in a multitude of instances; and so, from the very nature of man, it must continue to be.

I might mention also, as another important hindrance to a revival, the want of a simple dependence on God; but as this will come up in another form in a subsequent discourse, I shall waive, for the present, a distinct consideration of it.

In closing this view which we have taken of the obstacles to a revival of religion, I know not, my Christian Brethren, how we can use the subject in a single word, to better purpose, than to gather from it a deeper impression of our own responsibility.— Christians, ye who profess to desire a revival of religion, and to make this a commanding subject of your prayers, let me ask whether, in view of what you have now heard, you have no reason to fear that you may yourselves be standing in the way of the bestowment of the very blessing for which you profess to plead. The great obstacles to the revival of God's work are no doubt to be sought in the church: what these obstacles are, at least some of the more prominent of them, you have now heard; and I appeal to each of your consciences, as in the presence of the Searcher of the heart, whether the guilt of hindering God's work, in some or other of these ways, does not lie at your door? Wherefore is it that the Holy Spirit is not now as manifestly in the midst of us, by his awakening and converting influences, as he has been in other days? Is it not because you have relapsed in some measure into a habit of worldliness; or because you value the blessing less; or because you are less united and vigorous in your efforts to obtain it? Or is it for any other of the reasons which have now been spread before you? Christians, awake, one and all, to a deeper sense of your responsibility. Let it not be told in heaven that God's people on earth are opposing obstacles to the salvation of perishing men. In doing this, ye parents, ye may be keeping your own children out of heaven. In doing this, ye who have unconverted friends sustaining to you the tenderest earthly relations, you may be assisting to fix their doom in wo forever. In doing this, ye Christians of every class and of every condition, you are opposing the interests of God's holy kingdom, opposing the design of the Saviour's death, opposing the salvation of immortal souls. But you cannot do this, and think what you are doing. It must be that you are acting incautiously. Awake then to solemn reflection. Awake to earnest prayer. Awake to faithful and persevering action.— Else there may be sinners who will greet you at the last day, as the stumbling blocks over which they fell into eternal perdition.

LECTURE IV.

DIVINE AGENCY IN REVIVALS.

HABAKKUK III. 2.

O Lord, revive thy work.

There are few, if any, who acknowledge the existence of a God, but will be ready to admit that he has some kind of agency in the government of the world. What the precise nature or extent of this agency is, however, it were rash even to attempt to determine. Part of it is direct; but much the greater part of it, at least so far as we are concerned, is mediate; and it is not easy for us accurately to draw the line between the one and the other. Besides, he has created a vast multitude of agents, and moral agents; but though he has given them the power of action, he has not made them independent beings; though they act with perfect freedom, yet he acts in them and by them. Is not every man in this respect a mystery to himself? Who will venture to determine, in reference to his own conduct, precisely the measure of influence that is exerted upon him by that Almighty agent, in whom are all the springs, not only of physical, but intellectual and moral being ?

As it is admitted by all except the downright atheist that God has some kind of agency in the government of the world, while yet there is much in respect to the nature and extent of that agency which we cannot understand, so also it is admitted by all Christians that he exerts an influence in the sanctification of men, though they do not pretend exactly to define the character of that influence. On the same general principle, those who believe in revivals of religion, believe that God is the grand agent in producing them; though they are well aware that here, as in other departments of his agency, he " moves in a mysterious way ;" and that this is no field for a roving fancy or rash speculation. Something however may be known on this subject from God's word; and on a matter of such deep and awful concern, while we are to take heed that we keep fairly within our own province, it surely becomes us to gather up with devout attention even the most obscure of the divine intimations. I design therefore in this discourse, to bring this subject before you ; and keeping an eye on the law and the testimony in connection with the unequivocal dictates of experience, reverently to inquire respecting THE AGENCY OF GOD in revivals of religion. The passage which I have read to you, taken from the prayer of Habakkuk, may be a fit introduction to this subject; for though the petition is made up of five words—" O Lord, revive thy work"—it recognises the fact of God's agency in a revival in two different ways:—it declares that the work is God's; and it is the direct expression of a desire that *he* would revive it.

This agency may be advantageously considered under two distinct heads :—

I. The agency of *Providence*.

II. The agency of the *Spirit*.

I. Of *Providence*. It is one of the most simple deductions from the perfections of God, that he orders all things according to the counsel of his own will; in other words, that he has a plan which includes all events; which extends even to the numbering of hairs and the falling of sparrows. Of course, nothing ever occurs to an individual, but is designed to answer some purpose in the chain of events; and it is reasonable to consider the less important events as ordered in reference to the more important ;—the one sustaining to the other the relation of means to an end; though it must be acknowledged that if particular events are viewed in relation to the whole system of Providence, our views are too limited to enable us to judge of their comparative importance. Now it will readily be acknowledged that no event ever occurs in the life of an individual so important to him as his conversion ; the change of his character—from being a subject of pollution to a subject of holiness ; and of his destiny—from being an heir of misery to an heir of glory. It is reasonable therefore to suppose that many events in his life which, taken by themselves, may

seem of little moment, may nevertheless be designed
by Providence to lead to this wonderful change.
And if I mistake not, every Christian, especially
every one whose first experience has been strongly
marked, will find, on review, that he was led to the
fountain of atoning blood by a path which he knew
not; that God was working by circumstances of
which, at the time, he himself made no account, to
prepare him to come out of darkness into marvellous light. Perhaps his serious impressions originated in what seemed an accidental conversation
with some friend;—a conversation which he did not
court, and which would have been avoided, if he had
happened to walk on the opposite side of the street;
or perhaps he was brought to reflection by some
discourse which he had gone to listen to from mere
curiosity; or possibly some circumstance may have
occurred where he would least have looked for it—
in connection with his amusements or his excesses,
which God has overruled as a means of stopping
him in his career of guilt. I doubt not that there
are those among you, Christian friends, who may,
at this moment, be going back in your thoughts to
some event which, at the time, you scarcely noticed,
as having marked the era of your first setting your
face towards heaven; and now that you can look
at that event in some of its more remote influences,
you are ready in devout thanksgiving to the providence of God, to connect with it all the joy that
you have in believing in Jesus, and in the hope of
hereafter seeing him as he is.

Now if it is right to consider God as ordering the events of his providence with reference to the conversion of a single individual, it is certainly safe to form the same conclusion in respect to the conversion of many individuals; in other words, in regard to a revival of religion. There may be obstacles to be removed which seem to lie beyond all human power; but these God not unfrequently puts aside by an agency so silent and simple that men do not even observe it; while in other cases, though more rarely, he accomplishes the same end by some signal dispensation which almost bears the aspect of a miracle;—waking up even the careless mind to the reflection, "What hath God wrought!" Sometimes by the death of an individual, there is an organized and efficient opposition to the gospel put down; and sometimes by an individual changing his residence, there is a large accession of religious influence to some community; and the means of grace are multiplied; and a revival of religion succeeds. There may be some alarming dispensation of providence to arouse many simultaneously to reflection; or some one whose influence is extensively felt may become the subject of renewing grace, and may be a kind of central point from which good influences shall extend in every direction. It is fully believed that, in all ordinary cases in which a revival takes place, it would be no difficult thing to mark a distinct providential agency preparatory to it; and especially where the cause of religion has greatly languished, and the means of religion are but partially enjoyed, this agency is sometimes so manifest as to constitute of itself a distinct and solemn call to sinners to awake out of sleep.   But

II. There is also an agency of the *Spirit*.   This we proceed now to contemplate.

Of those general facts in relation to this subject, which are clearly matter of revelation and experience, we may mention the following:—

1. The fact that *the Spirit actually does operate in the whole work of man's sanctification.*   Hear the Spirit's own testimony on this subject:—"Not by works of righteousness which we have done, but according to his mercy he saved us, by the washing of regeneration, and the renewing of the Holy Ghost." "But as many as received him, to them gave he power to become the sons of God; even to them that believe on his name. Which were born not of blood, nor of the will of the flesh, nor of the will of man, but of God." "God hath from the beginning chosen you to salvation, through the sanctification of the Holy Ghost." "A new heart also will I give you, and a new Spirit will I put within you: and I will take away the stony heart out of your flesh, and I will give you an heart of flesh."

But beside many passages of scripture, of which those now recited are a specimen, in which the doctrine of the Spirit's agency is clearly taught, there are many *facts* recorded in the Bible, by which the same truth is abundantly confirmed.   How will you account for it, for instance, that the preaching of the Son of God produced so little effect, and the preaching of his apostles so much? How was it that multitudes were aroused, and pricked to the heart, and actually converted, under the preaching of Peter, who had sat with indifference, or rather been excited to opposition, under the preaching of Him who spake as never man spake? Whence was it that the jailor, who had doubtless often heard the Apostle before the night of his conversion, remained indifferent till that time; and then evinced so much anxiety and alarm, and finally a disposition to own Jesus as his Saviour and his Master, and to walk in his steps? And in general, whence was it that such marvellous success attended the ministry of the apostles; that by preaching a doctrine which enlisted against it the strongest prejudices and worst passions of the heart, they undermined the thrones of Paganism, and caused tens of thousands to gather around the standard of the cross? Here is a problem that has always been too hard for the jeering infidel to solve; and which most infidels have manifested but little disposition to encounter. There is no solution of it except in the fact that God works in the hearts of men by his Spirit; and that he dispenses it in the sovereignty of his wisdom.

2. Another fact in relation to this subject, of which we have the fullest evidence, is, that *the Spirit, in performing his work upon the hearts of men, has respect to the laws of their moral nature.*

God has made man what he is—a voluntary, accountable agent. He has given him the power not only of distinguishing, but of choosing between good and evil, has constituted him in such a manner that he is susceptible of the influence of motives; and every one must perceive that this involves responsibility. Inasmuch then, as this constitution of our nature is derived from God, it were to be expected that whatever influence he should exert upon the mind would be consistent with it; in other words, that he should not contradict his own works. It would do little honor to infinite wisdom to suppose that he should have formed man with such a nature, that he could not have access to it, without violating the laws which he had himself established.

But the conclusion to which we should arrive on this subject from the very perfections of God, is abundantly corroborated by the testimony of his word. Says Joshua to the people of Israel, "*Choose* you this day whom ye will serve; whether the gods which your fathers served, that were on the other side of the flood, or the gods of the Amorites, in whose land ye dwell; but as for me and my house, we *will* serve the Lord." And again, our Saviour says, "Mary hath *chosen* that good part which shall not be taken away from her." Indeed, what are all the exhortations, and promises, and threatenings, of the Bible, but a mass of evidence that God operates upon the hearts of men as moral agents; that he takes for granted that they are to be active in the work of their sanctification, notwithstanding he is himself the efficient cause of it? Admit that men are operated upon as mere machines, and then read any part of the Bible, and see what meaning you can find in it.

And I may add that the experience of Christians on this subject is in exact correspondence with the teachings of God's word. Let the Christian who is just entering heaven, give himself to the work of reviewing his own experience; let him look back to the hour when he first trembled under a conviction of his guilt; or to the time when he first felt the preciousness of the Saviour's love; or to his subsequent conflicts with corruption and temptation; or to any or every part of his progress in holiness; and while he will acknowledge with gratitude and delight that the Spirit has been active in it all, and deserves all the glory, he will be completely satisfied that there has never been the least interruption of his moral agency. He will find that he has been working out his salvation with fear and trembling, while God has wrought within him both to will and to do.

3. Another fact on this subject, which is ascertained to us by the best evidence, is, that *the Spirit operates by means of the truth.* It is partly in reference to this that He is called " the Spirit of truth;" and so also men are said to be " sanctified by the truth;"—not by the truth independently of the Spirit, but by the Spirit operating by means of the truth. Sometimes the agent alone is mentioned, and sometimes the instrument; but where one is spoken of, the other is always implied.

In the work which the Holy Spirit performs upon the heart, he makes use of every part of the

great system of truth which God has revealed. But
particular truths are adapted to accomplish particular ends: some are especially fitted to alarm the
conscience: others to bring peace and joy into the
soul: others to quicken and encourage to a course
of vigorous activity and Christian self-denial: and
the Spirit, in different parts of his work, uses these
various truths discriminatingly, according to the
particular end he may design to accomplish. When
we say, however, that God's truth is adapted to the
work of man's sanctification, we must beware of
the idea that the efficacy resides ultimately in the
instrument: it is the great agent who produces the
effect; and the truth wielded by any other power
than his, would never sanctify a single heart, even
though it might be preached to every creature. It
is indeed a well adapted—a divinely adapted instrument; but it is an instrument still; and it is only
through God that it is mighty to the pulling down
of strong holds.

We will contemplate for a moment the work of
the Holy Spirit in some of its distinct parts: in
conviction of sin; conversion to God; and subsequent progress in the divine life.

1. The Spirit is active *in convincing men of sin.*
Our Saviour distinctly recognised this among the
great purposes for which the Spirit was to be sent
into the world. "And when he is come," said he,
"he will reprove the world of sin." This office he
performed in the case of the three thousand who
were pricked in the heart on the day of Pentecost,
and said unto Peter and the rest of the Apostles,

" Men and Brethren, what shall we do ?" A similar
effect was produced in the case of the jailer, who,
at midnight, called for a light, and sprang into the
prison, and came trembling, and fell down before
Paul and Silas, and said, " Sirs, what must I do to
be saved ?" And the same thing substantially occurs in the case of every awakened sinner. And
the agent to whom this work is, in every instance,
to be ultimately referred is the Holy Spirit. This
is always the first step to the effectual application
of the benefits of Christ's death ; though there are
multitudes who experience this, and perish notwithstanding.

That faculty or principle of the soul which is
especially the subject of the Spirit's operation in
conviction of sin, is the conscience. It is this
which recognises the difference between right and
wrong, and passes a sentence of approbation or
disapprobation on our own actions. This, therefore, is the appropriate principle to be brought into
exercise in the work of conviction ; and to this the
Spirit always addresses itself. Hence conviction is
uniformly attended by remorse; and not unfrequently so pungent as to amount to agony. Hence, too,
convinced sinners are said to be " pricked in the
heart;"—an expression which denotes the most ex-
cruciating anguish.

The kind of truth which the Spirit uses in accomplishing this work is primarily the law of God.
" By the law," says the Apostle, " is the knowledge
of sin." God's law is nothing else than a transcript

of his moral character; requiring all his creatures to be holy, according to their measure, as he is holy. It is the eternal standard of right; and every departure from it is sin;—the abominable thing which God hateth. But if men are practically ignorant of this standard, they will of course be in the same degree ignorant of their sins; and it is only in proportion as the law is brought home to them in its high and awful bearings, that they can have any conviction of sin. And the more they view the law in its amazing extent, as reaching to the thoughts, affections, purposes—as taking cognizance of the whole inner man; and during every period of their existence;—the more they view it in connection with the awful attributes of Jehovah—especially his omnipotence, his omniscience, his holiness and his truth; so much the more black and dreadful appears the guilt of sin; so much the more numerous and appalling their own personal transgressions. I say, then, that the law is the great instrument which the Spirit of God wields in producing conviction of sin. Let that never be brought in contact with the conscience, and the sinner would go slumbering to his grave. If we might suppose the case that it should be kept out of view in the next world, the hell which the Bible describes could not exist.

There are indeed other parts of divine truth besides the law, which the Spirit uses in the work of conviction; but they are subordinate to this. For instance, the great doctrine of Christ crucified for the sins of men, has often a powerful influence in

convincing men of sin ;—for herein the honors of
the law are maintained; and the argument which
the Spirit uses with the sinner's conscience is, that
if sin be such a tremendous evil as to demand for its
expiation the death of the Son of God, then repentance of sin must be an immediate and imperative duty.   And I doubt not that many a sinner,
while he has yet been blind to the glories of redemption, has derived his deepest conviction of sin
from the views which he has taken of this doctrine:
and the question has forced itself upon his conscience with fearful urgency, "If these things be
done in the green tree, what shall be done in the
dry ?"

The same is true of various other parts of divine
truth: the Spirit in his gracious sovereignty uses
them to convince men of sin ; and sometimes even
those truths which might seem to us least adapted
to that end; but the influence which they exert is
indirect; and uniformly terminates in bringing God's
law to bear upon the conscience.

2. There is also an agency of the Spirit *in the work
of conversion ;*—in the turning of the soul from sin
to holiness.   This is what is referred to by our Saviour when he says, "Except a man be born of the
Spirit he cannot see the kingdom of God."   The
work which the Spirit here performs is the renovation of man's moral nature ; changing an enemy of
God into a friend of God ;—and if we have a right
to compare the different kinds of influence which
he exerts upon the children of men with each other,

perhaps it is a reasonable conclusion that more of his omnipotence is exerted here than in any other part of his work. What is done in conviction is only a preparation for this : what is done in sanctification is but a continuation of it. As the act of conversion may be considered in some respects the most decisive in its bearing upon man's destiny, so, we may suppose that it brings him more closely into communion with the almighty energies of God's Spirit than any other.

The Spirit, in his converting influences, instead of bringing the truth to bear directly upon the conscience, addresses it to the will and the affections. The will, or the faculty by which we determine our actions, has naturally a wrong direction; and in regeneration it is set right : the affections are naturally placed upon forbidden objects; and in regeneration they are recalled to objects which are worthy of them. Or to avoid all appearance of philosophical distinctions, the soul that has hitherto loved and chosen sin, experiences a change, in consequence of which it will hereafter love and choose holiness. Hence, the scripture speaks of it as a change of heart, by which we mean in common language, a change of disposition. Man in his natural state is said to possess " a heart of stone ;" in his renewed state " a heart of flesh," or " a new heart." As this then is the part of his nature in which the change primarily takes place, to this we must suppose the agency of the Spirit in performing the change, is especially directed.

And as the work of conversion is performed on a different department of man's nature from that of conviction, so also it is accomplished through the instrumentality of a different part of the system of divine truth. It is not only of the incorruptible seed of the word of God that men are born to newness of life, but it is by the gospel, in distinction from the law, that this work is effected. It was the law that made the jailer tremble: it was the gospel that brought peace and gladness to his soul. It was the law that caused the three thousand to be pricked in the heart; it was the gospel—Christ crucified—that melted them into contrition, and transformed them into disciples. And you see the reason of it—the law speaks terror, and nothing else: it points to a most eventful trial; and anticipates the eternal wrath of God. The gospel proclaims good news. It tells the sinner that his case though deplorable, is not desperate; and hope encourages exertion. It holds up the glorious truth, that through the merits of Christ's atoning blood, there is eternal life; and the sinner, through the agency of the Holy Ghost seizes hold of this truth as of life from the dead; and in view of it, he melts down, in humble submission, at the foot of the cross. I do not mean that the gospel, in its more particular, and even less important doctrines, may not sometimes be directly instrumental of producing this change; though certain it is, that wherever it takes place, it is the gospel, in distinction from the law, that accomplishes it. As it is not a common thing, to say the least, for men to know, with absolute assurance, the precise period of their conversion, so they cannot ordinarily determine what particular part of divine truth was then directly before the mind ; but if it were possible to ascertain, they would doubtless always find that it had a more or less intimate connection with the cross of Christ.

3. There is moreover an agency of the Spirit *in the whole progress of the soul in holiness*. Says the Apostle to the Thessalonians, "We are bound to give thanks alway to God for you, brethren, beloved of the Lord, because God hath from the beginning, chosen you to salvation, through sanctification of the Spirit and belief of the truth." The regenerating act leaves the soul far from a state of perfect holiness. The general current of its desires and purposes is changed ; but notwithstanding this change, the Christian finds a law in his members warring against the law of his mind, and bringing him into captivity to the law of sin. Hence there is much to be done subsequently to his regeneration, to prepare him for heaven ; and in every part of this work, the Spirit has a more or less direct agency. Sometimes he is to be reclaimed from a course of backsliding ; sometimes to be fortified against the influence of temptation ; sometimes to be stimulated to great and arduous enterprises ; now there is to be enkindled a spirit of elevated devotion, and now a spirit of stirring activity ; but in all this, and in all which belongs to the work of sanctification, a divine influence is to be exerted. All the various pow-

ers of the soul—the conscience—the will—the affections—the whole spiritual man—are to be brought into exercise, according to the particular end which the Spirit may design to accomplish. And so also every part of revealed truth—the law and the gospel, and each particular doctrine of the gospel, are used by this divine agent in carrying forward his work. And thus the whole man becomes more and more pure, until he reaches at last the fulness of the stature of a perfect person in Christ.

I have thus given you what I suppose to be a scriptural view of the agency of the Spirit, in respect to a single individual, who finally reaches heaven. Now what I have here described in respect to a single case, takes place, in a revival of religion, in many cases. Many sinners are the subjects of conviction and conversion; and God's people are advanced in the spiritual life. Nevertheless there are some points of view in which the divine agency in a revival deserves to be more particularly contemplated.

In every revival we are distinctly to recognise *the sovereignty of God*. As this is displayed in the influence by which a single soul is converted, it certainly is not less manifest in those copious showers of influence by which hundreds are converted. He who causes it to rain on one city and not on another, directs the motion of those clouds in the spiritual world from which descend the blessings of reviving and quickening grace. " The wind bloweth, where it listeth; and thou hearest the sound thereof; but canst not tell whence it cometh, or whither it goeth. So is every one that is born of the Spirit." And so too is every revival of religion.

There is one grand principle of our nature, which the Holy Spirit makes great use of in a revival, that is not brought into exercise in a single conversion; and which perhaps, more than any thing else, distinguishes the character of his agency in the two cases—I mean the principle of *sympathy.* The operation of this principle is familiar to us all in the common intercourse of life. You all know what it is to have a fellow feeling;—to be affected by the affection of another with feelings correspondent with those you witness in him. Who, for instance, has not been made to feel joyful, merely by coming in contact with those whose countenances have worn the aspect, and whose conversation has breathed the spirit of joy? And who has not felt his heart melting with sorrow, and even his eyes suffused with tears, merely from being cast into a scene in which there were bleeding hearts and streaming eyes? Now this principle with which we are all so perfectly familiar in common life, is brought into exercise with great effect in a revival of religion. A brother, for instance, sees a sister, or a husband a wife, or a parent a child, weeping under a sense of sin; and inquiring, it may be with agony, in respect to her salvation. That brother, or husband, or parent, must be destitute of all natural sensibility, not to be moved by such a spectacle: But the first exercise of the soul in such a case will not be

repentance—it will not be conviction; but it will
be simply a fellow feeling for a beloved friend in distress. Now it is acknowledged that there is no natural affinity between this state of mind and religion;
nevertheless, the former constitutes a happy preparation for the latter, and often the first step towards it.
For how natural for the sinner to inquire at such a
moment, whether there be any adequate cause for
this distress; and how probably will the answer to
this inquiry bring up the solemnities of eternity before the mind, and set the conscience at work; and
then the dream of thoughtlessness is interrupted,
and the cord which binds the soul to the world is
loosed; and having advanced so far, there is reason to hope that he will hold on his way, till he
comes into the marvellous liberty of a child of God.
The same principle is often brought into exercise in
the worshipping assembly. Let there be that deep
and awful solemnity pervading a congregation that
is induced by the special presence of the Spirit of
God; let there be many countenances and many
eyes that shall betray a deep, though silent anxiety;
and believe me, every anxious countenance, every
fixed eye, will preach; and it will utter a mysterious language that will not improbably waken up the
sensibilities of the careless sinner; and this will
naturally serve to open his ear to God's truth; and
thus conviction may take the place of sympathy, and
in the train of that may soon follow the clean heart
and the right spirit. I know, Brethren, that this is
a true description of the manner in which many a

sinner has passed from thoughtlessness to alarm;
from darkness to light. And I doubt not that the
same principle is often brought into exercise in advancing the believer's sanctification; especially in
rousing him from spiritual sloth, and in stirring him
up to a higher tone both of feeling and of action.

Let no one dream that there is any thing in this,
which casts suspicion on the reality, or derogates
from the dignity of a revival of religion. I repeat,
mere sympathy is not religion; though no doubt it
is sometimes mistaken for it. It has no one of all
the ingredients of religion; and may exist, and
does exist, in connection with rank hatred and bitter
opposition to the gospel. Nevertheless, it is an
original principle of human nature, which, when
operating on other subjects than that of religion, is
considered amiable and even noble; and wherefore
is it that, in respect to this, it degenerates into a pitia-
ble weakness? It is manifestly adapted to bring men
to a sense of religion; and why should not the Holy
Ghost use it for the accomplishment of that end?

There is yet another influence which the Spirit
renders subservient to sustaining a revival of religion—I mean that of *example*. There is no department of human action in which this influence is
not powerfully realized; and there is as little mystery in respect to the manner in which it operates
in a revival as any where else. Here are individuals becoming impressed with religious truth, and
inquiring what they shall do to be saved, and actually believing on the Lord Jesus Christ that they

may be saved. How natural that this fact should speak to the consciences of others, not merely through sympathy, but through the understanding, and thus put them upon a course which will terminate in genuine conversion. Besides, every one knows that one of the most formidable obstacles to entering on a religious life is a false shame—a dread of being singular; but in a revival the current of example is in favor of religion; and the anxious sinner has nothing to fear from the shafts of ridicule being pointed at him;—or if they *are* pointed at him, they fall powerless at his feet. It is not uncommon on these occasions for men of great worldly influence and distinction to come out from the world, and openly proclaim themselves on the Lord's side; and every such event almost of course makes an impression upon many minds; and others in the same walks of life, who have been accustomed perhaps to regard religion as a matter chiefly for the lower classes, are waked up to serious reflection; and begin to conclude that it is at least worth while to inquire whether that which receives the sanction of the intelligent, and the learned, and those who are best qualified to judge, may not be a serious reality. And this may lead to examination; and examination to conviction; and conviction to an actual renovation of heart. The history of revivals records many facts, like the cases which I have here supposed; and I should hazard little if I were to say that there are probably individuals before me, whose hearts are full of Christian joy and hope, who refer their first religious impressions to the influence of example in the midst of some revival of religion. I hardly need add, that there is no natural connection between such an influence and true piety; nevertheless the Holy Spirit renders the one subservient to the production and the advancement of the other.

Moreover, the Spirit of God operates during a revival to bring into exercise a far *more vigorous and efficient human instrumentality*, than on ordinary occasions. He impresses ministers more deeply with their responsibility, causing them to bring home the truth to the consciences of their hearers with unwonted earnestness. He renders Christians more circumspect, more active, more earnest in prayer, more ready to warn the sinner of his wicked way, more desirous of abounding in all respects in the work of the Lord. In short, he causes the whole system of means to be wielded with a greatly increased energy. The truth of God bursts forth upon the conscience of the sinner on every side; and the reason is that God is making his ministers and his people feel their responsibility, by impressing them more deeply with their obligations to Christ, and by carrying them forward to the solemnities of the judgment day.

With two inferences we shall conclude the discourse.

1. We may see, in view of our subject, that *it is possible to attribute to the Spirit too little agency, and too much, in revivals of religion.*

There are those, on the one hand, who attribute too little to this Almighty Agent. They do
this by the manner in which they speak of revivals
—as if they were produced altogether by man; and
if the Spirit is mentioned at all, it is in a way that
would indicate that we had little to do with it. They
do this by the measures which they adopt in carrying forward revivals; substituting human inventions
for divinely appointed means; and urging the doctrine of moral agency not in connection with that of
a divine influence, but in a great degree to the exclusion of it. On the other hand, there are those who
attribute too much to the agency of the Spirit.—
They do this who speak of revivals, as if God only
was at work in them, and man a mere passive reci-
pient of impressions. They do this who do not exert themselves to the utmost to co-operate with God,
on the ground that a revival is a mere matter of
sovereignty, and that God is able to carry forward
his own work independently of means. They do
this also who speak of every thing that may happen
to be connected with a revival as the immediate effect of divine influence;—who set down to the account of the Holy Spirit peculiar tones of voice,
and expressions of countenance, and violent gestures, which are supposed to indicate deep and
strong feeling; and any thing that is harsh, or boisterous, or in any respect irregular, even though it
may seem to be associated with the greatest imagi-
nable fervor. These things no doubt may all exist in

connection with a true revival; but they are the work of men—not the work of God.

The two evils of which I have spoken may possibly co-exist in respect to the same persons; that is, the same individuals may attribute too much to the Spirit in some respects, and too little in others. His agency in carrying forward the great work may practically be recognised but little; and yet he may be familiarly spoken of as being present in particular scenes, and as prompting to particular actions, which he could not fail to disown. Brethren, we honor the Holy Spirit most, when we give him precisely the place which he claims; when we recognise him as the efficient author of conviction, conversion, and sanctification; but he is offended when we undertake to palm upon him what we ought to take with shame to ourselves.

2. Our subject teaches us that *if we would labor successfully in the cause of revivals, we must labor with a spirit of dependence on God.*

This is the spirit that is most likely to bring success to our labors, because it is most likely to render us active and faithful. He who depends upon his own strength, has but a feeble motive to exertion; for his strength is but weakness; and when viewed in relation to the object to be accomplished—the conversion of the soul—it is the weakness of an infant. But he who depends on God has the most powerful motive for action that can be presented; for he realizes that the almighty and everlasting arm is round about him in his work; and this is the only pledge of success that he needs. With this encouragement he is prepared to labor vigorously and perseveringly ; to labor in the face of appalling obstacles ; to labor even in the darkest times ; for he knows that God's grace is sufficient to render the feeblest of his efforts mighty to the pulling down of strong holds.

Besides, it is a spirit of dependence that honors God. In it there is a practical acknowledgement of our own weakness, and of his greatness and goodness, of his ability and readiness to help. In the exercise of it, man sinks down before the throne as nothing, and with the confidence of a child, lifts up his heart to God as all in all. And them that honor him in the exercise of this spirit, he will honor by sending down in answer to their prayers the blessings of his grace. And on this subject I appeal with confidence to facts. Wherever God's people have been truly humbled before him, and have been brought deeply to feel their own impotence, and have been willing to be used as mere instruments, and to let him have all the glory, there you will find that a rich blessing has usually been bestowed ; and on the other hand, where they have had little sense of their need of divine influence, and have addressed themselves to their work with a spirit of self-confidence, however diligently they may have labored, they have ordinarily been compelled to witness barrenness and lethargy in the train of their efforts ; or, if there has been the appearance of a revival, there is much reason to apprehend that there is in it little of the presence or power of God.

What then, Christians, is the great practical inference which you ought to deduce in respect to yourselves? It is that in all your labors for the revival of God's work in the midst of you, or for the promotion of the general cause of revivals, you should feel more deeply that the Lord Jehovah is your strength. Every effort that you make in the spirit of self confidence, is an insult to the Holy Ghost. Go forth then, leaning upon the Almighty arm. Go and do your duty to each other and to the world; go and instruct the ignorant, and guide the inquiring, and put forth every effort you can to bring souls to Jesus; but remember after all, and remember for your rich encouragement, the doctrine of sovereign grace. Yes, even in the moments when you feel the weakest, and when your work seems the greatest, and when obstacles the most appalling rise up in your path, and when your heart is driven from every other source of hope, even then, remember the doctrine of sovereign grace, and hold on your way laboring, yet rejoicing.

LECTURE V.

GENERAL MEANS OF PRODUCING AND PROMOTING
REVIVALS.

———

PHILIPPIANS I. 27.

—Striving together for the faith of the gospel.

The Apostle uniformly manifested a cordial regard and complacency towards all who loved the
Lord Jesus Christ. But there were reasons why
the Philippian Christians occupied a higher place in
his affections than many others. It was through
his instrumentality that they had been converted to
the faith of the gospel. They had manifested a
faithful adherence to their principles in the midst of
much opposition. They seem moreover to have
given some special evidences of sympathy and attachment towards him, during his imprisonment at
Rome—such as became the relation they sustained
to him as his own children in the gospel. Hence
it is not strange that he should have honored them
with an epistle ; or that it should have been characterized by expressions of most affectionate regard,
and of the deepest concern for their spiritual welfare. At the date of the epistle, he was still con-

fined in prison; and it does not appear that the time
of his release was then fixed: hence, in exhorting
them to fidelity and perseverance, he alludes to the
fact that he might or might not make them a visit;
but in either case, he earnestly desires that they
may continue stedfastly engaged in the cause to
which they were devoted. "Only let your conversation be as becometh the gospel of Christ: that
whether I come and see you or else be absent, I
may hear of your affairs, that ye stand fast in one
spirit, with one mind, *striving together for the faith
of the gospel.*"

The direction contained in the text may properly
be considered as pointing in a general manner to
the duty of Christians in relation to a revival of religion. In a preceding discourse, we have contemplated the agency of *God* in a revival: in the present, we are to contemplate the agency of *man;* in
other words, we are to consider some of the more
prominent MEANS in the hands of the church, which
the Holy Spirit honors in reviving, and sustaining,
and advancing his work.

These means may be considered as of two kinds:
those which are expressly prescribed by God, and
those which are adopted by men professedly in accordance with the spirit of the gospel.

In respect to the former, viz. *the instituted means
of grace*—we must suppose that they are fitted to
accomplish their end in the best possible manner.
He who devised them, made the mind, and is perfectly acquainted with all its moral disorders, and

knows by what means it can be best approached, and what kind of instrumentality is most in accordance with its constitution. Unquestionably then, in all our efforts to cure the disorders of the mind, or what is the same thing, to produce or promote a revival of religion, we are to depend chiefly on the means which God himself has appointed; and we are to expect the greatest and best effect from them, when they are used in their greatest simplicity—precisely in the manner in which God designed they should be used. It is possible, no doubt, that a divine institution may be so perverted, that nothing more than the form of it shall be retained; and it is possible that it may be so incumbered with human additions that, though the substance of it may be said in some sense to remain, yet it loses in a great degree its life and power. In opposition to this, we are to retain both the substance and the form of God's institutions: let his word be preached; let his worship be celebrated; let all the appointed means of grace be used, exactly in accordance with his own directions, and then we may expect, with the greatest confidence, that he will honor them with his blessing.

But God has not limited his people, in their efforts to advance his cause, to what may properly be called divine institutions: he permits them to adopt means to a certain extent *of their own devising;* though, in exercising this liberty, they are to take heed that they depart not at all from the spirit of the gospel. In all the departments of benevolent

action, the invention of man is, in a greater or less
degree, laid under contribution: the great system
of moral machinery which has been put in operation in these latter days for evangelizing the world,
is to be attributed immediately to the wisdom and
energy of the church; and every one knows that
this has been crowned with the special favor of
God. In the same manner, he permits his children
to exercise their own judgment, to a certain extent,
in the adoption of measures for carrying forward a
revival; and if those measures are in accordance
with the general tenor of his word, though not in
all cases expressly enjoined by it, they have a right
to expect that he will affix to them the seal of his
approbation: but if they are contrary to the spirit
of the gospel, they must inevitably incur his displeasure.

What then are some of the *general characteristics*
of those measures which the Bible authorizes in
connection with a revival of religion? The true
answer to this question may not only enable us to
distinguish between right and wrong measures of
man's devising, but also to decide when the instituted means of grace are, or are not, used in a scriptural manner.

1. All the means which God's word authorizes,
are characterized by *seriousness*.

It will be admitted, on all hands, that if any subject can be presented to the mind which claims its
serious regard, it is religion; or if any occasion
ever occurs, in which the semblance of levity is un-

seasonable and revolting, it is a revival of religion. For then the world, for a season at least, falls into the back ground; and the interests of the soul become the all engrossing object. Then men are letting go the things which are seen and are temporal, and grasping after the things which are not seen and are eternal. The work which is attended to then, is deep reflection, and earnest prayer, and agonizing conviction, and effectual repentance, and the forming of holy resolutions, and the renewing of spiritual strength. Many sinners are coming into the kingdom; and saints, and no doubt angels, are looking on with deep concern lest others should abandon their convictions, and provoke the Spirit to depart from them forever. I may appeal to any of you who have been in the midst of a revival, whether a deep solemnity did not pervade the scene; whether, even if it is your common business to trifle, you were not compelled to be solemn then? And if you have wished at such a moment to be gay, have you not felt that that was not the place for it; and that before you could get your mind filled with vain thoughts, and your heart with light emotions, you must withdraw and mingle in some different scene?

Now then, if there be a high degree of solemnity belonging essentially to a revival of religion—if there never be a scene on earth more solemn than this—surely every measure that is adopted in connection with it, ought to partake of the same character. It were worse than preposterous to think

of carrying forward such a work by any means
which are not marked by the deepest seriousness,
or to introduce any thing which is adapted to awaken and cherish the lighter emotions, when all such
emotions should be awed out of the mind. All ludicrous anecdotes, and modes of expression, and
gestures, and attitudes, are never more out of place
than when the Holy Spirit is moving upon the hearts
of a congregation. Every thing of this kind is fitted to grieve him away; because it directly contra-
dicts the errand on which he has come;—that of
convincing sinners of their guilt, and renewing them
to repentance. Nor is the case at all relieved by the
occasional introduction of what may be really solemn and weighty; for its legitimate effect is almost
of course neutralized by the connection in which it is
presented; and that which might otherwise fall with
awful power upon the conscience, is thus rendered
utterly powerless and unimpressive. And not only
so, but there is often in this way an association
formed in the mind, which is exceedingly hostile to
subsequent religious impressions;—an association
between solemn truths which ought to make the
sinner tremble, and ludicrous expressions which
will supply him with matter for jests.

I doubt not that in reply to this, I shall be referred to the wonderful success of Whitfield and a few
others, whose preaching has been characterized by
what I have here set down as an exceptionable pecu-
liarity. But I would say that these cases constitute
exceptions from the common course of human ex-

perience. God had given to these men a power
over the human passions altogether peculiar; so
that they could sometimes make use even of the
lighter feelings in giving to divine truth its deepest
impression. But they are not in this respect an example for other men. All experience proves that
when men of common minds attempt to tread in
their footsteps, they acccomplish nothing to any
good purpose : and even in the case of the individuals referred to, it may reasonably be doubted
whether the good effect of their labors was not often diminished, rather than assisted, by the use
which they made of this extraordinary power: certainly this was true in every instance in which the
lighter emotions were ultimately left to preponde-
rate.

But surely no one will say that the Bible treats
the subject of religion otherwise than in the most
serious manner. Every thing that is there said respecting it, takes for granted that it is a concern of
the deepest moment. So too, in all the accounts
which the Bible records respecting revivals of religion, there is nothing that even approaches the confines of levity. All that is recorded as having been
spoken or done on these occasions, was of a deeply
serious character; and as these revivals were conducted by inspired men, we have a right to conclude that the course which they adopted, was, in
all respects, most in accordance with the designs of
infinite wisdom.

2. Another characteristic of those means for promoting a revival, which are authorized by God's
word, is *order*.

The Apostle, in his first epistle to the Corinthians, dwells at length on the importance of avoiding all irregularities in religious worship; declaring that "God is not the author of confusion;"
and exhorting that "all things be done decently,
and in order." And what the Apostle hath said
on this subject is in entire correspondence with
the general tenor of God's word; and I may add,
with all just and rational views of the divine character. In every thing that God has done there is
perfect order; insomuch that it has been said by
a poet, with inimitable beauty, that "order is heaven's first law." In the pure and elevated worship
of heaven, though there are ten thousand times ten
thousand, and thousands of thousands who join in
it, yet each harp and each voice is in unison with
every other; and there is not the semblance of disorder in that whole glorified community. Surely
then, in all our religious services, and in all the measures we adopt for co-operating with the Holy Spirit in the great work of saving men, it becomes us
to take heed that we never violate even the spirit of
the Apostle's precept; that we do every thing not
only with sincerity and zeal, but with that reverent
decorum which so well becomes *us* when engaged
in the immediate service of the infinite God. And
hence we are obliged to look with strong condemnation on that indecorous familiarity which is some-

times manifested in prayer; on expressions which, to say the least, border upon vulgarity, and would scarcely be regarded decent in common intercourse between man and man; on every thing like groaning, or shrieking, or shouting, during a religious service; on the praying of females in meetings composed of both sexes; on the speaking, whether in prayer or exhortation, of several individuals at the same time; on every thing in short which contributes to render a religious exercise, in the least degree, boisterous or irregular. We do not doubt that many of these evils may exist, not only where there is sincerity, but more or less of genuine Christian feeling; but we insist that they are totally inconsistent with the decorum that belongs essentially to religious worship; and therefore ought to be discouraged.

But possibly it may be asked whether the fervor which often exists in connection with these irregularities is not to be admitted as an apology for them; and whether we ought not to be slow in condemning the one, lest we should seem to pass sentence against the other? I answer unhesitatingly—No. The highest degree of genuine religious fervor, even that which the redeemed experience, while they cast their crowns at the Saviour's feet, is consistent with perfect order; and I venture to say that their worship, full of elevated rapture as it is, is associated with a degree of reverence, of which even Isaiah and Paul could here form no adequate conception. But that kind of fervor which is the parent of irregularities, which makes an individual apparently forget that he is on earth, and the Being whom he addresses, in heaven, is, to say the least, of exceedingly doubtful origin, and there is too much reason to fear that it will be found at last to have been a mere earthly affection. But even if it be admitted that a truly Christian fervor may be associated with gross irregularities, we maintain that there is no natural connection between them: the one is right and the other wrong; and whenever they are found together, the true way is to hold fast the one, and let go the other. I observe,

3. That another characteristic of the means which God authorizes in connection with a revival is *simplicity;*—and by this I mean the opposite of all parade and ostentation.

It is admitted that, under the Jewish dispensation, there were many things connected with religious worship, which were adapted to make a strong appeal to the senses; but all that machinery was abolished at the introduction of the Christian economy. *Now*, every thing in relation to the worship of God is simple; even the ordinances which are addressed to the senses, though they are full of meaning, are yet capable of being understood by a child. And all the means which are adopted for the advancement of religion, ought surely to correspond with the general spiritual character of the dispensation. And wherever there is a departure from this principle in reference to a revival, there is not only a palpable violation of scripture precept, but there is a bad influence exerted, as well upon those who are Christians as those who are not. The effect upon Christians is to awaken or cherish spiritual pride, and to lead them to lose sight of the great Agent in their own self-complacent instrumentality. Its effect upon those who are mere spectators will probably be, to lead them to pass severe judgment on the revival itself; or else, admitting what they see to be scriptural, to lower their views of the humility of the gospel. And if it be admitted that in the use of such means, persons become truly regenerated, is there not much reason to fear that they will be born into the kingdom with an overweening self-confidence; and that they will exhibit from the beginning a cast of character, not the most favorable either to Christian enjoyment or Christian usefulness? Let all our means for sustaining and advancing revivals be simple and unostentatious, and while we shall be acting in consistency with the spirit of the gospel, we may hope to do most and do best, for our Master's honor, and the salvation of our fellow men.

4. Another characteristic of the means which God approves for carrying forward a revival, and closely connected with the preceding, is *honesty;*— by which I mean the opposite of all worldly artifice.

It is true, indeed, that mere sincerity does not constitute religion; because a man may be very sincere in that which is very wrong; nevertheless there is no religion without sincerity; and while the gospel abounds in direct exhortations to cultivate it,

the general tendency of the gospel is to form a perfectly honest character. Now in accordance with
this general feature of Christianity, every measure
which is adopted for bringing sinners to repentance,
ought to be marked by entire Christian sincerity.
The maxim that the end justifies the means, has
sometimes been adopted in this department of Christian duty; and there is reason to fear that ministers,
and good ministers too, have acted under its influence; and instead of preaching God's truth in all its
length and breadth, have selected some particular
parts of it to the exclusion of others, thus separating things which God hath joined together; and instead of preaching God's truth just as it is, they
have made high-wrought and overstrained statements, which the Bible does not authorize; and this
they have done from a conviction that such statements are best adapted to produce powerful impression, as if the word of God would be tame and
powerless if it should come forth in its native simplicity. I confess I know not how to characterize
this in juster terms, than that it is "handling God's
word deceitfully." It were presumption in any one
to suppose that God has revealed any thing which
is not profitable, or that he has omitted any thing
which is important. What God requires his ministers to do, is not to frame any thing new, or even
to correct or revise his own word, but to dispense
it just as they receive it at his hands: and if they
do this, he will take care for consequences. But
if they adopt any different course, they may fairly

expect that, in some way or other, the divine displeasure will be visited upon their presumption.

And what is true of the preaching of the word, is equally true of all other means for carrying forward a revival—they must all be characterized by Christian honesty;—honesty as well towards God in whose service they are professedly employed, as towards the immortal souls whose salvation they are designed to effect.

5. The last general characteristic which I shall notice of the means which God's word authorizes for promoting a revival, is *affection.*

The gospel is pre-eminently a system of benevolence. The great object which it designs to accomplish—viz. the redemption of sinners, is the most benevolent object for which the heart of man or angel ever beat. And it is directly fitted to form in man a spirit of benevolence. It enjoins the exercise of kindness and good will in all circumstances, and all relations. And surely if there be any occasion on which the tenderness which the gospel inculcates ought to be exercised, it is in the efforts which are made to bring men to conviction and repentance; in other words, to carry into effect the gracious purpose of God in their redemption. Witness the exhibition of this spirit in the ministry of the holy Apostle, who, with all his firmness and energy, (and no man ever had more,) was uniformly courteous and affectionate. Witness too, a greater than Paul—even our great model and Master;—observe the meekness and gentleness that character-

ized all his conduct; listen to his pathetic excla-
mation over the guilty city of Jerusalem, and to the
inimitably tender petition which he offered in his
last moments in behalf of his enemies and murderers;
—and then say whether the benevolent spirit which
he inculcates in his instructions, does not shine forth
with unparalleled brightness in his character? But
who does not know that all this is the exact opposite of what has sometimes appeared among the
professed followers of Christ, even in their labors
to advance his cause? And who does not see that
it conveys a pointed rebuke to all those ministrations which are characterized by unhallowed severity;—to all addresses, whether public or private,
designed to waken up the bad passions, and draw
forth expressions of resentment;—to every thing,
in short, which is not according to the meekness and
benevolence of the gospel?

Let no one suppose that I am pleading for a tem-
porizing course, either as it respects ministers or private Christians; or that I object to the use of great
plainness of speech. I would have the naked sword
of the Spirit brought directly in contact with the
sinner's conscience. I would have no covering up,
or softening down, of plain Bible truth. I would
have the terrors of the invisible world, and the fearful depravity and doom of the sinner, held up in the
same appalling terms in which they are represented
in God's word. But never was there a greater mistake than to suppose that all this may not consist
with an affectionate and inoffensive manner. Let

the benevolent spirit of the gospel have its legitimate operation in a minister, and it will lead him to proclaim the most solemn and alarming truths with a tenderness which will be well fitted to open a passage for them to the heart. Let the same spirit possess the breast of a private Christian, and he too will earnestly exhort sinners to flee from the wrath to come ; but while he commends himself to their consciences on the one hand by his fidelity and honesty, he will ordinarily commend himself to their feelings of good will on the other by his kindness and affection.

Having thus noticed some of the characteristics of those means which God's word authorizes in connection with a revival of religion, we are now prepared to inquire more particularly *what those means are*. We shall consider indiscriminately those which are of divine appointment, and those which are not.

1. And the first we notice is, *the faithful preaching of God's word*.

As divine truth is the instrument by which the work of sanctification is accomplished, so we have a right to expect its greatest influence, when it is wielded by means of an institution which God himself has ordained. Accordingly we find that God honors the preaching of the gospel in the conversion of men more than all other means ; and if this institution were to be abolished, even though the Bible should still be left in the world, there is no reason to doubt that the great cause of moral renovation would be arrested, and a darkness that could be felt speedily settle over the earth.

But in order that the preaching of the gospel may exert its full influence, especially as a means of promoting revivals, it is necessary that the institution should be maintained in all respects agreeably to the design of its author. Particularly, it is essential that the great doctrines of the gospel should be distinctly and fairly exhibited; in opposition to human philosophy on the one hand, and to mere exhortation on the other. I acknowledge that by earnest and impassioned addresses, in which there is little or nothing of God's truth, there may be produced a feverish excitement of the mind; and *that*, through the influence of sympathy, may be extended over a congregation; but if the great doctrines of the Bible are not brought in contact with the conscience and the heart, I expect to look in vain for any thing like an intelligent conviction of sin; much less for the peaceable fruits of righteousness. It is when the law of God is exhibited in all its extent and spirituality, and the gospel in all its grace and glory, that we may expect to see men brought to a sense of guilt, and believing on the Lord Jesus Christ that they may be saved. Other things being equal, you may calculate with confidence on the best effect of the preaching of the gospel, when its distinguishing doctrines are exhibited with the greatest prominence.

But then these doctrines must be held up in their practical bearings. They may be stated ever so clearly, and defended ever so skilfully, in the form of abstract propositions, and yet all this will be to little purpose, unless men can be made to feel that they describe their own character, and condition, and relations, and prospects. When the law of God is exhibited, the aim should be to bring it home to every conscience as the standard of duty, and to make each one estimate his own character in view of it. When the doctrine of depravity is proclaimed, it should be in that spirit of direct and personal application, which is adapted to bring up before the sinner his own pollution and guilt. When the great doctrine of Christ's atonement is held up, it should be exhibited in its most practical relations, and brought directly in contact with the feelings of the heart, and urged as a rebuke to impenitence on the one hand, and an encouragement to exertion and a foundation of hope on the other. It is only when men are brought to contemplate the gospel as a practical system, bearing directly on all the interests of both worlds, that it can become, in respect to them, the power of God unto salvation.

Much also depends on the right adaptation of divine truth. In a season of revival especially, one of the most difficult duties which devolve upon a minister is the selection of appropriate topics of public instruction. Suppose, at such a time, he were to bring before his people that fundamental truth in all religion—the existence of a God, and should attempt by a process of reasoning, to vindicate it against the objections of atheism; or suppose he were to discuss, in an elaborate manner, the historical evidence of Christianity;—this, in certain circumstances, might be very proper; but it would be ill adapted to guide inquiring souls to the Lord Jesus Christ; or to prevent them from grieving away the Holy Spirit. It is obvious that the great peculiarities of the gospel should, in some form or other, at such a time, constitute the whole burden of a minister's public instructions; nevertheless there is great wisdom requisite to determine in what form, and in what combinations, these truths will be likely to come with the greatest power;—what proportion of effort should be employed to alarm the careless, to guide the inquiring, and to prove and establish those who are hopefully born of the Spirit.

In order to prepare the way under God for a revival of religion, it is proper that those truths should be urged with special prominence, which involve most directly the great subject of Christian obligation; and which are best fitted to awaken sluggish and backslidden professors to a sense of their duty; for so long as Christians remain asleep, it cannot be expected that sinners will be awake: so long as Christians do not pray, or pray only in a formal manner, there is little reason to hope that sinners will begin to inquire. And in the progress of a revival, the duties of Christians should still be frequently pressed upon them, that they may not become weary in well doing; and the law should be proclaimed with all its thunders, that there may be a constant waking up from the dreams of self security among sinners; and the gospel should be constantly exhibited, in all the richness and adaptation of its provision, and in the full extent of its conditions, that inquirers may not mistake the way to the fountain of atoning blood. I do not say indeed that God in his sovereignty may not work, and work powerfully, where his ministers fail exceedingly in rightly dividing the word of truth; nevertheless, as the truth is the instrument by which he works, and as particular parts of it are adapted to particular ends, we have a right to conclude that when it is preached in its right adaptation, and with a judicious reference to circumstances, it will ordinarily be preached with the greatest effect. And, if I mistake not, this remark is confirmed by the history of revivals. Wherever ministers have selected their subjects with the greatest wisdom, addressing different classes with proper discrimination, and in due proportion, *there* have usually been witnessed the greatest displays of divine power, in the conviction and conversion of sinners, in the edification of Christians—in short, in a consistent and glorious revival of religion.

I only add farther, under this article, that during a season of revival, a larger amount of public religious instruction is demanded, than in ordinary circumstances. For then there is a listening ear; and the understanding and conscience are awake; and the truth of God tells with mighty effect upon all the powers of the soul. Indeed men *will* hear the gospel preached at such a time; and if they cannot hear it in one city they will flee to another; and if they cannot hear it in its purity, take heed lest they should put themselves under the ministrations of some fanatic or heretic. And this demand for religious instruction *must* be met;—not indeed, in all cases, to the full extent; for it is possible, even in a revival, that public services may be multiplied to such a degree as to prevent their good effect; and men under the influence of strong excitement are not always best qualified to judge;—nevertheless, while there is room here for the exercise of wisdom, it admits not of question that the truth ought to be kept, so far as may be, constantly before the mind; and this is to be effected principally by means of public instruction.

It has long been a practice in some parts of the church, and has recently become common in this country, to hold a succession of religious exercises through a period of several days. In respect to this measure, though I am aware that it is liable to great abuse, yet in itself considered, I confess that, in certain circumstances, and with certain limitations, it seems to me unobjectionable. One principal reason why sinners are not converted, is, that the impression which the truth makes upon them in the house of God, yields almost instantly to the cares and levities of the world. Now then, if before this impression can have time to escape, it be followed up by another exhibition of truth, and another, there is reason to hope that it may become permanent; and that the result may be a genuine conversion to

God: and this effect, it cannot be denied, is likely, in many cases, to be secured by a succession of several public religious services. But while I am free to express my conviction that such a meeting may be—has been, an important means of good, I think it cannot be questioned that the benefit to result from it must depend greatly on the circumstances in which it is introduced, and the manner in which it is conducted. Let it be regarded as an extraordinary measure, not frequently to be repeated; let it be held when the minds of a congregation are waking up to God's truth; and let it be conducted with solemnity and decorum becoming the exercises of the sanctuary on the Sabbath; and I doubt not it may be rendered truly and even greatly subservient to a revival of religion. But on the other hand, let it be regarded as a common measure often to be repeated; let it be held without any reference to the peculiar circumstances of a congregation, and especially let it be conducted with an irreverent disregard to the order of religious worship, or in a spirit of forwardness, or censoriousness, or fanaticism; and then it becomes a measure which the adversary wields with powerful effect against the purity of revivals and the interests of the church.

2. Another important means to be used in connection with a revival, is *private and social prayer.*

It is in the closet especially that Christians must expect to get the flame of devotion enkindled; and if the closet be neglected, whatever of a devotional frame they may suppose themselves to possess while

mingling in public exercises, they have great reason
to suspect is the mere operation of sympathy or animal feeling. And while that spirit of prayer in
which a revival begins, usually originates in the closet, there the Christian may wrestle in behalf of
Zion with as much earnestness as he will; there he
may pour out his whole soul in tears, and sighs, and
broken petitions, and the ear on which his importunity falls will never be offended by it. There too
he may bring before God the cases of his individual
friends, and even plead for them by name, and mention minute circumstances of their condition, (which
would be entirely inconsistent with the decorum of
public worship,) and earnestly supplicate for them the
convincing and renewing influences of the Spirit.
It is probable that, during every true revival, the
most fervent and effectual prayers that are offered,
go up from the closet; and are never heard by any
other ear than that which hears in secret.

But there should be much of social, as well as
private prayer, connected with a revival. Much
may be effected by the frequent meetings for this
purpose of a few friends, whose hearts are closely
joined together, who have a common interest not
only in regard to the general cause, but in respect
to particular individuals; and whose communings
together serve to increase that interest, as well as
to heighten in each other the spirit of earnest intercession. The record of these retired meetings,
noiseless and unknown to the world, will, I have no
doubt, show, at the last, that there was often mighty

energy there; and that the Spirit made intercession with groanings which could not be uttered. And in larger circles too, God's people are often to meet, for the express purpose of supplicating the influences of his Spirit; and though, on these occasions, the prayers must necessarily be more general, yet they should have direct reference to the advancement of God's work. And these prayers, instead of being offered in the spirit of formality, should be the deep and earnest longings of the soul; should go up from hearts bathed with the reviving influences of the Holy Ghost.

Prayer, as a means of grace, or a means of promoting revivals, is distinguished, in one respect, from every other: all other means are addressed immediately to men—this, directly to God. And all others are dependant in no small degree for their success on this; for ministers and Christians may labor, no matter how faithfully, and it will be to no purpose without a divine influence; and that influence is to be secured only by prayer.—God has said that he will be "inquired of by the house of Israel to do it for them." Prayer then, let it never be forgotten, secures the blessing on every other means which the church employs. Prayer too may reach individuals whom the preaching of the gospel could never reach; because they will not come within the sound of it. You may have irreligious friends to whom you dare not open your lips concerning their salvation; and yet you can go and pour out your whole soul before God in their behalf; and that prayer, for aught you can say, may carry the Holy Spirit to their hearts to work a genuine work of conversion. Believe me, Christians, you cannot, at any time, estimate prayer as a means of saving the souls of your fellow men too highly. Though it cannot take the place of other means, it is that without which all others would be utterly in vain; and besides it has a direct influence, the extent of which it is impossible fully to estimate.— Therefore, Brethren, pray without ceasing.

3. Much is to be done in producing and sustaining a revival by means of *conversation.*

This is a duty which devolves not only upon the minister and other officers of the church, but upon all private Christians according to their ability. And it is a duty which may be performed in a great variety of circumstances. There may be frequent opportunities for it in the common intercourse of life; and no doubt a suitable degree of attention would discover many opportunities which are suffered to pass without observation. But this is a duty which, especially in a season of revival, should hold a distinct and prominent place among Christian duties; and should not be left to the control of any contingency. There should be, so far as possible, a regular system of visiting, especially on the part of church officers; with a view to alarm, to direct, or to quicken, according to the circumstances of each individual with whom they may converse.

It belongs to Christians on these occasions to stir up the minds of each other; to endeavor to make each other feel more deeply their responsibility, and the value of the souls around them, and the danger of their being lost: and if there be among their number any who are sluggish, and disposed to excuse themselves from coming up to the help of the Lord, they are to be entreated affectionately, yet earnestly, to shake off their apathy, and give themselves actively to the great work. And while Christians are to be faithful in their conversation with each other,—to encourage, to arouse, to quicken, so also are they to be faithful in warning the wicked of his wicked way, and in endeavoring to open his eyes on the destruction that threatens him. And those whose consciences are awake they are to press with the obligation of immediate repentance; explaining to them, if need be, the terms of the gospel, and endeavoring to lead them without delay to the cross of Christ. They have an important duty to perform also in respect to those who have professedly come out of darkness into light; in assisting to detect false hopes and confirm good hopes; to guard against temptation, and establish principles of holy living, and form plans for future usefulness. Many a Christian has had occasion, through his whole religious life, to reflect that much of his usefulness and much of his happiness, was to be referred under God, to an unreserved intimacy, or perhaps to a single conversation, with some judicious Christian friend, at that critical moment subsequent to his conversion, when he was adopting principles for the regulation of his conduct.

You will not understand me here as recommending that every one should assume the office of a religious teacher; or that all Christians indiscriminately should take it upon them to give particular counsels and directions to the awakened sinner.— The general direction to exercise repentance toward God and faith in the Lord Jesus Christ, it may come within the scope even of the humblest intelligence, to give; but to counsel an inquiring sinner aright sometimes becomes an exceedingly delicate and difficult duty, and may well put in requisition the experience and wisdom of the most advanced and judicious Christians: and the assumption of this office by those who are inadequate to it, it is easy to see, must greatly jeopardize the souls of men. While therefore, every Christian, however circumscribed his field, or however limited his attainments, has something to do, by his conversation, in helping forward God's work, let every one take heed that he attempt nothing in this way which his knowledge or experience will not justify.

4. Another important means for producing and sustaining a revival is *Sabbath school and Bible class instruction.*

As the work of sanctification is begun and carried forward by means of the truth, it is manifest that the greater the degree of truth that is lodged in the mind, the greater the probability, other things being equal, that the individual will become a subject of conversion. And as the mind is far more easily impressed and directed in the period of childhood and youth, than after it has reached maturity and its habits have become fixed, so it is in the morning of life that the truth is likely to exert its greatest influence. Now then, as it is the design of the Sabbath school to throw the light of truth into the mind, and into the youthful mind; in other words to wield the great instrument of moral renovation in circumstances most favorable to its success, it cannot be doubted that this institution is a most powerful auxiliary to the cause of revivals. A child who could gain but little from the ordinary instructions of the pulpit, in consequence of their exceeding his capacity, may, from the more simple and familiar instructions of the Sabbath school, be learning at least the elements of Bible truth; and at a very early period, no one can say how early, may have truth enough in his mind for the Spirit to use in the sanctification of his heart.

But there is a still more direct influence exerted by Sabbath schools in favor of revivals. It ought to be, and we doubt not, is, to a great extent, regarded as the duty of every teacher, not merely to enlighten the understanding, but to impress divine truth upon the heart and conscience of each of his pupils; aiming at nothing short of a thorough moral renovation. Here is the best possible opportunity for the teacher to find his way to the heart. If, in the intercourse which he holds with his pupils, he is amiable and conciliatory, he will almost of course secure their confidence; and this is a most important preparation for their listening to him with at-

tention and profit. And then let him, from time to
time, commune faithfully with their consciences;
let him show them how the truths which he inculcates involve their interests and destiny for eternity;
let him press them frequently with those considerations which are most fitted to make them feel that
religion is the one thing needful, and that there is
no apology for neglecting it. Let him carefully
watch every serious impression, following it up by
suitable admonitions and counsels; and finally let
him bear the interests of these children before the
throne of the heavenly grace; and he has good
reason to expect that such instrumentality will be
honored in saving souls from death. It is familiar
to you all that the records of Sabbath schools and
the records of revivals are to a great extent identified; that the noblest triumphs of God's grace have
often been found in these nurseries of knowledge,
virtue and piety.

There is another point of view in which the
influence of Sabbath schools on revivals appears
most desirable—I refer to the fact that they contribute to their purity. One principal reason why
revivals are sometimes corrupted is, that there
is so much ignorance and error at work in the midst
of them; and every one knows that this is the natural food of fanaticism. Let the Sabbath school
exert its proper influence in imbuing the minds of
children with a knowledge of God's word, and in
establishing them in the great principles of the gospel, and it will constitute the best security against

those false and fanatical notions which tend so directly to fatal self-deception. Let God's Spirit be poured out upon a community well instructed in the truths of the gospel, and the happiest results may confidently be expected; for here is the natural preparation for a revival on the one hand, and the best pledge against all perversion and abuse on the other.

The remarks which have been made in respect to Sabbath schools, apply, in general, with equal force, to Bible classes. Indeed, the latter may, in one point of view, be considered as more intimately connected with revivals than the former; inasmuch as those who attend them are usually somewhat more advanced, and of course more capable of understanding and improving doctrinal instruction. Hence, revivals have perhaps, of late, more frequently commenced in Bible classes than any where else; and not a few instances have occurred, in which all or nearly all the members of a class have become hopefully the subjects of renewing grace; while the work, which had its beginning here, has extended on the right hand and on the left, till multitudes have experienced its quickening and renovating influence.

5. The faithful discharge of *parental duty*, is another important means of promoting a revival.

There is no human influence ever exerted in forming the character, more decisive, whether for good or evil, than that of parents; and if it be a well directed religious influence, we have a right to expect, both from the nature of the case and from actual experience, that it will secure the happiest results. Let a parent train up his children in the way which the Bible prescribes; let him faithfully instruct them in the truths of God's word as soon as they are capable of being taught; let him render his instructions as familiar and practical as possible, mingling with them appropriate counsels and admonitions; and let him pray with them, and for them, and teach them to pray for themselves; and if all this is not immediately instrumental of their conversion, it will, at least in all ordinary cases, render them peculiarly promising candidates for converting grace; will be a happy preparation for the effectual work of God's Holy Spirit.

I know it has been sometimes said that the subjects of revivals are most commonly selected from the haunts of open irreligion and profligacy; while those who have been educated under the benign influences of Christian instruction and example, more commonly remain entrenched in a habit of mere morality and self-righteousness. But I appeal to the whole history of revivals for evidence that this is not so. I know, indeed, that God glorifies his sovereignty, by extending his renewing grace to *some* who would seem to be at the greatest distance from him; but as a general rule, he puts direct and visible honor upon his own institutions, by bringing those to experience the sanctifying influence of his truth, who have been in the way of hearing and studying it. If it be asked, whence come the greater number of the subjects of our revivals, we answer, from our Sabbath schools, and Bible classes, and from families in which the parental influence is decidedly religious ; and the reason why some have held a different opinion, is, that when a profligate or an infidel is hopefully converted, it excites much attention and remark ; and thus the number of such conversions is frequently estimated far higher than it should be. Go into any place you will, where the Holy Spirit has been extensively and powerfully at work, and you will find that the families which have been specially blessed, are those in which God has been honored by the faithful discharge of parental duty, and the general influence of Christian example ; while only here and there one is taken from those families in which there is no parental restraint, nor instruction, nor prayer; and in which, as a natural consequence, the youthful mind is pre-occupied with sentiments and feelings most unfriendly to the work of the Holy Spirit.

It deserves also to be remarked that much devolves upon Christian parents in immediately sustaining and carrying forward a revival. If they see their children, at such a time, manifesting an indifference to the things of religion, they are to press them most earnestly and affectionately with its obligations. If they see in them the least anxiety, they are to endeavor by every means, to cherish it, and put them on their guard against grieving away the Holy Spirit, and take them by the hand, and lead them, if possible, to the Lamb of

God. If they see them rejoicing in the hope that their sins are forgiven, they are to aid them by lessons from God's word and their own experience, to ascertain the true character of their religious exercises, and to avoid the hope of the hypocrite. It is a reproach to many Christian parents, that they suffer a false delicacy to prevail against the faithful discharge of their duty in these most interesting circumstances. As God has constituted them the guardians of their children, it devolves upon them to be especially watchful in respect to their immortal interests; and never is neglect more culpable, than when the Holy Spirit is offering to co-operate with them to secure their children's salvation.

6. The last means for promoting a revival which I shall notice, is, *an exercise designed particularly for awakened sinners.*

It is generally admitted, I believe, by those who are friendly to revivals, that there should be some occasion on which persons of this class should be distinctly addressed; and which, by bringing them together as inquiring souls, may serve in a measure to get them over their indecision, and commit them to a course of successful striving to enter in at the straight gate; though special care should be taken that this act of commitment is not perverted to yield aliment to a self-righteous spirit. What the precise character of this exercise should be, you are aware, is a point in relation to which there is a diversity of opinion. I confess the result of my own reflection and observation on this subject, has been a conviction that no better course could be adopted, than that with which you, as a congregation, are already familiar. At the close of a public service in which God's truth has been exhibited and enforced, let those who have been impressed by it, and who wish to have their impressions deepened, and to be instructed in reference to their duty and salvation, be requested to remain after the rest of the assembly have retired. And then let the minister, or some other competent person, address them earnestly and affectionately in reference to their peculiar condition; connecting with the address one or more prayers; and afterwards, so far as circumstances may admit, or occasion require, let them be met in a more private way, and let the particular state of each mind be ascertained; and let each receive appropriate counsel and instruction. In all this there is nothing ostentatious, nothing which peculiarly exposes to self-deception, while yet the individual commits himself as truly as he could by any more public act, to cherish his serious impressions, and places himself in a condition in which the prayers of Christians, and scriptural instruction and counsel, are effectually secured to him. I do not say that some different course may not appeal more strongly to the passions; but I confess that I know of none which seems to me better adapted to impress upon the conscience and heart Bible truth; and thus subserve a genuine revival of religion.*

---

* From the experience I have had on this subject, I am inclined to think that this mode of treating inquirers is to be preferred to that which has been

With two or three remarks, by way of inference, we shall conclude the discourse.

1. Our subject may assist us to *form a correct judgment of any particular measures, which may be proposed in connection with a revival.*

There may be danger on this subject of erring on the right hand, and on the left. It is wrong to decide against any particular measure merely because it is new; and it is equally wrong to *adopt* it merely because it is new. It would be strange when the invention of the church is so constantly in exercise, if there should not be some new things connected with religion which are good; and it would be strange in view of the waywardness and extravagance that pertain to human nature, if there should not be others of evil tendency. Here, then, is an argument for our examining carefully every measure or course of measures that is proposed to us, and referring it to the proper standard. If it will abide that standard, it were an unworthy prejudice not to adopt it. If it will not abide that standard, to adopt it were at once a weakness and a sin. It were to refuse the privilege which God has given us of judging for ourselves what is right.

---

common, and which I have myself formerly adopted—of holding a meeting of a *more public nature* for the express purpose of inquiry. It is no doubt of great importance that an opportunity for inquiry should be given; but the more private, other things being equal, the better. In an extensive revival of religion, however, especially where the burden of conducting it devolves chiefly on a single individual, it may sometimes be a matter of necessity for him to meet a greater number of inquirers at a time than would otherwise be desirable.

If you will know then whether it is safe and proper to adopt any particular measures in connection with revivals, which may be comparatively new in the church, bring them to the test which has been presented in the former part of this discourse. Are they characterized by seriousness; by the entire absence of every thing that approaches to levity? Are they marked by that order, and decorum, and reverence, which God requires in every thing connected with his worship? Is there the absence of all ostentation, of all pious fraud, of all unhallowed severity; and is there godly simplicity, and Christian honesty, and sincere affection? If these be the characteristics of the measures proposed, then you may safely adopt them; but if any of these characteristics are wanting, they are not in accordance with the spirit of the gospel, and you cannot consistently, in any way, give them your sanction.

But it may be asked whether there is not a much better test than this; whether the *effect* produced by particular measures does not more clearly determine their character? I answer, if the *entire* and *ultimate* effect be intended, the standard which it furnishes will always be in consistency with that to which we have just referred; though it must after all furnish an inadequate rule for judging; for in many cases at least, it is so general in its character that it is not easy to be traced. If only the *immediate* and *partial* effect be intended, then I insist that this is no standard at all; for it admits not of question that there may be a violent religious excitement

which, at the moment, may seem to many to be doing good, which, nevertheless, may pass over like a
hurricane in the natural world, marking its course
with the wrecks even of God's own institutions.—
Judge not then by this uncertain standard. If you
are to judge of any great change by effects, you
must wait till they are fully developed, till you can
see not only the more immediate but the more remote
effects; the latter of which are often the most important; and these are usually developed gradually.
Hold fast then to the law and the testimony as your
rule of judging ; and as, in so doing, you will honor God most, so you will be most likely to be kept
out of the mazes of error.

2. Our subject may assist us *to discover the causes
of the decline of a revival.*

I admit that there is more or less of sovereignty
here ; and that the Spirit of God operates whenever
and wherever, in infinite wisdom, he pleases. I acknowledge too that the strong excitement which often attends a revival cannot, so far as respects the
same individuals, be kept up for a long time ; nor is
it at all essential, or even desirable, that it should be.
But so far as a healthful and vigorous state of religious feeling is concerned on the part of Christians, and I may add, in view of the promises of
God to answer prayer, so far as the conversion of
sinners is concerned, it is not irreverent to say that
while he is himself the great agent, he commits his
work in an important sense, into the hands of his
people; and if it decline, there is blame resting upon

them. It is because they have grown weary in their
supplications, or because they have relaxed in the
use of some other of the means which he has put
within their reach. Let Christians then tremble in
view of their responsibility; and when God is sending down his Spirit to work with them, let them
take heed that they render a hearty and persevering
co-operation. Let them take heed that they grieve
not this divine agent to depart either from their
own souls, lest they should be given up to barrenness; or from the souls of inquiring sinners, lest
there should fall upon them the curse of reprobation.

3. Once more : *How great is the privilege and the
honor which Christians enjoy, of being permitted to co-
operate with God in carrying forward his work.*

When you are laboring for the salvation of sinners around you, when you are using the various
means which God has put into your hands to waken
them to conviction and bring them to repentance,
you are laboring in the very cause which is identified with the success and the glory of Christ's me-
diation. Nay, you are a fellow worker with the
Holy Ghost ; and while he honors your efforts with
his saving blessing, they are set down to your account in the book of God's remembrance. Yes,
Christian, all that you do in this cause brings glory
to God in the highest, contributes to brighten your
immortal crown, and subserves the great cause of
man's salvation. What remains then but that you
take these considerations to your heart as so many

152LECTURE V.

arguments, to labor in this holy cause with more untiring zeal, with more holy fidelity? Is it a cause that demands sacrifices? You can well afford to make them, for it brings happiness, and glory, and honor in its train. Let it be seen on earth, and let the angels report it in heaven, that you are co-workers with God, in giving effect to the purposes of his grace, and in training up immortal souls for the glories of his kingdom.

LECTURE VI.

TREATMENT DUE TO AWAKENED SINNERS.

ACTS III. 19.

Repent ye therefore, and be converted.

There is scarcely a period of so much interest in the life of an individual, as that in which he is brought to earnest inquiry respecting the salvation of his soul. It is a state of mind which comes between the utter neglect of religion and the actual possession of it. The dream of thoughtlessness is disturbed. Conscience wakes to its office as an accuser. This world holds the soul with an enfeebled grasp, and the realities of another weigh upon it with deep and awful impression. But then, on the other hand, there is as yet no submission to the terms of the gospel;—no melting down in penitence at the feet of mercy;—no yielding up of the heart to God;—no thankful, cordial acceptance of Christ and his salvation. But between these two states of mind there is no uniform connection; for though conviction is essential to conversion, yet the sinner who is only convinced, may, instead of being converted, return to the world, and thus his last state be worse than his first. It is reasonable to suppose, in any given case of conviction, that the sinner who is the subject of it, is on the eve of having his destiny decided for eternity: for if he press forward, he secures his salvation; but if he linger and fall back, there is, to say the least, an awful uncertainty whether he is ever again the subject of an awakening influence.

Now you will readily perceive that it is a most responsible office to counsel and direct an individual in these interesting circumstances. The mind is in a state to be most easily influenced; and influenced on a subject that involves all the interests of eternity: there is a sort of balancing of the soul between religion and the world, between heaven and hell; and no one can be certain that the weight of a single remark may not turn the scale one way or the other. Of what vast importance is it that all the suggestions and counsels that are offered at such a time should be scriptural—seasonable—the very instructions of the Holy Ghost.

But if it be a responsible office for an individual to direct a single inquiring sinner, what shall be said of the responsibility of the church during a revival of religion; in which there are many, on every side, pressing the inquiry, 'what they shall do to be saved?' And how important is it that members of the church should be so enlightened as to be safe guides on this momentous subject; that thus they may never put in still greater jeopardy the interests of those whom they attempt to direct. A large part of the conduct of a revival consists in COUNSELLING THE AWAKENED; and on the manner in which this duty is performed, as much as any thing, depend both the character of the work and its results. It is proper, therefore, that in a series of discourses like the present, this should be made a distinct and prominent topic; and this is what I am about to bring before you for our present exercise.

The direction which the Apostle in our text gives to the Jews—that they should repent and be converted—is applicable to sinners of every description; and especially to those who are in any measure awakened. It is proper to direct every inquiring sinner to repent and turn to God in a way of holy obedience; and this may be considered an epitome of all appropriate teaching in such circumstances: nevertheless this direction is to be given in a variety of forms, adapted to a diversity of cases, and accompanied with many cautions and admonitions. My design will be,

I. To consider *in general the treatment due to an awakened sinner:* and

II. To contemplate *some of the most prominent cases which require more special counsel and instruction.*

I. I am to present before you *the general course proper to be taken with an awakened sinner.*

When a person in these circumstances comes to ask your counsel, the first thing you have to determine is, *what is his amount of knowledge, and his amount of feeling.*

It is possible that he may have much feeling, and little knowledge. He may have learned so much of God's law, as to have wakened up his conscience, and brought him to a sense of danger, and made him tremble in anticipation of a fearful hell. But his knowledge even of the law may be very limited; and how to secure the forgiveness of his sins, and an escape from the tremendous doom that threatens him, he may be utterly ignorant? Of the nature of the gospel salvation, of the conditions on which it is offered, of the repentance of sin, of the faith in the Lord Jesus Christ, of the life of holy obedience, he may know almost literally nothing. Possibly his habits of life may have rendered him a voluntary exile from the means of religious knowledge; but it is by no means certain that he may not have been a regular attendant on Christian institutions; for facts prove that it is possible for an individual to sit under the faithful preaching of the gospel during a long life, and yet to hear with such entire inattention, that there is gained no distinct knowledge of any one of the doctrines of the Bible. Yes, it has often happened in respect to men of general intelligence, and high worldly consideration, that when they have been awakened, they have themselves acknowledged that they were entirely ignorant of Bible truth; and with all their talents, and learning, and maturity, have had to begin at the very alphabet of the gospel. Now wherever you discover in an anxious sinner such gross ignorance, whether he be a man of high or low degree, your first business

should be to instruct him. And let your instructions be characterized by the utmost plainness;
for a mind to which the subject of religion is
in a great degree new, (no matter how familiar it
may be with other subjects,) will find it difficult to
apprehend the truth, unless it is presented in its
most simple form. Teach him what God has done
for his salvation; and what God requires him to do;
and the reasonableness of that requirement; and
the necessity of its being complied with. It may
be necessary, in some cases, that these things should
be presented in different forms, and by a succession
of efforts, before they come to be fairly understood:
nevertheless, it were wrong to withhold any thing
that is essential to salvation, on the ground that the
mind is not thoroughly enlightened in all those truths
which have the precedence in the order of nature;
for if you leave an awakened sinner without having
set Christ distinctly before him, as the only foundation of hope, and without having taught him in what
manner the benefits of redemption may be secured,
before you see him again, he may have been brought
to a stand by not knowing what to do, and may have
actually settled down with a determination that he
will do nothing. Or else your next meeting with
him may be at the judgment; and you may be compelled to reflect that the last opportunity which was
enjoyed on earth of directing him to the cross of
Christ, you enjoyed, but neglected.

It is possible, on the other hand, that you may
find a good degree of knowledge, and comparatively

little feeling.　There may even be a correct and intelligent view of all the evidence and doctrines of the gospel, which has resulted from laborious, critical and long continued examination ;—there may be an ability rarely to be met with to confound skeptics and gainsayers; and yet the impression of divine truth may be feeble, and the conscience only partially awake.　There may be conviction enough to bring the sinner to you for counsel, when there is not enough to bring him to Christ for salvation. In this case, your duty manifestly is, to endeavor to impress more deeply upon his mind the truths which he understands and admits; to bring him to examine his heart more closely by the searching light of God's law; and to look at every doctrine in its practical bearings in connection with his own character and destiny.　The amount of conviction necessary to conversion may vary in different cases, according to the character of the mind, and its previous opportunities for acquiring religious knowledge; but conviction there must be in every case; and wherever it is feeble and wavering, it is fair to presume that something more is necessary in this way in order to bring the soul to rest upon its Saviour.

The awakened sinner may be benefitted by some such counsels and cautions as the following :—

Let him be admonished, first of all, that *the duty of devoting himself to God by a compliance with the terms of the gospel, is of immediate obligation ; and that he is guilty, and becoming more and more guilty,*

in the neglect of it.   For is not this duty reasonable?
Is it not due to God as a Creator, as a Preserver,
and especially as a Redeemer, that every human
being should love him with all his affections, and
serve him to the extent of his powers? And if the
sinner has never done this hitherto, nay if he has
never ceased from a course of rebellion against
God, and has not performed a single act from a regard to his authority, surely it is reasonable that he
should change his course without delay; that he
should at once wake, not only to a sense, but to a
performance, of the duties which God requires of
him.   Would it be right that a child who had broken away from parental restraints, and set at naught
parental love, when pressed to submit to a father's
authority, and return to a father's arms, should
plead that he had not wounded and insulted that father as long as he wished; and that though he felt
the obligation to yield, yet he did not consider it as
binding him to do so immediately?   Would it be
right for a rebel, when urged to throw down arms
against a wise and benevolent sovereign, to acknowledge the reasonableness of the requisition for
a future day, but to deny it in respect to the present? Let not the sinner then dream that he has any
excuse for continuing unreconciled to God for an
hour.   Press him with the obligation of *immediate*
repentance, and faith, and submission to God.   Endeavor to make him feel that apart from all considerations of personal interest, this is a duty which he
owes to God, and which ought to press upon him

with the weight of a mountain, until he has discharged it.

Let the awakened sinner be admonished farther that *the present is the best time for securing his soul's salvation.* For then there are facilities for becoming religious which do not exist at any other period. Supposing him, as I here do, to be in the midst of a revival, there is an energy and efficiency in all the means of grace which is, to a great extent, peculiar to such a scene. Ministers are encouraged to preach with unaccustomed earnestness, and are enabled to bring out the truth of God with great pungency and effect. Christians too pray with unwonted fervor, and converse with peculiar fidelity; and there is the current of example setting strongly in favor of religion; and the very atmosphere around seems to be pervaded by deep solemnity; and with all this the sinner's own attention is awake; and the Holy Spirit is striving with him to bring him to repentance. Let him be inquired of what circumstances can exist more favorable to his conversion than now exist. Let him be reminded that he has no reason to expect that such an assemblage of circumstances will again occur in the course of his life; and that even if they should, the same disposition which would lead him to resist the Spirit now, might lead him to resist it then. Dwell upon the appalling fact, that trifling with divine influences must serve greatly to harden the heart; and that if he return to the world from the point which he has now gained, he will in all probability, go back to a

point of obduracy at which he will be left, without
any farther divine interposition, to take his own
way down to the chambers of eternal death.

Admonish him, farther, that *he is in danger, from
various causes, of losing his serious impressions.* This
is a point in relation to which he may not improbably think himself safe; and though he may not be
able to anticipate any favorable result of his convictions, yet so pungent and overwhelming are they,
that he cannot realize that there is any danger of
their leaving him. But even the strongest religious
impressions are sometimes driven away from the
soul almost in an hour; though in general the process is a gradual and almost imperceptible one. Admonish him to beware of the levities of the world;
for one light conversation with a careless friend,
may change decisively the current of his thoughts.
Guard him against the influence of worldly care—
even of his necessary daily employments; for any
thing of a mere worldly nature that occupies the
mind, is liable to turn it off from the great subject
of salvation. Caution him, also, against yielding
to a false shame; for this cannot long prevail without grieving away the Holy Spirit. Urge upon him
the importance of holding God's truth to his mind
as constantly as possible, that thus the impressions
which have already been made by it, may have no
opportunity to escape. And to give the greatest
effect to all these cautions, point him to examples
in the way of illustrating them; and let him know
that there are multitudes now in the ranks of profli-

gacy and infidelity, who once even trembled under
the awakening influences of God's Spirit. In view
of the tremendous evil which must result from the
departure of this divine agent from the soul on the
one hand, and of the ease with which he may be grieved away on the other, you are to ring a monitory peal
in the ear of the awakened sinner, adapted to make
him cherish his impressions with the most watchful
diligence.

And then, again, you are to put him on his guard
*against seeking salvation in a spirit of self-righteous-
ness.* There is no natural predilection in man
for the gospel plan of salvation: on the contrary, there is a strong original bias in favor of being saved by the deeds of the law; though unhappily there is no disposition to perform the deeds
which the law requires. Hence the sinner, when
he is first awakened, almost always puts himself
upon a course of self-righteous effort; and practically asks with the young man in the gospel, " what
good thing he shall *do* that he may inherit eternal
life." He forthwith begins an attendance upon all
the means of grace, if he has neglected them before, or if he has been accustomed to attend upon
them, he does it now with an increased degree of seriousness. He listens attentively to God's word; is
found in the meeting for social prayer, and religious
conference; passes much time in his closet, and in
conversing with Christian friends: and in short,
aims to perform externally every duty which God
requires of him. And in all this the secret feeling of

his heart is, even though he may not always be sensible of it, that he is performing something meritorious, which will catch and please the eye of God, and cause his name to be enrolled in the Lamb's book of life. Now it devolves upon you carefully to guard him against this error; for so long as it is retained, it must be an effectual barrier to a compliance with the terms of the gospel. Do not discourage him from striving; but admonish him to strive in the spirit of the new covenant, and not of the old. Tell him that there is no merit in any of his striving, and that he can never be saved till he becomes convinced of this, and falls down helpless at the feet of mercy, and is willing to accept of salvation as the free gift of God through Christ, without any respect to his own deservings. The mistake to which I here refer may be made by those who speculatively understand the way of salvation, as well as those who do not; and the only means by which it is discovered, is faithful communion with one's own heart. To the duty of self-communion then, with special reference to this point, every inquiring sinner should be earnestly exhorted.

Counsel him, moreover, to beware of *making comfort rather than duty an ultimate end.* A state of conviction is a state of anxiety and alarm, and of course unhappiness. As the sinner, from the very constitution of his nature, desires happiness, it is not strange that in the agony of conviction he should often fasten his eye upon that as an ultimate object; though nothing is more certain than that, so long as he pursues it as such, true religious comfort will never be attained. In doing this, he places himself before God merely as a sufferer desiring to be relieved from distress; whereas, the attitude which he ought to assume is that of a guilty offender, acknowledging and forsaking his evil courses, and turning unto the Lord. What God requires of him is the discharge of duty;—repentance, faith, obedience; and in this way only has he a right either to seek or to expect comfort. He is to regard himself first as a sinner, and then as a sufferer: if he repent of his sins he has reason to expect relief from his sufferings; but if he hold fast his sins, how much soever he may supplicate God's mercy, he will either experience no relief or none which he ought to desire. He must understand that it is the economy of God's grace that true Christian comfort can never be gained except as it is made a secondary consideration. He must keep his eye constantly fixed on duty: he must stir himself up to do what God requires of him; and God will take care that he is no stranger to the joys of his salvation.

It may be well to caution him also *against seeking aid from too many advisers; especially where their religious views do not harmonize.* There are among Christians, we all know, shades of difference in their views of the truths of the gospel; and though they all hold the Head, and recognize each other as members of the same family, yet on some minor points they do not speak the same language; and indeed, though the real difference may not be great, yet they may differ in their phraseology even in respect to the essentials of religion; and may be accustomed to contemplate these great truths in different relations and combinations. The consequence of this may be that several persons who are really agreed on all fundamental doctrines, may counsel an awakened sinner, each in his own way, and each substantially in the right way; and yet there may be, after all, to his apprehension a disagreement, which may be the source of much painful perplexity. His mind will be liable to become confused by the variety of directions which he receives; and will be far less likely to profit by any, than if this confusion had been avoided. It were better for the awakened sinner that he should have a single judicious counsellor, or at the extent a few such, than to be soliciting or receiving the advice of every one indiscriminately.

I add, once more, that he should be advised to *pass much of his time in the closet.* It is proper, indeed, that he should avail himself of frequent opportunities to hear the preaching of God's word; and that he should mingle in the social prayer meeting; and should receive appropriate counsels and instructions from Christian friends; but this can never take the place of private meditation and self-communion. The searching and probing of his own heart, and the recollection of his sins, is a work peculiarly for the closet; because there the mind is least likely to be diverted by external objects and

circumstances. I know there is a strong tendency
in most persons who are awakened, to mingle continually in public religious exercises. This may be
the easiest, but it is not the safest or most desirable
course. I do not say that many who adopt it do
not become true Christians; but, to me at least, it
appears that there is more danger of a spurious
conversion, or if it be not spurious, that the principle of spiritual life will be feeble and sickly, than
if there had been more of that knowledge of the
hidden abominations of the heart, which is to be
acquired especially by private self-examination.

While you are giving to the awakened sinner
these various directions, you can hardly repeat too
often the caution that *he should not mistake the de-*
sign of the means which you are recommending. Let
him understand clearly that the only end to be answered by them, so far as respects himself, is to
bring him to the conviction that he is all pollution,
and guilt, and unworthiness; and that he can do
nothing toward his salvation but throw himself
into the arms of sovereign mercy. When he is
brought to this state of mind, means have done all
that they can do for him as an impenitent sinner;
and if, instead of yielding himself up to God, he
goes on still in the use of means, there is great reason to fear that they will prove the stumbling block
over which he will fall into perdition.

II. Having now marked out a general course of
treatment adapted to an awakened sinner, I proceed, secondly, to contemplate *some of the great*

*variety of cases which require more special counsel and
instruction.*

Suppose the sinner says that, though he is aware
that his case is as bad as you represent it, yet *he can
do nothing to render it any better, and therefore must
be contented to remain where he is.* You are to endeavor, in the first place, to convince him, by a direct
appeal to his conscience, that the inability under
which he labors is nothing more than a settled aversion of the heart from God; and therefore is entirely without excuse. Let him see that he has all
the powers of a moral agent; that he has a conscience to distinguish between right and wrong, and
a will by which he may choose the one and refuse
the other. Let him see that in withholding his heart
from God, he is as free as in any other course of
action; and therefore blameworthy; and therefore
condemned in the plea which he sets up for doing
nothing.

But let it be admitted, as it certainly must be,
that every sinner, if left to himself, will perish;
that though the inability is of a guilty sort, yet it
really does prevail;—still you are to show the awakened sinner that this is nothing to him in the way of
discouragement, for he is not left to himself: the
Holy Spirit has already come to his aid; and is offering not only to convince him of guilt, but to re-
new him to repentance. What if it be true that, by
his unassisted powers, he will never enter in at the
straight gate, yet so long as the almighty energy of
divine grace is actually proffered to his assistance,

how can he stand still on the plea of inability? Let the sinner bring his own powers into exercise to the utmost, and he need have no fear but that God will work within him both to will and to do, to secure his salvation.

But suppose he should say that *he has made thorough trial of his own powers, and yet has accomplished nothing*—Let him be inquired of, in what manner he has been striving? Is it not more than possible that the secret of his ill success lies in the fact that he has been trying to do too much; or rather that he has done nothing with a right spirit; that the influence of all his exertions has been neutralized by the self-righteous notion of merit being attached to them? Or may not his striving have been inconstant; frequently interrupted by the cares of the world; and never so earnest as the object of it demands? But suppose it really appears to him on reflection that he has done all that he can do—inasmuch as the interests of his eternity are suspended on the result, he surely will not think it prudent to adopt a course which he *knows* must land him in perdition. If he give up all effort, his case is certainly hopeless: if he continue to strive, he can *but* perish; and he *may* be saved. It were better that he should sacrifice a thousand worlds, were they in his possession, than to forego the possibility, if there were nothing more, of his escaping hell and obtaining heaven.

But what if he should plead still farther, as a ground of discouragement, that *many of his friends who were awakened at the same time with himself, have apparently given themselves to the Saviour, and are rejoicing in hope ; and that hence he has no reason to believe that there is any mercy for him*—Answer this plea by showing that God has given the same powers of moral agency to him as to them; that he has made the same gracious provision for him as for them ; and that in both cases the offer is equally free, equally sincere. Remind him that God has no where promised that he shall have the comforts of a good hope at any particular time, but he *has* promised that they who seek in a proper manner shall find ; and that promise he will certainly fulfil. If his friends have come into the kingdom before him, instead of ministering to his discouragement, let it be an argument with him to press forward ; for He who has had compassion on others is equally ready to extend compassion to him.

But suppose the sinner allege as another ground of discouragement *the doctrine of election* ; presuming that he is not among the elect, and therefore all efforts to secure his salvation must be in vain. Take care that, in reply to this, you say nothing to bring this doctrine into question. Instead of even seeming to doubt it, or to treat it as if it were a mere speculation, admit it, prove it, and show that if it be not true, God has not spoken plainly in his word, and that he does not even exercise a providence. But show him, at the same time, that the secret purposes of God do not in the least infringe the moral agency of man. Appeal to his own con-

sciousness for the truth of this; and then confess
to him your ignorance of the manner in which these
two doctrines harmonize; and at the same time expose to him the folly of rejecting any truth which
is susceptible of absolute proof, only because we
cannot discover its harmony with some other truth
which is no less clearly proved.   And you may go
farther still, and show him that this very doctrine of
election, when rightly understood, so far from being a discouraging doctrine, lies near the foundation
of the sinner's hope; for if all, when left to themselves, are inclined to reject salvation, where is
there hope for any, independently of God's sovereign grace?   But this is nothing more nor less than
the scripture doctrine of election.

If however, the sinner, under the influence of an
awakened conscience, should be disposed to indulge
in cavils respecting this or any other doctrine, it
were better not to attempt to follow him.   The safest course in such a case, were to appeal from the
speculations of his understanding, to the honest
dictates of his conscience.   If you undertake to
answer all his objections, and do not answer them
to his satisfaction, he may regard your supposed
defeat as proving the weakness of the cause you
have attempted to defend; and in this miserable delusion he may find a refuge from his convictions.
Or let the result of your conversation with him, in
this respect, be as it may, the very fact of his being
engaged in such a dispute, would be fitted to diminish his anxiety, and not improbably might be the

first step in his return to his accustomed carelessness.

Suppose the sinner *should complain of great insensibility, and should express an earnest desire that
he might have more pungent convictions*—While you
endeavor to keep his thoughts fastened upon those
great truths which are most fitted to convince and
to dissolve, such as the holiness of God, the perfection of his law, the deep depravity of the heart,
and the compassion and grace of a dying Saviour,
you are to institute a faithful inquiry as to the
ground of this desire; and it is not improbable that
you will discover that its leading element is self-
righteousness; that the sinner desires conviction
because he imagines that there will be something of
merit in it, to recommend him to the divine favor.
He may not, indeed, be sensible of this, and it may
not be easy to convince him of it; for so deceitful
is the heart, and so busy is the adversary, at such a
moment, that inquiring sinners are exceedingly apt
to mistake their own feelings; but wherever you
discover any evidences of the workings of this spirit, you must endeavor, if possible, to make the individual perceive it, that he may escape from its influence. Let him fully understand that he is just
as depraved, just as worthy of eternal death in the
sight of God, when he is in an agony of conviction,
as he was in the depth of his carnal security;—
that the difference in the two cases is precisely the
difference that exists between two criminals who
are sentenced to die, one of whom views the reality

of his condition, and anticipates with horror the appalling scene of execution; while the other, in the confident expectation of a pardon, gives himself up to absolute unconcern. Let him see that in conviction he only looks at himself as he is; and let his own conscience decide whether there can be any merit in merely beholding his guilt. The man who is convinced that his house is on fire, and that he shall be burnt to death, if he remain in it, will make a hasty escape; and his conviction of danger will have brought him to it; though no one would say that there was any thing of merit in that conviction. In like manner, the sinner who is effectually convinced that he must perish if he remain impenitent, and that he can be saved only by the free grace of God in Christ, actually throws himself a guilty and helpless creature into his Saviour's arms; and it is the conviction he has of his ruin that leads him to do this; but will the sinner himself say that there is more of merit in this case than in the other?

Suppose the sinner to be *sinking down under the burden of his guilt into a state of despair*, with an impression that his sins have been so aggravated that mercy cannot be extended to him—what you have to do in this case is to give him juster views of the gospel. He has practically lost sight of the truth that the blood of Christ cleanseth from all sin; and this is the doctrine which you are to hold up to him in all its extent and glory. Bring to his mind God's own declarations, that he is able and willing to save all that come unto him; that whosoever

believeth on the Son hath everlasting life; and whosoever will may come and take the water of life
freely. Tell him that a bloody Manasseh and a
persecuting Saul, and even some of the murderers
of the Son of God, have obtained mercy; and if
he will have it that his guilt is more aggravated than
theirs, urge upon him the fact that there is a bound-
lessness in the compassions of God, and an infinite
value in the blood of Christ, which no measure of
guilt and pollution can possibly transcend. Dwell
moreover on the wonderful consideration that, as
God is glorified in the forgiveness of every penitent
sinner, so he is most glorified in the forgiveness of
the greatest sinners; for then each of his moral
perfections, and especially his grace, shines forth
with the brightest lustre: and hence it is the privilege of the penitent to urge the greatness of his
guilt before God, as an argument for his being forgiven. Endeavor to make him realize that if his
guilt, instead of having risen to the height of a
mountain, had been limited to a single transgression,
he could never have atoned for it by any exertions
or sufferings of his own; but that the sacrifice
which Christ has offered, forbids him to despair,
notwithstanding his guilt appears so appalling. His
eye has been already fixed long enough exclusively
upon his guilt: it is time that it should be turned
away to the cross of Christ. Hold him, if you can,
to the blessed gospel. Let him see the richness,
the preciousness, the freeness of its provision; that
it exactly meets the exigencies of those who feel

that they are great sinners, and can do nothing but
sink away into the arms of mercy. Admonish him,
moreover, that despair is in itself a sin of fearful
magnitude ; that though it may excite the compassion of man, it awakens the abhorrence of God;
that one of its primary elements is cold distrust of
the offers and promises of the gospel; and that the
indulgence of it is only putting the soul at a more
awful distance from Christ, and clouding still more
deeply the prospect of its salvation.

Suppose the sinner to become impressed with the
idea that *he has had no conviction of sin*, and that all
that he supposed to be conviction was delusion ;
when at the same time he furnishes the most conclu-
sive evidence that he is really a subject of powerful
divine operation—in a case of this kind, I would
endeavor to convince him, what is beyond all peradventure true—that the adversary is at work, trying to drive away his convictions, by making him
believe that he has none. I would show him how
reasonable it were to expect that it should be so ;—
that the great enemy of all good should be upon the
alert, in the use of his wiles, when he sees that he is
in danger of losing one of his subjects. And I would
refer to the experience of many others, who have
passed through similar trials, and who have at length
become fully satisfied that they were suffering under
a delusion, which was the effect of satanic influence.
And when the point is once gained, that the sinner
really believes that this impression in respect to his

having no convictions is from below, he is prepared
to resign it, and the delusion vanishes.

It may be useful sometimes, in order to correct
his views on this subject, to set him to account for
his own unhappiness on the ground that he has no
conviction.   The fact that he has no peace, that he
is even wretched, he will be willing enough to acknowledge.   He is not as he was in other days,
when his spirits were gay and buoyant, and no
thoughts concerning the salvation of his soul ever
rose in his mind.   There is some cause in operation now, which did not operate then; else there
would have been no change in his feelings—no
change in his conduct.   Suppose he could exclude
the subject of religion from his thoughts;—suppose
he could regard it with the same indifference he formerly did;—suppose he could revert to the former
impression that there was little or no danger in his
case;—and would not all the unhappiness which he
now feels instantly fly away?   If he reflects, will he
not acknowledge that this would be the case?   Let
him say then what else it is than the conviction that
he is a sinner, that disturbs the peace of his mind?
If he had no conviction of the truth of religion, and
of the interest which he has in it, and of his exposure to the woes of perdition in consequence of having offended God, why is it that he is thrown into a
state of wretchedness from which he would give the
world, if it were at his command, to be delivered?

But if the awakened sinner persevere in the mistaken notion that he has no conviction, I know of no

other course than to hold up to his view those great
truths which are fitted to produce it. If he will have
it that he has hitherto had no just sense of sin, we
can only proclaim to him the evil of sin, and point
him to the fountain that is opened for sin and un-
cleanness. It is desirable, however, in such cases,
to dwell chiefly on the glorious provision of the
gospel; for though the soul is unwilling to admit
that it feels its need, yet it actually does realize it;
and if Christ be continually held up, it may let go
its favorite delusion long enough to embrace him;
and when Christ is really received, the delusion is
gone forever.

There is yet one more attitude in which we may
contemplate the awakened sinner—I mean *as gradually falling under the power of a settled melancholy.*
As this is an evil greatly to be deprecated, so the
very first tendencies to it, ought, if possible, to be
promptly counteracted; for unless it be early check-
ed, it may soon become habitual, and may lead to
the most disastrous and even fatal results. Where-
ever this state of mind exists in connection with the
subject of religion, it will usually be found to have
been occasioned by an erroneous view of some particular truth. It is a matter of much importance
therefore to ascertain what is the error to which the
individual is yielding himself; and this may ordinarily be done by close and diligent inquiry. It is,
however, often more easy to ascertain the error than
to remove it; for the very fact that it operates so
powerfully as to destroy, in some measure, the ba-

lance among the faculties, proves that it has gained
a strong hold of the mind, and is not probably to be
dislodged by any feeble effort.   In attempting to
remove it, it is often wisest to avoid coming, at once,
to the point; lest the mind should take the alarm,
and put itself into the attitude of defence.   Let the
effort be directed first to impress upon the disordered intellect some of the great truths which it may
not be disposed to question, but which are utterly inconsistent with the notion which has plunged it into gloom; and let it be left, in some measure, to its
own reflections and conclusions; and when the particular error is approached, let it be in an easy and
delicate, and not in a harsh and revolting manner;
and there is good reason to hope that it may be delivered from its bondage to the error, and thus the
clouds of melancholy may go off, and light, and
peace, and comfort, may succeed.

It sometimes happens that the calamity of which
I am speaking is connected with great physical derangement; and that it would never have existed,
but for some predisposing cause in the bodily system.   In this case, the mind and body have a mutual action and re-action upon each other;—the mind
becoming more gloomy on account of the disease of
the body; and the body more diseased on account
of the gloom of the mind.   Sometimes important
benefit may be derived from medical aid, and still
more frequently perhaps from gentle relaxation and
exercise.   It has not unfrequently happened that
change of scenery, change of surrounding objects,

change of daily associates, has helped to restore the
health of the body, while it has contributed in the
same degree to bring back the balance of the mind.

There is one caution which ought always to be
diligently observed, but which there is reason to
fear is too often overlooked, in the treatment of a
person in these painful circumstances—I refer to the
fact that no measures should be taken which are fitted to carry his mind ultimately away from religion.
It is not uncommon for those whose friends have
fallen into this state, to manifest a strong disposition to separate them from all religious influences;
to divorce them from the company of Christians;
and to urge them into the society of the gay and
thoughtless. But never was there a greater mistake. The contrast which, in that case, exists, between the world without and the world within; between the cheerless and wretched state of the soul
and the joyous bounding of hearts amidst the vani-
ties of life, instead of relieving melancholy, is fitted to change it into agony. But if the point be ultimately gained by such a course, let me ask, what
is it that is gained? It is not merely relief from
gloom; but it is freedom from all concern for the
soul. It is a deliberate rushing back upon the va-
nities and gaieties of life. It is turning away the
thoughts from God, and from Christ, and from salvation, in a manner which renders it extremely probable that they will never in this world be seriously
directed to these objects again; at least not in circumstances in which reflection will be likely to be

availing. If, instead of this violent course there should be adopted one which should be fitted to break up gloomy associations on the one hand, without driving away serious thought on the other; which should surround the individual with cheerful and yet with religious influences; there might be just reason to hope that, in escaping from the dominion of melancholy, he would pass, not into the thoughtlessness of the world, but into the peace and joy of the true Christian.

Two brief remarks, by way of inference, will conclude the discourse.

1. Our subject *exposes two opposite errors, both of which, it is believed, are common, in the treatment of awakened sinners.*

The first is the error of those who limit themselves to the simple direction to repent, or believe, or submit to God. Any thing beyond this they consider as putting the sinner upon the use of the means of grace; and they ask how they can consistently do this, when the sinner is liable to die every moment, and thus be alike beyond repentance and beyond mercy? And then again, they say that all that he does while he remains impenitent is sinful; and that by exhorting him to do any thing before repentance, they exhort him to sin. But it is not difficult to see where lies the mistake in this matter. All will admit that it is the duty of a sinner to repent without delay. But he cannot repent until he knows what repentance is, and until he understands those great truths in view of which repentance is exercised. And to this end, if he be ignorant, he must be instructed out of God's word;—either by reading the Bible himself, or hearing its truths presented by others;—in other words, he must be put upon the use of the means of grace. True it is that he may die before he has knowledge enough to exercise evangelical repentance; but even if it should be so, they who direct him are not responsible for the event; because some degree of knowledge is essential to repentance. And can it reasonably be said that any thing is sinful, which is necessarily involved in a compliance with God's command? If he commands the sinner to repent, he commands him to do all that is necessary to enable him to repent; and as some knowledge of his truth is necessary, if he do not possess it already, he is bound to gain it; and surely there can be nothing in that to excite the divine displeasure.

The other error is that of directing inquiring sinners to use the means of grace, without, at the same time, enforcing the obligation of immediate repentance. This direction is fitted to abate a sense of guilt, and finally to bring back to the soul its accustomed spiritual torpor. One of two results from such a direction you may confidently expect;—either that the sinner will lull himself to sleep in the use of means, and will soon be disposed to abandon them, or else that he will put himself upon a course of self-righteous effort, and imagine that he is going rapidly towards heaven, when he has totally mistaken the path that leads thither. Means are nothing to an awakened sinner, except to bring before him those truths which are necessary to the exercise of repentance. To exhort him to the use of means with reference to any other end than this, were undoubtedly to mistake their design, and to expose him to be dangerously and fatally misled.

Take heed then, Brethren, that you avoid both these errors. Before you put off the sinner with the simple direction to repent, be sure that you are not speaking to him a language which he does not understand. Be sure that he understands those truths without a knowledge of which, your direction, though true and good, would leave him to grope in the dark. And on the other hand, when you direct him to study his Bible and attend on the various means of religious instruction, take care that you do not leave the impression that this is a substitute for repentance, instead of the means of it; or at least that repentance will by and by come along in the train of these means without any more direct personal effort. In short, endeavor to put him in the best way for understanding those truths which are involved in the exercise of repentance; but at the same time, let him distinctly know, that it is of such vital importance and such immediate obligation, that if he dies a stranger to it, he must reap the fruit of his neglect in a scene of interminable anguish.

2. Finally: Our subject teaches us *what are the best qualifications for directing and counselling awakened sinners.*

It is essential that a person who undertakes this office should have a good knowledge of God's word; for this is the great instrument by which the whole work is to be accomplished. It will not suffice that there should be a mere superficial acquaintance with divine truth; but it should be deep and thorough;— the doctrines of the Bible should be understood in their various bearings and connections. There should also be an intimate knowledge of the human heart—the subject on which this work is to be performed. There should be an ability to guide the sinner in the work of self-examination; to ferret sin out from its various lurking places; to bring principles and motives to bear upon the various faculties and affections of the soul, with discrimination and good effect. In short, there should be an intelligent and devoted piety; for this secures a knowledge of divine truth on the one hand, and an acquaintance with the springs of human conduct on the other. I hardly need say that the knowledge necessary to the right discharge of this office, is especially of an experimental character; for he who undertakes to direct an inquiring sinner in a path in which he has never walked, is as the blind leading the blind. A man may be destitute in a great degree of human learning, he may be a babe in the wisdom of the world, and yet he may have that divine and spiritual knowledge which shall render him a competent guide to inquiring souls. And on the other hand, he may be a proficient in every branch of human knowledge, he may have even studied thoroughly the philosophy of the mind, and the criticism of the Bible, and yet, from having never felt the power of divine truth upon his own heart, he may be a most unskilful and unsafe guide in the concern of the soul's salvation.

Wherefore, Christian Brethren, be exhorted to larger attainments both in knowledge and in piety. I might urge you to this on the ground that it will increase your comfort here, and brighten your crown hereafter. I might urge you to it also on the ground of general usefulness; for there is no department of benevolent action for which such attainments would not better prepare you. But I exhort you *now* to aim at these attainments from the consideration that your lot is cast at a period, when much devolves upon you in the way of directing inquiring souls; and while on the one hand, they may keep you from being instrumental, even in your well meant efforts, of great evil; on the other, they may secure to you the blessing of accomplishing great good. Go then, Christian, often into your closet, and study your own heart. Open God's blessed word, and apply yourself to its precious truths. Keep your soul constantly imbued with its spirit. Then the inquiring sinner may find in you a safe and skilful guide. Then you may hope that God will honor you as an instrument of saving souls from death, and hiding a multitude of sins.

LECTURE VII.

TREATMENT DUE TO YOUNG CONVERTS.

---

2 Corinthians, XIII. 5.

Prove your own selves.

This exhortation was addressed by the Apostle to professed Christians. It takes for granted that they were not absolutely assured of their discipleship, and were liable to be deceived in the views which they formed respecting their own character. It enjoins the duty of referring their character to the proper test; proving whether Christ is in them by the sanctifying influences of his Spirit, or whether they are mere nominal Christians, finally to be cast off as reprobate.

The advice contained in the text was addressed to the Corinthian church indiscriminately; and it may properly apply to all Christians, without any reference to age or standing. It is, however, especially applicable to those who have just entered, or professedly entered, on the Christian life; for if they mistake their own character then, there is reason to fear that the mistake will be fatal. It there-

fore becomes every minister, and every private
Christian, who undertakes the office of a counsellor
and guide, during a revival of religion, to make
much use of the exhortation—" Prove your own
selves."

It is, if I mistake not, becoming a somewhat
popular notion, that nearly all the efforts which are
made during a revival, should be directed to the
awakening and conversion of sinners; and that
comparatively little attention is needed by those
who have indulged the hope that they have become
reconciled to God.   Far be it from me to say, or
to think, that too much is done to effect the former
of these objects; but I am constrained to believe
that there is far too little done in reference to the
latter.   True it is that the sinner, while trembling
under a conviction of guilt, is in circumstances of
awful interest; for if the Spirit of God depart from
him, it may be the eternal death of his soul: but it
is no less true, that the period of his first cherishing a hope in God's mercy is an exceedingly critical one; for if he build on a sandy foundation, he
may never discover it, until it slides from beneath
him, and lets him into the pit.   Let no Christian
then imagine that his responsibility in connection
with a revival terminates in the duty which he owes
to awakened sinners: let him remember that there
is another class who as truly claim his attention as
they; and who cannot be neglected but at the peril
of encouraging self-deception, and corrupting the
purity of the church.   Lend me your attention,

therefore, while I endeavor in this discourse to exhibit an outline of THE TREATMENT WHICH IS DUE TO THOSE WHO HAVE BEEN HOPEFULLY THE SUBJECTS OF A RECENT CONVERSION.

We will consider the *object* which ought to be kept in view; and the *means* by which it may be most successfully accomplished.

I. The *object* to be aimed at in all our treatment of those who hope they have been recently converted, is twofold: *to save from self-deception*, and *to build up in faith and holiness.*

1. *To save from self-deception.*

That there is danger that many persons will practise deception upon themselves in these circumstances, must be obvious to any one who gives the subject the least consideration. For the mind is then in an excited state, when it is most liable to misjudge of its own exercises: and the heart has been burdened with anguish; and has been longing for relief; and is prepared to welcome with transport the least evidence of pardon; and of course is in danger of grasping at a shadow, and mistaking it for the substance. Besides, there is a chapter in the record of experience which teaches a most impressive lesson on this subject; which exhibits instances innumerable, of persons who have, for a season, felt confident of their own conversion, and have been hailed by Christians as fellow helpers in the work of the Lord, who have, nevertheless, subsequently been convinced themselves, and forced the conviction upon others, that what they had call-

ed Christian experience was mere delusion. And
while there is danger that self-deception will take
place in these circumstances, no one can doubt that
this is an evil greatly to be deprecated; for there is
comparatively little reason to hope, in any given
case, that it will be removed; and if it be not removed, it is in the very worst sense fatal. Surely
then it devolves upon all who are active in conducting a revival of religion, to guard those who hope
they have been recently converted, against self-deception. Even amidst all the peace and rapture
which they may experience, in connection with
what they suppose to be a conversion to God, it is
the duty of those who counsel them, though they
may rejoice in their joy, to rejoice with trembling,
lest it should prove that the hope with which their
joy is connected, should be the hope of the hypocrite, which shall finally prove as the giving up of
the ghost.

2. The other great end to be kept in view in respect to the class of which I am speaking, is, *to build
them up in faith and holiness.*

If they have actually been regenerated, they will
certainly, in a greater or less degree, bring forth the
fruits of holiness; for it is impossible that a gracious principle should exist in the soul, and be habitually and entirely inoperative. Nevertheless, it
is not every Christian who lets his light shine as he
ought; not every one that exerts any thing like the
amount of influence in favor of the cause of Christ,
that is fairly within his power. It therefore becomes

a matter of great moment that, at the very beginning
of the Christian life, each one should be impressed
with his obligations to labor for his Master to the
extent of his ability ; and should be assisted so far
as may be, to form a character which will ensure
at once the highest degree both of comfort and of
usefulness. Whatever is done *then* to mould the
character, will probably exert a far more decisive
influence, than any thing which could be done at a
future period ; and upon the counsels and directions
which an individual receives, at such a moment,
may depend in a great degree, the amount of good
which he is to accomplish during his whole future
life. Surely then, it is no unimportant office, to
counsel and guide the young Christian. He who
does it aright may be instrumental of opening fountains of blessing, which shall send forth their purifying streams in every direction.

II. We proceed, secondly, to consider some of
the *means* by which this twofold object is to be attained.

1. Let those who hope they have been the subjects of a recent conversion be put on their guard
*against too confident a belief that they have been truly
regenerated.*

I remember to have heard of an individual, who
was afterwards greatly distinguished for piety, going to the elder Jonathan Edwards, to whose congregation he belonged, to tell him what God had
done for his soul ; and after that great and good
man had listened to the account of his supposed

conversion, and had heard him speak with rapture of the new and delightful views which he had of spiritual objects, and when the individual was expecting that he would do nothing less than congratulate him upon having become a child of God, he was disappointed beyond measure by simply hearing him say that what he had experienced was an encouragement to him to persevere; though the man himself, in relating the circumstance many years after, when he had come much nearer the fulness of the stature of a perfect person in Christ, cordially approved the course which his minister had adopted. It is not always easy to satisfy persons in these circumstances, even of the possibility that the hope and joy which they experience may be spurious; but it is much to be desired, both as it respects their safety and their usefulness, that this should be effected; that while they acknowledge with devout gratitude to God the least evidence that he has extended to them a gracious forgiveness, they should fear lest a promise being left of entering into rest, they should seem to come short of it.

You cannot do better service to those who believe themselves to have been recently converted, than by presenting distinctly before them the evidences of Christian character. Let them clearly understand that the mere fact that the clouds which hung over their minds are dispersed, and that they are rejoicing in bright sunshine, constitutes no sufficient evidence of their regeneration. Encourage them to analyze their feelings, to examine the motives and principles of their conduct, especially to inquire whether they have the humility of the gospel, whether they cordially approve its conditions, and whether they glory in sovereign grace as it is manifested in the gospel scheme of salvation. Show them moreover, that the evidence of Christian character in order to be decisive, must be progressive ; that it consists especially in a fixed purpose, and a steady course of endeavors in reliance on God's grace, to do whatever he would have them to do ; that they must add to their faith all the virtues and graces of the Christian ; and that if they fail of this, whatever other experience they may have, must be set down as nothing. Caution them against the wiles of their own hearts, and the wiles of the great adversary ; and urge them to settle the question respecting their claim to Christian character, by referring their experience to the simple standard of God's word.

It is matter of great moment that they should be impressed, from the beginning, with the importance of habitual self-examination; for this is not more essential to ensure them against self-deception, than it is to all their attainments in holiness. Let them be exhorted not only to inspect narrowly their motives and feelings from day to day, with a view to give a right direction to their prayers, and to ascertain the measure of their growth in grace, but also frequently to revolve the great question whether they have really been born of the Spirit. Such a course honestly and faithfully pursued in the light

of God's word, is hardly consistent with cherishing
the hypocrite's hope, or with making low attainments in piety.

2. Endeavor to impress them with the consideration that *if they have really been renewed, they are
just entering on a course of labor and conflict.*

It too often happens that, in the rapture which
the soul experiences when it emerges suddenly into
light from the gloom of deep conviction, there is
little else thought of than its own enjoyment; and
the bright visions of heaven by which it is well
nigh entranced, occasion a temporary forgetfulness
of the trials and conflicts, and all the more sober
realities, of the Christian life. Now it is highly
important that an individual should not, at this interesting moment, take up the idea that he is born
into the kingdom to enjoy a state of perpetual sunshine; that he has nothing to do but fold his arms,
and sit quietly down in the cheering and bright
light of God's countenance. Let him once get this
impression, or any think like it, and the effect in
the first place will be painful disappointment; for
it is almost certain that, at no distant period, he will
have to encounter days of darkness; and he will
find a law in his members warring against the law
of his mind; and not improbably he may be ready
to give his hope to the winds, and resign himself to
the conviction that all the joy he had experienced,
was the effect of delusion. Besides, such an impression, there is reason to fear, might exert an influence that would be felt through life, unfavorable

to his Christian activity; and might abate, in no small degree, his zeal, and efficiency, and usefulness, in the cause of his Master.

Strive then to impress the young convert, from the very beginning, with the conviction that God has called him into his kingdom to struggle with the corruptions of his heart—to war with principalities and powers. Admonish him that there is still an evil principle within him; and that if its operations seem to be suspended for a season, it yet retains a deadly energy, which will call him ere long to severe conflict. Admonish him also of the temptations of the world; tell him how insidious they are; in what a variety of forms they present themselves; how many who have imagined themselves secure against their influence, have nevertheless been assailed by them with success. Remind him also that he has a powerful, invisible enemy to contend with—the enemy of all good;—against the influence of whose wiles no condition in life can secure him. Let him understand that he is never so much in danger of falling into the hands of his spiritual enemies, as when he yields to a spirit of self-confidence or carelessness; and either practically forgets that such enemies exist, or else thinks to encounter them in his own strength. He cannot be girded for conflict too early; or observe their movements too vigilantly; or meet them too resolutely and boldly. Let him determine that he will wear the whole armor of God at all times, and especially in every scene of temptation into which his duty may call him, and then he may be able to stand.

But he has something more to do than merely to contend with enemies; he has to labor directly for the advancement of Christ's cause. His lot is cast in a world lying in darkness and wickedness; and it is for him to lend his aid to enlighten and reform it. At home and abroad there are multitudes thronging the road to perdition; it is for him to put forth a hand to arrest them, and by God's blessing upon his efforts, to turn them into the path of life. The Lord Jesus Christ has given to the world his gospel; and he has left an injunction upon his people to carry it to the ends of the earth; that its light may every where be diffused, and its influence every where felt; and every one who is born into his kingdom, becomes specially obligated to lend himself to this glorious work; and to continue in it, till he shall be taken from his labors to his reward. Every young convert should be made to feel that this is a matter of personal concern with himself; and that from the hour of his conversion to God, all his affections, and faculties, and possessions, are in some way or other to be consecrated to his glory.

Let it further be impressed upon him that it is most unworthy of any one who believes himself called into the kingdom of Christ, even to desire an exemption from labor and trial. For what were the sufferings and sacrifices of him, to whom the Christian looks as the foundation of his hopes and joys?

And what is the utmost that he can do or suffer, when compared with the exceeding and eternal weight of glory which awaits him in heaven? It is a law of God's providence that, on the whole, the highest degree of happiness is connected with the most faithful discharge of duty ; so that while he calls the Christian to glory, he calls him also to virtue ; in other words, he brings him into his kingdom to find his enjoyment in a course of obedience to his commandments. And while these commandments in themselves are not grievous, the keeping of them brings peace to the soul, inasmuch as it furnishes the best, the only satisfactory evidence of true discipleship. Surely the young Christian cannot resist, will not desire to resist, the force of such considerations.

3. Let it be impressed upon the mind of the new convert that *much of his comfort and usefulness in the religious life will probably depend on the resolutions he forms, and the principles he adopts, at the beginning.*

It is in religion as in every thing else—the first steps that are taken are usually the most decisive. The man who sets out well in any worldly enterprize, who carefully counts the cost, and engages in it with a prudence and zeal, and resolution, corresponding to its importance, we expect, in all ordinary cases, will succeed ; and we calculate that the amount of his success will be very much in proportion to the discretion and energy which characterize his earliest efforts. On the other hand, let an

individual engage in the same enterprize with but
little reflection and zeal, and instead of making it,
at the beginning, a commanding object, let him regard it as a matter to be taken up and laid aside as
circumstances may seem to dictate, and you may
expect with confidence that the end will be like the
beginning;—little attempted, little accomplished.
In like manner, suppose the young Christian to set
out with a decided purpose formed in the strength
of divine grace, to do the utmost in his power for
the advancement of the Redeemer's cause;—suppose he adopt fixed principles for the regulation of
his whole conduct, and begin with a firm resolution
that he will never yield them up in any circumstances; and you may hope with good reason to see him
holding on his way in the face of appalling obstacles, and exhibiting through life the character of a
good soldier of Jesus Christ. But if he begin, satisfied with some general intentions to do his duty,
and without any definite plan for the regulation of
his conduct; if he adopt the principle of yielding
improperly to circumstances, and endeavor to make
a compromise with conscience for the neglect of
duties that require great self-denial, rely on it, his
course will, in all probability, be marked by little
either of comfort or usefulness; and if he is saved
at the last, it will be so as by fire. I acknowledge,
indeed, that there are some cases in which an un-
promising beginning is followed by an active and
useful life; in which an early course of conformity
to the world is terminated by means of some dis-

pensation of providence, and is followed by a course of exemplary and devoted obedience; but in all ordinary cases, the man who adopts a low standard at the beginning, never rises to a more elevated one at any subsequent period.

Let the young convert, then, be admonished to begin the Christian life with such resolutions and principles, as will be likely to secure the greatest amount of activity and usefulness. Let him contemplate the importance of doing the utmost in his power for the honor of his Master, and the advancement of his cause, as well as of reaching the highest attainable degree of personal holiness;—let him determine that nothing shall divert him from the purpose of following Christ through bad as well as good report, and that in the strength of his grace, he will march on in his service in spite of any obstacles that may lie in his way—let him resolve that he will keep the eye of faith steadily fixed now upon the Saviour's cross, and now upon the crown of glory;—in short, let him form a plan of holy living that shall reach onward to his entrance into the abodes of light; and in these holy resolutions and purposes, I expect to find the germ of an actively useful and eminently happy life. I expect there will prove to have been that which will reflect an additional lustre on his immortal crown.

4. Let him be exhorted farther *to draw all his religious opinions, and all his maxims of conduct, directly from God's word.*

I know there are many human productions in which the doctrines of the gospel are stated and defended with great ability; and he would do himself injustice, as well as evince a criminal ingratitude for God's goodness, who should refuse to avail himself of them as helps towards building himself up in the most holy faith. But let them always be considered as subordinate to God's word; and let them be tried by it; and let whatever will not stand that test be thrown among the wood, and hay, and stubble. He who derives his views of religion from any uninspired works, however much of general excellence they may possess, will, of course, be liable to an admixture of error; and besides, even if he should chance to gather from them the uncorrupted truth, he could not have the same deep and powerful conviction of it, as if it had been drawn directly from the lively oracles. And how much less is God honored in the one case than in the other! How much less by believing the truth because we may have been taught it in our catechisms and confessions, than because it has beamed forth upon our own intellectual eye, from the very page on which the mind of the Spirit has been recorded!

I would say then to every one just entering on the Christian life—study the Bible for yourself. Study it with humility, diligence and prayer. What you find written there, believe; whatever is not written there is either not true or not important. And be not discouraged in your efforts to ascertain the truth for yourself, by the fact that the world is

full of different opinions respecting it;—for the
truth is clearly revealed; and besides, most of the
disputes which exist among Christians relate rather
to human philosophy than to the matter of God's
word. Remember that God himself hath said that
" the meek he will guide in judgment; the meek he
will teach his way."

But it is not less important that the new convert
should derive the rules of his *conduct*, than the principles of his faith, directly from the Bible. There
are, indeed, many particular cases in which men
may be called to act, in relation to which there are
no express directions given in God's word; but
there are general rules to be found there which admit of application to every possible case; and which
an enlightened conscience will always know how
to apply. Let the young Christian then be exhorted to study the Bible diligently as a rule of duty;
to ascertain from God's own word what he would
have him to do in the various conditions in which
he is placed; and to refer every question of right
and wrong which he is called practically to decide
to this standard, and no other. Let his character
be formed under this influence, and it cannot fail to
rise in fair and goodly proportions. There will be
in it a dignified stability which will secure it from
the undue influence of circumstances. Its posses-
sor will be enabled to act not only with rectitude,
but with confidence and decision; and while he
keeps a conscience void of offence, he will commend himself to the good will of his fellow men,

and to the special favor of God. The current of
public opinion not unfrequently sets in a wrong direction, and yet is exceedingly rapid and powerful;
and he who attempts to resist, may be obliged to do
it, at the expense of bearing a heavy load of obloquy; but he who makes God's word the rule of his
conduct, will be able to do this notwithstanding;—
to stand firm, even when the waves of opposition
are rolling over him. Many a young Christian has
been carried, by the influence of custom and example far into courses over which he has subsequently
had just occasion to weep; when, by having ad-
hered to the scriptural standard of duty, he would
have kept a conscience void of offence, and prevented the occasion for bitter repentance.

You then who may be called to counsel those
who are just setting out in the Christian life, should
charge them by a regard to their comfort, their
character, their usefulness, to have nothing to do
with any other standard of conduct than that which
they find in the Bible. Let them be exhorted to
adhere to this, even though it should subject them
to the greatest temporal inconvenience. Let them
determine that they will regulate by it the whole conduct of their lives;—not only what may seem to them
their most important, but also their least important
actions. When they have settled the question,
" Lord what wilt thou have me to do ?" then, and
only then, are they prepared to act with freedom
and confidence; in a manner that is fitted to keep

peace in their consciences, and to bring down upon them the blessing of God.

5. Let the young convert be admonished *to ascertain, as soon as possible, his besetting sin ; and to guard against it with the utmost caution.*

It is true of every Christian that there is some one sin to which he is more inclined than any other : what that sin will be in any particular case, may depend on tne previous moral habits of the individual, or on the circumstances in which he is placed, or on some original infirmity or obliquity of constitution ; for as bodily disease is most likely to seat itself in the part which is originally the weakest, so the depravity of the heart usually concentrates its energies in some passion or appetite which is marked by the greatest degree of natural perverseness. He, therefore, who ascertains in his own case what this sin is, and who regards it as the most formidable enemy to be encountered in his conflict, and succeeds in gaining a victory over it, accomplishes much in the way of his sanctification. He who neglects to guard against the besetting sin, while he takes care to avoid sins to which he is not specially inclined, acts as unwise a part as a general who should employ all his skill and energies to prevent an attack from some scattered and unimportant part of a hostile army, while, without any effort at resistance, he should suffer the main body to move toward his ranks, and open upon them in a fierce discharge of artillery.

There is no difficulty in ascertaining the besetting sin in any given case, provided there is a faithful use of the means which God has put within our
power : nevertheless, from a neglect of these means,
there is no doubt a lamentable degree of ignorance
on this subject.   Let the young Christian then be
exhorted to watch closely all the tendencies of his
mind ;—to observe on what forbidden objects his
affections most readily fasten ;—in what manner
his thoughts are occupied when his mind is most at
leisure and subject to the least restraint ; and what
circumstances and occasions operate most powerfully upon him in the way of temptation ; and the
result cannot fail to be, that he will know what is
the sin which most easily besets him.   And when
he knows it, he is prepared to guard against it.
This he must do by keeping a watchful eye upon
that particular part of his moral nature in which
this sin has its operation ; by avoiding, as much as
possible, those objects and occasions which are
likely to furnish temptations to it ; or if called into
scenes of temptation in the providence of God, by
placing a double guard at the vulnerable point ; by
earnest prayer for grace to be enabled to gain the
victory ; and by cultivating, in a high degree, general spirituality of character.   As the indulgence of
the besetting sin, whatever it may be, is unfavorable to the growth of all Christian affections, so the
general culture of these affections, the abounding in
all the virtues and graces of the gospel, is the most
certain means of destruction to the besetting sin.

It can never flourish in a soil which is habitually watered with heavenly grace.

6. Impress the young convert with *the danger of the least departure from duty ;—of taking the first step in the way of spiritual decline.*

It rarely happens that an individual becomes a great backslider at once : on the contrary, it is usually the work of time, and generally has a small and almost imperceptible beginning. When the first step is taken, there is probably, in most cases, an intention not to take another—certainly not to go far; but it is a law of our moral constitution that one step renders the next easier ; and hence the facility with which we form our habits, especially evil habits. The young convert, upon the mount of Christian enjoyment, is able to form but an inadequate idea of the conflicts of the religious life ; he realizes then, much less than in subsequent parts of his course, the need of constant watchfulness against temptation ; and this lack of vigilance throws open the doors of the heart, and not unfrequently the tempter has planted himself there, and begun his work, before any danger has been apprehended. And the soul which was just now burning with ecstacy, wakes to the fact that not only its joys are rapidly upon the wane, but that its desires are becoming earthly, and its impression of invisible things feeble and inconstant.

Caution the young Christian then, against the least allowed violation of duty. Admonish him that, if he enter on such a course, he can never know where it will end. Point him to examples of those who have taken the first step with a firm purpose never to take another, who have nevertheless continued to backslide, until there was scarcely the semblance of Christian character remaining. Let him understand that no degree of joy, or even of spirituality, which he can possess on earth, can be any security against his losing his evidences and his comforts, and sinking into a state of the most chilling spiritual indifference. And if, at any time, he find that he has actually begun to wander, let him know that he has the best reason to be alarmed, and that every hour that he continues his wanderings, he is making work for bitter repentance, and bringing a dark cloud over his religious prospects.

7. Put the young convert on his guard *against neglecting the duties of the closet.*

It is in the closet especially that every Christian must labor to keep alive the flame of devotion in his own soul. Here, more than any where else, is carried forward the work of self-examination: here are the silent communings of the soul with its God, in acts of confession, and thanksgiving, and supplication: here the believer becomes acquainted with his sins and his wants; and while he unburdens his soul before the throne of mercy, gathers strength and grace, by which he is sustained and carried forward amidst the various duties and trials which meet him in the world. Hence it always happens that, in proportion as the duties of the closet are neglected, religion languishes in the heart, and the exhibition of it in the life becomes faint and equivocal. It is manifest to those who see him and converse with him, that there is a canker corroding the principle of his spiritual life. And he himself knows that his joys have fled, and his conscience has become his accuser, and he has no evidence which ought to satisfy him that he is walking in the path to heaven.

But this evil—that of neglecting the closet—is one to which the young convert is exceedingly liable. He may not be liable to it in the very earliest stage of his Christian experience; for then the duties of the closet are usually a delight to him; but when his first joys have partially subsided, and he has begun to be conversant with the more sober realities of the religious life, there is great danger that he will find some apology for a partial and irregular attendance on these duties. One source of danger is found in the fact that he may neglect them, and still be unobserved by the world;—that he may neglect them without forfeiting, even in the view of his fellow Christians, who of course are ignorant of it, his claim to Christian character. And then these duties being of a peculiarly spiritual kind, are the very first to lose their attractions to a Christian who is losing his spirituality. Other duties bring him before the world: these bring him only before his own conscience and the searcher of his heart. And besides, where circumstances may seem to render it inconvenient to engage in closet devotion, it is too easy a matter to satisfy

the conscience with an indefinite resolution that it
shall be attended to at a subsequent period; and no
resolution is more easily broken than this; and let
it be broken in a few instances, and a habit of comparative indifference to the closet is the consequence. I doubt not that I might appeal to the
experience of a large part of those who have professedly entered on the Christian life for evidence
of the fact, that no habit is formed with more ease
than that of neglecting, in a greater or less degree,
this class of duties.

If then the faithful discharge of private religious
duties be so essential to a vigorous and healthful
tone of religious feeling and action, and if there be
peculiar temptations to neglect them, then every
person at the commencement of the Christian life,
ought to be admonished of his danger on the one
hand, and exhorted to fidelity on the other. Counsel him to have his stated seasons for private devotion, in which nothing but imperative necessity shall
keep him out of his closet. Counsel him to take
heed that he do not substitute the form for the spirit of prayer; that he do not satisfy his conscience
by appearing before God with the bended knee,
without the broken heart. Counsel him to mingle
with his private prayers self-examination and the
reading of God's word; that thus his communion
with God may be more intelligent on the one hand,
and more spiritual on the other. Counsel him never to turn his back upon his closet, because he
may find his affections low and languid, and may

imagine that he should have little enjoyment in attempting to pray: let this rather be urged as an argument for hastening to his closet, and confessing and lamenting his indifference, and endeavoring to get the flame of devotion rekindled in his bosom. In short, urge upon him the importance of private meditation and devotion in all circumstances; urge him to redeem time for that purpose under the greatest pressure of worldly care; and keep him mindful of the connection which this duty has with every thing that belongs to Christian character and Christian enjoyment.

8. Admonish him to *beware of the world.*

Every one who has made much progress in the Christian life, has been taught by his own experience that the world is a deadly enemy to the believer's growth in grace. It is not easy for an advanced Christian to be very familiar with it and retain a high degree of spirituality; and accordingly you will find that there are few comparatively whose secular callings keep their faculties under an almost constant contribution, who habitually evince a deep and strong religious sensibility. Even the cares of the world—to speak of nothing more, are exceedingly apt to mar the Christian character; but there are, in addition, the pleasures of the world, the honors of the world, the riches of the world; all of which in turn seize hold of the heart with a mighty grasp. And sometimes the world laughs and scoffs at the young Christian, and tries to persuade him that he is giving himself to fanaticism

and folly.   Sometimes it flatters and caresses him,
and by its artful blandishments, seeks to draw him
aside from the plain path of duty.   And sometimes
it would fain persuade him that he is right in the
general, but unreasonably scrupulous in respect to
particulars; and that the self-denial to which he is
disposed to yield, is little better than pharisaical
austerity; and that if he will go, at least to a moderate degree, into the amusements of the world,
there is enough in the Bible in favor of cheerfulness
and joy to bear him out in it.   Indeed the world
will assume any form, or turn into any thing, to
draw the Christian, especially the young Christian,
away from God and from duty.

How important then that you put him on his
guard, at the very beginning, against this dangerous
enemy! If he is in the morning of life as well as
young in Christian experience, there is reason why
you should caution him especially against the levities and amusements of the world; for this is the
point at which he will be most in danger.   Let him
beware of the influence of former careless associates: not that he should say to them by his conduct—" Stand by, I am holier than thou;" not that
he should be encouraged to assume a single distant
or unsocial air towards them; but he *should* take
heed that they do not imperceptibly draw him into
forbidden paths; that they do not either by flatter-
ies on the one hand, or sneering insinuations on
the other, prevail over his scruples, and bring him

under the lash of his own conscience in consequence of unjustifiable and unchristian complian-
ces.

9. Another important part of duty towards those
who are just entering on the Christian life, is to
*encourage them gradually to bear a part in social re-
ligious exercises.*

I do not mean that this is to be done in every
case; for I well know that there are a few persons
who, from some difficulty of utterance, or some pe-
culiarity of constitutional temperament, are disqualified to conduct the devotions of an assembly to edification; and wherever cases of this kind exist, it
were wrong to urge, or even to encourage the individuals to attempt this service. But these cases,
I believe, are not frequent; in far the greater number of instances where they are supposed to exist,
the individuals, I doubt not, mistake their own powers. Wherever there is the gift of prayer in a common degree, it is exceedingly desirable that its pos-
sessor should be trained to the exercise of it in public; for if he improve it in that way discreetly, it
cannot fail greatly to increase his usefulness. I
would not, however, advise, in ordinary cases, that
a young Christian, especially if he be a very young
person, should be brought at once to conduct the
devotions of a large assembly; for I should expect
that it would serve to embarrass and dishearten
him on the one hand, or to puff him up with spiritual pride on the other; and withal that there would
be little to edify those whose devotions he should

attempt to conduct. I would advise, therefore, that
his first attempts to lead in social prayer, should be
on some occasion where there are literally but two or
three gathered together ; and it were well that those
should be persons whose feelings correspond with his
own, and whose presence would be least fitted to embarrass him; and from leading occasionally in such
an exercise, he might soon acquire that composure
and self-command, which would enable him to guide
in a proper manner the devotions of a larger circle; and ultimately, and at no distant period, to perform the duty of public prayer, wherever he should
be called to it. Let him be preserved from the extreme of being driven to this service, prematurely,
on occasions altogether public, and let him be kept
from the opposite extreme of yielding to a timidity
which shall prevent him from engaging in it at all;
and the greatest amount of good will be secured to
him, the greatest amount of good will be secured to
the church and the world through his instrumentality.

10. I observe, once more, that every young convert should be encouraged, *at a proper time, to make
a public profession of religion.*

This is a duty which he owes to himself, to the
church, and to his Master; and he cannot deliberately and voluntarily neglect it, but at the expense
of his comfort, his usefulness, and even his claim to
Christian character. It is his *privilege* to come into
the church; for it is refreshing to sit under the shadow of its ordinances, and in the communion of

saints on earth, to anticipate the more elevated and rapturous communion of heaven. It is his *duty* to come into the church ; for hereby especially he is enabled to let his light shine before men, so that they seeing his good works may glorify our Father who is heaven.

But while every young Christian should be encouraged to make a profession of religion, he should be encouraged to do it at the proper time—neither too early nor too late.

There is a possibility of doing this too early. In this case there would be no sufficient opportunity of testing the character; or of guarding against self-deception; or as the case may be, of understanding what is implied, and what is required, in a Christian profession. On the other hand, it may be deferred too long ; and then the desire for it may become feeble, the mind clouded, and all the Christian graces languish for want of that appropriate nourishment which is supplied by Christian ordinances. It is not easy, nor indeed possible, to establish any certain rule which shall apply in all cases, in respect to the time of admission to the privileges of the church ; because there must needs be a difference corresponding with the variety of constitutional temperament, external advantages, degrees of knowledge, and degrees of evidence of Christian character ; but it is manifest that either extreme is fraught with danger ; that great precipitancy, or long delay, may be the occasion of serious evils.

The young convert should be well instructed in
relation to the nature and obligations of a Christian
profession; and should be encouraged to come
with humility in view of his unworthiness; with
gratitude in view of the greatness of the privilege;
with strong resolutions of holy living in view of the
peculiar obligations of acknowledged discipleship;
and with full dependence on divine grace in view of
his own weakness on the one hand, and the arduous
duties of the Christian life on the other. Let him
come with this spirit, at the proper time, and we
may reasonably hope that it will be good for him,
that it will be good for the church, that he joins
himself to her communion.

Let it not be thought, however, that the church
owes no peculiar duty to young Christians, after
she has received them into her fellowship, or that
the same cautions and counsels which she has given
them before, are not to be repeated subsequently
to this act. She is to bear in mind that they are
new in the duties and conflicts of the Christian life;
that they are peculiarly exposed to the temptations
of the world; that they need to be counselled and
instructed with Christian fidelity and affection;—
to be assisted in forming and executing their plans
of usefulness; and encouraged to come up pru-
dently, and yet fearlessly and decidedly, to the help
of the Lord against the mighty. As a tender mother cherisheth her children, so she is to cherish
them. Like the great Shepherd, she is to take the
lambs in her arms, and carry them in her bosom.

Without extending my remarks farther on this subject, I think we are fairly brought to the conclusion, that every revival of religion is dependent for its good effect, in no small degree, upon the course which is adopted with those who are professedly its subjects. Whether the effect of a revival is to be that the purity of the church shall be increased, as well as its numbers, or that with what is truly good it is to receive a large amount of dross and chaff; whether those who have really been renewed are to begin and hold on a course of consistent, active, Christian obedience, or are to have their religious character marred, and their usefulness abridged, by being conformed to false and unscriptural standards;—depends, in no small degree, upon the instruction and counsel they receive, while they are yet babes in Christ. Let every Christian, then, who undertakes to perform this important office, realize deeply his responsibility. Let him bear in mind that the influence which he exerts, will tell, not only on individual character, but on the future efficiency and purity of the church. And let all seek to qualify themselves for this arduous work, (for there are none upon whom it may not at some time devolve,) by the faithful study of God's word, by earnestly supplicating divine grace, and by constantly aiming at a high standard of Christian experience. With the furniture thus acquired, you may mingle among your younger brethren and sisters in Christ with delight and profit, both to yourselves and them. You may be increasing in the know-

ledge of God, while you are building them up in
the most holy faith. You may be walking in the
path of eminent usefulness towards the abodes of
immortal glory.

LECTURE VIII.

EVILS TO BE AVOIDED IN CONNECTION WITH REVIVALS.

———

ROMANS XIV. 16.

Let not then your good be evil spoken of.

This direction of the Apostle was suggested by a particular case, which was the subject of controversy in the church at Rome, when this epistle was written. You will instantly perceive, however, that the rule here prescribed, is of universal application; and that it is founded in general principles of Christian prudence and charity. The design of it is not only to direct us in the practice of that which is good, but to lead us to unite wisdom with our pious activity; that we may, so far as possible, prevent incidental evils from being connected with our well meant efforts, and that our good may be inoffensive and irreproachable.

As there is no part of Christian conduct in relation to which this direction is not applicable, so, if I mistake not, it applies especially to the part which the church is called to take in a revival of religion—indeed to the whole economy of a revival. For as there is no department of religious action in which even good men are not liable to err, so there is no other field in which the Christian is called to labor, where there is greater danger of his being misled. There is in the minds of most men a tendency to extremes; and that tendency is never so likely to discover itself as in a season of general excitement. When men are greatly excited on any subject, we know that they are in far more danger of forming erroneous judgments, and adopting improper cour- ses, than when they are in circumstances to yield themselves to sober reflection. Now as there is often great excitement in connection with a revival, there is the common danger which exists in all cases of highly excited feeling, that our honest en- deavors to do right will result in more or less that is wrong; in other words, that we shall give occa- sion for our good to be evil spoken of.

The conclusion to which we should be brought on this subject from the very constitution of human nature, is in exact accordance with what we know of the history of revivals. There always has been, mingled with these scenes of divine power and grace, more or less of human infirmity and indis- cretion; and in some cases, no doubt, in which there have even been many genuine conversions, there has been just reason to say, "what is the wheat to the chaff?" To say nothing of revivals in modern times—whoever will read the history of the early revivals in New-England, while he will find evidence enough that the presence and power of

God was in them, and if he be a Christian, will regard the record of them as occupying one of the
most blessed chapters in the history of the church,
will nevertheless find just cause to weep that they
should have been clouded so much by the mistakes
and infirmities even of good men. But those good
men (some of them at least) lived to be satisfied
that they were in the wrong; and it is to their honor
that they acknowledged it; and it were impossible
to read the record of their acknowledgment, without feeling a sentiment of veneration for their characters, and without wishing that the errors into
which they fell, might, so far as they were themselves concerned, be blotted from the memory of
the church.

I am aware, my friends, that in endeavoring to
present before you the abuses to which revivals are
liable, and with which they have always been, in a
greater or less degree, connected, I am undertaking
a task of peculiar delicacy; and I confess to you,
that nothing but a strong and honest sense of duty
would have led me to attempt it. I will state to
you the considerations which have arisen to occasion this reluctance, and the manner in which I
have felt myself obliged to dispose of them.

In the first place, I can hardly doubt that an attempt to expose these evils, may appear to some
unnecessary. But so thought not the illustrious
Edwards, when his discriminating and mighty mind
was occupied in framing some of the most judicious
treatises which the world has seen, for the very

purpose of guarding against the abuses of revivals. On the title page of those books the church has written her own name, and she claims them as her property in a higher sense than almost any thing else except the Bible. And is it not manifest that that illustrious man judged rightly in composing them; and that the church has judged rightly in the estimate she has formed of them? For who does not perceive that if revivals of religion become corrupted, there is poison in the fountain whose streams are expected to gladden and purify? And who that is competent to judge, will doubt that those treatises have done more than any other un-inspired productions, to maintain the purity of re-vivals, from the period in which they were written to the present? If Edwards has rendered good ser-vice to the church by writing these immortal works, then surely it cannot be unnecessary for other mi-nisters to direct their humbler efforts to the same end. It is just as necessary now to distinguish be-tween true and false experience, and between right and wrong conduct in a revival of religion, as it ever has been in any preceding period; and the manner in which this duty is practically regarded, must always determine, in a great degree, the amount of blessing which any revival will secure.

But it may be said also that what I am about to attempt should be avoided, because it is *fitted to awaken controversy*. I acknowledge that controver-sy on the subject of religion is not in itself desira-ble; for it is exceedingly liable to wake up the bad passions of men. Nevertheless, there are some cases in which we shall all agree that it is necessary to hazard the evils that may result from it. No being on earth ever awakened a more violent religious controversy than Jesus Christ; but if it had not been for this, where now would have been our blessed Christianity? So also Luther, and Calvin, and Zuingle, and Knox, and the whole host of Reformers, excited a controversy concerning religion which had well nigh set the world on fire; but if it had never existed, what evidence have you that the church would, to this hour, have witnessed the glorious Reformation. President Edwards published his " Thoughts on Revivals," and other invaluable works in connection with the same subject, at the expense of being denounced, even by some of his own brethren, as an enemy of revivals; but these publications have served to correct and prevent great abuses ever since; and if he had rendered the church no other service, for this alone she would have embalmed his memory. Controversy, then, though it is never to be desired for its own sake, cannot always be declined in consistency with Christian obligation; or without putting at fearful hazard the best interests of the church.

In the present case, however, permit me to say that I have no intention to excite controversy by attacking any man or body of men. The evils which I shall endeavor to expose, are none of them peculiar to any one denomination of Christians, or to any particular period of the church; but they have existed at various periods, and among different sects; and there is always danger that they will exist from the very constitution of human nature. If it should be said that some of the remarks which I shall offer ought to be withheld, on the ground that they admit of application to an existing state of things in the church, I acknowledge that that seems to me a strong reason why they should *not* be withheld; for if the abuses of which I shall speak actually do exist in our own times, we are in the greater danger of falling into them; and in the greater need of being guarded against them;—whereas, if they were only evils of other days, I might, in speaking of them, seem to be beating the air. But I utterly disclaim all responsibility in respect to any particular application. I only say that such abuses have existed—do exist; but my province in respect to them is, not to charge them upon any individuals, or upon any particular portion of the church, but to endeavor to guard *you* against them. The only point for which I hold myself responsible is, that these are really evils, and ought to be avoided.

It may also occur to some, that an exhibition of the evils which are sometimes connected with revivals, may be fitted *to injure the general cause*, by leading many to the conclusion that if ministers themselves acknowledge that there is so much chaff in them, probably the whole is delusion; and worthy to be regarded only with indifference or contempt. That some men may have taken refuge from the convictions of conscience in this miserable delusion, far be it from me to question; never-theless, I am constrained to believe that it is a rare case in which any good cause is ultimately injured, by telling the honest truth respecting it. Besides, you may be assured that the cause of revivals is far more likely to suffer by an attempt on the part of its friends to pass off every thing for gold, than by giving to that which is really dross its proper name. Suppose you should introduce a mere man of the world—if you please a man of high intellectual culture, into a revival in which there should be gross disorder and fanaticism; and you should endeavor without any qualifying remarks, to impress him with the importance of the work that was going forward—it is altogether probable he would say, or at least think, if that were a revival, he had seen enough of it; and if that were religion, the less he had of it, the better. But suppose you should say to him of all that is disorderly—" *that* is the mere operation of human infirmity or passion—the chaff mingling with the wheat;" and of all that is good and praise-worthy—" *that* is the genuine operation of the Holy Spirit;" and he would not improbably, in view of that distinction, acknowledge the reality and im-portance of the work. You cannot, even if you would, make sensible men think, in ordinary cases, that that is religion, or part of a revival of religion, which is not so; and any attempt of this kind is exceedingly liable to awaken their hostility to the whole subject. Irreligious men are generally ready enough to admit the correctness of any distorted accounts of religion, especially if they get them on so good authority as that of Christians themselves; for every such account furnishes them with an argument against the whole subject, and puts their consciences into a still deeper lethargy.

And finally, I can suppose it may appear to some that any attempt to expose the evils incidentally connected with revivals, may be fraught with danger, inasmuch as it is acknowledged, on all hands, that *these evils exist among good men, and withal are connected with much that is praiseworthy;* and it may be thought safest to let the tares and wheat flourish together, lest an attempt to remove the former should expose the latter. As to the fact that the evils to which I refer have been found among truly devoted men, there is no ground for question. Even the well known Mr. Davenport, who was for awhile, an apostle of fanaticism, and who publicly denounced, and prayed for by name, many of the most eminent ministers of New-England as the enemies of revivals, was nevertheless beyond a peradventure a good man; and thought that in all his irregularities he was faithfully serving his Master: but he did not think so always; for he afterwards penitently and publicly acknowledged his error, and even justified the severest censure which his conduct had received. Yes, I repeat, good men do fall into these excesses; and so also good men are sanctified but in part. And as we do not fear that any scriptural endeavors to purify them from remaining corruption will exert a bad influence upon their

Christian graces, so we ought not to apprehend that
any judicious efforts to correct the errors to which
I refer, will serve in any degree to abate their truly
Christian zeal and activity. There are cases, I acknowledge, in which great evils must be tolerated
for a season, because any attempt to remove them
would only make way for greater ones; but nothing
is more certain than that to tolerate evil in good
men because they *are* good men, is directly contrary both to the spirit and letter of the gospel. And
besides the very fact that there is much that is
praiseworthy in their characters, and much that is
benign in their influence, is a reason why we should
do all in our power to remove whatever may, in
any degree, impair their usefulness. We would
treat good men in this respect as in every other :
while we would acknowledge them good, we would
strive to make them better and more useful.

I have now stated to you the grounds of the delicacy which I have felt in bringing this subject before you on the one hand, and the grounds of my
conviction that my duty as a Christian minister
would not permit me to pass it by, on the other.
Some of the evils to which I have referred in general, I proceed now more distinctly to consider.

1. One prominent evil to be guarded against in
a revival, is *the cherishing of false hopes.*

I surely need not undertake to prove that this is
an evil, and one of appalling magnitude; for a false
hope, at the gate of eternity, is a passport to hell;
and such a hope once indulged, is exceedingly apt

to hold its place till the last, though it sometimes lurks in the bosom, almost unobserved, even by the individual who is the subject of it. And where it is given up, it more commonly makes way for a kind of vague scepticism in respect to all experimental religion; and steels the conscience, in a great measure, against future conviction. There are doubtless some who indulge a false hope, that are subsequently awakened, and become true Christians; but in general such a hope is undoubtedly the best security which the adversary could desire for keeping the soul under his entire dominion.

Now I admit that in every case of supposed conversion, there is a liability to a false hope. Let a revival be conducted with as much wisdom as it may, and there is danger that there will be some cases of self-deception. And the reason is obvious. For the first evidence upon which the mind fastens, is a change of feeling. But some of the operations of animal passion appear so much like truly gracious affections, that even advanced Christians often mistake, in their endeavors to distinguish between them. Certainly then, there is far greater danger that those who have had no experience in religion, and who withal are eagerly looking out to catch the first gleam of evidence that they have been renewed—there is far greater danger that they will mistake some accidental and joyous, yet temporary, commotion of the animal feelings, for the exercise of a principle of true piety. I am sure that every person who has been conversant with revivals, must acknowledge that this is in accordance with fact.   Who that has mingled even in the most genuine revival, has not witnessed, in some instances at least, a painful exemplification of the character of the stony ground hearers; in whom, for a while, there was much that looked like religion, but because the principle was wanting, it all gradually withered away.

Now if there is danger of the indulgence of a false hope in every case, there is special danger of it under particular circumstances. The change which takes place in conversion is of a moral nature; it has its seat in the soul, and no where else. There is no natural connection between this change and any bodily postures or movements. If then the idea be held out, that conversion is usually associated with the loss of bodily strength, or with any remarkable bodily motions, or that it is more likely to happen to an individual in one place or one posture than another, where the same truths are proclaimed, and the same prayers offered, there is great danger that this will lead to self-deception;—that, with unreflecting minds at least, that bodily exercise which profiteth little will be put in place of that godliness which has the promise of eternal life. There is danger that the individual will substitute what is considered an external expression of anxiety for his soul, for the internal workings of genuine conviction; or if there be something of true conviction, there is danger that he will mistake the physical act of taking a particu-

lar place or posture which is spoken of as peculiarly favorable to conversion, for the spiritual act of
yielding up the soul to the Saviour.

Again: The instrument by which every conversion is effected is God's truth. If then ministers,
during a revival, fail to hold up the truth in its
distinctive and commanding features, and confine
themselves principally to impassioned addresses, and
earnest, exhortatory appeals, there is great reason
to apprehend many spurious conversions. God
requires, indeed, that the truth should be preached
in an earnest manner; but it must be *the truth* that
is preached; and that only he will honor in the
conversion of men. I appeal to the whole record
of revivals for evidence, that where any thing has
been substituted to any extent in place of this—
where exhortation, instead of holding its proper
place, has taken the place of instruction, *there* has
been the least of sound, deep, abiding religious impression; and *there* have been found the greatest
number of hopeful converts, whose subsequent experience has proved that they had no root in themselves.

Still farther: The change which the soul experiences in regeneration is a change of mighty import—nothing less than a new creation—old things
passing away, and all things becoming new. Any
course of instruction then, which should leave the
impression that it may be accomplished independently of a divine influence; or that a man has nothing to do but to wish himself a Christian in order

to become one; or that it is as easy to change one's heart from the love of sin to the love of holiness, as to change one's purpose in respect to any worldly concern, or to perform any physical act;— any such course of instruction, I say, must necessarily expose to self-deception: because it represents the conversion of the soul to God as comparatively a small matter; and if that impression be gained, how reasonable to expect that the individual should suppose himself converted when he is not so! The way of effecting true conversions, no doubt, is, to represent the work to be done in all its magnitude; and then to bring out the very mind of the Spirit in respect to the manner of doing it, and the means by which it is to be accomplished.

I think you will agree with me, my friends, that in any of the circumstances which I have here supposed, there is special danger that sinners will *take up* with false hopes. There is yet another course of treatment which is extremely well adapted to *cherish* and *confirm* such hopes. Let the sinner who has actually deceived himself, hear his supposed conversion spoken of with as much confidence as if it were known to be a genuine one; let him hear himself constantly numbered among the converts, and by those in whose judgment and experience he confides; let there be little or nothing said that implies the possibility of his being deceived, and let every thing that is done in respect to him, seem to take for granted that he stands on safe ground; and above all let him immediately be introduced into the church; and if he ever wakes out of that delusion, believe me, it will be little less than a miracle. This last step particularly is fitted, more than any other, to entrench him in a habit of self-security, which he will probably carry with him to his death-bed.

2. Another of the evils to be guarded against in a revival is a spirit of *self-confidence*.

Even advanced Christians are liable to this; and sometimes exhibit it in a degree that is truly humiliating. While they are witnessing the powerful operation of God's Spirit in the conviction and conversion of sinners, and are actively engaged in helping on the work, they lose sight in some degree, of the fact that they are but unworthy instruments; and though there may be an acknowledgment of divine agency occasionally upon their lips, yet in their hearts they are really taking to themselves the glory. I need not speak of the manner in which this spirit discovers itself in the part which they bear in a revival, for no one who witnesses its operation can easily mistake it; but I may say with confidence that wherever it exists, it mars the beauty, and detracts from the purity, and hinders the efficacy of the work.

But I refer here more particularly to a self-confident spirit, as it is often exhibited by young converts; and let me say that the very same course of treatment to which I have just adverted as being fitted to cherish and confirm a false hope, is adapted to awaken even in those who have been truly converted a spirit of self-confidence. This is a great evil, as it respects their own growth in grace. Wherever it exists there will be little of self-examination; little sense of the need of being constantly taught and guided by the Holy Spirit; little of that humility which becomes a sinner redeemed by the blood of Christ, and saved by sovereign grace; and I may add, little of that gratitude which looks in acts of faith and praise toward the Lamb that was slain. That there may be much of zeal connected with self-confidence in a young Christian, cannot be questioned; though it may reasonably be doubted whether even that is altogether of heavenly origin: but whether it be so or not, it usually happens, where it is found in connection with this spirit, that the flame burns with diminished brightness until it has nearly died away.

Nor is this spirit less prejudicial to the young Christian, as connected with his usefulness. In a young convert especially, nothing is so lovely as humility. Let him show by his deportment rather than by his professions, that he often turns his eye upon the hole of the pit from which he hopes he has been taken; that if he has obtained mercy he feels that he deserves nothing but wrath; and that for aught he knows he may be indulging the hope of the hypocrite—certainly that he has much to do to make his calling and election sure;—I say, let him manifest such a spirit in his conduct, and it will give him favor with all with whom he associates; and it will secure him access to many hearts which might otherwise be barred against his influence. But let him, on the other hand, speak of his conversion as if he were sure it was genuine; let him refer with confidence to the very moment when it occurred; let him talk of it as an event that has been brought about by mere human agency; and let him say to others by his deportment, " Stand by, I am holier than thou ;"—and you may rest assured, especially if he be a young person, that he can have little hope of accomplishing much for the cause of Christ. There will be something in his very manner to repel those whom he should desire to win; and though he may console himself in view of his unsuccessful efforts, by thinking and speaking of the obstinacy of sinners, yet it were more reasonable that he should humble himself that, if he be a Christian, his conduct, in this very particular, indicates so much of remaining infirmity and corruption.

3. Another lamentable evil incident to revivals, is a spirit of *censoriousness.*

No doubt there is much in the conduct of many Christians and ministers, at such a time, to give just occasion for regret; and if they appear cold and worldly, it is only a Christian duty that we should affectionately admonish them of their error, and endeavor to render them more spiritual and active. But this is something quite different from that censorious, denouncing spirit, to which I here refer; which, though it be exercised in reference to religion, is nothing better than the spirit of the world.

And it is easy to see how it gets into operation even in good men. Their minds are awake to the great subject of the soul's salvation; and they are oppressed by its amazing weight. They feel that something efficient ought to be done—*must* be done to wake up a slumbering world; and they desire that all Christians should go along with them in their efforts. In this state of mind they are prepared for nothing but cordial co-operation; and where they do not find it, corrupt nature takes advantage of the excitement they have reached, and the disappointment they feel, and perhaps withal of a naturally ardent temperament, to discharge itself not only in grievous complaints, but sometimes even bitter invective. This is the most favorable account of the exercise of this spirit. There are other cases, no doubt, in which it is identified with a spirit of self-righteousness; in which the secret and prevailing feeling of the heart is, that heaping censure upon others is an easy way of laying up treasure in heaven; that to complain of the coldness and worldliness of our fellow Christians, is an evidence of zeal and devotion in ourselves. But let this spirit have its origin in whatever state of mind it may, we shall all agree that it is a serious evil; and ought to be guarded against with the utmost care.

It is not uncommon to find this spirit marking the conduct of private Christians towards each other. There are some who will condemn their brethren as cold Christians, or perhaps even no Christians at all, because, with less of constitutional ardor than themselves, and possibly more prudence, they are not prepared to concur at once in every measure that may be suggested for the advancement of a revival; or because they talk less of their own feelings than some others; or because they attend fewer public religious exercises than could be desired; or because from extreme constitutional diffidence they may, either properly or improperly, decline taking part in such exercises. Many a Christian who has been laboring faithfully and judiciously for the salvation of sinners, whose closet has witnessed to the fervor of his devotion, and whose conversation has been according to the gospel of Christ, has not only been suspected by his brethren of coldness, for some one or other of the reasons just mentioned, but has been marked, and denounced, and even prayed for, as dead to the interests of revivals, if not dead in trespasses and sins.

On the other hand, it is not to be questioned that men of a cautious habit, who are constitutionally afraid of excitement, sometimes unjustly accuse their more zealous brethren of rashness, and impute to spiritual pride what really ought to be set to the account of an honest devotedness to Christ. Especially, if real and great abuses actually exist, they may be so much afraid of coming within the confines of disorder, that they may rush to the opposite extreme of formality; and from that cold region they may look off upon the Christian who evinces nothing more than a consistent and enlightened zeal,

and hail him as if he were burning to death in the
very torrid zonȩ of enthusiasm.

The same spirit which discovers itself in private
Christians toward each other, is also frequently
manifest in respect to different churches.   A church
which is abundantly blessed with revivals, may condemn with a high hand another church, in which,
though religion may not be in a languishing state,
yet there may never have been any general and
sudden effusion of the Holy Spirit.   And this may
be attributed most unjustly to a cold ministry, or to
some signal want of faithfulness in the members;
when the fact that the church is really in a flourishing state, (its interests being sustained by gradual, rather than by sudden accessions,) is entirely
overlooked.   And where there is not only the absence of revivals, but the spiritual interests of a
church are really depressed, it is still more common to hear the case spoken of with an air of unchristian severity; and not unfrequently there is
something like a sentence of reprobation passed
upon the whole body, as if they were indiscriminately a company of backsliders.   Or where a
church differs from another in its views of the economy of revivals, it may denounce that other as
chilled with the frost of apathy on the one hand,
or scorched with the fires of fanaticism on the
other; when, as the case may be, the church that
is the object of censure may hold correct and scriptural ground.   Any church, whether it be distinguished by its zeal or its want of zeal, that takes

the responsibility of dealing out violent censures upon its sister churches, especially if they are walking in the faith and order of the gospel, certainly assumes a degree of responsibility which it can ill afford to bear; and it will have no just ground for surprise, if it should meet a painful retribution, not only in bringing back upon itself the censures of men, but in bringing down upon itself the displeasure of God.

And I am constrained to go farther, and say that ministers have sometimes erred in the same manner; judging each other as fanatics or as drones; some supposing that their brethren were setting the world on fire, when they shed around them no worse light than that of sober consistent zeal; and others that their brethren were in the very valley of death as it respects religious feeling, when the principle of spiritual life was beating in strong and vigorous pulsations. I will say nothing of what exists on this subject in our own day; but I refer you to what has been in other days. I point you for examples to men who have long since been in their graves, and whose joy in the world of glory will not be interrupted by our learning wisdom from the imperfections of which they are now entirely free, and which they lived bitterly to lament. In the revivals which are recorded in the early part of the history of New-England, there were a considerable number of ministers, and among them the individual to whom I have already referred as distinguished for his extravagance, who declared the

mass of their brethren to be unconverted men; who
denounced them as leading souls to hell; and who
endeavored, by every means in their power, to
alienate from them their congregations, that they
might bring them under the influence of what they
regarded a more faithful ministry. This unhappy
faction, from the nature of the case, was not of
long continuance; it could not be, because it lived
upon the highest excitement;—but it lasted long
enough to counteract, to a melancholy extent, the
benign effects of that work of grace; long enough
to entail upon at least two generations, its destructive consequences. If you read the history of
those days, or rather of those men, there will be
every thing to make you weep, until you come to
the delightful fact that they saw their error, and acknowledged it, and wept over it themselves.

I know of no way in which a censorious spirit
can discover itself, whether in ministers or private
Christians, that is so revolting, and I may say,
dreadful, as in prayer. The fact must be acknowledged, humbling as it is, that men have sometimes seemed to be pouring out at the foot of the
throne their resentments against cold Christians and
ministers; and have even assumed the office of
judging their hearts; and have told the Almighty
Being, apparently for the sake of telling the congregation, that they were as dead as the tenants of
the tomb. Brethren, no apology can be offered for
this—not even the semblance of an apology. Christian charity herself can record nothing better con-

cerning such a prayer, than that it breathes the spirit of the world in one of its most odious forms. Whatever degree of religious indifference may have called it forth, it certainly cannot furnish a juster cause for humiliation than does the prayer itself.

4. *Inconstancy in religion* is another evil to be avoided in connection with revivals.

Men are exceedingly prone to vibrate from one extreme to the other; and it is a law of human nature that a very powerful excitement, in respect to the same individuals, cannot long be sustained. Hence there is danger that Christians, from the excitement to which they are liable during a revival, will gradually fall into a state of spiritual languor, and will even give occasion for the cutting inquiry, " What do ye more than others ?"

Now what might be expected, from the very tendencies of human nature to happen, we find, actually does happen ; both in respect to individuals and churches. Who has not seen the Christian, during a revival, seeming to be constantly on the mount both of enjoyment and of action ; willing apparently to wear himself out in the service of his Master, and for the salvation of souls ; and in a few months after, comparatively silent, and inactive, and insensible on the great subject which had so lately occupied him almost to the exclusion of every other ? And who that has been much conversant with revivals, has not seen a church, during one of these seasons of special blessing, waking up to a lively sense of obligation, sending up united, and holy, and strong supplications, and laboring incessantly with an eye now on the cross, and now on the judgment seat, and now on the crown of life; and the same church, at a subsequent period, apparently forgetting their responsibility, becoming cold in their devotions, and relaxing in all their efforts for the salvation of men? In the one case, you would have supposed from their fidelity, that they were marching on to a high seat in glory: in the other, you would, especially if you had turned your eye off from the Bible, have almost been ready to doubt the perseverance of the saints.

Now wherever this state of things exists, it is a serious evil, both as it respects the church and the world. It is so to the church, because it mars the consistency and beauty of her character; lessens the amount of her communion with her Head; and renders her light comparatively dim and feeble, when she is commanded to let it shine with a steady brightness. It is an evil to the world, inasmuch as it casts an air of suspicion, in the view of many, over the reality and importance of revivals; and leads them to imagine that Christians work hard one day to purchase the privilege of doing nothing the next; and that a revival is a matter to be got up and laid aside, at the pleasure of those who engage in it. It leads them, moreover, to think less than they otherwise would of the good influence of Christians when they attempt to exert it; and when, in more favored seasons, they show themselves active and endeavor to rouse up the sinner's slumbering conscience, not improbably their exertions will be unavailing from his recollection of their indifference at other times, and his impression that their zeal is a mere creature of circumstances.

You will all agree with me that this is a great evil, and ought to be guarded against with the utmost caution. One means of avoiding it is, by endeavoring to keep down animal passion, especially at the height of the revival, when it is most likely to be awakened; for the stronger the excitement of the animal nature, the greater the tendency to a universal re-action. Another means is, by endeavoring to keep up spiritual feeling when the general excitement attending a revival begins to pass away; for that is the critical time when religious languor usually first creeps over the soul. By using the proper caution at these two points, the church may effectually avoid the evil which I am considering; and instead of becoming listless at the close of a revival, she may show that she has renewed her strength for subsequent labors and conflicts.

5. Another evil to be guarded against in connection with revivals, is *ostentation*.

I refer not here to the manner in which revivals are sometimes conducted, (having adverted to that already,) but to the manner in which they are represented, both in common intercourse, and through the press: and I cannot doubt, that, in respect to both, there is much that no discreet Christian can contemplate without regret and disapprobation.

It is not uncommon, during the progress of a revival, and sometimes in an early stage of it, to hear its glorious results spoken of with as much confidence as if they had actually been realized. Particular religious exercises which may have been attended with unusual solemnity, are represented as having secured the conversion not only of a great, but a definite number of souls. One is represented as having preached, another as having prayed, another as having talked, so many sinners into the kingdom. Perhaps the infidel has professed suddenly to renounce his infidelity, and embrace the Saviour; or perhaps the profligate has wept in view of his profligacy and resolved to enter upon a new life;—these cases are confidently spoken of as instances of genuine conversion; and what is still worse, they are too often spoken of as such in the presence of the very persons who are the subjects of them. It is easy to see that, if the individuals are true converts, the effect of this must probably be to inflate them with spiritual pride; if they are not true converts, it must fearfully aid the work of self-deception. It leaves a bad impression also upon the world; for it is the exact opposite of that humility, that sense of dependance, that disposition to acknowledge God in every spiritual blessing, which constitute some of the loveliest features of Christian character.

But what I chiefly refer to under this article, is the ostentatious complexion, and the premature date, of many of those narratives of revivals, which

are given to the world through our religious periodicals. It is only honest to acknowledge that many of them, though evidently dictated by a desire to
do good, are yet eminently fitted to do evil. They
are written in the midst of strong excitement, when
the mind is most in danger of mistaking shadows
for substances; when its strong hopes that much is
about to be done, are easily exchanged for a conviction that much has been actually accomplished.
Hence all who are supposed to appear more serious than usual, are reckoned as subjects of conviction; and all who profess the slightest change of
feeling are set down as converts. And particular
instances are detailed, in which very obstinate sinners have been made very humble, and then have
become entranced with bright visions of the Saviour; and other cases are mentioned, in which a
child has pressed forward into the kingdom, in
spite of the opposition of a wicked parent; or a
wife, notwithstanding she was persecuted by an ungodly husband. Now the narrative containing these
particulars goes abroad into the world; and almost
of course comes back immediately into the congregation whose religious state it professes to describe.
And what think you will probably be the effect?—
What will it be upon those who here find it announced to the world that they have been converted; and perhaps read a high wrought and glowing story of their conversion? What especially
must it be on those who are represented as having
been the subjects of a miracle of grace; as having

been great sinners, and now having become great saints? If they are really converted, the effect of this must be, as in the case just mentioned, to lessen their humility, and open their hearts to temptation. If they are cherishing a false hope, it cannot fail to add to its strength. And if, before the narrative meets them, as is a very supposable case, they have cast off their serious impressions and returned to the world, it must provoke and irritate them; and thus fearfully increase their obduracy, and render their salvation still more improbable.— And what effect will this be likely to have upon those who are designated, (if not by name, yet so as to be identified,) as having been distinguished for their malignant opposition to the work? It will awaken in them the spirit of fiends. It will embolden them to fight still more furiously against God and against his people; and not improbably to do that which will seal their perdition. And what must its effect be upon the surrounding world? What, when they compare the written statement with what has fallen under their own observation, and find a sad disagreement? Must it not be to create and cherish a prejudice against all revivals? Must it not throw an air of suspicion over every statement respecting them which they either hear or read? Must it not even bring in question the veracity of good men?

You will by no means understand me as intimating any disapprobation of publishing at a proper time even detailed accounts of revivals. So far from this, that I regard it as due to the church, due to the honor of him whom we acknowledge as the great Agent in revivals, that such accounts should in due time be sent forth. But let them not, in ordinary cases, be written, until the true results of the revival are in some measure known; certainly, let them be confined to palpable facts which no one can gainsay. Let them be framed with a deliberate recollection that they are to be scanned by multitudes; that they are to exert an influence either for or against the cause of revivals; and that God is not honored, but offended, by the least attempt to go beyond the truth, even in recording the triumphs of his grace. It is a matter of importance that all narratives of this kind should be furnished by competent and responsible persons—those who have opportunity to know the facts, and ability properly to estimate them. While it cannot be questioned that there are many instances at the present day, in which the evil of which I am speaking is strikingly exemplified, it is an occasion for joy that there are many other cases, in which revivals are detailed seasonably, judiciously, and in a manner fitted in all respects to subserve the cause of truth and piety.

6. *Undervaluing divine institutions, and divine truth,* is another evil, which often exists in connection with revivals.

It is common, and no doubt right too, during a season of special attention to religion, to increase the number of occasional services during the week; and especially the number of meetings for social

prayer. And it is desirable that Christians should
feel a deep interest in these exercises; and should
regard it as not less a duty than a privilege to engage in them, as their circumstances may admit.
But they are not to be considered in the strict sense
as divine institutions; for though there is a fair
warrant for them in the general spirit of the gospel,
and, as we believe, even a direct sanction in apostolic usage, yet the regulation of them is a matter
which God has been pleased to leave to the wisdom
of the church; and whenever Christians exalt them
to an equality with those institutions which are
strictly divine, they may expect to incur the displeasure of the Master, as well as lose the benefit which
these exercises are adapted, when kept in their proper place, to impart. But there is reason to apprehend that many Christians, during a season of revival, actually do in their feelings, attach an importance to these services which is even paramount to
that which they recognise as belonging to the public exercises of the Lord's day. The secret feeling
of the heart, there is reason to believe, often is,
that to attend public worship on the Sabbath, though
it is a duty, has yet too little in it that is distinctive
and out of the common course, to be regarded with
very deep interest; whereas those services which
are observed during the week, and which seem more
like a free will offering, rise in their estimation to
the highest degree of importance. There is in all
this no doubt more or less of self-righteousness;—a
sort of unacknowledged and perhaps undetected

feeling, that the eye of God rests upon them even with more favor, when they are rendering him a service which he has left in some measure to their own discretion, than when they are walking in the plain and broad path of his direct commandments. These occasional services, I repeat, are not to be undervalued ; for they are important helps, in every point of view, towards sustaining and carrying forward a revival ; but that we may reap the benefit they are designed to secure, we must give them no higher place than the great Head of the church has manifestly assigned to them.

And while there is danger that the social exercises which the church may establish during a revival, may lead to too low a comparative estimate of the stated services of the sabbath, there is perhaps equal danger that they may bring into some degree of disregard the duties of the closet. Especially if these occasional exercises are greatly multiplied, the time which is requisite for attending them beside other duties of a more secular nature, may leave but little opportunity for self-communion, reading the scriptures, and private prayer; and there is reason to fear that, sometimes at least, the Christian makes a compromise with his conscience for at least a partial neglect of these latter duties, by calling to mind his exemplary diligence and constancy in respect to the former. And besides, there is no doubt that it lays his powers under far less contribution, to be engaged in a constant round of social exercises which are fitted to excite the mind, than to enter into his closet, and commune with himself, and apply the truths and precepts of the gospel for the regulation of his affections and conduct. It is to this practical error, I doubt not, that we are to attribute in a great degree, the fact, that many Christians, who engage with much interest in a revival, still seem to turn it to so little account as it respects their own personal piety. Nothing is more certain than that the neglect of closet duties, whatever other duties may be performed, must wither the believer's graces, and render his Christian character sickly and inefficient.

If you would avoid the evil which is here contemplated, and secure the good which is aimed at by those who incur the evil, let God's institutions be kept in their proper place. Regard the public services of the sabbath as far the most important which you can attend. Think it however a blessed privilege that you may meet for religious purposes frequently at other times; but never let such meetings be a substitute for secret devotion. And if the effect of them should ever be to keep you away from your closet, or to give you a disrelish for its duties, you need no other evidence that there is something wrong;—either that your attendance on these social services is too frequent, or not with the right spirit.

Nor is there less danger that a revival may be perverted to the undervaluing of God's *truth*. At such a time especially men love to be excited; and while those who hear the preaching of the word are apt to delight in those stirring and earnest appeals which are most fitted to rouse the feelings, there is a strong temptation on the part of ministers to feed this passion for excitement by limiting themselves to a few topics of exhortation, rather than by holding up gospel truth in all its extent and fulness. And in this way it often comes to pass, that there is an aversion contracted to instructive preaching; the doctrines of the Bible come to be regarded, both by people and ministers, as comparatively tame; and I hardly need say that, as a consequence, the ministry loses much of its real efficiency, and the piety of the church languishes for want of its appropriate nourishment.

Nor is this all. It cannot be questioned that revivals are sometimes made the occasion not only of inspiring a disgust for sober scriptural doctrine, but of introducing into the church a flood of error. Ministers in seasons of great excitement, and in the desire of saying something that shall seize hold of the feelings, sometimes make unguarded expressions which involve some important error; and if these expressions *seem* to be followed by good effects, they are in danger of repeating them until they come really to adopt the error which is thus involved. And then again, the excited multitude in such circumstances are usually carried away by the appearance of great zeal and earnestness; and he who evinces the most of these qualities is almost sure to be the favorite preacher; and if he be disposed to commingle error with truth, there is every

probability that, in many instances at least, the one
will be received with the other without inquiry or
suspicion. Such has been the history of the introduction and progress of some of the wildest reveries and grossest errors which have disturbed the
peace and marred the purity of the church. Let
ministers and private Christians, those who preach
and those who hear, be alike on their guard against
this tremendous evil.

7. There are certain things which sometimes occur during a revival, that are *fitted to impair the dignity and lessen the influence of the ministerial office;*—
an evil which should always be guarded against
with great caution.

It must be acknowledged that ministers themselves
not unfrequently contribute to this unhappy result.
Sometimes they are carried away by strong excitement into the region of extravagance and even gross
fanaticism; and say and do things under this influence, which in their cooler moments will take them
to their closets for confession and humiliation. In
other cases, they come perhaps honestly to the conclusion that some new expedient is necessary to
secure attention; and the result is, that they come
out with something which not only offends a correct taste, but shocks all the finer sensibilities, or
as the case may be, convulses the audience with
laughter. Let a minister be as plain, as earnest, as
faithful as he will;—but the moment he violates the
decorum due to the place in which he stands, or the
work in which he is engaged; the moment he in-

troduces or even tolerates any thing like confusion in the worship of God; then, rely on it, he sins against the dignity of his office. He does that which is fitted not merely to lessen his own influence with all men of discreet and sober minds, but in the view of multitudes, he brings the ministerial office itself into contempt. There are enough who would be glad to take such a mistaken course as a sample of the deportment of ministers in general; and a single instance of this kind furnishes them with a text book for censure and ridicule which they are sure to use to the best advantage.

The same evil also frequently results from a virtual assumption of the sacred office, by men who have neither the proper warrant nor the requisite qualifications. Not that I would intimate that judicious and intelligent laymen have nothing to do in public, beyond merely conducting the devotions of the congregation: I would have them, in many instances at least, ready to impart the word of exhortation; and in private their labors may turn to great account in the way of counselling persons in different states of mind: but I would have it always borne in mind, that the ministry is an institution of God's appointment, and that the man who performs the appropriate duties of this office, without being regularly called to it, is chargeable with running before he is sent. And just in proportion as this is actually done—just in proportion as men set at naught the scriptural rules pertaining to order on this subject, you may expect to see the influence of the ministry paralyzed. Let this be generally done, and who will yield to it the reverence which it claims as an institution of God?

8. There is danger, during a revival, of *setting up false standards of Christian character.*

Men are perpetually prone to mistake the circumstantials of religion for the substance of it. If this is owing partly to human infirmity, it is owing still more to human corruption;—to an aversion from that self-denial which is involved in the practice of the genuine Christian virtues. This tendency frequently discovers itself even in good men; and perhaps never more frequently than during a season of revival.

There is special danger that, at such a time, the means of religion will be substituted for religion itself. As means are of no importance in any other department of action, except as they are related to the end and may tend to secure it, so they are of no use in any other point of view in the department of religion. Means are of use as it respects the sinner, when they bring him to repentance; and as it respects the Christian, when they build him up in faith and holiness; and any use of them which does not lead to these results, will aggravate the condemnation of the one, and retard the sanctification of the other. But there is great reason to fear that, in seasons of revival, many Christians, in examining themselves, and estimating their growth in grace, do not go much farther than to inquire how many meetings they have attended, or how many they have failed to attend. Instead of asking themselves whether the means they are using are accomplishing their end; whether their love, and faith, and humility, and all other Christian graces, are quickened, or deepened, or brightened, by what they are doing, they satisfy themselves with the bare use of the means; and mistake a secret self-complacency for the testimony of a good conscience.

It is not uncommon to place the evidence of Christian character, especially during a revival, in talking abundantly and fervently on the subject of religion. True it is that out of the abundance of the heart the mouth speaketh; and it is impossible that religion should be in lively exercise in the soul, without giving a character to the conversation. But, at the same time, the mere fact that an individual makes the subject of religion a constant topic in certain circumstances, and even dwells upon it with great fervor, is the most equivocal evidence of true piety that can be imagined. Who has not heard the man actually under the influence of the intoxicating cup, talk of his experiences and of his joys, as if he thought himself on the threshold of heaven? And who has not been sometimes shocked in hearing glowing statements in respect to revivals of religion, and deep lamentations over the coldness of Christians, and strong expressions of devotedness to Christ—who has not been shocked, I say, to find himself listening to a man, whose character he knew to be openly stained with pollution, or marked by fraud or falsehood? I say then that while an entire silence on the subject of religion reasonably subjects one's Christian character to great suspicion, a disposition to converse much upon it does not of itself constitute any evidence of piety, or of growth in piety, that can be relied on. This is a matter which often depends more on constitutional temperament than any thing else. Of two Christians who have the same degree of grace, and have it in the same degree of exercise, one will speak out his feelings far more readily than the other, owing solely to a difference of original constitution. And what is a more striking case still, one being of a self-confident turn, may talk like an angel about his hopes and his joys, and another, being constitutionally distrustful, may speak hesitatingly, and rarely at all, of his religious experience ; and yet the former may be a miserable hypocrite, the latter a devoted Christian. But is it not true that in revivals especially, we are too prone to estimate the piety, both of ourselves and others, by this most uncertain standard ? Is there not often at least a lurking feeling that when we have talked most on the subject of religion, we have had the most evidence, and have given the most evidence, of being under its power?

I cannot avoid here adverting, in one word, to the use of a sort of technical phraseology relating to Christian experience and revivals of religion, which in some instances, is not only an outrage upon taste, but is destitute of meaning. It may be said that it matters little what language we use on this subject, provided it be understood : but this is not true; for if two expressions convey the same idea, and one is fitted to awaken prejudice or disgust in a large class of people, and the other is entirely unexceptionable with all, then it is not a matter of indifference which of them should be used. Now it is not to be questioned that the cant phraseology which has gained such extensive prevalence in the church, in connection with revivals, is exceedingly revolting to men of taste; and there is reason to fear, in many instances, awakens a permanent prejudice against the whole subject. And there is nothing gained to the lower classes by the adoption of this phraseology; for no language can be more intelligible than that of the Bible and common sense. But if I do not greatly mistake, the use of this phraseology which I am condemning, is in in many instances identified with a high tone of spiritual feeling. It is evidently regarded by many as indicating a deeper spirit of devotion, a more earnest desire for the salvation of souls, in short more of the spirit of a revival, than would be indicated by the use of the simple and pertinent language supplied by God's word. But never was there a greater mistake. The best that can be said of it is, that it is a departure from the dignity that belongs to the whole subject of religion.

You will perceive at once that the effect resulting from these arbitrary standards of Christian character, must be unfavorable to the cause of truth and holiness. It is unfavorable upon Christians; for while it greatly interferes with their own reli-

gious improvement, it usually awakens among them
a spirit of censoriousness towards each other.   Its
tendency in respect to sinners is to put them on a
course of self-righteous effort, and thus to expose
them fearfully to self deception.   Let this evil then
ever be cautiously avoided.   Let Christians remember that, in a season of revival as well as in a season of coldness, the evidence of piety is to be sought
in the fruits of the Spirit.   And let sinners remember that no degree of attendance on means, no degree of animal fervor, can be substituted for repentance of sin and faith in the Saviour; that the existence of the former does not constitute the least evidence of the existence of the latter.

9. The last of the evils against which I would
put you on your guard in connection with revivals,
is *corrupting the purity of the church.*

We have indeed no right to expect that the church,
during its militant state, will ever be entirely free
from corruption ; though this does not at all lessen
our obligations to do all we can to render it so.
The efficiency of a church depends greatly on its
purity.   Even if it consist of only a little band, and
yet be eminent for its consistency and spirituality,
it will exert an extensive and salutary influence.
But let its numbers be increased to any extent, if
it embrace a great amount of spurious religion, it
will diffuse around it but a feeble and uncertain
light.   Every such accession is an accession of
fresh weakness.   Men who are destitute of religion
had far better be out of the church than in it; for

whether they come in as cold formalists or heated
fanatics, they will bring with them the spirit of the
world in some form or other; and whatever their
worldly rank may be, their influence will injure
rather than assist the cause of piety. Let the
church receive to her communion a large number
who have deceived themselves with false hopes,
knowing nothing of the power of religion; and it
will be strange if she does not soon find that her
most formidable foes are those of her own household. She may calculate that the time is not distant when she will find her own members corrupting the purity of the faith;—when she will see them
bound up in the frost of a heartless formality, and
even resisting so far as they dare, her own efforts
to promote the cause of Christ; when, in a word,
she will be compelled frequently to exercise her
discipline, or grievously to neglect her duty.

Now there is one course which is often adopted
in connection with a revival which is sure to bring
in its train this great evil—I refer to the practice of
admitting persons to the communion with little or no
probation. Experience has long since taught us
that there are many at such a time whose feelings
are excited and apparently changed, and who give
promise of being devoted to Christ, who nevertheless within even a short time, relapse into their former indifference, and neither consider themselves,
nor are considered by others, as furnishing the least
evidence of Christian character. These persons
not being received into the church, are ready enough

to acknowledge that they have lost their interest in religion; but let them be thus received, and though you will hear from them no such acknowledgment, the real fact in respect to their condition will be the same. Hence we are forbidden to doubt that where the custom prevails of admitting persons to the communion almost immediately after they are supposed to be converted, many must be received who are no better than were the stony ground hearers. I know it is said in favor of this practice that it originated with the Apostles; and that Peter received to the church the three thousand who were converted on the day of Pentecost, without waiting to test their characters. But I know too that that case cannot be pleaded as a precedent for a similar course now, because the circumstances by which it was marked, do not exist at the present day. To make a profession of Christianity then, was to expose one's self, not merely to reproach and obloquy, but to the rack and the stake; and it were impossible to conceive of any higher evidence of sincerity than such a sacrifice would involve. But now the fact of confessing Christ before the world injures no man's character in the view of any one; and it is a rare case that it exposes to any personal inconvenience; so that, of itself, it can scarcely be said to furnish the least evidence of Christian character. Let the church, then, as she values her own purity and efficiency, beware of prematurely receiving those whom she considers the fruits of revivals to her communion. Not that she will be able, at any period, to make an exact separation between the chaff and the wheat: but it is a duty that she owes not only to herself but to her exalted Head, to make that separation as accurately as she can.

Such are some of the evils with which revivals of religion may be—have been connected. I have dwelt upon this subject at considerable length, not because it is a subject the most grateful to Christian contemplation, but because, to my own mind at least, it possesses an importance of which we can scarcely form too high an estimate. It were far more pleasant to speak of the blessings of revivals, and of the triumph of the cause of revivals, than of the evils which, through the weakness or corruption of human nature, may be associated with them. But I cannot resist the impression that, in order to realize the highest amount of blessing which they are fitted to secure, we must testify against their abuse, and endeavor to keep them in their purity. I invite you then, my Brethren, one and all, to labor according to your ability, not merely in the promotion of revivals, but in preventing the evils with which they are so often connected; for in doing so, you not only contribute greatly to the ultimate good influence of every such work of grace, but you disarm men of their prejudices against the cause of revivals, and thus remove at least one obstacle in the way of their salvation. If we knew all who had rushed into infidelity in consequence of what they have seen and heard in connection with revivals, I fear we should be overwhelmed by the discovery; and as we would save souls from death rather than multiply the temptations to self-destruction, we are bound to watch, and pray, and labor, that whatever assumes the sacred name of a revival, may be worthy of the character which it professes to bear.

Do you ask what you have to do in relation to this subject? I answer, when God pours down his Spirit in the midst of you, you have much to do in preventing some or other of these various evils; and this you are to effect by a constant and watchful observation of the state of things around you, and by subjecting every thing that is proposed to be done to the simple test of God's word. You may also exert a general influence beyond your own immediate sphere; by having your views of this subject clear and settled, and expressing them temperately, yet firmly, as occasion may require. But be careful never to mingle in the expression of your views, the least unkind or unchristian feeling. Though you may consider your brethren in some respects wrong, and may frankly tell them so, yet you are to do it in the spirit of Christian charity, and cheerfully give them credit for their full amount of usefulness. It were greatly to be lamented if any of us, in our endeavors to correct the errors of others, should fall into a still greater one; should forfeit our claim to that charity which hopeth and beareth all things.

Brethren, I anticipate for the cause of revivals a glorious triumph; and one ground of this expectation is, that the friends of revivals will labor diligently for the promotion of their purity. I cast my eye toward the millenial age, and I witness these scenes of divine love and mercy going forward with such beauty and power, that the eyes of angels are turned towards them with constantly increasing delight. I see the pure gold shining forth in its brightness, and the dross thrown aside and estimated at nothing. I see the chaff burnt up in the fire, or flying off on the winds, while the wheat is pure, and ripe, and ready for the garner. I see Christians every where co-operating with God for the salvation of men, in the very ways he has himself marked out; and while he pours out his rich blessings on the church, the church sends back her thanksgivings and praises to Him in the Highest. May God in mercy hasten this blessed consummation! And may you and I, whom he permits to labor in his cause, count it an honor that we are privileged to direct our efforts towards this high end, and to anticipate with confidence a glorious result!

LECTURE IX.

RESULTS OF REVIVALS.

————

REVELATION v. 13.

Blessing, and honor, and glory, and power, be unto him that sitteth upon the throne, and unto the Lamb, forever and ever.

This is the new song that was heard by John in vision, as a response from the whole creation, to the sublime anthem which had just before trembled on the harps and lips of the general assembly and church of the first born. The heavenly host, including the angels and the redeemed, shout forth their praises in this noble song:—"Worthy is the Lamb that was slain, to receive power, and riches, and wisdom, and strength, and honor, and glory, and blessing." All nature instantly becomes vocal, and sends back her amen to this loud, and thrilling, and extatic acclamation. "And every creature which is in heaven, and on the earth, and under the earth, and such as are in the sea, and all that are in them, heard I saying, Blessing, and honor, and glory, and power, be unto him that sitteth upon the throne, and unto the Lamb forever and ever."

In the series of discourses of which the present is to form the conclusion, I have endeavored to present before you what seems to me the scriptural view of most of the leading topics connected with revivals of religion. I have attempted to show the nature of a genuine revival, and the characteristics by which it is distinguished; to defend revivals against the cavils of those who oppose them; to note the circumstances which are unfavorable to their progress; to consider the agency of God on the one hand, and the instrumentality of the church on the other, in carrying them forward; to exhibit an outline of the treatment that is due both to the awakened sinner and the hopeful convert; and last of all, to guard you against the evils to which revivals, through the weakness and corruption of human nature, are liable to be perverted. It only remains to direct your attention, in the present discourse, to the RESULTS of revivals; partly in their gradual and partial developement, and partly as they will be seen, when the cause shall have gained its complete triumph. And in taking up this subject in this connection, we pass from a theme the least grateful to one that is most grateful to the Christian's heart: we turn our back upon a region of misgivings, and difficulties, and discouragements, and enter a field of hope, and light, and glory.

But you will ask, perhaps, in what manner the glorious hymn of praise which I have selected as a text, can be considered as pointing to the results of revivals of religion? I answer, it is a hymn in

which the church on earth may very properly unite
in celebrating the triumphs of God's grace as they
have been manifested in the blessed effects of
revivals already. It is the tendency of revivals
to prepare multitudes for taking up this noble song
even here, and continuing to repeat it with increasing melody and rapture for ever. And moreover it is the song in which the ransomed in glory
are to celebrate through eternity the praises of redemption; and of course the triumph of the cause
of revivals, in which the purposes of God's redeeming mercy will have gone so wonderfully into effect.
Whether, therefore, we consider this as a song of
triumph from the church on earth, or as the everlasting song of the redeemed in heaven, it will, in
either case, justify the train of thought into which
I purpose to lead you in respect to the results of
revivals. These results I will endeavor to present
before you as they are developed,

I. *In the present world:*
II. *In the world of glory.*
I. *In the present world.*

The grand result to which revivals are here tending is *the complete moral renovation of the world.* This
result is to be accomplished,

1. *By their direct influence, in elevating the intellectual, spiritual, and social condition of men.*

There is a sluggish tendency in the human mind
which it often requires a severe shock effectually
to counteract. Most men choose almost any other
labor rather than the labor of thought; and hence

no doubt many an individual in whom there is the
germe of a noble mind, never actually rises above
a very moderate intellectual stature.   Now it is the
tendency of a revival of religion to bring the faculties into vigorous exercise.   Let the Spirit of God
be poured out upon a community, and you will find
that the public mind there is in a wakeful state;
that men seem to have lost their aversion to thinking, and have shaken off their accustomed sluggish-
ness, and are earnest in making inquiries, and cannot rest till those inquiries are answered.   There is
an intellectual excitement at such a time pervading
the whole community; for while convinced sinners
are set upon a course of deep and earnest thought
in respect to their salvation, the minds of Christians
are laid under contribution by the demand that is
made upon them for counsel and aid; and even
those who are not specially awakened by the Holy
Spirit, are usually to a greater or less extent, brought
into the posture of reflection or inquiry.   And the
subject which occupies the mind in this case, let it
be remembered, is of the noblest kind.   The intellect no doubt may be vigorously employed upon
subjects of an unimportant character, and the exercise which it thus receives, may serve to develope
and quicken its powers ; but in a revival of religion,
the subject also is fitted not only to develope and
quicken, but to elevate ; for it brings the mind in
contact with higher orders of being and higher
states of existence.   Yes, in such a scene, men are
not only trained to deep reflection, but to reflection

upon matters of infinite moment ; and the intellect and the heart get warm together; and while the deep and strong sensibilities of the soul are roused by means of the light that blazes in the understanding, the feelings in turn send back into the mind an influence that is fitted to render its perceptions more distinct and vivid. I appeal to the subjects of revivals every where for evidence of the fact, that the mind is never more active than during a season of the special outpouring of the Holy Spirit.

But revivals of religion are favorable to intellectual culture, not only as they bring the mind at the time into vigorous exercise, but as they originate in the subjects of them moral feelings and habits which are peculiarly favorable to the acquisition of useful knowledge. Every true subject of a revival has been brought to realize that his intellectual powers and all the means he enjoys for their improvement, are a talent from the great Master, for which he will be responsible ; and this impression will of course be favorable to the highest degree of diligence. And then again, that calm state of the affections which is thereby induced, is peculiarly favorable to a habit of intellectual abstraction, and to all high mental efforts : and hence I should expect with great confidence that of two individuals, one of whom had been a sharer in the blessed effects of a revival, and the other was a stranger to the power of religion—other things being equal—the former would be far more successful in acquiring any branch of useful knowledge than the

latter; besides the fact that in the one case there
would be a security, and in the other none, that the
acquisitions which were made would be consecrated
to the cause of truth, virtue and happiness. And
what would be true of a single subject of a revival,
would be true of its subjects generally: they have
experienced an influence which is fitted more than
any thing else to bring out their intellectual energies, and give them a right direction.

Moreover, as it is the tendency of a revival to impress those who share in it with their obligations to
cultivate their own powers as God gives them opportunity, it is adapted also to awaken in them an active
desire for the general promotion of useful knowledge. For though they know that knowledge is capable of being perverted to the worst purposes, and
renders a bad man a much more formidable enemy to
the cause of virtue and happiness than he could be
without it; yet they also know that knowledge in
itself is an important auxiliary to that cause; and
that it were as unreasonable to object to it because
it is occasionally perverted to bad ends, as it would
be to call in question the utility of the sun, because
in his march through the heavens he sometimes
lights the path of the robber or the assassin. Hence
we find that in our own country at least, many of
the most active promoters of useful knowledge at
the present day are to be found among those who
have been practically taught the great lesson of human responsibility in a revival of religion; and it is
reasonable to conclude that in the progress of re-

vivals not only religious knowledge, but every other species of knowledge that is fitted to adorn and bless society will be regularly advanced.

But if revivals serve to elevate the intellectual condition of men, they operate still more benignly as well as powerfully upon their *spiritual* condition. All who are the subjects of them, were previously lying under the curse of God, and exposed to his everlasting displeasure. They were polluted in their whole moral nature ; were liable not only to the fierce upbraidings of a guilty conscience, but to the tyranny of worldly lusts, and sometimes even to a storm of malignant passion. In the hour of affliction they had no refuge; in the prospect of death, they saw nothing but agony—to say nothing of the agony of dying forever. And what has the revival done for them ? It has changed their relations to God, and brought them within the arms of his forgiving mercy, and filled their hearts with the spirit of adoption, and opened their lips in thanksgiving and praise. It has clothed them with the beauties of a renovated nature, has delivered them from their bondage to the earthly, and brought them into close alliance with the heavenly ; it has secured to them living consolation in all their trouble, and given them a pledge that there shall be nothing to harm them even in the valley of death. And those who had already begun to live for God, it has quickened to a higher tone of feeling and action, impressing upon them more deeply their Redeemer's image, and rendering them more fit to breathe the atmosphere of heaven. This it has done not for a solitary individual, or for a few individuals only, but for a multitude ; thus changing the spiritual condition sometimes of entire families, and not unfrequently of a large part of an extensive community. True it is that this change relates especially to the hidden man of the heart, and is for the most part beyond the reach of mortal vision ; but it is not the less real—not the less momentous : indeed it may be considered in an important sense, as the germe of all the blessing which a revival of religion secures.

Equally true is it that the influence of a revival extends to the *social* condition of men. Intelligence and virtue are the the two main springs of public happiness. But we have already seen that it is the tendency of revivals to put the mind into active operation on the one hand, and to purify the fountains of moral conduct on the other. If the heart is changed from the love of sin to the love of holiness, it must necessarily result that this change will discover itself in all the Christian virtues ; in that very course of conduct which makes man a blessing to his fellow man, and converts all his social relations into so many channels of benign and healthful influence. Hence it is found, in point of fact, and in instances almost innumerable, that a revival has renovated not only the moral but physical aspect of a community ; has driven away vice ; has encouraged industry ; has given a spring to intelligence ; and has caused the social virtues to

look forth in smiles, where chilling selfishness, or
hateful discord, or unblushing crime, seemed to
have established a perpetual reign.

Revivals also exert an influence in favor of social
happiness, somewhat less direct, but not less efficient, as they have a bearing on the whole machinery of civil government. This is an engine of
tremendous power; and must almost of course secure to a people great good or bring upon them
great evil; and which side of the alternative is to
be realized in any given case, must depend on the
character of the rulers on the one hand, and the
character of the people on the other. Revivals
number among their subjects not a few men of
intellectual distinction, who are qualified for the
higher stations in society; and there are many
others equally gifted, whose character they help to
form and elevate, who nevertheless do not profess
to have realized their highest benefit. And while
the influence of revivals eminently fits these men
for office, by bringing them under the power of moral or Christian principle, it is also some pledge of
their elevation to office, as it serves to enlighten
and purify moral sentiment throughout the community. And after they are actually elevated to public stations, the same influence will make them honest, and resolute, and faithful to their convictions
of duty, even in the worst of times; while on the
other hand it will cherish in subjects a spirit of
obedience, and lead them to co-operate with their
rulers for the accomplishment of all the good ends

of government. Let the true spirit of revivals prevail through our land, and we shall deserve, in respect to our social and civil interests, far more than
we now do, the appellation of " a happy people."

But while such is the immediate effect of revivals
upon our own public interests, I can not resist the
impression, that the revivals in this country are
destined to exert a more remote influence in advancing the general cause of human society throughout the world. Where is even the superficial observer of human affairs, who does not perceive that
the signs of the times, in respect to the European
nations, tell fearfully of revolution? Who needs
be told that the fabric of society in those nations,
which has stood firm amidst the shocks of past
ages, begins now perceptibly to totter; and that
the day is probably at hand, when their civil institutions will be remodelled, and the whole face of
society receive a new aspect? Now I do not suppose that I claim too much for our country, when
I say that the eyes of the nations will be more likely
to be directed to her as a model of social and civil
renovation than any other country on earth. It is
no improbable supposition then that the influence of
our revivals—these very scenes of divine power
and grace in which we are permitted to mingle—
may dart across the Atlantic, and be felt at the very
springs of society there. Yes, those institutions
to which, under God, we owe so many of our blessings, and which are sustained, in a degree at least,
by the influence which comes from revivals, may

be adopted by other nations, until there shall be no
nation that does not rejoice in their light. The
testimony of God forbids us to doubt that there is
a period approaching when the social state of man
every where, will have reached a point of improvement far beyond what has ever yet been attained by
any people. When the light of the millenial morning dawns upon the world, it may be easier than
now to form an estimate of the results of revivals
in giving proportion, and beauty, and strength, to
the edifice of human society. But,

2. Revivals tend towards the complete moral
renovation of the world, *by enlarging the moral resources, and quickening and directing the moral energies of the church.*

The church is much indebted to revivals for *the
increase both of her numbers and her graces.* Observe this influence as it is often exerted in individual cases, and on the spiritual interests of particular communities of Christians. It were no difficult matter to find many instances which have occurred in these latter years, in which hundreds,
during a single revival, have hopefully become the
subjects of renewing grace; and a large proportion
of them at least, have subsequently evinced the reality of their conversion by a holy life. And in
many of these cases, a church which before barely
had an existence, has not only been saved from utter extinction, but has been enlarged by great accessions to its numbers and influence ; and not unfrequently has been enabled to supply itself with

what before it did not enjoy—the stated administration of Christian ordinances. And if the influence of a revival be so great and good as it respects particular instances and individual churches, what shall we say of the influence of all the revivals which take place during a single year; much more of all which have hitherto existed, as well as those which are hereafter to exist, before the world shall be filled with the glory of the Highest? How many new churches are probably destined to grow up under this influence! How much is the standard of Christian character—of humility, of zeal, of devotion, of every thing that pertains to practical godliness, yet to be elevated in consequence of these glorious effusions of the Holy Ghost! What an immense number will have been brought to the table of the Lord, and will have been enlisted actively in his service, and will count it an honor to wear themselves out in his cause, who, but for revivals of religion, might have continued to turn their backs upon the Saviour, and even have openly opposed the interests of his kingdom! And how much is our idea of the influence of revivals heightened, when we recollect that it is constantly accumulative; that those who are the subjects of one revival, are prepared to labor, and actually do labor, for the promotion of others; and the subjects of these revivals in turn address themselves to the same work; and so on in an uninterrupted succession, until the Redeemer shall have seen the travail of his soul, and been fully satisfied.

Again: Revivals *increase the efficiency of the Christian ministry;* both by increasing the qualifications of those who are engaged in it, and by bringing others to give themselves to the work. They serve to raise the tone of ministerial qualification. A minister can learn that in a revival which he can scarcely learn in any other circumstances. There he enjoys advantages which he can have no where else for becoming acquainted with the windings of the human heart; for ascertaining the influence of different truths upon different states of feeling; for learning how to detect false hopes, and to ascertain and confirm good hopes; and I may add, for getting his soul deeply imbued with the true spirit of his work. Accordingly, it has often been remarked that ministers, after having passed through a revival, have preached, and prayed, and done their whole work with far more earnestness and effect than before; and they themselves have not unfrequently acknowledged that what they had gained, during such a season, has been worth more to them than the study of years.

But revivals contribute also to increase the number of ministers. They are the means of introducing many young men of talents and promise into the kingdom of Christ; not a small part of whom consecrate themselves to him in the ministry of reconciliation. As the population of our own country is so rapidly advancing, and as the church is waking up to the spiritual desolation both of Christendom and of the Pagan world, it is mani-

fest that an immense number of ministers are wanted, and are likely to be wanted, to meet this constantly increasing demand. Now then if it were
not for our revivals, we can see no alternative but
that the great work must stand still for want of laborers, or else it must be prosecuted by men who
lack the most essential of all qualifications. But
here, blessed be God, we are saved from both sides
of this miserable alternative. We have young
men—truly devoted, as well as in many instances,
eminently gifted young men, offering themselves to
the work; and most of the younger ministers of the
present generation—as well those who have gone
abroad as those who labor at home—date their conversion to some revival; and as the cause of revivals advances in coming years, we cannot doubt
that there will be a constantly increasing number
directing their eye towards the sacred office, until
the Saviour's command shall actually be obeyed to
preach the gospel to every creature.

Revivals also *lend an important influence to the support of our benevolent institutions.* It is by means of
these especially that the gospel is to be sent abroad
to the ends of the earth; and the kingdom of Christ
every where to be established. When you view the
inroads which have already been made upon the territories of darkness and sin; when you cast an eye
toward the wilderness, and see it beginning to assume
the aspect of moral renovation; when you look
off upon the dominions of Paganism, and see how
many idol gods have fallen from their thrones, how

many have exchanged rites of superstition and cruelty for a pure and rational worship of the true God, how many Christian churches and Christian schools are already established, and how many Bibles and tracts are in circulation ;—when you witness all this, I say, you behold nothing which has not been accomplished by the benevolent institutions either of this or of other lands. Now, this moral machinery, so far as our own country at least is concerned, is evidently to be sustained and increased chiefly through the influence of revivals. Each individual who is converted to God is a new laborer in this glorious cause ; and the multitudes who already are, or hereafter will be, born into the kingdom, must bring to it an amount of influence of which we can form no adequate conception. Besides, it is the tendency of revivals to make those who are already Christians address themselves with more vigor and efficiency to this work ; for while, what they witness and experience in such a scene is fitted to increase their general spirituality, it is especially adapted to make them feel more deeply the value of the soul, and the importance of laboring for its salvation abroad as well as at home to the extent of their power. Yes, my friends, it is amidst the effusions of the Spirit of God that men are trained to engage actively and efficiently in the great enterprise of Christian benevolence : here they are to have their hearts and their hands opened in behalf of those who are sitting in the region and shadow of death : here they are to catch that spirit of zeal, and self-denial, and holy resolution, which will lead them to attempt great things, and by God's blessing to accomplish great things, towards the moral renovation of the world. I hardly need say that all our great benevolent institutions— our Missionary, and Bible, and Tract, and Education, and Temperance, and all kindred societies, have flourished most where the influences of God's grace have been most abundantly experienced; and I am sure that every thing in the aspect of Providence indicates that the spirit of revivals and the spirit of public charity are hereafter to go hand in hand—the one being sustained and cherished in a great degree by the other, until the earth shall be filled with the Redeemer's glory.

There is one institution which the church uses with greater effect than almost any other, which, in this country, at least, derives its efficiency in no small degree from the influence of revivals—I mean *the sabbath school*. In order to impart to this institution the greatest moral energy, it is necessary that there should be a sufficient number of teachers able and willing to discharge their duty in the best manner, and that all who are the proper subjects for sabbath school instruction should be brought within its influence. You will easily see how revivals contribute to the accomplishment of both these ends. They multiply the number of adequate teachers, by bringing many persons of intelligence and discretion to a practical knowledge of the gospel; and they not only enlist them in the enterprise, but impart to them a tender concern for the salvation of their pupils; and lead them to regard this rather than the bare communication of scriptural knowledge, the ultimate end of their efforts. They serve also greatly to increase the number of those who are brought within the reach of the benefits of this heaven-born institution. Let sabbath school teachers become deeply imbued with that spirit which a revival is fitted to impart to Christians,—a spirit of love to the Saviour and love to the souls whom he died to redeem, and it will carry them out to the hovels of wretchedness, and lead them to gather into this sacred enclosure as many as they can: and let parents feel the influence of a revival, either in reclaiming them from a course of backsliding, or in bringing them for the first time to an acceptance of the Saviour, and they too will stand ready to cooperate in this noble enterprise by encouraging not only their own children, but all with whom they have influence, to be found regularly in the sabbath school. It were easy to point to many instances of this institution being first established in consequence of a revival, and that too where no effort of this kind could have been made at any preceding period with the least prospect of success; and to many more instances in which a revival has raised a sabbath school from a state of extreme depression to that of great prosperity. Its numbers have been greatly increased; its teachers have been rendered more efficient and faithful; the church have come to regard it with renewed interest; and even the world have looked upon it with favor, and extended to it a cordial and cheering patronage.

I must not omit to say in this connection, that the sabbath school furnishes a most interesting field for the direct action of a revival. I will say nothing here of the peculiar advantages which this institution furnishes for carrying forward a work of divine grace, having adverted to that in a preceding discourse; but I refer to the fact, that the pupils in the sabbath school are generally in the morning of life, and that a revival in numbering them as its subjects, secures in every instance the influence of nearly a whole life to the cause of truth and piety. We are accustomed to feel, and very properly, that there is special reason for thanksgiving to God, when the man who has nearly worn out his life in sin, is arrested in his guilty career just as he is on the borders of the tomb; but the peculiar interest which we take in such a conversion arises not from any expectation we can have of very extensive subsequent usefulness, but from the fact that it occurs at so late a period, as to furnish a signal instance of sovereign mercy, and to be in a peculiar sense as life from the dead. But when an individual comes into the kingdom, bringing with him the full freshness and vigor of youth, there is occasion for joy not merely because, from an heir of hell he has become an heir of heaven, but because there is reason to hope that he may be long useful in the church, and do much for the advancement of the cause of Christ. And when the dews of divine grace descend copiously upon a sabbath school, there is an amount of influence secured in favor of the interests of the church, which outruns calculation. There are many youth saved, it may be, from exerting an influence unfriendly to the Redeemer's cause—possibly from being its open enemies; and they enter at once on a course of vigorous effort for its advancement; and some of them may be destined to high places of trust, and their influence, whether it be greater or less, whether it be exerted for a longer or shorter period, is brought as an humble offering to their Saviour and Lord. It is a delightful thought that, while the sabbath school is an important auxiliary to the cause of revivals, revivals in turn do much to direct and increase the influence of the sabbath school; rendering it a still more efficient helper to all the great and holy interests of the church.

There is yet another way in which revivals increase the moral energies of the church—I mean *by cherishing a spirit of prayer for the success of the gospel.* The Christian who has the true spirit of a revival, cannot limit his prayers any more than his efforts, to the salvation of those who are immediately around him. As he wakes to a more impressive sense of the value of the soul, and to the fact that the gospel offers the only effectual remedy for its moral disorders, he feels a stronger desire that that remedy may every where be known and applied, and this desire carries him often to the throne of the heavenly grace. And no doubt the prayers of

Christians for the general diffusion of the gospel, which are drawn forth by revivals, have much to do instrumentally in setting in motion and keeping in motion the great moral machinery of the age; as well as in securing the blessed effects which we see produced by it. And as it is now, so we have reason to believe it will be in all coming years—the prayers of the church which her revivals will secure, will have much, very much to do, in carrying forward the triumph of the gospel, until the church shall be able to recognise the whole world as her habitation, and to record that the work that was given her to do has been accomplished.

Who then but will acknowledge, in review of this article, that revivals have already, both by a direct and indirect influence, accomplished wonders toward the renovation of the world? And what Christian's heart will not bound with joy in the prospect of what is yet to be done through the same instrumentality? Let your imagination anticipate a period, (how near or how remote I will not venture to say,) in which the wilderness, instead of presenting here and there a spot of moral verdure, shall every where be as the garden of the Lord; in which Paganism, and Mahomedism, and every other false religion, shall have fled from the world; in which every hill and valley shall echo to the Redeemer's praises, and the bright light of millenial glory spread itself over the whole earth;—let that period come, and let the question be asked, whether on earth or in heaven, by what means this

glorious triumph has been secured, and it requires
no spirit of prophecy to predict that the answer
must be, that it has been, in a great degree, by revivals of religion.   Such then is the grand result
of revivals as it respects the present world—

II. And what is it, as it respects *the world of
glory?*

It is *a vast accession to the felicity of that world.*
For,

1. Revivals *minister directly to the joy of the heavenly inhabitants.*

The *angels* are by no means indifferent spectators
of these scenes.   Our Saviour himself hath declared
that " there is joy among the angels over one sinner
that repenteth."   Much more then must they rejoice, when multitudes repent and believe, and have
their destiny for eternity reversed.   These exalted
beings are represented as eagerly penetrating into
the mysteries of redemption; as employing their
noble faculties to the utmost to become acquainted
with this wonderful work ; because, more than any
other, it brings out to view the perfections of Jehovah.   But it is in a revival especially, that this work
as it respects individuals, and even the whole church,
advances rapidly towards its consummation.   Here
the provision which has been made for sinners is
appropriated; the remedy is applied and proved to
be efficacious.   The wisdom, the power, the grace,
the faithfulness of God, shine forth amidst every
such scene, with a distinctness and an effulgence,
which angels cannot contemplate without burning

with a loftier and more admiring regard for the divine character. Yes, we have no reason to doubt that when they cast an eye towards our world which is the theatre of redemption, and towards our revivals in which this redemption so wonderfully takes effect, they gain deeper, and brighter, and nobler views of God, than when they look directly at the glories of his throne.

Another reason of their joy on these occasions is, that the benevolence of their nature leads them to delight in the happiness of men. Though they know nothing by experience of the evils from which the sinner is redeemed, yet they know much of the glory to which he is destined: they know that he is saved from the miseries of the second death;—that he has a title to an incorruptible inheritance secured to him;—that during his residence on earth, some beams of heavenly glory will be let down into his soul;—and that ere long he will be taken up to be their companion, and will advance through everlasting ages, from one degree of purity and bliss to another. Inasmuch as, during a revival, the change takes place in respect to many individuals, which secures to them an exemption from so much misery, and the possession of so much glory, how natural that the angels, in contemplating this change, should rejoice; how reasonable that their native benevolence should lead them to turn an eye of transport toward the earth, while they bend with deeper reverence before the throne, in view of these wonderful displays of divine mercy.

But while revivals are a source of rich joy to the angels, we may suppose that they are so in a still higher degree to that part of the population of heaven who have *washed their robes and made them white in the blood of the Lamb.* It is with them, in common with angels, a reason for joy that, in these triumphs of divine grace, they gain the most glorious view of the divine character; and also that they contemplate in them a mighty addition to the amount of human happiness. But there are other circumstances to operate in their case, the influence of which angels cannot be supposed to feel. They know by actual experience the misery of a life of sin, and the danger that is connected with it of being cast off forever, and the fearful forebodings of eternal torment which have risen under the influence of a waking conscience; and they know too on the other hand the sweet hope that accompanies the sense of forgiveness, and the sustaining influences of piety in the hour of trial, and the cheering prospect that greets the eye of faith as it respects the future, and the aid which the soul experiences from the everlasting arm in the valley of death, and finally they know something of the exceeding and eternal weight of glory in which the sinner's redemption is consummated. They are able therefore to form a far more perfect estimate than the angels, of the real importance of a revival of religion, so far as it is connected with the happiness of its subjects; because their experience enables them to put the joy that is gained in more

striking contrast with the wo that is avoided. They
look back to the hole of the pit from which they
were themselves taken, and then consider their present condition as kings and priests unto God, and
the gain of bliss and glory which is secured by one
revival defies the utmost reach of their laboring
conceptions.

Moreover, it is reasonable to suppose that the joy
which the redeemed feel in view of the triumphs of
God's grace on earth, must be heightened in many
cases by the relations which they have themselves
sustained to those who are the subjects of a gracious
renovation. Suppose the glorified parent looks
down and sees the children whom he left walking
in the broad road to death, turning into the path to
life and setting their faces firmly towards heaven ;
or suppose the wife beholds her husband, or the
sister her brother, for whom she had offered a
thousand prayers but had died without seeing them
answered, now waking up to a concern for his salvation, and laying hold on the hope set before him
in the gospel, and solemnly dedicating himself to
the Lord ; or suppose the faithful pastor to have
gone down to his grave mourning over the obduracy of hearts which he could never reach, and to
look down from Mount Zion above and see them
pierced with conviction, and melted in penitence,
and rejoicing in hope ; and I ask you whether you
do not believe that in each of these cases, there
would be a new and deeper thrill of joy in the
breast of that glorified immortal ? Do you not be-

lieve that he would strike his harp to a higher and nobler note of thanksgiving, that those whom he loved while he was on earth and whom he still loves though he is heaven, have not only been redeemed by the blood but renewed by the Spirit of Christ, and are training up to be his companions through ages of happiness that will know no end.

I may say too, reverently, that Jehovah himself rejoices in a revival of religion; for he beholds in it the most precious of his own works. In such an event each person in the adorable Godhead is eminently glorified by an exhibition of the various attributes of the divine character. The Father is glorified in the display of that love and wisdom in which the plan of redemption originated: the Son is glorified in the honor which hereby comes to his mediatorial work, and especially in the efficacy which is thus proved to belong to his atoning blood: the Holy Ghost is glorified in the effectual energy of his operation on the heart; in changing stone into flesh—in new-creating the whole man. Here is power, wisdom, mercy, faithfulness, holiness, every attribute of God, brought out in a living—I had almost said, a palpable form. If Jehovah rejoices in his own glory, and if that glory is illustrated in the conversion of even a single soul, what shall be said of his rejoicing in view of a revival of religion—much more of all the revivals which will have taken place when the whole number of the ransomed of the Lord shall be gathered home.

2. Revivals tend to the same grand result, *by increasing the number of the heavenly inhabitants.*

Who can estimate the number that have already not only had their names written among the redeemed, but have actually entered through the gate into the city, and taken up the anthems of heaven, who but for revivals of religion would have had no part nor lot in the matter ? Limit your view, if you will, to the result of a single year, and think what a mighty accession to the heavenly host is furnished by one year's revivals. And then with the promises of God and the signs of the times in your eye, let your thoughts travel down the tract of coming years, and see how much the revivals of each successive year serve to increase the population of heaven. And finally anticipate the time when this earth shall no longer exist as a theatre for the triumphs of redemption, and the ransomed shall all be assembled on the plains of immortality ; and behold in that vast community a multitude which no man can number who date their change of character and destiny to revivals of religion. And then think of what has been done for these myriads of immortals. Fix upon the moment when the scene of dying was over, and the spirit was rushing forth to meet its God ; and estimate the importance of the change it has experienced, by all the horror which it henceforth avoids, and all the bliss which it henceforth attains. All this countless multitude have escaped the pollution, and degradation, and wailing of the pit, and have risen to the purity, and glory, and ecstacy of heaven. The day of the resurrection and the judgment which, but for the renovation they have experienced, would have awakened in them nothing but shame and agony, is a signal for exultation and triumph. They walk in the light of the Lamb. They know how to use angelic harps. They are kings and priests unto God. They go on from glory to glory, constantly approaching the perfection of the Highest, while immortality endures. Whose mind is not lost in contemplating the amount of felicity which revivals will secure to their subjects through all the ages of eternity?

Pause now for a moment on the eminence to which we are brought, and so far as you can, let your eye take in at a glance the results of revivals, as they respect both worlds. Under their influence see the cause of moral renovation advancing, until this earth every where brightens into a field of millenial beauty. Behold also the inhabitants of heaven kindling with higher rapture in view of these wonderful works of God! Not only those who have been subjects of revivals, but those who have not, not only the ransomed of the Lord but the principalities and powers in heavenly places, and even Jehovah who is over all blessed forever, rejoice, and will eternally rejoice, in these triumphs of redeeming grace. And this joy and glory is not only to be perpetual, but to be perpetually progressive. Say then whether such results will not justify the church even now in beginning her song of triumph? Which of the angels will think she is premature in her praises, if, when she looks abroad, and sees what God has wrought for her already in her revivals, she should begin to ascribe blessing, and honor, and glory, and power, unto him that sitteth upon the throne and unto the Lamb? Be this then the song of the church as she travels on here in the wilderness, while she rejoices in the smiles, and leans upon the arm, and looks forth upon the gracious triumphs of her living Head. Be this her song on the morning of the millenial day. Let that bright jubilee be ushered in by the echoing and re-echoing of this hymn of praise all round the arch of heaven. Let the church on that glorious occasion count up if she can all the revivals which have contributed to her enlargement, and brought glory to her Redeemer, and say what so well becomes her as to take this language of thanksgiving upon her lips. Let this be her song when her enemies have all gone into confusion and taken up an eternal wailing; when she is herself glorified and enthroned on the fields of immortality, and privileged to walk in the full vision of God; when the complete triumph of redemption shall every where be acknowledged, and shall awaken joy or agony that is to endure forever. From the most distant point in eternity which an angel's mind can reach, let the church, when she remembers these scenes of mercy through which she is now passing, still shout forth her high praises in the same noble song ; and let seraphim and cherubim, and the whole angelic choir of the third heavens, join to increase the melody :—" Blessing, and honor, and glory, and power, be unto him that sitteth upon the throne, and unto the Lamb forever and ever, Amen !"

APPENDIX.

LETTER I.

FROM THE REVEREND ARCHIBALD ALEXANDER, D. D.

Professor of Theology in the Theological Seminary, Princeton, New-Jersey.

Princeton, March 9, 1832.

REVEREND AND DEAR SIR,

In compliance with your request, I send you a few thoughts on revivals. I am gratified to learn that you are about to publish some Lectures on this interesting subject. I hope they will be extensively useful; and if you should judge that any thing which I may write would subserve a valuable purpose, you are at liberty to make use of this letter as you may think best.

1. A revival or religious excitement may exist and be very powerful, and affect many minds, when the producing cause is not the Spirit of God; and when the truth of God is not the means of the awakening. This we must believe, unless we adopt the opinion that the Holy Spirit accompanies error by his operations as well as truth, which would be blasphemous. Religious excitements have been common among Pagans, Mohammedans, heretics and Papists. And in our own time there have been great religious excitements among those who reject the fundamental doctrines of the Gospel; as for example, among the *Christ-ians,* who are Unitarians, and the *New-lights* or Schismatics of the west, and the Çampbellites, who deny the proper divinity of our Lord, and the scriptural doctrine of atonement. The whole religion of the Shakers also, consists in enthusiastic excitement. Hence it is evident, that revivals ought to be distinguished into such as are genuine and such as are spurious. And the distinction should depend on the

doctrines inculcated, on the measures adopted, and the fruits produced. "Beloved," says the apostle John, "believe not every spirit, but try the spirits, whether they are of God."

2. Again, a revival or religious excitement may take place when a few persons only are under the saving operations of the Holy Spirit: but when many are affected by sympathy, and by the application of extraordinary means of awakening the feelings. I have seen a powerful religious impression pervade a large congregation at once, so that very few remained unaffected; and most expressed their feelings by the strongest signs; and yet, as it afterwards appeared, very few of them became permanently serious. Besides, when the Spirit operates savingly on some, there is reason to think that his common operations are experienced by many. The minds of the people generally become more serious and tender; and many are deeply convinced of the necessity of religion, and engage earnestly in prayer, and in attendance on other means of grace. Now while so many are affected, but few may be truly converted; and no human wisdom is adequate to discern between those who are savingly wrought upon, and those who are only the subjects of the common operations of the Holy Spirit. The tree which is covered with blossoms often produces little fruit. The wind which agitates the whole forest, may tear up but few trees by the roots. Thus there may be great and promising appearances, and yet very little fruit. Temporary believers may use the same language, and exhibit to others precisely the same appearance as true converts. This consideration should be sufficient to prevent the practice lately introduced, of admitting persons to the communion of the church at the very meeting at which they were first awakened. There may be cases in which well instructed persons of known good character, may be received to the Lord's table, as soon as they profess a hope of acceptance with God, but these should be considered exceptions to the general rule. Often the impressions produced at a public meeting, where strong excitements are applied to awaken the feelings, are as evanescent as the morning cloud or early dew. And many of those who become truly pious, entertain for a while, hopes, which they afterwards are convinced to be unfounded; and to pronounce such persons converted at once, and hurry their admission to the Lord's table, would be the most effectual

method of preventing their saving conversion. There may be an error on the other side, of too long a delay, and of discouraging real believers from approaching the table of their Lord ; but the error is on the safest side. As to apostolical precedent, it is just as strong for a community of goods ; and after all, there is no undoubted case of any convert being immediately received to the Lord's supper. They were baptized instantly on their profession, but this in our view is a different thing ; for we admit infants to baptism, but not to the other sacrament. And the fact is, that in every part of the world, the plan of placing young converts in the class of catechumens, to be instructed even prior to their baptism, was adopted. God often leaves his servants to find out by experience what is most expedient, and does not teach every thing by inspiration ; as in the case of Moses in judging the people of Israel. And if experience has uttered her monitory voice clearly on any point, I think she has in regard to this ; and I have no doubt that future experience will fully corroborate the lessons of the past.

3. A real work of the Spirit may be mingled with much enthusiasm and disorder ; but its beauty will be marred, and its progress retarded by every such spurious mixture. Thus also, individuals who are the subjects of special grace, may for a while, be carried away with erroneous notions and extravagant feelings. We must not, therefore, condemn all as deluded souls, who manifest some signs of enthusiasm. But under the same revival or general excitement, while some are renewed and ingrafted into Christ, others may be entirely under the influence of error, spiritual pride, and delusion. When the Son of man sows good seed in his field, will not the enemy be busy in sowing tares ? And doubtless it often happens, that by the rashness, fanaticism, and extravagance of a few persons, especially if they be leaders, an ill report may be brought up against a work, in which the Spirit of God has been powerfully operating. The opinion that it is dangerous to oppose fanaticism, lest we hinder the work of God, is most unfounded. We cannot more effectually promote genuine revivals, than by detecting and suppressing fanaticism ; which is their counterfeit, and injures their reputation among intelligent men, more than all other causes.

4. Often also, there may be much error mingled with the evangelical truth which is preached in times of revival; and while God blesses his own truth to the conversion of men, the baleful effects of the error which accompanies it will be sure to be manifest. It may be compared to the case, where some poisonous ingredient is mingled with wholesome food. I might here, perhaps, refer to some sections of our own church, where the truth is not clearly inculcated; and it might be shown that there is danger of error on both extremes. But I choose rather to refer to those churches, which we all think to be erroneous in certain points. No denomination among us has had more frequent and extensive revivals than the Methodists, and we have no doubt that multitudes have been truly converted under their ministry; but the effect of their errors is manifest to an impartial observer. The same remark holds good respecting the Cumberland Presbyterians, who greatly resemble the Methodists in their doctrines, and modes of promoting and conducting revivals. And as an example from the opposite extreme, I would mention that portion of the Baptist church, which is tinctured with Antinomianism. They have revivals also, but their mode of treating the subjects is widely different from that of the sects last mentioned.

5. But I come now to speak of genuine revivals, where the gospel is preached in its purity, and where the people have been well instructed in the doctrines of Christianity. In a revival, it makes the greatest difference in the world whether the people have been carefully taught by catechising, and where they are ignorant of the truths of the Bible. In some cases revivals are so remarkably pure, that nothing occurs with which any pious man can find fault. There is not only no wildness and extravagance, but very little strong commotion of the animal feelings. The word of God distils upon the mind like the gentle rain, and the Holy Spirit comes down like the dew, diffusing a blessed influence on all around. Such a revival affords the most beautiful sight ever seen upon earth. Its aspect gives us a lively idea of what will be the general state of things IN THE LATTER-DAY GLORY, and some faint image of the heavenly state. The impressions on the minds of the people in such a work are the exact counterpart of the truth; just as the impression on the wax corresponds to the seal. In such re-

vivals there is great solemnity and silence. The convictions of sin are deep and humbling: the justice of God in the condemnation of the sinner is felt and acknowledged; every other refuge but Christ is abandoned; the heart at first is made to feel its own impenetrable hardness; but when least expected, it dissolves under a grateful sense of God's goodness, and Christ's love; light breaks in upon the soul either by a gradual dawning, or by a sudden flash; Christ is revealed through the gospel, and a firm and often a joyful confidence of salvation through Him is produced: a benevolent, forgiving, meek, humble and contrite spirit predominates—the love of God is shed abroad—and with some, joy unspeakable and full of glory, fills the soul. A spirit of devotion is enkindled. The word of God becomes exceedingly precious. Prayer is the exercise in which the soul seems to be in its proper element, because by it, God is approached, and his presence felt, and beauty seen: and the new-born soul lives by breathing after the knowledge of God, after communion with God, and after conformity to his will. Now also springs up in the soul an inextinguishable desire to promote the glory of God, and to bring all men to the knowledge of the truth, and by that means to the possession of eternal life. The sincere language of the heart is, " Lord what wouldst thou have me to do?" That God may send upon his church many such revivals, is my daily prayer; and many such have been experienced in our country, and I trust are still going forward in our churches.

6. But it has often occurred to me—and I have heard the same sentiment from some of the most judicious and pious men that I have known—that there must be a state of the church preferable to these temporary excitements, which are too often followed by a deplorable state of declension, and disgraceful apathy and inactivity. Why not aim at having a continuous lively state of piety; and an unceasing progress in the conversion of the impenitent, without these dreadful seasons of deadness and indifference? Why may we not hope for such a state of increasing prosperity in the church, that *revivals* shall be no longer needed: or if you prefer the expression, when there shall be a *perpetual revival?* Richard Baxter's congregation seems for many years to have approximated to what is here supposed; and perhaps that of John Brown of

Haddington, and Dr. Romaine of London.   And in this country, I
have known a very few congregations in which a lively state of
piety was kept up from year to year.

7. We cannot, however, limit the HOLY ONE, nor prescribe
modes of operation for the Spirit of God.   His dispensations are in-
scrutable, and it is our duty to submit to his wisdom and his will;
and to go on steadily in the performance of our own duty.   If He,
the Sovereign, chooses to water his church by occasional showers, rather than with the perpetual dew of his grace; and this
more at one period, and in one continent, than at other times and
places, we should rejoice and be grateful for the rich effusions of
his Spirit in any form and manner; and should endeavor to avail
ourselves of these precious seasons, for the conversion of sinners,
and the edification of the body of Christ.   In the natural world
the cold and barren winter regularly succeeds the genial and grow-
ing seasons of spring and summer; and there may be an analogy
to this vicissitude in the spiritual world.   One thing we are taught,
that believers stand in need of seasons of severe trial, that they
may be purified, as the precious metals are purged from their
dross in the heated furnace.   Paul says, " For there must be heresies among you, that they which are approved may be made
manifest."

8. As genuine revivals are favorable to truth and orthodoxy, so
spurious excitements furnish one of the most effectual vehicles for
error and heresy.   The church is not always benefitted by what
are termed revivals; but sometimes the effects of such commo-
tions are followed by a desolation which resembles the track of
the tornado.   I have never seen so great insensibility in any people as in those who had been the subjects of violent religious excitement; and I have never seen any sinners so bold and reckless
in their impiety as those who had once been loud professors, and
foremost in the time of revival.   If I had time, I might illustrate
this remark by a reference to the great revival of the west, which
commenced about the close of the year 1800 in the south part of
Kentucky; and by which the Presbyterian church in that region
was for so many years broken, distracted, and prostrated—but I
must forbear.   When people are much excited, their caution and
sober judgment are diminished; and when preachers are ardently

zealous in revivals, serious people do not suspect them of holding errors, or of entertaining the design of subverting the truth. It is also a fact that the teachers of false doctrine, do sometimes artfully associate their errors with revivals, and by continually insinuating or openly declaring, that revivals only take place in connexion with their new theology, they succeed in pursuading those who have more zeal than knowledge, that all who oppose their errors, are the enemies of revivals. This artifice has often been played off with much effect; and they have sometimes gone so far as to deny the genuineness of great revivals which occurred under the ministry of those holding opinions different from their own ; or who neglected to bring into operation all the newly invented apparatus of revivals.

You may, perhaps, expect me to say something respecting what are called *new measures;* but as I am out of the way of witnessing the actual operation of these means, I will not venture on a discussion which is both delicate and difficult, farther than to mentiòn some general results, which from a retrospect of many facts, I have adopted, in regard to revivals of religion. On each of these I might largely expatiate, but my prescribed limits forbid it.

All means and measures which produce a high degree of excitement, or a great commotion of the passions, should be avoided; because religion does not consist in these violent emotions, nor is it promoted by them ; and when they subside, a wretched state of deadness is sure to succeed.

The subjects of religious impressions ought not to be brought much into public notice. It ought not to be forgotten, that the heart is deceitful above all things, and that strong excitement does not prevent the risings of pride and vain glory. Many become hypocrites when they find themselves the objects of much attention, and affect feelings which are not real ; and where there is humility and sincerity, such measures turn away the attention from the distinct contemplation of those subjects which ought to occupy the mind.

On this account, I prefer having the anxious addressed and instructed as they sit undistinguished in their seats, rather than calling them out to particular pews, denominated *anxious seats:* and if the pastor can visit the awakened at their houses, it would be better than to appoint meetings expressly for them. But as this cannot be done, when the number is great, these meetings may be necessary; but instead of attempting to converse with each individual, let the preacher address suitable instruction and advice to all at once; and if any are in any great trouble and difficulty, let them come to the minister's house, or send for him to visit them.

All measures which have a tendency to diminish the solemnity of divine worship, or to lessen our reverence for God and divine things, are evidently wrong; and this is uniformly the effect of excessive excitement. Fanaticism often blazes with a glaring flame, and agitates assemblies as with a hurricane or earthquake; but God is not in the fire, or the wind, or the earthquake. His presence is more commonly with the still small voice. There is no sounder characteristic of genuine devotion, than reverence. When this is banished, the fire may burn fiercely, but it is un-hallowed fire. Fanaticism, however much it may assume the garb and language of piety, is its opposite: for while the latter is mild, and sweet, and disinterested, and respectful, and affectionate, the former is proud, arrogant, censorious, selfish, carnal, and when opposed, malignant.

The premature and injudicious publication of revivals, is now a great evil. There is in these accounts often *a cant* which greatly disgusts sensible men; and there is an exaggeration which confounds those who know the facts; and it cannot but injure the people concerning whom the narrative treats. But I must desist.

I am respectfully and affectionately
Yours,

A. ALEXANDER.

REV. W. B. SPRAGUE, D. D.

LETTER II.

FROM THE REVEREND FRANCIS WAYLAND, D. D.

President of Brown University, Providence, Rhode-Island.

Providence, March 7, 1832.

REVEREND AND DEAR SIR,

You have requested me to give you some account of the revivals with which I have been acquainted, and specially of those which have occurred in the denomination to which I belong. So large a portion of my life has been devoted to the business of instruction, and having been permitted to witness but one general revival in a literary institution, I regret to say, that I am far less able to comply with your request, than many others of my brethren. I have, however, frequently visited congregations and places during seasons of revival, and have been in habits of intimacy with many of my brethren who have enjoyed such seasons, and have been thus, in various instances, acquainted with the whole progress of the work. I merely mention these circumstances to shew you just how far the subsequent opinions are worthy of credit. Having done so, I will proceed, and offer such remarks as my limited observation and experience have suggested on the subject.

I. I believe in the *existence* of revivals of religion, as much as I believe in any other fact, either physical or moral. By revivals of religion I mean special seasons in which the minds of men, within a certain district, or in a certain congregation, are more than usually susceptible of impression from the exhibition of moral truth. The effects of this special influence are manifest on *ministers* and *hearers*, both converted and unconverted. *Ministers* are more than usually desirous of the conversion of men. They possess, habitually, an unusual power of presenting the simple truths of the gospel directly to the consciences of their hearers, and feel a peculiar consciousness of their own weakness and insufficiency, and at the same time a perfect reliance upon the efficacy of the gospel, through the agency of the Spirit, to convert men. Every minister of the gospel has, I presume, enjoyed this feeling occasionally in his addresses to his fellow men, and every one has,

I fear, felt that to possess it habitually is one of his most difficult attainments. *Christians*, during periods of revival, are characterized by an unusual spirit of penitence, of confession of sin, and of prayer, by a desire for more holiness, and specially by a tender concern for the salvation of souls. Unconverted persons are more desirous to hear the gospel, and particularly the plainest and simplest exhibitions of it; they readily listen to conversation on the subject, and seem to expect it. Truths which they have frequently heard with total unconcern they now hear with solemn and fixed attention; and in many cases, for days together, scarcely a sermon will be preached, or an exhortation offered, which is not made effectual to the conviction or conversion of one or more souls.

Seasons of this sort commence in various ways. Sometimes a whole congregation is simultaneously impressed with the importance of religion. At other times a single striking conversion spreads its effect gradually over the whole. Sometimes the unconverted are awakened while the church yet slumbers. But more frequently Christians become convinced of their lukewarmness, and return to God by repentance, and through them the Holy Spirit is shed abroad upon the unconverted. That such seasons as these have been and still are witnessed, in almost every part of our country, can no more be doubted than the shining of the sun at noon-day.

II. I next inquire what *means* have been most successfully used for the obtaining of this blessing.

1. On the part of the church, putting away all known sin. The enforcement of strict discipline, the universal engagement in behalf of temperance, the renewal of covenant engagements with God, more universal separation from the world, have all been frequently followed by seasons of revival.

2. Setting apart seasons of fasting, and prayer, and humiliation, both individually and collectively, has very commonly been attended with a blessing. Those seasons which have been followed by most powerful revivals, have been marked by unusual confession of sin, deep humility, earnest longing for the salvation of others, specially of parents for children, and of relatives for relatives. In innumerable cases, such prayers have been in a remarkable manner answered.

3. The more frequent and more faithful preaching of the gospel, has been generally followed by increase of religious attention in a congregation. Ordinarily, ministers in New-England have formerly preached twice on the sabbath day, and once on an evening of the week. Of late, however, the number of services has much increased. Most churches have three services on the sabbath, when they can be procured, and meetings for religious improvement frequently during the week. These meetings have been of various kinds. Sometimes the families in a neighborhood have been invited to spend an hour in religious services. At other times, particular classes of society have met separately for this purpose. For instance, parents, fathers, mothers, young men, young men in business, persons in middle age, have met and have been addressed in relation to their own particular case. Meetings for conference, or for exhortation and prayer, by lay brethren, have been very common, and have been very useful. Perhaps few means have, however, been attended with more invariably good effect, than the establishment of bible classes. These, I need not say, are associations for the purpose of studying the sacred scriptures, conducted by a minister, or some competent person. I perhaps should not err in saying that revivals have more commonly commenced in bible classes than any where else. Within a few years also, protracted meetings, or meetings for the purpose of continuing religious services for three or four days in succession, have been attended with good success. Such meetings have rarely been held without being followed by hopeful conversions. Like any other special means of religious improvement, however, they need to be carefully guarded to prevent their falling into abuse. I have no doubt that experience will suggest such rules concerning the best mode of conducting them, as will enable Christians to derive the benefit which they confer, without suffering the evil which in some cases, it has been said, they have produced. That they have, in most instances with which I have been personally acquainted, been attended with a decided preponderance of good effect, so far as their results have been at present developed, I have no reason to doubt.

The doctrines which have been most successfully exhibited in the promotion of revivals of religion, I think have been those which are peculiar to the gospel of Christ. Of these I believe the following to be some of the most important—The entire want of holiness in all men by nature ; the justice of God in the everlasting condemnation of sinners ; the exceeding sinfulness of sin ; the total inability of man, by his own works, to reconcile himself to God ; the sufficiency, freedom and fulness of the atonement ; the duty of immediate repentance, and faith in Jesus Christ ; the inexcusableness of delay ; the exhibition of the refuges of lies under which sinners hide themselves ; the sovereignty of God in the salvation of sinners ; the clear exhibition of the truth that he is under no manner of obligation to save them ; and the necessity of the agency of the Spirit of God to the conversion of any individual of the human race.

III. The *objects* that should be aimed at in conducting a revival of religion, are few and simple. Some of them are, I think, the following :

1. To cultivate the deepest piety in Christians. Hence they need to be exhorted frequently to self examination, secret prayer, self denial, and the cultivation of the special graces of the Spirit. At such times the temptation is strong to exhibit our religion before the world. When this becomes the case, it soon languishes, and the power of a revival passes away.

2. To improve the season as faithfully as possible to the conversion of sinners. This will be accomplished, 1. By rendering all the preaching as plain, scriptural, faithful and affectionate as God shall enable us. 2. By extending the means and increasing the amount of religious instruction. I see no reason why judicious laymen, provided they are experienced Christians, should not, under the general direction of the pastor, hold neighborhood meetings in various parts of a congregation. In this manner multitudes in every place, and especially in large towns, would be brought within the hearing of the gospel, who never enter a place of worship. 3. By personal conversation, to as great an extent as possible, with those whose minds are at all impressed with the importance of religion, for the sake of removing difficulties, dispelling ignorance, and leading them to the Savior.

3. I suppose we should aim so to conduct our efforts during a revival of religion, as to prolong it as much as possible ; or what is still better, to render it the permanent religious state of a congrega-

tion. Several means will probably conduce to this. 1. We may so multiply religious meetings, as to weary men's minds and bodies by the continuous effort of attention. When this effect is produced, their capacity for feeling is exhausted. On the contrary, by keeping within the limit designated by the laws of the human constitution, men's attention may be directed to the subject for any period whatever. 2. By creating no collision between religious and other duties. If other duties are neglected for a season, the conviction of this neglect will soon form an excuse for a subsequent neglect of the duties of religion. 3. By avoiding the mere excitation of the passions, and striving simply to arouse and quicken the conscience. Duty is, in its nature, fixed, permanent, stable; passion noisy, variable and uncertain. It is from want of this distinction that the results of many revivals have so greatly disappointed the hopes of the church.

IV. There are *some things* which experience has taught us the importance of *guarding against*, in revivals of religion. Such are the following:

1. Reliance on means, instead of reliance upon the Spirit of God. Seeing particular, and sometimes unusual means attended by a blessing, both ministers and people are prone to indulge the feeling that the efficacy resides in the means. They see particular exhibitions of truth, protracted meetings, &c., followed by conversions, and they are too likely to feel as though there were some combination of means by which men may certainly be converted. Thus reliance on the Spirit of God is forgotten; a spirit of self-confidence succeeds to a spirit of prayer, and God leaves the work in the hands of men. I need not say that it immediately ceases.

2. A tendency to exaggeration is specially to be avoided. Men who desire to convince others, are always liable to use stronger language than the cool consideration of the case will warrant. It is so here. I do not mean to assert that the *truth* is represented too strongly. This cannot be. But a stress is frequently laid upon trivial circumstances, for the sake of immediate effect; plain truths are often represented in so novel a light, or surrounded with so unusual imagery, that they have the effect upon a plain congregation, of false doctrine. We can never improve upon the sayings of Christ, nor present the doctrines of the gospel in a dress

better adapted to the human mind than he has done.   As an illustration of the nature of this tendency to exaggeration, I would remark that I have known ministers urge persons to wait, after the congregation was dismissed, for the purpose of being prayed for, in such terms as would have led us to believe that their salvation absolutely turned upon this very point.   Now I will not say that a person's salvation may not turn upon such a point as this, but I ask, is this *the general rule*? Does the Bible authorise us to state it thus to a congregation ?

3. A tendency to spiritual pride needs frequently to be corrected. Young converts are often put forward too rapidly, and induced to address congregations. These exhortations are sometimes attended with good effects, and are, by the injudicious, applauded.   Hence they are prone to vanity, self-exaltation and censoriousness.   The same effect is produced in Christians who are trusting to the means of grace, instead of relying on the Spirit of God.   These indications need to be repressed by faithfulness and independence on the part of the ministry.   In opposition to all this, I know it may be said, that a revival is a season of harvest, and we must labor differently from our usual manner.   I answer, granted.   But I ask, are we to work harder in a season of harvest than in a season of seed time ?   Should we not always work for God with our *whole might*, and should we, or others, work, or can we work, *beyond that might* ?   Should a man work so, on the first day of his harvest, that he and *all his fellow laborers* would be disenabled from labor during the remainder of the season ?   And, secondly, Whether it be seed time or harvest, God expects us to labor according to the laws, to which he has subjected this and every other labor.   What should we think of a farmer who went to work upon his wheat field, cutting down and trampling under foot the rich blessings of autumn, and alleging as his reason, that it was *harvest time*, and he must work hard, for it would soon be over ?   If it will soon be over, the reason is the stronger why we should lay out our labor to the greatest effect.   And our labor will be laid out to the greatest effect, by conducting it according to the laws which God has enacted.

These, my dear sir, are a few of the reflections which have occurred to me in attempting to comply with your request.   I have been obliged to study brevity, and fear that, in many cases, I may not have made myself perfectly understood.   I have been obliged to write in haste, and in imperfect health.   Should any thing have been written which can be of the least use to any of my brethren, I shall have cause for thankfulness.   That this may be the result, is the sincere desire of,

Dear sir,
Yours truly,
F. WAYLAND.

The Rev. Dr. Sprague, Albany.

LETTER III.

From the REVEREND DANIEL DANA, D. D.

Newburyport, Massachusetts.

Newburyport, March 22, 1832.

Reverend and dear sir,

I rejoice that you have been led to preach at large on the subject of "Revivals;" and still more, that the instruction you have given your people, is likely, through the press, to become the common property of the religious public.

The unparalleled mercy with which God has visited, and is still visiting, his American churches, excites our increasing wonder. It should pour a tide of holy gratitude and joy into every heart.

Still we have reason to "rejoice with trembling." Spiritual prosperity, not less perhaps than temporal, has its peculiar dangers. Should those revivals which seem to be over-spreading our land, lose their heavenly character; should they degenerate into mere animal, or enthusiastic, or artificial excitements; they would cease to be blessings. Their progress would be marked with desolation and spiritual death. To preserve them, then, in all their genuine, unsullied purity, should be the first object. This, I know, is your favorite object; and in its pursuit, you have the concurring wishes and prayers of every enlightened friend of God and man in the community.

On this most interesting point, you have been pleased to request some thoughts from me. And though I have little sanguine hope of meeting your expectations, yet as your request has the force of a command, I will offer a few desultory hints.

If all genuine religion is based on *truth*, it follows that every departure from truth, and every admixture of error, in religious instruction, tends to undermine the foundations of piety. Nor can it be denied that even the concealment of truth has a similar general tendency. These remarks are of universal application. But to no subject do they apply so forcibly, as to our protracted meetings. To these scenes multitudes resort to learn more of religion than they ever knew before. Numbers bring with them an unwonted seriousness and candor. Others are softened on the spot; and for the first time, begin to hear without prejudice. All are liable to receive impressions which will attend them through life, and accompany them to the eternal world. From the bare statement, this is the time which pre-eminently demands a plain, energetic, undisguised exposition of scripture doctrines. This is the time to pour TRUTH in all its effulgence, and in all its fulness, on the mind. Shall we refuse to these immortal listeners, the gos. pel; the pure gospel; the whole gospel? This, we assuredly know, is just what they need; and is all they need. Other things may amuse the fancy; but this will save the soul. Other things may be more palatable; but they may be poisonous too. Shall we, in inculcating religion, suppress any thing, either of its humbling doctrines, or its arduous duties, or its costly sacrifices? Shall we for a moment suspect that any part of our Master's message will be improved by any curtailment, or addition, or modification of our own?

Does not a disposition prevail, to depart from the simplicity of gospel truth; to fritter away its substance; to soften down its harsher lineaments; and to give it a form and features less offensive to the fastidious taste of the age? Do not many who value themselves on their orthodoxy, coalesce with latitudinarians in their grand error; and make reason the final umpire in matters of religion? Is not a *false philosophy* exercising a most baneful influence on Christian doctrines—repeating, in fact, the old experiment of Procrustes, and stretching or mutilating them into an agreement with its own model? That between genuine philosophy, and the doctrines of the gospel, there can be no real discrepancy, is perfectly obvious. Both emanate from the same eternal fountain of truth. But the philosophy of the mind, it is truly observed, is yet in its infancy. And no attempt to make an accurate and rigid application of its principles to the doctrines of the gospel, has hitherto succeeded. This, however, proves not that the attempt is utterly impracticable. Some master spirit may yet arise, deeply studied in the human mind, and deeply studied in the Bible; powerful enough to seize the best truths of philosophy, and to grapple with its errors; and humble enough to learn every thing anew at the feet of Jesus. Such a spirit might do much to pour light on

the long-gathering darkness of Christian metaphysics, and to re-
duce the chaos to order.   To such a teacher we might listen with
safety, and with delight.

While the enterprising spirit of the age is accomplishing such
wonders in art, and even in science, numbers seem to anticipate
corresponding improvements in theology.   But with little reason.
If any essential truths are to break out from the Bible in the nineteenth century of Christianity, the Bible has been given in vain.
It has failed to accomplish its grand object.   We hope, indeed,
that many of its great doctrines will be better understood.   In
other words, we hope that the darkness with which a false learning
and a false philosophy have shrouded them, will be dispelled, and
they will be *seen by their own light*.   Improvements in religious
knowledge come in a different way from most other improvements.
They are the fruit, not of ambitious toil, or of bold speculation ;
but of humility, of self-distrust, of calm reflection, of ceaseless inquiry at the Heavenly Oracle, and of fervent prayer to the Father
of lights.   The fear of the Lord is the beginning of *this* wisdom.
To approach the Bible, or any of its sacred truths, without reverence, without a holy, trembling caution, is to be disqualified, not
only to *teach*, but even to *learn*.   Here, men are ordinarily bold and
self-confident in proportion to their ignorance.

> Where men of judgment creep, and feel their way,
> The positive pronounce without dismay.

How disastrous is it for religion, when men of this stamp become
the oracles of the day ; teaching what they have not learned ; condemning what they have never understood ; confident, where a
little reflection would teach them to doubt ; and breathing their
own spirit into their admiring, deluded followers.

A special cause of doctrinal error and corruption is found in that
excitement which frequently attends revivals of religion ; and particularly, lengthened religious meetings.   In these cases, the ima-
ginations and feelings of men being powerfully roused, the plain
truths of the gospel pall upon their ears, and they demand something more novel, more startling, more overwhelming.   The con-
tagion reaches the preacher.   His own imagination and feelings
are kindled ; and he longs to utter something which shall irresisti-

bly seize every heart. In the ardor of the moment, and perhaps
with the best intentions, he utters a sentiment which his cool judgment would have condemned, and which the Bible condemns.
But it enkindles thought and feeling. It thrills a whole assembly.
Thus sanctioned, it flies forth on every wind; and it remains to
trouble the church for ages.

If doctrinal errors are to be deprecated, as hostile to the purity
of revivals, errors in experimental and practical religion are still
more immediately dangerous and fatal.

In the extraordinary meetings to which we have alluded, the
preaching generally assumes the hortatory character. Undoubtedly it ought to embrace powerful and affecting appeals to the conscience, and the heart. But this is not enough. It should abound
in instruction respecting the distinguishing nature and evidences of
genuine piety. Such instruction, so far from being, as is sometimes supposed, unsuited to the occasion, is eminently appropriate
and needful. If men are to be urged to religion with unusual energy, let them know what religion is. If the very circumstances
under which they assemble, expose them to mistake mere natural
excitement or *sympathy* for piety, let the mistake not be cherished,
but counteracted. Religion should, indeed, be exhibited in all its
beauty and loveliness; in all its divine and attractive charms.
But we may not conceal its spirituality, its difficulties, or its self-
denials. We may not depress its high demands, nor narrow its
broad requisitions. We cannot speak to sinners too emphatically
of their obligation to immediate repentance; of the guilt and danger of delay; nor of their encouragement to give themselves to religion; nor of the absolute certainty that if they truly seek, they
shall obtain its blessings. Nor can we employ too much pains to
wrest from them their ten thousand excuses for impenitence. Still,
we may not suffer them to forget their deep depravity; their insufficiency; their dependence on sovereign mercy; nor the necessity of divine influence to change their hearts. True; these things
are regarded by many, as *over-statements* of gospel doctrine; points
which the Christian preacher is called, not so much to expound
and enforce, as to explain away. But the great majority of the
Christian church have ever viewed them as simple Bible truths;
and they have considered it as most honorable to the Bible to re-

ceive them in their simplicity, and open their hearts to their influence. Others, too, who cannot but confess that these are plain and prominent points of scripture, are much disquieted as to their *tendency;* and think that, if inculcated at all, they should be inculcated with much caution, and much qualification. But is it not safe to declare the gospel message? Is there any danger like that of concealing or distorting it? If truth *may* be perverted to men's ruin, is not error *necessarily* destructive? If, from the very doctrines which should alarm, and rouse to action, they will draw argument for sloth, or despondence, or presumption, will not the error be voluntary and criminal on their part, and their destruction entirely of their own procuring?

Are there not certain characteristics of the age, which threaten, in a greater or less degree, the purity of religion?

It is eminently an age of *action.* On every subject, in every department of science, and of life, the human mind seems roused to an unwonted energy; an almost unparalleled activity. The religious world has awoke from a long and most lamentable slumber. Not content with barren wishes and prayers for the conversion of the impenitent, and of the heathen world, it puts its faculties to the work. It vigorously employs the appropriate means. This is matter of the liveliest gratitude and joy. Yet even here, there arises danger. If, through multiplied active engagements, ministers or private Christians shall be drawn away from their closets; from communion with their hearts, and their God; their piety will languish and decline. With new converts; with those whose characters and habits are in the forming state, the case is still more critical. They too must prepare for action; vigorous, benevolent, holy action. And this preparation must be made in the closet. It must be the fruit of retirement, of meditation, of self-converse, of prayer. Without these, they may have the form, the features, and apparently the activities, of living Christians; but the informing, animating spirit will be absent. Without these, they may do something to save the souls of others; but too probably, they will lose their own.

This is likewise an age of *display.* Almost every thing new pushes itself into notice, courts the public gaze, and claims the public admiration. But religion, genuine religion, is modest, unobtrusive and humble. It seeks not public applause. It is content with the notice and approbation of God. These characteristics constitute not only its beauty, but in some measure, its very essence. A vain, ambitious, popularity-seeking Christian is almost as great a solecism as a profane, or prayerless Christian. Should this spirit once enter our churches, it will sadly mar their beauty, and consume the very vitals of their religion. Let us beware of it in all its forms, and all its approaches. Let us especially, in all the arrangements of our protracted meetings, and in all our treatment of inquirers, and young converts, avoid and discountenance, as much as possible, the pernicious spirit of display.

In adverting to the causes by which religious revivals are corrupted, I intended to have noticed the evil of precipitate admissions of supposed converts into the church. But I have already protracted my remarks beyond my intention; and this topic, as well as some others, must be waived.

In reviewing what I have written, I perceive that the spirit of *animadversion* has been somewhat freely indulged. Yet I humbly hope that nothing has been marked with disapprobation, which the great Head of the church approves. If any thing is to be found on earth, which has much of heaven in it, it is a genuine revival of religion. But in this imperfect state, nothing can pass through human hands entirely unsoiled. It is a delightful thought, that He who loved the church, and gave himself for it, will finally present it to himself, a glorious church, without spot or wrinkle. It is my prevailing hope and belief, that the great things which God has already done for his American Israel, are precursors of still greater things. May He cleanse our Zion " by the spirit of judgment, and by the spirit of burning." And may He " purify the sons of Levi, that they may offer to the Lord an offering in righteousness." May our beloved land, and may the whole earth, soon behold the glory of the Lord, and rejoice in his salvation.

Adieu, my dear Sir. Accept my sincerest wish, that all your efforts to do good, and especially the present, may be crowned with an abundant blessing.

> With much esteem and friendship, I am
> > Your brother in the gospel,
> > > D. DANA.

Rev. Doctor Sprague.

LETTER IV.

From the REVEREND SAMUEL MILLER, D. D.

Professor of Ecclesiastical History and Church Government in the Theological Seminary at
Princeton, New-Jersey.

Reverend and dear brother,

The pious and devoted Mr. *Baxter* somewhere remarks—" The
Word of God is divine ; but our mode of dispensing it is human :
and there is scarcely any thing we have the handling of, but we
leave on it the prints of our fingers." The justness of this remark
we shall probably all acknowledge. And although the contemplation of the fact which it expresses, ought by no means either to
discourage the Christian, or lead him to depreciate the real importance of human instrumentality in extending and building up the
Church ; it ought to lead us all to " cease from man" as an ultimate
guide in divine things ; to " search the Scriptures daily ;" to walk
with a scrupulous care in their light ; and to pray fervently and
unceasingly that both those who administer and those who receive
the ordinances of God, may constantly go " to the law and to the
testimony" for guidance in every thing.

As the remark in question applies to every department of sacred
things, in which men act ; so it may be considered, perhaps, as
applying particularly to Revivals of Religion. In those precious seasons, so dear to every pious heart, and so much to be desired by every one who loves the prosperity of Zion ;—when the
graces of Christians are revived ; when many who have been
slumbering in sin are awakened for the first time to a sight of their
guilt and danger ; when the awful realities of eternity begin to be
revealed to the minds of multitudes who never saw them as realities before ; when human sympathies and passions as well as gracious feelings, are called into exercise, and sometimes into very
powerful and morbid exercise ; and when those who are yet " babes
in Christ," and who, of course, have no experience, are ready to
listen to every suggestion which may indicate some new method of
" winning souls," and of extending the Redeemer's kingdom ;—
can it be wondered, that, in such a season of deep interest, and
powerful excitement—feeling should often predominate over judg-

ment ; and enthusiasm, fanaticism, and various forms of spurious emotion, mingle with genuine exercises ; and, in the view of superficial observers, throw a suspicious appearance over the whole work ? In many instances, there can be no doubt, that genuine effusions of the Holy Spirit, by means of which large additions have been made to the Church of Christ, have, in their progress, been tarnished by human management, and unhallowed mixtures ; and, in not a few cases, arrested by transactions and appearances, which pained the hearts of intelligent Christians ; disgusted and alienated serious inquirers ; grieved away the Spirit of God ; left the state of the population thus graciously visited, perhaps less favourable than it was found ; and greatly strengthened the hands of the enemies of the revival cause.

This is so far from being a rare occurrence, that it is presumed an extensive and strongly marked revival of religion has seldom occurred, in any age or country, and even under the ministry of the most prudent and pious pastor, in the course of which some things did not take place adapted to grieve the enlightened friends of the cause of Christ. Public services, perhaps have been, with the best intention, so inordinately multiplied as, in a measure, to defeat their own object. Means have been resorted to, in the fulness of ardent feeling, which scriptural wisdom and experience could not justify. Irregularities and excesses have insensibly crept in, which, though meant for the best, and promising, at the time, to be useful, proved far otherwise in their influence. Expression has been given, in public and private to feelings, which, though sincere and unaffected in those in whom they were first witnessed, were by no means of a similar character in all subsequent imitators. A few, perhaps, who were deeply impressed with the importance of religion, and with the danger of the impenitently wicked, began, without permission, to give vent to their honest zeal in warm public addresses. Those whose zeal and knowledge were less, and whose vanity was greater, soon imitated their example ; until lay-preaching became prevalent, and extravagance and folly were the most prominent features in the scene. Meetings for prayer were protracted to an unseasonable hour. Judicious and sober-minded Christians were grieved to see plans adopted, and practices indulged, which, though intended for good, were by no means adapted to promote it. Many who saw and lamented these evils were backward to oppose them, lest they should be thought unfriendly to what was really excellent and commendable in the passing scene. Thus revivals have lost some of their lustre with all ; have been altogether discredited in the eyes of many ; and have, perhaps, been succeeded by long seasons of prevailing carelessness, and even of hardened opposition to the special work of the Holy Spirit.

But not only are the seeds of human infirmity and corruption to which I have referred, quite sufficient to produce, and to explain the evils which have been mentioned :—not only are the honest mistakes, and the remaining imperfections of the best men apt to betray them, in seasons of excitement, into language and plans which will not stand the test of enlightened reflection ; but there can be no doubt that the great adversary of souls makes it his constant study, by working on the minds of hypocrites and fanatics, and by leading good men, as far as possible, into his snares, to counteract and to discredit revivals of religion. " If we look back"—says the eminently wise and experienced President *Edwards*—" If we look back into the history of the Church of God in past ages, we may observe that it has been a common device of the devil, to overset a revival of religion, when he finds he can keep men quiet and secure no longer, then to drive them into excesses and extravagances. He holds them back as long as he can ; but when he can do it no longer, then he will push them on, and, if possible, run them upon their heads. And it has been by this means chiefly, that he has been successful, in several instances, to overthrow most hopeful and promising beginnings : yea, the principal means by which the devil was successful, by degrees, to overset that grand religious revival of the world, that was in the primitive ages of Christianity ; and, in a manner to overthrow the Christian Church through the earth, and to make way for, and bring on the grand anti-christian apostacy, that master-piece of all the devils work, was to improve the indiscreet zeal of Christians ; to drive them into those three extremes of *enthusiasm, superstition*, and *severity towards opposers*, which should be enough for an everlasting warning to the Christian Church. And though the devil will do his diligence to stir up the open enemies of religion ; yet he knows what is for his interest so well, that in a time of revival of religion, his main strength shall be tried with the friends of it, and he will chiefly exert himself in his attempts upon them to mislead them. One truly zealous person, in the time of such an event, that seems to have a great hand in the affair, and draws the eyes of many upon him, may do more (through satan's being too subtil for him) to hinder the work, than an hundred great, and strong, and open opposers."*

One would think, at first view, that a single series of mischievous disorders, strongly marked; exhibited in a day of great public interest ; and distinctly recorded, would be sufficient to instruct and warn the Church in all succeeding times. But, unhappily, this is by no means found to be the case. Human nature being the same in all ages, the tendencies, infirmities and temptations of men are the same. One generation forgets the experience of that which preceded it. Few read the record of that experience, and fewer still are qualified to profit by it. The consequence is, that every few years, the same occurrences take place. Good men are ensnared and led astray in the same manner. Hypocrites manifest the same arts and unhallowed ebullitions. Similar mistakes are made, and similar irregularities are indulged, without recollecting, or, perhaps, knowing, that they were ever witnessed before, and, of course, without being admonished by the painful instructions of former times. Thus it is that children profit so little by the experience of their fathers. It were well, indeed, if the fathers themselves always profited as they ought by their own.

The truth of these remarks has been exemplified, in a greater or less degree, in almost every age of the Church, from the day of Pentecost, until the present hour. Even under the eyes of the inspired Apostles themselves, some of the evils of which we have spoken occurred, and were formally reproved as disorderly and mischievous. For example, no one can read the fourteenth chapter of the first Epistle to the Corinthians, without perceiving that the extraordinary gifts of the Holy Spirit were greatly abused by some of the members of that Church, and the exercise of these

---

* Some Thoughts concerning the present Revival of Religion, &c. Part IV. p. 190.

gifts connected with much disorder. It is perfectly evident that there was a considerable excitement among the people : and it is quite as evident that this excitement was not conducted with decorum and wisdom. The following paraphrase of Dr. *Doddridge,* on the twenty-sixth verse of that chapter, is decisive as to his view of the subject. " I might also urge, upon this head, the great disorder which is introduced into your assemblies by this ostentatious manner of proceeding ; for, indeed, if you think seriously, *what a* shocking *thing it is,* my *brethren,* that *when you come together* for the purposes of social worship, in which all hearts should unite, each of you is desirous himself to officiate publicly, in such a manner as best suits his present inclination, without any regard to decency and order ? *Every one of you hath a psalm* to read, *hath a doctrine* to inculcate, *hath a tongue* in which to preach or pray, *hath a revelation* of some mystery to produce, *hath an interpretation,* which perhaps he immediately begins, while the person from whom he is to interpret, hath but begun to speak ; and thus five or six, if not more, may be speaking at the same time ; in consequence of which no one can be distinctly heard, and the assembly degenerates into a kind of tumultuous riot. I beseech you, my friends, to rectify this, and to proceed upon the general canon, which I would recommend to you upon all such occasions,—*let all things be done,* not for ostentation, but *for edification,* in such a manner as you do in your consciences believe will be most like to do good to the souls of men, and to build up the Church of Christ." To this paraphrase, the pious author adds, in a note—" It seems probable that some of these Christians were so full of themselves, and so desirous of exercising their respective gifts, that, without waiting for the permission and direction of him who presided in the assembly, several began speaking, or singing in the same minute, and some began while others were speaking. The manner in which discourses were carried on in the schools of the philosophers, where several little knots of disputants seem to have been engaged at the same time, and what happened in Jewish synagogues, after worship was completed, might possibly have given some occasion to an irregularity which to us seems so shocking." So much for the case of the Corinthian Church. The diligent reader of the New Testament will see in the accounts given of other churches, indications of similar disorders, evidently spoken of as offensive to infinite wisdom.

Concerning the partial or more extensive revivals of religion which took place, in different countries, from the Apostolic age to the Reformation, we know so little in detail, that we cannot undertake to speak particularly of the disorders with which they were attended. But that there *were* such disorders, in a number of instances, cannot be doubted by those who read ecclesiastical history with the smallest share of either attention or discernment. I have no doubt, that many of those serious people, who are represented by *Mosheim* and others, as having fallen into irregularities; and who are set down by these historians as " heretics" or " schismatics;" were really among the " Witnesses of the Truth;" who connected with their testimony, some wildness in opinion, or disorder in practice, which tarnished their profession, and virtually threw their influence into the scale of the enemy. The fact is, we seldom read of the minds of men being roused and excited, even by a good Spirit, without some testimony that pride, vanity, enthusiasm and fanaticism, in various degrees and forms, mingled with the good work, and produced effects which grieved the hearts of intelligent and solid Christians. It seems to have been the lot of " the sons of God," in all ages, that whenever they assembled in greater numbers, and with greater zeal than usual, to "present themselves before the Lord," " Satan came also among them."

The glorious revival of religion which we are wont to designate by the emphatic title of THE REFORMATION, can never be too highly estimated, or too gratefully acknowledged by those who love the purity and prosperity of the Redeemer's kingdom. That wonderful impulse from the Spirit of God, which electrified western Christendom, and which, at once, convulsed and purified so large a portion of the church; was made productive of blessings in which we yet rejoice, and which will be matter of fervent thankfulness to the end of time. But even the lustre of *that* scene was tarnished by various disorders, which deeply grieved intelligent and judicious Christians, and, in some places, for a time, greatly hindered the progress of the good cause. When I see *Carolostadt*, the friend, and, for a time, the affectionate coadjutor of *Luther ;* a man

of respectable talents and learning ; who had exposed the tyranny
and superstition of the Pope with great effect ; and who has been
pronounced to have deserved well of the Protestant cause :—when
I see such a man acting the unwise and turbulent part which history reports of him—I could almost sit down and weep over poor,
frail human nature.   When I see him entering the Churches of
the Romanists, breaking in pieces their images, throwing down
their altars, and trampling their crucifixes under his feet :—when
I find him denouncing human learning, as useless, if not injurious
to the student of the holy Scriptures ; going into the shops of the
lowest mechanics, and consulting them about the meaning of difficult passages of Scripture ; ostentatiously renouncing the title of
" doctor," and all names of ecclesiastical distinction ; insisting that
ministers ought not to study, but to support themselves by the labor
of their own hands ; filling the minds of young men with his eccen-
tric and mischievious opinions ; persuading the students of the University of *Wittemberg*, to abandon their studies, and even the boys,
in the lower schools, to throw aside their books, and enter immediately on the business of religious teaching ;—and when I find him,
in addition to these irregularities, declaring that he had not the least
regard for the authority of any human being, but must pursue his
own course ; and that no man could be a real Christian who disapproved of that course :—I say, when I find him acting thus, amidst
the entreaties and the tears of far wiser and more pious men than
himself ;—I cannot help exclaiming—" Lord, what is man !"
These proceedings, it is unnecessary to say, were matter of great
grief to *Luther*, and all his judicious friends, and evidently injured
the cause of the Reformation.   But, in spite of all the remonstrances and entreaties which could be presented to *Carolostadt*, he
persevered in his unhappy course for several years.   And although
he afterwards came, in a great measure, to his senses, acknowledged his fault, and professed to mourn over it ; still the cause of
truth had been dishonored, and incalculable mischief done, which
it was impossible to recall.

The revival of religion which took place in the former part of
the eighteenth century, in this country, is generally considered, I
believe, and with great justice, as the most extensive and powerful that American Christians ever witnessed.   The labors of the

Apostolic *Whitefield*, and his coadjutors, the *Tennents*, &c. and also of the venerable *Stoddard*, President *Edwards*, and others, in *New-England*, were connected with triumphs of gospel truth, which the friends of vital piety love to remember, and which they can never call to mind without gratitude and praise to Him who has "the residue of the Spirit." Many thousands of souls, there is reason to believe, were brought into the kingdom of Christ, during that revival, and a new impulse and aspect given to the Church in the American colonies.

Yet, here again, some of the managers in this heart-elevating scene,—to recur to the expressive language of *Baxter*,—"left upon it the prints of their fingers," and thus created unsightly spots in a "blaze of glory." He who will take the trouble to consult the *fourth part* of the venerable *Edwards's* treatise on that revival, as well as some other contemporaneous publications, will find evidence of this fact as painful as it is unquestionable. He will find, that, amidst the most gratifying evidence that good seed, and good fruits predominated, the enemy was permitted to "sow tares," which sprung up with the wheat, and, in some cases, almost "choked it." The disorders of *lay-preaching* well nigh brought the ministry, in many places, into contempt. The outcries, the praying and exhorting by *females* in public, grieved the hearts of judicious Christians. The language of *harsh censure*, and of uncharitable *denunciation*, as "unconverted" persons,—as "blind leaders of the blind,"—as "devout leaders to hell"—was directed towards some of the best ministers of Christ in the community, because they disapproved of these irregularities. Public *confessions* of secret sins were warmly urged, and actually made, and crimes altogether unsuspected brought to light, to the disgrace of Christian character, and the destruction of domestic peace. Thus scenes which were no doubt intended to make a deep and salutary moral impression, were made the subjects of unhallowed speculation, and the themes of a thousand tongues. All these things were urged with the confidence of oracular wisdom; and whoever ventured to lisp any thing like doubt or opposition, was publicly stigmatized as an enemy to revivals, and an opposer of vital piety.

Among those who took the lead in this fanatical and disorderly conduct, one individual obtained such an unhappy eminence, that his case ought to be kept before the public mind as a salutary warning. I need not tell *you*, that I refer to the Rev. Mr. *James Davenport*, great-grandson of the venerable and excellent *John Davenport*, the first minister of *New-Haven*, and at that time pastor of a church at *Southhold*, on *Long-Island*. Mr. *Davenport* was then a young man, and had been for some time esteemed a pious and faithful minister. Hearing of the signal effusions of the Holy Spirit with which God had been pleased to favor many parts of *New-England*, he, about the year 1741, made a visit to *Connecticut*, and shortly afterwards to *Massachusetts;* and every where preached abundantly, and entered with warmth into the spirit of the prevailing revivals. Soon, however, becoming animated by a furious zeal, and imagining that he was called to take a *special lead* in the work, he began to set at nought all the rules of Christian prudence and order, and to give the most unrestrained liberty to his fanatical feelings. He raised his voice to the highest pitch in public services, and accompanied his unnatural vehemence, and cantatory bawling, with the most violent agitations of body. He encouraged his hearers to give the most unrestrained vent both to their distress and joy, by violent outcries, in the midst of public assemblies. He pronounced those who were thus violently agitated, and who made these public outcries, to be undoubtedly converted persons. He openly encouraged his new converts to speak in public, and brought forward many ignorant and unqualified persons, young and old, to address large assemblies, in his own vehement and magisterial manner. He led his followers in procession through the streets, singing psalms and hymns. He claimed a kind of prescriptive right to sit in judgment on the character of Ministers of the Gospel. He went from place to place, undertaking to examine ministers, as to their spiritual state, and to decide with confidence whether they were converted or not; and when his judgment was unfavorable, he would often, in his public prayers, denounce them as graceless persons, and call upon the people to pray for their conversion. Those who refused to be examined by him, he, of course, placed on the reprobated list. He made his public prayers the medium of harsh, and often indecent attack on those ministers and others whom he felt disposed, on any account, to censure. He taught his followers to govern themselves by impulses and impressions, rather than by the word of God ; and represented all public services in which there was not some visible agitation, or some audible outcry, as of no value. He warned the people against hearing unconverted Ministers, representing it as a dreadful sin to do so ; and on more than one occasion publicly refused to receive the Sacramental symbols in particular churches, when he had an opportunity of doing it, because he doubted the piety of the pastors.

Mr. *Davenport's* elder and more judicious brethren, who trembled for the interests of religion, and who were especially anxious that no dishonor might be cast on the revivals which were going on around them ;—remonstrated against these proceedings ; warned him of their consequences ; and begged him to examine whether he was not under the influence of a wrong spirit. But he was deaf to all their remonstrances and entreaties ;—encouraged bodies of people, in a number of places, to withdraw from their pastors, and establish separate societies, in which all his peculiarities and extravagancies might be freely indulged ;—scattered division and strife in every direction ;—increased the number of the enemies of the revival ;—discouraged and disgusted not a few of its friends ;—and, in a word, created disorders, alienation, bitterness, and division, the consequences of which remain, in many parts of that country, to the present day.

In this deplorable state of things, some of the most eminently wise and pious ministers in the land raised a warning voice against extravagancies which seemed likely to bear down all before them. They were heard by some, and their preaching and writings did much good. But they were denounced by many as enemies of the revival ; and, in spite of every thing they could say or do, the infatuation of *Davenport* and his followers could not be arrested. Like other diseases, it ran its course, until the virulent matter which gave it aliment was in a measure expended. The Holy Spirit, in the mean time, was grieved and took his departure ; and a spirit of discord, contention, and animosity took the place of his hallowed influence.

It is true, Mr. *Davenport*, in 1744, became sensible of his folly and sin, and published an humble confession and recantation, in which he acknowledged that he had been actuated by a wrong spirit; lamented many parts of his conduct; and was in some measure restored to the fellowship of his injured brethren. But to repair the mischief which he had done was beyond his power. The friends of Zion had been clad in mourning. Her enemies had triumphed. Truth lay bleeding in the streets. Congregations had been torn in pieces and scattered. New societies had been established upon fanatical principles, and could not be reclaimed. Immortal souls had been disgusted with what claimed to be religion, driven from the house of God, and probably lost forever. The enemies of real revivals of religion, who were many and powerful, had become confirmed and hardened in their hostility. And many personal and ecclesiastical desolations had been produced, over which their author might mourn and weep, but which he could not remedy.*

Scenes in some measure similar have been repeatedly exhibited since that time. Of these, I have neither time nor inclination to speak of more than one. The case to which I refer is that of the remarkable revivals which took place in the years 1800, 1801, and 1802, in the western country, and more particularly within the bounds of the Synod of *Kentucky*. My impression is, that the most enlightened and sincere friends of vital piety, who had the best opportunity of being intimately acquainted with the revivals referred to, believe them to have been a real work of the Holy Spirit, or at least to have been productive of a number of genuine conversions. But that this work of grace was attended, and finally overshadowed, disgraced and terminated by fanaticism and disorders of the most distressing character, will not, probably, now be questioned by any competent judges. This excitement began in *Logan* county, in *Kentucky*, but soon spread over all the state, and into the neighboring states. Besides increased attention to the usual seasons, and the ordinary means of religious worship, there were, during the summers of the years just mentioned, large *camp-meetings* held, and a number of days and nights in succession spent in

---

* See Prince's Christian History, Nos. 82, 83, 103, &c. Trumbull's History of Connecticut, Book ii, Chapter 8.

almost unceasing religious exercises. At these meetings, hundreds, and, in some cases, thousands of people might have been seen and heard, at the same time, engaged in singing and prayer, in exhortation and preaching, in leaping, shouting, disputing and conversing, with a confusion scarcely describable. This wonderful excitement may be considered as standing related, both as cause and effect, to several other deplorable irregularities.* A love of excitement and of agitation seemed to take possession of the people. They began to suppose that when these were absent, nothing was done. A number of hot headed young men, intoxicated with the prevailing element of excitement, and feeling confident of their own powers and call to the work,—though entirely destitute of any suitable education,—assumed the office of public exhorters and instructors. These were soon afterwards licensed to preach ; a majority of the Presbytery hoping that, although not regularly qualified, they might be useful. When once this door was opened, it was found difficult to close it. Candidate after candidate, of this character, and on this plan, was licensed, and subsequently ordained, until this description of ministers threatened to become a majority of the whole body. As might have been expected, a new source of trouble now appeared. A number of these raw and ignorant young men, and a few of the older ministers, began to manifest great laxness as to their theological opinions. And a *new Presbytery* having been set off, consisting chiefly of those who were friendly to the new opinions and measures, became a sort of *mint* for issuing, in great abundance, *similar coin.* Candidates were freely licensed and ordained who declined adopting the Confession of Faith of the Presbyterian Church, in the usual form. They were received on their declaring, that they adopted that Confession " *only so far as they considered it as agreeing with the word of God.*" On this plan, it is manifest, subscription was a piece of solemn mockery. Persons of all conceivable sentiments might freely enter at such a door. The consequence was that Arminians and Pelagians actually entered the Presbyterian Church, and went on rapidly to multiply, until the decisive measures of the Synod of *Kentucky,* and of the General Assembly arrested the

---

* See President Bishop's Outline of the History of the Church in Kentucky, p. 117.

progress of the evil. By means of the measures referred to, these disorderly intruders, with their pertinacious adherents, were finally separated from the Synod of *Kentucky.* A majority of them formed the body known by the name of the " Cumberland Presbyterians," now consisting of a number of Presbyteries, professing to adopt the Presbyterian form of government, but avowedly embracing Semi-pelagian principles in theology. Another, but smaller portion, formed a new body, denominated " Chrystians," and sometimes " New-Lights," or " Stoneites," (from the name of their principal leader) and became a kind of enthusiastic, noisy Socinians. While the remainder, under the same lawless impulse, took a third course, and fell into all the fanatical absurdities of " Shakerism."

In this case, indeed, as in some of those before recited, several of the ministerial brethren, more advanced in life, who had lent their names and their influence to these deplorable disorders, became, after a while, sensible of their mistake; acknowledged their fault; and were restored to the bosom of the Presbyterian Church. But, as in former cases, not until mischiefs then beyond their control had been consummated. The mournful results of their course had been predicted, and they were entreated to guard against the division and corruption to which it could not fail of leading. But they would not be prevailed upon to pause, until the Church had been rent in pieces;—until heresies of the grossest kind had been engendered and embodied;—and until they had effectually scattered, in that country, the seeds of deep and extended ecclesiastical desolation. No intelligent Christian, it is believed, who has any adequate acquaintance with the course of the events in question, has any doubt, that these revivals, on account of their sad accompaniments, *left the churches in the west in a far worse state than they had been before.* Anterior to the occurrence of these scenes, their state had borne chiefly a *negative* character. There was a lamentable *absence* of religious knowledge, privileges, and feeling. But now there was generated a bitter hostility to revivals of religion; a systematic, bold and wide-spread infidelity; and such a division and alienation of the sound materials for ecclesiastical organizations which were left, as to throw them back for many years, as to any desirable religious order. As to the disorders

which have marked some revivals of still more recent date, I dare
not trust myself either to recount or discuss them. But enough,
I trust, has been said to answer my purpose. I have stated the
facts of other times just as they are recorded by the pen of impartial history, without allowing myself, to the best of my knowledge
and belief, to disguise, or to caricature a single feature in any por-
trait. Every discerning reader will be able to apply the past to
the present, and to see, in the errors and sufferings of our fathers,
some of those mistakes which we ought carefully to avoid. God
grant that we may none of us reject the lesson, until it shall be
too late to profit by it!

It was remarked, on a preceding page, that the disorders which
occurred in the Synod of *Kentucky* were early connected with
Camp-meetings. It is my impression that Camp-meetings began
in the Presbyterian Church; that they were first adopted from a
kind of *necessity*, in a country where houses for public worship
were few, and of small size, and, of course, altogether insufficient
for receiving the great crowds which collected on particular occasions, and who were in a state of mind which prompted them to
remain a number of days at the place of meeting. In such circumstances, encamping in the open air seemed to be unavoidable.
But what was begun from *necessity*, was afterwards, in many cases, continued from *choice.* Camp-meetings were found to furnish
admirable means for the propagation of strong excitement. The
evils, however, to which they naturally led, soon diminished their
popularity with calm and impartial observers. Our Methodist
brethren, it is believed, took this plan from us; and retained it for
many years, as one of their favorite methods of conducting worship for the purpose of effect. But, although not yet wholly dis-
carded from that body, it is no longer so great a favorite, or so extensively employed, as formerly. Hence a pious and judicious
minister of that denomination lately said to a friend of mine—" I
am a little surprised at you Presbyterians. *We* tried the machine
of Camp-meetings for a number of years, and have but recently dis-
mounted from it, scarcely escaping with whole bones; when, lo,
you are disposed to mount again, and once more to venture on the
perilous experiment!"

I confess I deeply regret that the use of Camp-meetings should be resumed in our body. Where they are *necessary*, that is, where an assembled multitude cannot be accommodated in any other way,—as was evidently the case with some of the audiences of John the Baptist, and afterwards, in some cases, with those of our Lord,—and as, doubtless, has happened in a number of instances since ;—let them be freely employed. I am far from supposing that they are necessarily, and always injurious. Far less that all the converts which have been numbered on such occasions, were of a spurious character. By no means. Wherever the word of God is faithfully and powerfully presented, it never fails, I believe, of doing some good. It has never been my lot to see a Presbyterian Camp-meeting. But I have had an opportunity of personally witnessing the effects of such a scene, as they appeared among our Methodist brethren. And the general impression which they made upon me, was, I acknowledge, by no means favorable. To say nothing of the irregularities and abuses which it is difficult, if not impossible, in ordinary cases, wholly to avoid, on the skirts, and sometimes in the interior, of such camps ;—they have always appeared to me adapted to make religion more an affair of display, of impulse, of noise, and of animal sympathy, than of the understanding, the conscience, and the heart. In short, they have always struck me as adapted, in their ordinary form, to produce effects on our intellectual and moral nature analogous to those of *strong drink* on the animal economy ;—that is, to excite, to warm, and to appear to strengthen for a time ; but only to pave the way for a morbid expenditure of " sensorial power," as we say concerning the animal economy—and for consequent debility and disease.

Some of my brethren, I am aware, honestly, and I have no doubt, piously, entertain a different opinion. I judge them not. " To their own Master they stand or fall." I have merely ventured to pour out on paper the fulness of a heart intensely solicitous, if I do not deceive myself, for the extension and the honor of true religion ; and desiring, as sincerely as any friend of Camp-meetings in the land, the multiplication, and the universal triumph of genuine revivals. I claim no particular skill, or extent of information on this subject ; and am cordially willing to sit and learn at the feet of any brother who has lessons of sound and adequate experience, and, above all, of inspired wisdom, to offer on this subject. But until such can be produced to my satisfaction,—I must be allowed, as a commissioned and sworn "watchman on the walls of Zion," (however incompetent) to give warning, "according to the best of my knowledge and understanding."

While I speak thus candidly on the subject of *Camp-meetings,* allow me to volunteer a word in relation to what are commonly styled *Anxious Seats.* They are connected, and not very remotely, with the subject I have undertaken to discuss. Far be it from me to undertake to pronounce on those brethren who have thought it their duty to countenance them, a sentence of condemnation; or to question that good has sometimes been done where they have been used. But this, I must insist, is not, in all cases, a safe criterion of duty. Men may be savingly benefitted by the instrumentality of means which all would unite in condemning. The decisive question is, can this method of proceeding be considered as the best mode, nay as a really eligible mode, of drawing to a point, and ascertaining, the exercises of serious inquirers? Is it the best way of deciding on the digested feelings, the deliberate purpose of persons, whose attention has been aroused, it may be for the first time, and perhaps only a few minutes before, to the great subject of religion? If, indeed, I were called upon to address one or more individuals on a *journey,* as *Philip* was, in the case of the Ethiopian Eunuch;—individuals whom I never expected to see again, after the passing hour;—I might, without impropriety, call them to declare their decision *within that hour,* and baptize them, as *Philip* did. Or, if I had occasion to speak to a mixed multitude, the greater part of whom could only remain a few days in the place where the Gospel was preached to them,—as was the situation of many in the city of *Jerusalem,* on the day of *Pentecost;*—it would strike me as proper to call them, not merely to an *immediate decision*—between the claims of God and the world, which indeed OUGHT ALWAYS TO BE DONE BY EVERY MINISTER;—but also to an IMMEDIATE MANIFESTATION OF THAT DECISION, that they might be conversed and prayed with accordingly, in the few hours of opportunity which they were permitted to enjoy. But it would by no means occur to me as the most judicious way, in ordinary cases, of drawing the line between the careless, and the truly anxious inquirer, to request all who were disposed to think seriously, to rise and present themselves before a public assembly, in the character of persons who had resolved, or were desirous, to devote themselves to the service of Christ,—and this, perhaps, at the close of the very sermon by means of which it was hoped they had, for the first time, begun to feel and inquire about salvation ; and, of course, in a few minutes after they thus began to feel. If I were to make such a request, I should expect to find the persons rising and presenting themselves in compliance with it, to be, for the most part, the forward, the sanguine, the rash, the self-confident, and the self-righteous; and that many, who felt more deeply, and yet hesitated about announcing themselves so suddenly as anxious inquirers, and, of course, kept their seats, would prove to be the modest, the humble, the broken-hearted, who had a deep impression of the deceitfulness of the heart, and who considered the importance of pondering well the solemnity of every step on a subject of such unutterable moment.

I am aware that the advocates of the system of " anxious seats," urge, with some plausibility, that, in consideration of the natural tendency of the impenitent to stifle convictions, and to tamper with the spirit of procrastination, it is desirable that they should be prevailed upon, as soon as possible, to "commit themselves" on this great subject. That a decisive step in relation to this subject is *desirable*, and that it ought to be taken *without delay*, is certain. But, at the same time, that it ought to be taken without rashness, with knowledge, with due consideration, and with sacred care not to mistake a transient emotion, for a deep impression, or a settled purpose, is equally certain. Suppose, after a solemn and pointed sermon, an invitation to be given to all present who felt the importance of an immediate attention to " the things which belong to their peace," to come forward and take the seats provided for them near the pulpit. Suppose *two hundred* individuals to avail themselves of this invitation, and to present themselves before the church as objects of attention and prayer. And suppose, at the end of three months, *fifty* of these to unite themselves with the professing people of God, on the ground of " a good hope through grace ;"—*fifty* more to take the same step, not because they were

satisfied of their Christian character ; but because they had "committed themselves," and did not wish to appear fickle, or apostates :—and the *remaining hundred* to return, with greater obduracy than before, to their former careless and sinful course. I say,
suppose such steps, and such a result as I have stated to occur ;—
would it be deemed, by judicious Christians, a result, on the
whole, more favorable for the best interests of the Redeemer's
kingdom, than if, in pursuance of what are called the " old measures," in such cases, none but *the fifty genuine converts* had ever
been brought forward to public view at all, and not even these until they had enjoyed an opportunity to bring their exercises to the
test of time ; to gain and digest the elements of Christian knowledge, and to "count the cost" of their undertaking ?—The
Church indeed, in the latter case, might not grow in numbers
quite so rapidly ; and her movements might not be quite so audible and imposing :—but, methinks, her growth would be more
likely to prove healthful. She would be less burdened with spurious members. She would be more likely to escape the multiplied
evils naturally arising from the fact of a large portion of her members being hurried forward in such a school of agitation, immature
training, and noisy excitement ; and much less in danger of placing
both the *fifty* who insincerely took upon themselves the vows of
Christ, and the *hundred* who " drew back," in a state far more perilous than ever, with regard to their final salvation.

Let it not be said, that inviting to " anxious seats" is the only
effectual method of ascertaining who are under serious impressions,
and who are not. Why is it not quite as effectual to give a public invitation to all who are in any degree seriously impressed, or
anxious, to remain after the congregation is dismissed, or to meet
their pastor the next evening, in some convenient apartment, for
the purpose of disclosing their feelings, and of being made the subjects of instruction and prayer. Nay, why is not the latter method
very much preferable to the former ? It surely gives quite as good
an opportunity to ascertain numbers, and to distinguish persons
and cases. It affords a far better opportunity to give distinct and
appropriate instruction to particular individuals. It prevents the
mischief of dragging into public view, and even into the highest
degree of publicity, those whose exercises are immature, and per-

haps transient. And it avoids the danger, which to many, and especially to young people, may be very formidable;—I mean the danger of being inflated by becoming objects of public attention, and by being forthwith addressed and announced, as is too often the case, as undoubted "converts." Surely the incipient exercises of the awakened and convinced, ought to be characterized by much calm self-examination, and much serious, retired, closet work. If there be any whose impressions are so slight and transient that they cannot be safely permitted to wait until the next evening; it will hardly be maintained that such persons are prepared to "commit themselves" by publicly taking an anxious seat. And if there be any whose vanity would dispose them to *prefer* pressing forward to such a seat in the presence of a great assembly, to meeting their pastor and a few friends in a more private manner, the Church, I apprehend, can promise herself little comfort from the multiplication of such members.

I have just said, that, among those who came forward on such an extemporaneous invitation, I should expect to find the sanguine, the self-confident, the superficially informed and exercised, as a matter of course. On a late occasion, and in a house of worship, not very far distant from this place, when, after a solemn discourse, a request was made that all who were anxious, or resolved to attend to their spiritual interests, should immediately arise, and signify their determination; the *first* person that arose was a young man, in whom the odour of strong drink was very offensive; who was evidently more than half drunk at the time; and who never, before or afterwards, manifested any serious concern on the subject. In another place, and on another occasion, when a similar request was made, the *only* person that arose was a woman of very dubious character, who is not supposed, I believe, by any one, to have been, either then, or since, under any thing that deserves to be called real anxiety of mind. The great Searcher of hearts is my witness, that I do not mention these facts for the purpose of casting any unfair odium on the practice to which I refer; but merely for the purpose of exemplifying the principles which I wish to inculcate, and of showing that the dangers which I deprecate are not the mere phantoms of a disordered fancy.

In fine, I suppose the truth concerning both " Camp-meetings," and "anxious seats" to be about this: That however useful they may have *really* been in a few cases, of very peculiar character; and however they may have *appeared* to some honest but ardent minds, to operate favorably in a still greater number of cases; yet, as means of stated and promiscuous use, or, in fact, as means to be *used at all*, unless in very special circumstances, they are eminently adapted to generate fanaticism; to give a taste for ostentatious display in the service of the sanctuary; to favor the rapid multiplication of superficial, ignorant, untrained professors of religion; and to prepare the way for almost every species of disorder.

I have been acquainted with more than one Church in which the extemporaneous mode of introducing members, of which I am speaking, has been extensively practised. And I must say, the result has been in no degree adapted to recommend the practice. The great numbers thus added made a most animating figure in the religious periodicals of the day; but, after a year or two, a large portion of them were not to be found. " Their goodness, like the morning cloud and the early dew," had passed away. They had, in a great measure, withdrawn from the house of God, and from all attendance on sealing ordinances; and needed as much as ever to be gathered in from the " highways and hedges," and to be made the subjects of a new conversion. The truth is, any plan, in the house of God, for separating the precious and the vile; for drawing a line between the Church and the world, which does not provide for an intelligent and deliberate, as well as serious entrance into the body of Christ; which does not make some good degree of knowledge as well as feeling necessary in the candidate for admission; however it may gratify one whose "ruling passion" is to multiply professed converts to the greatest possible extent; and however plausibly it may appear in the public journals of the day;— will disclose miserable results in the end, as to any genuine building up of the Redeemer's kingdom.

But I will not run the risk of wearying your patience by farther enlarging on this subject. I shall, therefore, after two or three general remarks, which appear to me to be suggested by the foregoing facts, close this long letter.

The *first* remark is, that there is a *striking similarity* in the disorders which have attended and marred revivals of religion in all ages. As in *doctrine*, what is thought by many a *new opinion*, is frequently found, upon inquiry, nothing more than the revival of *an error long ago exploded;*—so in *measures* of practical disorder, what wears to many all the attraction of *novelty*, is a repetition—perhaps the *fiftieth time*—of some old contrivance for producing a sudden and strong impression on the feelings of a popular assembly. In fact, as real religion is the same in all ages, so its counterfeits are the same; human nature is the same; and the symptoms and morbid results of enthusiasm, superstition and fanaticism are substantially the same. We need not be surprized, then, to find ancient irregularities so remarkably resembling the modern. We have seen that whenever masses of men became excited, and especially when this excitement seized the minds of those who had been bred in ignorance and thoughtlessness;—as they were brought into a new world; so they were apt to think, as a matter of course, that some new and bold measures must be adopted; that exigencies which are as old as human nature, but which appear to them new, call for new modes of proceeding; and that the counsels of age and experience, like the exploded theories of by-gone days, are no longer seasonable or adequate. Hence the inordinate love of novel contrivances for arresting the popular attention, and impressing the popular mind; the spirit of rash and uncharitable denunciation; the remarkable fact, that, in all ages, *young, and, of course, inexperienced ministers*, have commonly taken the lead, and discovered the most headstrong obstinacy in commencing and pursuing measures of an innovating character; a tendency to undervalue the settled order of the Church, and to usurp the functions of the sacred office; yielding the mind to impulses and enthusiastic impressions; denouncing all who refused to concur in these things as graceless formalists; encouraging *females* to take the lead in social prayer; calling upon penitents to make *public confession* of their private sins, as indispensable to forgiveness, and spiritual prosperity; claiming to have a gift, unknown to others, of promoting genuine revivals, to be the only real friends of true, spiritual religion; —These are some of the fruits of human corruption which attended and marred revivals of religion centuries ago; and which have appeared every few years since, in similar connection, and with end-less repetition. It is an undoubted fact, that most of those well meant irregularities, on which some truly pious people now look with approbation and interest, as means pre-eminently adapted for promoting religion, have been confidently proposed, tried, found in in the end to work badly, and exploded, over and over again ;—and yet there are those who still dream that they can be made to ac-complish what all experience has pronounced to be impossible.

The *second* remark which I would make, as the result of the the whole, is, that, as we may confidently take for granted that *en-lightened and stable Christians* will not be shaken, either in their faith or hope, by the occasional and even prominent exhibition of these disorders in connection with revivals of religion ; so it is im-portant to put *inquirers* on their guard against " stumbling at this stumbling stone." Some, when they see what claims to be reli-gion, and even a genuine and precious revival of religion, tarnished by management, or extravagances which they cannot approve, are apt hastily to conclude, that vital piety, and revivals of religion are all a dream. I fear that this fatal delusion is often adopted ; and cannot but also fear that the disorders which often attend revivals frequently minister to it. But it *is* a delusion. The very exis-tence of counterfeits, shows that there is true coin. In every de-partment of affairs, temporal or spiritual, in which men are called to act they discover their imperfection. The Bible teaches us to expect this. And if we did not find it so, the Bible representation of human nature would not be verified. When, therefore, any are tempted to doubt the reality or the importance of what are called by intelligent Christians, revivals of religion, because they have been often tarnished by unhappy admixtures or accompaniments ; they adopt a conclusion which does as little credit to their scriptu-ral knowledge, and their historical reading, as it does to their Chris-tian experience. The work of the Holy Spirit, in renovating and sanctifying the heart, is the glory and hope of the Church. That there should be seasons in which this work is made to appear with peculiar lustre and power, so entirely falls in with all the works and ways of God, that the only wonder is, that any one who reads the New-Testament, or looks abroad on the face of Christian socie-ty, should cherish a remaining doubt. And although the Spirit is a divine Person, and all his influences infinitely pure and holy ; yet, when we recollect that its subjects are sinful men, who remain, after they become the subjects of his power, but imperfectly sanctified ; and that those who preside over the dispensation of the various means of grace, are also sinful, fallible men ;—though we may mourn and weep, we certainly cannot wonder, that marks—sad marks of our weakness and fallibility should appear in our most precious seasons, and in our holiest services.

The *last* remark with which I would trouble you, is, that we ought to guard against undertaking to condemn, as of course lacking piety, those who favor some or all of the disorders to which reference has been made. We have seen that one of the characteristics which seldom fail to mark those brethren, is a disposition to anathematize as unfaithful or graceless, all who cannot adopt their views, and pursue their plans. It is important that we guard against imitating this unworthy example. While we avoid, with sacred care, all participation in their faults ; while we bear testimony faithfully and openly against whatever we deem unfriendly to the cause of genuine religion ; let us remember that some zealous and active servants of Jesus Christ ; brethren whose piety we cannot doubt, and whose usefulness we can have no disposition to undervalue or abridge ;—have appeared, for a time, as the patrons of these mistakes. Let us honor their piety, rejoice in their usefulness, forgive their mistakes, and pray that they may be brought to more correct views.

That you and I, my dear Friend, may have grace given us to love and promote, with our whole hearts, genuine revivals of religion, and to guard against every thing which tends to impede or mar them ; and that we may speedily enjoy the unspeakable pleasure of seeing the power of the Gospel in its choicest influences pervade our land, and the world ;—is the unfeigned prayer of your affectionate brother in Christ.

SAMUEL MILLER.

Rev. W. B. Sprague, D. D.
Princeton, March 8, 1832.

LETTER V.

From the REVEREND ALVAN HYDE, D. D.

Pastor of a Congregational church in Lee, Massachusetts.

Lee, March 22d, 1832.

DEAR BROTHER,

In compliance with your particular request, I now commence a concise narrative of the work of God's Holy Spirit, in reviving religion, at several periods, among the people of my pastoral charge. Conscious of the many defects which have been attached to my ministry, I engage in this service with diffidence, and yet I humbly hope, with a sincere desire, that the great Head of the church may thereby be glorified. What I shall communicate, will be a simple and unvarnished statement of facts, which my own eyes have seen and my own ears have heard, taken from minutes which I made, at the time they occurred. These facts will develope the astonishing mercy of God to a guilty people, and to the unworthy instrument, who has stood for so many years as their spiritual teacher and guide. It will be seen, as I proceed in the narrative, what *doctrines* were preached, and what *means* and *measures* were adopted, both before these revivals commenced, and while they were in progress.

The first season of "refreshing from the presence of the Lord," which this people enjoyed, commenced in June 1792, a few days after the event of my ordination. There was, at this time, no religious excitement in this region of country, nor had I knowledge of there being a special work of God's grace in any part of the land. The church here was small and feeble, having only twenty-one male members belonging to it. It was, however, a little praying band, and they were often together, like the primitive christians, continuing with one accord in prayer. Immediately on being stationed here, as a watchman, I instituted a weekly religious conference, to be holden on each Wednesday, and, in succession, at the various school houses in the town. These were well attended in every district, and furnished me with favorable opportunities to instruct the people, and to present the truths of the gospel to the old and young in the most plain and familiar manner. This weekly meeting has been sustained to the present time, without losing any of its interest; and when I have been at home, has carried me around the town, as regularly as the weeks have returned.

With a view to form a still more particular acquaintance with the people committed to my charge, I early began to make family visits in different sections of the town. These visits, of which I made a number in the course of a week, were improved wholly in conversing on the great subject of religion, and in obtaining, with as much correctness as I could, a knowledge of their spiritual state, that my instructions on the sabbath, and at the weekly meetings, might be better adapted to their case. This people had been for nine years without a pastor, and were unhappily divided in their religious opinions. Some were Calvinists, and favored the church, but the largest proportion were Arminians. And as they had been in the habit of maintaining warm disputes with each other on the doctrines of the bible, I calculated on having to encounter many trials. Contrary to my expectations, I found, on my first visits, many persons of different ages, under serious and very deep impressions, each one supposing his own burdens and distresses of mind, on account of his sins, to be singular, not having the least knowledge that any others were awakened. It was evident, that the Lord had come into the midst of us in the greatness of his power, producing here and there, and among the young and old, deep conviction of sin, and yet it was a still small voice. A marvellous work was begun, and it bore the most decisive marks of being *God's work*. So great was the excitement, though not yet known abroad, that into whatever section of the town I now went, the people in that immediate neighborhood, would leave their wordly employments, at any hour of the day, and soon fill a large room. Before I was aware, and without any previous appointment, I found myself, on these occasions, in the midst of a solemn and anxious assembly. Many were in tears, and bowed down under the weight of their sins, and some began to rejoice in hope. These seasons were spent in prayer and exhortation, and in conversing with the anxious, and with such as had found relief, by submitting themselves to God, adapting my instruction to their respective cases. This was done in the hearing of all who were present. Being then a youth, who had seen but twenty-four years, and inexperienced, I felt weak indeed; and was often ready to sink under this vast weight of responsibility. But the Lord carried me along from one interesting scene to another. I was governed, in my movements, by what appeared to me to be the exigencies of the people.

As yet there had been no public religious meeting, excepting on the sabbath. A weekly Lecture, at the meeting-house, was now appointed, to be on Thursday, and though it was in the most busy season of the year, the house was filled. This Lecture was continued for more than six months, without any abatement of attention; in sustaining which, I was aided by neighboring ministers, and by numbers from a distance, who came to witness this display of sovereign grace. The former disputes of the people, respecting religious sentiments, in a great measure, subsided, their consciences seeming to testify in favor of the truth. The work spread into every part of the town, and what was worthy of special notice, it was entirely confined within the *limits* of the town, excepting in the case of a few families, which usually attended public worship with us, from the borders of the adjacent towns. Especially powerful was the work among those, who had taken their stand in opposition to the small church, and the distinguishing doctrines of grace. Many of this class were convinced, that they had always lived in error and darkness, and in a state of total alienation from God. They were compelled, notwithstanding their former hatred of the prominent truths of the gospel, to make the interesting inquiry, *what shall we do to be saved?*

The truths which I exhibited in my public discourses, and in the many meetings between the sabbaths, were in substance the following :—the holiness and immutability of God; the purity and perfection of his law; the entire depravity of the heart, consisting in voluntary opposition to God and holiness; the fulness and all-sufficiency of the atonement made by Christ; the freeness of the offer of pardon, made to all, on condition of repentance; the necessity of a change of heart, by the Holy Spirit, arising from the deep-rooted depravity of men, which no created arm could remove; the utter inexcusableness of sinners, in rejecting the kind overtures of mercy, as they acted freely and voluntarily in doing it; and the duty and reasonableness of immediate submission to

God. These are some of the truths, which God appeared to own and bless, and which, through the agency of the Spirit, were made "quick and powerful, and sharper than any two-edged sword."

All our religious meetings were very much thronged, and yet were never noisy or irregular, nor continued to a late hour. They were characterized with a stillness and solemnity, which, I believe, have rarely been witnessed. The converts appeared to renounce all dependence on their own doings, feeling themselves entirely destitute of righteousness, and that all their hope of salvation was in the mere mercy of God in Christ, to whom they were willing to be *eternal debtors*. To the praise of sovereign grace I may add, that the work continued, with great regularity and little abatement, nearly eighteen months. In this time, as appears from the records of the church, one hundred and ten persons of different ages, united themselves unto the Lord and his covenant people. All these were examined in the presence of the church, and were received, on the ground of their professing to have experienced a change of heart, and to have passed from death unto life. They appeared to exhibit the fruits of the spirit, and to exemplify the religion of Jesus in their subsequent lives. The instances of apostacy have been but few. Many of them have finished their course, and entered into the joy of their Lord. They gave evidence of enduring to the end, and of departing this life, in the triumphs of faith. Others remain to this day " burning and shining lights" in the church, some in this town, and some in the new settlements.

This revival of religion produced a surprising change in the religious sentiments and feelings of the people, and in the general aspect of the town. It effected a happy union; a union, which to an unusual extent, has continued to the present time. After the shower of grace had passed over, divine influences were not altogether withholden, nor did the people lose their relish for religious meetings. Insulated conversions to the cross and standard of the Redeemer, strongly marked as being genuine, frequently occurred. In the six following years, forty-two were added to the church, including some, who came from other churches.

In the year 1800, we were again favored with special tokens of God's presence, in a work of the Holy Spirit. This display of sovereign grace was witnessed, soon after I commenced a weekly religious conference, with particular reference to the *young people;* and it was noticed, that the *subjects* of the work were confined almost wholly to those who attended this conference. As in the former revival, I explained and enforced the doctrines of the gospel, showing the youth, who flocked together in great numbers, that sinners had brought ruin upon themselves, and were awfully guilty and justly condemned, and that all their hope of salvation was in a crucified Saviour. Prayer and praise accompanied this instruction. No attempts were made to produce an excitement, only in view of the plain truths of the gospel. The great body of the people, as they did not attend on these means, were not affected and solemnized, as they were in the first revival; but the convictions of the awakened were *clear, rational* and *pungent,* and those who received comfort, appeared understandingly to embrace the soul-humbling doctrines of the cross, and to be renewed in the temper of their minds. This revival occasioned an accession to the church of twenty-one persons, the most of whom were between the ages of sixteen and twenty-four.

A few years now passed, in which we had no revival; but many of our religious meetings were continued, and well attended, nor were we without evidence of the bestowment of God's special mercy, in rescuing sinners from deserved wrath. In this time twenty-nine persons, including a few who brought letters, were added to the church.

In September 1806, the Lord graciously visited us again. This season of the out-pourings of his Spirit followed the death of a youth, a respectable and promising young man, who had been for several years, a constant attendant on the conferences of young people, and had acquired an uncommonly good understanding of the doctrines of Christianity. His death, which took place, when at a distance from home, was unexpected; and his appearance, in the last days of his life, was peculiarly calculated to arouse the attention of his youthful companions. It pleased a sovereign God to accompany this providence, by the influences of the Holy Spirit. The effect was immediately visible and remarkable. On the sabbath succeeding the arrival of the afflictive intelligence, I preached to a crowded assembly from Heb. xi. 4. "He being dead, yet speaketh." It was indeed a memorable sabbath to many of this people. That divine influences were shed down upon us, that day, none could doubt. The solemn stillness and the flowing tears from many eyes evinced the presence of the Holy Spirit. More than twenty persons, who soon after exhibited evidence of having bowed in humble submission at the feet of Jesus, dated the commencement of their serious impressions, at that time. This work, in its progress, resembled a plentiful shower from a small cloud. It was powerful and refreshing indeed in one part of the town, affecting more or less in almost every family, before any deep impressions were noticed in other parts of the town. Eventually the work spread in some measure; but the most of the shower was apparently received, where divine influences first began to fall. The season was precious, and was continued to us about a year. Our meetings were the same as before, and they were characterized with the same stillness and solemnity. Many new family altars were erected, and many were embraced as the disciples of Jesus, who had practically set him at nought. During this revival, and soon after it, seventy-one persons were received to the communion of the church.

The six following years were years of coldness and spiritual dearth in the church, and of uncommon stupidity among the people. During this time twenty-two only were gathered into the church. We seemed to be ripening fast for the judgments of God.

It is proper, in this place, to mention what might have been introduced before, that the church, males and females, were frequently called together for the express purpose of uniting in prayer, whether we were favored with special divine influences or not. Many such meetings have been attended, in the course of every year of my ministry. On these occasions, the church have been by themselves, confessing their sins, and imploring God to build up Zion. I have always been present, and the brethren, as they have been called upon by the pastor, have readily taken an active part, and led in these solemn devotions. These meetings have been very precious, and when closed, I have often heard the members say, " It is good to be here." They have been the means of keeping religion *alive* in the church, and of promoting brotherly love and union. We have also been in the practice of observing whole days of Fasting and Prayer in the church, giving opportunity to any of the people, who were disposed, to attend with us. Great numbers have usually attended on these occasions, beside the members of the church, and God has appeared to bless these efforts. Many have acknowledged, that they felt their first convictions of sin at these meetings.

In 1813, soon after a distressing and mortal sickness, which, in a short time, swept off many of the inhabitants, God returned to us again in mercy. His special presence, in the gift of the Holy Spirit, was manifestly with us until sometime in the year following. We enjoyed another little harvest of souls. The same weekly meetings, in which prayer was a principal exercise, were continued, and the same course of instruction was pursued. As fruits of this work of the Lord, twenty persons were added to the church.

During the next seven years, though we were not favored with such tokens of mercy, as might be denominated a revival, (for stupidity greatly prevailed,) yet there were many insulated cases of awakening and hopeful conversion. Our meetings, on the Lord's day, continued to be full, and all other meetings were attended with interest. In this time seventy-six persons were received into the church, fifty-two from the world, and twenty-four by letter.

In the summer of 1821, there was an evident increase of solemnity in the church and congregation, and some individuals were known to be anxious for their souls. This appearance continued for several weeks, under the same means of grace, which the people had long enjoyed, but none were found who rejoiced in hope. The church often assembled together for prayer, and in the month of August, we observed a day of Fasting and Prayer. The meeting-house was well filled, and deep solemnity pervaded the congregation. The hearts of many seemed to " burn within them," and there were increasing indications from the rising cloud " of abundance of rain." We began to hear from one and another a new language, the language of submission to God.

At this interesting crisis, the Rev. Asahel Nettleton spent a few days with us. He preached five sermons to overflowing assemblies, and his labors were remarkably blessed. The Spirit of God

came down upon us, "like a rushing mighty wind." Conversions
were frequent, sometimes several in a day, and the change in
the feelings and views of the subjects was wonderful. At the
suggestion of Mr. Nettleton, I now instituted what are called
inquiring meetings. More than a hundred persons attended the
first. These meetings, as I found them to be convenient, were
continued through this revival; and I have ever since made use of
them, as occasion required, sometimes weekly, for many months
in succession. The church have always been requested to assemble for prayer, in the upper room of a large school-house, in
which the inquiring meetings have been attended. While the
church have been engaged in prayer, a sufficient number of the
brethren have been with the pastor to converse, in a low voice,
with every individual in the inquiring room, giving opportunity for
each one to make known the state of his feelings. This has been
followed by instruction addressed to them all, and adapted to their
cases, and by prayer. The ruined and helpless state of sinners,
the exceeding wickedness of their hearts, and the awful consequences of neglecting the great salvation, have been explicitly
stated, on these occasions, and pressed on the minds of the inquirers. They have not been directed to take any steps *preparatory*
to their accepting of Christ, but being acquainted with the nature
and terms of the gospel, repentance toward God, and faith in Him,
"who came to seek and to save that which was lost," have been
enjoined upon them, as their *immediate duty* and *only safe course*.
No language can describe the deep feeling, which has been manifested at some of these meetings.

The work of the Holy Spirit in 1821, was continued to us until the close of the year. Many young heads of families, and others in the midst of life were among the happy subjects. The
church received an accession of eighty-six persons as fruits of this
revival.

Between this revival, and that which took place in 1827, the
church received only twenty-four, and nearly half of these were
recommended to us from sister churches. The seasons of prayer
in the church were frequent, and occasionally whole days of Fasting and Prayer, which all the people were invited to attend, were
observed. The church also, by a large committee, selected from

their body, visited every family in the town, and conversed with parents and children and domestics on the concerns of their souls, and their prospects for eternity, closing these interviews with prayer. This has been repeatedly done, within the last ten years, and sometimes the whole has been accomplished in one day. The people have been publicly notified, on the sabbath, of the particular day on which these visits were to be made, and the brethren appointed for this labor of love have had their respective districts assigned them. These have been solemn days, pre-eminently days of prayer in every part of the town, and profitable both to the brethren, who made the visits, and to the people who received them.

On the sabbath preceding the first day of the year 1827, I invited the people, as had been our practice, to assemble, at the rising of the sun, in the sanctuary for the purpose of prayer and praise to that God, who had been our Preserver, and on whom we were dependant for all our blessings. Several hundreds convened, at that early hour, and some came from a distance of two and three miles. An uncommon interest was evidently felt in the meeting. Another display of the all-conquering grace of God commenced, which was extensive and very powerful. This work of the Holy Spirit continued through the winter and spring. Many stubborn hearts were bowed, and not a few of the subjects were from that class of people, who appeared to be far from righteousness. In the course of a few months, it was found that thirty new domestic altars were erected, and many of them near the house of God, and erected by a number of our active, businessmen. As the fruits of this revival, one hundred and twenty-five were added to the church.

During the next four years, we received fourteen into the church, the most of whom were from the world.

In the year 1831, which was a year memorable for the effusions of the Spirit, in almost every part of our land, this people were not passed by. In the fore part of this year, it pleased God again to arrest the attention of many. For a number of months, the excitement was very great, and our meetings were frequent, crowded and solemn. Some instances of conversion early occurred, which were more striking than any we had ever witnessed.

The almighty and sovereign power of God was remarkably displayed, evincing the truth of his own declaration, "I will have mercy on whom I will have mercy." This revival was followed by an accession to the church of forty-four persons.

The whole number received into the church, during my ministry, is six hundred and seventy-four. None of these have presented themselves for examination, under two and three months, after they began to cherish a hope of having passed from death unto life, and many have chosen to wait longer. Whenever we have been favored with a season of the out-pourings of the Spirit, meetings have been appointed with particular reference to the *young converts*, at which they have been freely conversed with, respecting the ground and reason of their hope, and they have had opportunity to test their characters, by having the great truths of the gospel presented clearly to their view. They have been warned of the danger of being deceived. The Confession of Faith has also been read and explained to them, and their full assent to it has been obtained, before they offered themselves to the church.

In all the revivals, of which I have given a brief account, it has been evident, that *God* and not *man* has selected the subjects of renewing grace; yet a large proportion have been taken from religious families. In some instances, heads of families, with their children and children's children, sit together at the table of the Lord.

I would here remark, that several praying meetings have been sustained in this town wholly by the female members of the church, and I have had no doubts of their utility. They have been the means of quickening those, who have attended them. What rich blessings these prayers may have drawn down upon us will be known in the great day, which is approaching. But while I have rejoiced, in knowing such meetings were holden, I have never countenanced the praying of women, in promiscuous assemblies, whether great or small, from a full conviction, that the practice is contrary to the spirit of God's word. Neither have I seen it to be proper, even in seasons of the greatest excitement, to call upon impenitent sinners, either in our public meetings, or in the inquiring room, to manifest their *determination* to seek religion, or to give any *pledge* that they would do it. This would be inconsistent with the views I entertain of the depravity of the heart. It would be a departure from the practice of Christ and his apostles. In *their* preaching, they inculcated repentance and submission to God, as the *immediate duty* of sinners.

Though all, who have been received into this church, have not appeared equally well, as being *devoted* and *established christians*, yet, generally speaking, they have exhibited evidence, in their walk, of a moral change, and of being on the Lord's side. We have had frequent calls for the exercise of christian discipline. Some of the members have been led publicly to confess their faults, from a consciousness of their having brought reproach on the precious cause of Christ, and some, refusing to be reclaimed, have been cut off from our communion. The number of the latter is small.

In conclusion, I will say, and I feel a pleasure in saying it, that the church have manifested a commendable zeal and liberality in supporting the various charitable institutions of the day, and in promoting the cause of temperance, which, for a few years past, has been regarded as a subject of the deepest interest to the cause of the Redeemer and to our country.

My only apology for the length of this letter is, that I have taken a survey of the labors and events of forty years.

From, Rev. Sir, your brother in Christ,

ALVAN HYDE.

Rev. WILLIAM B. SPRAGUE, D. D.

LETTER VI.

FROM THE REVEREND JOEL HAWES, D. D.

Pastor of the First Congregational church in Hartford, Connecticut.

Hartford, March 12*th*, 1832.

MY DEAR BROTHER,

You request me to "furnish some account of the revivals that have fallen under my observation, or have occurred within the sphere of my labors." My reply must be brief, but will, I trust, embrace the principal points which are of any importance to your object.

The church of which I am pastor, like most of the early churches of New-England, was planted in the spirit of revivals. This circumstance has had great influence on its subsequent history. Revivals of religion have always been held in high estimation by the church; and many have been the seasons of spiritual refreshing, with which God has visited this vine, since it was first planted by Hooker and Stone, and the faithful men who followed them into the wilderness. But passing over these, as not coming within the design of your request, it is more to the purpose to state, that when the *present series* of revivals commenced, in this part of our country, about forty years ago, this church shared richly in the blessing. Dr. Strong was then its pastor. He was a man of a clear and powerful mind, and of decidedly evangelical sentiments. During the last twenty-five years of his ministry, he witnessed three special seasons of revival among his people; in the progress of which large additions were made to the church, the tone of piety was much elevated, and the state of religion generally in the city greatly improved. The last of these seasons was of nearly two years' continuance, at no one time very powerful, but marked with a constant, silent descent of divine influence; producing general seriousness among the people, with frequent conversions and frequent accessions to the communion of the church. The fruits were decidedly good. The church was large and flourishing, happily united in sentiment, and "walking," in some good degree, "in the fear of the Lord and in the comfort of the Holy Ghost."

About the close of this revival in 1816, Dr. Strong died. I was called to take charge of the church in 1818. During the first three years of my ministry, though not entirely unattended with tokens of divine favor, I witnessed nothing like a revival among my people. Early in 1821, a work of great power commenced, and continued, with some variations of interest, during the year. As the fruits of this visitation of mercy, nearly two hundred were added to the church. Some of these, as was to be expected among so large a number, have since given painful evidence that they were deceived in regard to the foundation of their hope. But of the great body of them, I am happy to say, they have continued to adorn their profession by an exemplary Christian life. Since that period, we have enjoyed three other seasons of special religious attention ; but neither of them was of so long continuance, or productive of so abundant fruits as was the first. During the time I have been connected with the church, about five hundred and fifty have been added to its communion, not less than four-fifths of whom are to be regarded as the fruits of revivals.

I know not that there has been any thing in the mode of conducting the revivals with which we have been favored, or in the effects that have resulted from them, so peculiar as to be worthy of notice. It was the object of my predecessor, as it has been mine, to preach the doctrines of the gospel with great clearness and discrimination at such seasons ;—to guard against every thing like irregularity and noise and misguided feeling ; and to encourage none in the indulgence of a hope, that did not appear to be based on an intelligent conviction of truth and a sincere conversion of the heart to God. That the effects have, on the whole, been eminently happy, it is needless to affirm after what has now been stated. I have often said, in addresses from my pulpit, that the *church is what it is very much from the influence of revivals of religion.* And it is now my sober judgment, that if there is, among the people of my charge, any cordial belief and love of the distinguishing doctrines of the gospel; any serious practical regard to the duties of the Christian life ; any self-denial and bearing of the cross and following Christ according to his commands ; any active benevolence and engagedness in doing good; in short, any pious efficient concern for the glory of God and the salvation of

sinners, either at home or abroad, in Christian or in heathen lands,—
all this is to be traced, in no small part, to the influence of revivals of religion; and is to be found, in an eminent degree, among those who have been added to the church as fruits of revivals.

The above remarks, I doubt not, are equally applicable to the other churches, in this city, belonging to the Congregational denomination. A large proportion of their numbers date their Christian hope from some season of special divine influence, and the tone of religious feeling and action has risen in proportion to the frequency with which such seasons have been enjoyed. Nor is this remark to be confined to the churches of this city. It is applicable to the churches of our connexion throughout the State. In 1829 a letter was addressed to the Congregational ministers of Connecticut, proposing, among other inquiries, the following:— " 1. What was the whole number of professors of religion in your church at the commencement of the year 1820? 2. What number were added to your church by profession during the years 1820,–1–2–3–4? 3. Of those who are now members of your church, what proportion may be considered as the fruit of a revival, and what is their comparative standing for piety and active benevolent enterprize?" I have not by me, at this time, the documents that were communicated in answer to these or other similar inquiries. But I am able to state, that the answers were in a high degree satisfactory. It appeared that a very large proportion of all, who are now members of the Congregational churches in this State, became such in consequence of revivals; that the relative proportion of such, as revivals have been multiplying, has been continually increasing; that the most active and devoted Christians are among those who came into the church as fruits of revivals; that those churches in which revivals have been most frequent and powerful are the most numerous and flourishing; and that in all the churches thus visited with divine influence, there has been a great increase of Christian enterprize, and benevolent action. These results, stated by men who witnessed them in their own congregations, and many of whom, from long experience and observation, had the best means of judging, should silence the tongue of cavil and scepticism, and excite all Christians to pray, with warmer and holier affections, for the universal revival of God's work.

Though I have extended this letter beyond what I intended, I feel constrained to add a few particulars as the result of what little experience God has been pleased to give me in revivals of religion.

1. The theory of revivals is very simple. It is only the increase, and the extension to a number of sinners, at the same time, of that influence of the Holy Spirit, which is employed in the conversion of each individual sinner that is brought to repentance.

2. I see not how any man, who believes in the doctrine of divine influence, or has ever witnessed a revival of religion, can, either on scriptural or *rational* grounds, doubt the reality or the decidedly happy tendency of such a work.

3. It is pre-eminently important, that the preaching, during a revival of religion, should be clear, discriminating, instructive,—addressed to the understanding and conscience, rather than to the feelings and passions.

4. It is a great error to admit converts to the church before time has been allowed to try the sincerity of their hope. This is an error into which I was betrayed during the first revival among my people, and it has cost me bitter repentance. And yet none were admitted to the church under two months after they had indulged a hope.

5. It is of great importance, that young converts, immediately after conversion, should be collected into a class by themselves, and brought under the direct and frequent instruction of the pastor. I have pursued this plan for several years past, and with the happiest effect. Never are so great facilities afforded for pouring instruction into the minds of young converts and forming them for a high standard of Christian character, as during the time that intervenes between their conversion and admission to the church; and if they are continued from four to six months, in a course of judicious instruction and then admitted to the church, there is very little danger that they will afterwards fall away, or that they will not continue to shine as lights in the world till the end of life.

6. It is very important also, that young converts should early be trained to habits of Christian activity;—they should be drawn

out and encouraged in the way of doing good; and from the first, a deep and thorough impression should be made on their minds, that their great business in the world is to live and labor for Christ and his cause. The tone of piety and of action, which a young convert adopts during the first few months of his course usually goes with him through life.

7. A sinner may be converted at too great an expense. I mean, that measures may be adopted, that shall issue in the conversion of a sinner, which measures may, at the same time, by exciting prejudice and enmity, be the occasion of a vast deal more evil than good.

8. It should be the great aim both of ministers and Christians, in a time of revival, so to conduct the work, both in *affectionate* zeal, and in sound Christian wisdom and prudence, that the effect may be to prolong the season of mercy; to prepare the way for a return of it; and to cause all the true friends of Christ to regard revivals as the most precious blessings that God bestows upon a guilty world.

It would be easy to enlarge, but I forbear. May the blessing of the God of revivals attend the volume you propose to publish with a view to promote them, and hasten the day when he shall pour his spirit upon all flesh, and fill the whole earth with his praise.

I am, dear Brother, very truly and
Affectionately yours,
J. HAWES.

Rev. W. B. Sprague, D. D.

LETTER VII.

From the REVEREND JOHN M'DOWELL, D. D.

Pastor of the first Presbyterian Church, Elizabethtown, New-Jersey.

Elizabethtown, March 5, 1832.

REV. AND DEAR BROTHER,

Agreeably to your request, I will endeavor to give you a brief account of the revivals of religion, with which it has pleased a sovereign and gracious God to favor the church of which I am pastor. Of the early history of this church, I have been able to discover very little. It is an ancient church, having been founded about 160 years since. Whether it was visited with revivals, during nearly the former half of the period of its existence, I have not been able to ascertain. The first revival of which any account has been transmitted to us, was in the latter part of the ministry of that eminent servant of God, the Rev. Jonathan Dickinson, author of "the Five Points," and of many other valuable works.

Of this revival, a particular and very interesting account was given by Mr. Dickinson, in a letter to the Rev. Mr. Foxcroft, of Boston, which letter is in print. From this it appears, that this special work visibly commenced in June 1740, under a sermon addressed to the youth. "The inward distress and concern of the audience,'(Mr. Dickinson observes,) 'discovered itself by their tears, and by an audible sobbing and sighing in almost all parts of the assembly." On the character and effects of this revival, he goes on to remark—"Meetings for sinful amusements were abandoned by the youth; and meetings for religious exercises substituted in their place. Numbers daily flocked to their pastor for advice in their eternal concerns. More came to see him on this errand in three months, than in thirty years before. The subjects of the work were chiefly youth. A deep sense of sin, guilt, danger, and despair of help from themselves, preceded a hope in Christ. All the converts were for a considerable time under a law work, before they had satisfying views of their interest in Christ. The number of those who were savingly the subjects of this work was about sixty."

In 1772, this church was again blessed with a considerable revival of religion, under the ministry of the Rev. James Caldwell.

In 1784, this church was again visited in a special manner with the influences of the Holy Ghost. This was just after the close of the revolutionary war; and the people were without a house of worship, and without a pastor; the church having been burned and the pastor slain near the close of the war. This revival continued about two years; and time has abundantly proved that it was a genuine and glorious work of God. A number of the subjects are still living, and are truly fathers and mothers in Israel. Nearly all the session, and almost half the members of the church, when the writer settled here, were the fruits of this revival; and he has had an opportunity of knowing them by their fruits; he has been with many of them when about to pass over Jordan, and from their triumphant death as well as exemplary life, he can testify to the genuineness of the work.

From the time of this revival to the settlement of the writer, there were two seasons of more than ordinary interest, when the number of additions to the communion of the church was considerably increased.

The subscriber was settled as pastor of this congregation December 1804. In August 1807, a powerful and extensive revival commenced. The first decisive evidence of the special presence and power of the Holy Spirit, was on the Sabbath, under a powerful sermon on Prayer, by the Rev. Dr. Gideon Blackburn. A number were awakened that day; and new cases of conviction, and hopeful conversion were for a considerable time occurring at almost every religious meeting. The special attention continued for about 18 months, and the number added to the communion of the church as the fruits of this gracious work, was about 120. The subjects of it were generally deeply exercised; and most of them continued for a considerable time in a state of distress, before they enjoyed the comforts of the hope of the gospel. This revival was the first I had ever seen; and it was a solemn situation, for a young man, totally inexperienced in such scenes. It was general through the congregation, and in a few weeks extended into neighboring congregations, and passed from one to another, until in the course of the year, almost every congregation in what was then the Presbytery of Jersey, was visited.

The next revival with which the Lord favored my ministry, visibly commenced in December 1812. It was on a communion Sabbath. There was nothing peculiarly arousing in the preaching. I was not expecting such an event; neither as far as I have ever discovered, was there any peculiar engagedness in prayer, or special desire or expectation on the part of christians. I saw nothing unusual in the appearance of the congregation; and it was not until after the services of the day were ended, when several called in deep distress to ask me what they should do to be saved, that I knew that the Lord was specially in this place. This was a day of such power; (though I knew it not at the time,) that as many as *thirty* who afterwards joined the church, were then first awakened. And it is a remarkable circumstance that the same powerful influence was experienced, on the same day, in both of the Presbyterian churches in the neighboring town of Newark. It was also communion season in both those churches. This revival continued about a year; and the number of persons added to the communion of this church as its fruits was about one hundred and ten.—The subjects of this revival generally were deeply and long distressed, and in many instances, their distress affected their bodily frames. Frequently sobbing aloud was heard in our meetings, and in some instances, there was a universal trembling, and in others a privation of bodily strength, so that the subjects were not able to get home without help. In this respect this revival was different from any others which I have witnessed. I never dared to speak against this bodily agitation, lest I should be found speaking against the Holy Ghost; but I never did any thing to encourage it. It may be proper here to relate one case of a young man, who was then a graduate of one of our Colleges, and is now a very respectable and useful minister of Christ. Near the commencement of the revival, he was led for the first time, reluctantly, and out of complaisance to his sisters, to a meeting in a private house. I was present, and spoke two or three times between prayers in which some of my people led. The audience was solemn; but perfectly still. I commenced leading in the concluding prayer. A suppressed sob reached my ears—it continued and increased: I brought the pray-

APPENDIX.

er speedily to a close, and cast my eyes over the audience, when behold, it was this careless proud young man, who was standing near me, leaning on his chair sobbing, and trembling in every part like the Philippian jailer. He raised his eyes towards me, and then tottered forward, threw his arms on my shoulders, and cried out, "what shall I do to be saved?" A scene ensued, the like of which I never witnessed. The house was full, and there was immediately, by the power of sympathy I suppose, a universal sobbing through the assembly. He repeatedly begged me to pray for him. I felt so overcome with the solemnity of the scene, and fearful of the disorder which might ensue in the excited state of feeling, that I held this trembling young man for half an hour, without speaking a word. I then persuaded him to go home with me, and the audience to retire. His strength was so weakened that he had to be supported. From that hour he appeared to give his whole soul to the subject of religion. He continued in a state of deep anxiety and distress for nearly two months, when he settled down in a peaceful state of mind, hoping in the Saviour.

About the beginning of February 1817, this church was again visited with a great revival of religion. It commenced most signally, as an immediate answer to the united prayers of God's people. The session, impressed with a sense of the comparatively low state of religion among us, agreed to spend an afternoon together in prayer. The congregation were informed of this on the sabbath, and a request made that Christians would at the same time retire to their closets, and spend a season in prayer for the influences of the Spirit to descend upon us. The season appointed was the next afternoon; and that evening was the monthly concert of prayer, which was unusually full and solemn; and before the week was out, it was manifest that the Lord was in the midst of us, in a very special manner. Many cases of awakening came to my knowledge; and the work soon spread throughout the congregation. This revival was marked, not by the deep distress of the preceding; but by a general weeping, in religious meetings. There was doubtless much of sympathy. A larger proportion than usual of the subjects were young, and many of them children. Some were long in darkness; but most of them, much sooner than in either of the former revivals of my ministry, professed to have embraced the Saviour. The number in the congregation who professed to be seriously impressed, amounted to several hundreds. The special attention continued about a year; and the number added to the communion of the church during that time was about one hundred and eighty. It was during this revival that you visited this place, and spent some time with us while a student in Princeton Seminary.

About the close of the year 1819, it pleased a gracious God to grant to this church another season of special refreshing. This was not so general through the congregation as the former; but was confined to particular neighborhoods. Christians did not appear to be specially awake to the subject, either before it commenced or during its progress. The subjects were generally from among the most unlikely families and characters; from the highways and hedges; while the children of the kingdom were generally passed by. The special attention continued about a year; and the number added to the communion of the church as its fruits, was about sixty.

In the early part of the year 1824, there was a considerable increase of attention to the subject of religion, which continued through the year 1825. About sixty were added to the communion of the church during this time, as the fruits of this special influence. But the work did not terminate with this ingathering. These were but as drops before a mighty shower. About the beginning of December 1825, the work was greatly increased. It commenced visibly on a day of Fasting and Prayer, appointed by the Synod of New-Jersey, on account of the absence of divine influences from their churches generally. Within a few weeks many were awakened and brought to seek the Lord. This revival, with few exceptions, was not marked by deep distress, and the subjects of it, generally, soon professed to hope in Christ. It continued through the year 1826, during which time about one hundred and thirty were added to the communion of this church, as its fruits.

In the winter and spring of 1829, a partial season of refreshing was again experienced, and about twenty-five were added to our communion. Again it pleased a gracious God specially to visit some neighborhoods of the congregation, through the winter and spring of 1831. The fruits of this visitation, which have been gathered in through the year past, amount to about forty.

In 1820, a second Presbyterian church was organized in the town ; and in the revivals which we have experienced since that congregation was formed, a similar gracious influence has been enjoyed among them.

Thus I have given you a brief statement of facts respecting what the Lord has done among the people of my charge. Allow me now to close the narrative with a few remarks. Between these seasons of special refreshing we have constantly had additions to the church. As to the genuineness of the work, I have had time to form a judgment, especially with respect to the revivals in the earlier part of my ministry ; and I can testify that the subjects of them have generally manifested that they had experienced a true work of grace in their hearts. Very few apostacies have occurred among those who have been added to the church in revivals—quite as few in proportion to their numbers, as among those who have been brought in, when there was no special attention ; and the former have generally been as stedfast, and adorned their profession quite as well as the latter. Of the subjects of the revivals which have occurred under my ministry, a number have become ministers of the gospel. In looking over the list I find the names of twelve who have since entered the ministry, several of whom are now usefully occupying important stations in the church, and some have gone to their gracious reward. Nine more are now in the different stages of education preparatory to the gospel ministry.

Another remark I would make, is, that we have carefully guarded against a speedy admission to the privileges of the church. Seldom in times of revival have we admitted persons to the communion in less than six months after they first became serious. Again I would remark, that from what I have seen, I have drawn the conclusion, that it is wrong to prescribe any particular manner for the Spirit's operations. There has been a difference in this respect in almost every revival which I have witnessed. There have been diversities of operations ; but time has shown that it was the same Spirit. The subjects of these revivals and additions to the church, have, the great majority of them, been in the morning of life, and many while yet children have been impressed ; but we have very seldom received any very young persons to communion. The means which have been constantly employed during my ministry, and which God has blessed, besides the preaching of the word on the sabbath, and frequently on other days of the week in different neighborhoods of the congregation, have been catechetical and bible class instruction, and family visiting; and to these may be added meetings for social prayer.

In conclusion I would add, that appearances among my people at present are very favorable. There is much increase of attention to the means, and of solemnity in attending upon them. Many Christians appear to be much quickened in duty, and to be earnestly praying that the Lord would appear again in his glory in the midst of us to build up Zion ; and a number have recently been awakened to serious concern about their soul's salvation. We are anxiously looking for a time of general revival; but what will be the result time must show.

With sincere and fraternal respect, I am,

Dear Sir, yours,
JOHN M'DOWELL.

REV. W. B. SPRAGUE, D. D.

LETTER VIII.

FROM THE REVEREND NOAH PORTER, D. D.

Pastor of a Congregational church in Farmington, Connecticut.

Farmington, March 12, 1832.

DEAR SIR,

Revivals of religion, considered as the effects of a divine influence prevailing throughout a whole congregation at the same time, have not been as frequent in this town, as in many places around us. In different sections of the town, at different times, they have not, for a few of the last years, been unfrequent; but often, when we have hoped for a general revival, we have been disappointed. Perhaps, this may in part be ascribed to our circumstances. About one half of the inhabitants belong to the central village, and the other half to surrounding neighborhoods, distant from the centre, two, three and four miles. The latter, on account of their relative situation, have no free and easy intercourse with the rest of the town; and the former, for the last half century, have been divided, by adventitious circumstances into distinct classes, whose intimacies have been very much confined to their respective limits. Hence it has been difficult to diffuse a common sentiment and feeling, on almost all subjects, and on the subject of religion, as on others.

The era of modern revivals, in this country, is reckoned, I believe, from the year 1792. In the autumn of 1793 there appeared, in this place, a spirit of unusual seriousness and inquiry, on the concerns of salvation. It was under the preaching of Dr. Griffin. He was then a licentiate; and with all the ardor of his youth, together with the freshness of his "first love," he preached here the same system of truth, which he has continued so powerfully and successfully to inculcate. It was not another system than had been preached in this town from the time of its first organization; but there were certain leading topics, such as the radical defect of the best doings of the impenitent, the duty of immediate repentance, the freeness of evangelical offers, and the natural ability of men to accept them, and the consistency of all these with the purposes of God, the election of the heirs of life, and the grace of God in their regeneration, which he presented with a clearness and a force that were new. There was also a simplicity, a vividness and an affection in his manner, which gave the truth access to the mind. The careless were obliged to hear, and the young and the ignorant could understand. What number of conversions took place under his preaching I cannot say; but the spirit of religious inquiry silently increased, and under the labors of Rev. Mr. Washburn, who was installed as pastor of the church in 1795, the influences of grace came down "as the rain upon the tender herb, and as the showers upon the grass." The work was noiseless, and, in the common intercourse of life, an ordinary observer would scarcely perceive it; but for a whole year it was apparent in the prayerfulness, union and fidelity of the church, in the solemnity of religious assemblies, and in the conversion of sinners. Fifty-five, as fruits of the revival, were admitted to the communion of the church, in the course of that year, and the succeeding one; only two of whom have since given us any reason to distrust their sincerity.

In the year 1799, there was a revival in at least fifty adjoining congregations in this State; the character of which, in them all, was remarkably similar, and, I think I may say, remarkably happy. In some of these congregations, it commenced in the fall of 1798. In this town it began in February 1799, and first appeared in the solicitude of Christians for the restored presence of God. Hearing of the goings of their King around them, humbled with the sense of their backsliding, and anxious, though not disheartened, in view of forbidding circumstances in the state of the people, a number of them, after mutual consultation, solemnly agreed to devote themselves to renewed prayerfulness and diligence, casting themselves on the sovereign will of God. On the sabbath after their conference, the pastor addressed the congregation on the subject of a revival, and appointed public lectures to be attended, on the next day and evening, at the meeting-house. At the lectures two neighboring ministers were present, the sermons were followed by plain and pungent addresses—the assemblies were large, and the impression was general and solemn, so that from about that time, the commencement of a revival was manifest. Beside the customary services of the sabbath, a weekly lecture was delivered in the meeting-house; a meeting for the young was held on Monday evenings at the house of the pastor; and, as frequently as his other duties would allow, lectures were preached at the school-houses in the extreme neighborhoods; all of which were attended fully and eagerly. Persons of both sexes, and almost every age, and many from a distance of four and five miles, were seen, pressing through storms, and making their way over heavy roads, to hear the word of God; and the house of the pastor was almost daily the resort of the anxious. Beside these means, and such as naturally resulted from the feelings of the pious, in the ordinary intercourse of life, no others were employed. No meetings were publicly appointed for the anxious;—no invitation was given to them, or to new converts, in promiscuous assemblies, to relate their experience, or to address the people; no attempts of any kind were made to excite feeling or move sympathy, beside a plain exhibition and a close application of the truth of God. The work continued in progress seven or eight months. About one hundred persons were considered serious inquirers, of whom about seventy were reckoned subjects of deep conviction, and the same number, including a few who dated their conversion from the preceding revival, and were now established in hope, were gathered into the church. These were received, at different times, from August of the same year, till nearly the close of the year following. With a few exceptions, they have adorned their profession; many of them have been distinguished for their intelligence, stability, and substantial fruits of holiness.

After this revival, for more than twenty years, conversions were comparatively unfrequent. There were seasons of increased attention to religion, and with no long intervals there were instances of hopeful conversion; but the general tone of evangelical feeling gradually declined, and the whole number added to the church, both by letter and by original profession, but little exceeded two hundred, or about ten in a year—a number not equal to that of removals from the church, nor half the number of deaths in the parish. God, at the same time, rebuked our hardness of heart, by terrible dispensations; commissioning a fatal epidemic to enter our houses, and people our grave-yards. Scarcely a family was exempt; and yet our families were generally prayerless, and our hearts impenitent. I do not know of more than a single individual, who has ever professed to have come to repentance by means of the awful visitation. Our condition was the more affecting, because the showers of mercy had refreshed most of the congregations around us, and some of them repeatedly, while we remained, as the place on which there was, in the comparison, no rain. At the close of this period, the whole number in the church was about two hundred; the greater part of these lived in the remoter neighborhoods; and there were but few among them in younger life, and but few males of any age.

The year 1821 was eminently, in Connecticut, a year of revivals. Between eighty and a hundred congregations were signally blessed. From the commencement of the year, a new state of feeling began to appear in this town. On the first sabbath in February, I stated to the assembly the tokens of the gracious presence of God in several places of the vicinity, and urged the duties peculiarly incumbent on us at such a season. This I had often done before, but not with the same effect. Professors of religion now began evidently to awake. They had an anxiety for themselves and for the people, that would allow them no rest. In their communications with each other and with the world, they were led spontaneously to confess their unfaithfulness, and a few without the church, about the same time, were pungently convicted. In this state of things, Rev. Mr. Nettleton made us his first visit. His preaching on the evening of a Lord's day, in this month, from Acts ii. 37, was set home by the power of the Spirit upon the hearts of many; and his discourse on the Wednesday evening following, from Genesis vi. 3, was blessed to the conviction of a still greater number. As many as fifty persons, it was afterwards ascertained, dated their first decided purpose of immediately seeking their salvation from that evening; and it is worthy of remark, that the same sermon was preached on the following week to two other large and solemn assemblies, in adjoining parishes, with no special effect that could afterwards be traced. The fact probably was, that here it convinced numbers that the Spirit was already striving with them, and that then was their day. " A word spoken ·in due season, how good is it ?" At a meeting of the anxious on the evening of February 26, there were present about a hundred and seventy. Here were persons of almost every age and class— some who, a few weeks before, had put the subject of serious piety at scornful distance, and others who had drowned every thought of religion in giddy mirth, now bending their knees together in supplication, or waiting in silent reflection, for a minister of the Gospel to pass along, and tell them, individually, what they must do. Twelve were found to have lately become peaceful in hope, and a great number to be powerfully convicted of sin. From this time, so rapid was the progress of the work, that at the next simi- lar meeting, March 12th, there were present a hundred and eighty, (the room would hold no more,) of whom fifty supposed that, since the commencement of the revival, they had become recon- ciled to God; and, a week afterwards, I had the names of more than ninety, who indulged the same persuasion concerning them- selves.

The state of feeling which, at this time, pervaded the town, was interesting beyond description. There was no commotion; but a stillness, in our very streets; a serenity in the aspect of the pious; and a solemnity apparent in almost all, which forcibly impressed us with the conviction, that, in very deed, *God was in this place.* Public meetings, however, were not very frequent. They were so appointed, as to afford the opportunity for the same individuals to hear preaching twice a week, beside on the sabbath. Occa- sionally there were also meetings of an hour in the morning or at noon, at private dwellings, at which the serious in the neighbor- hood were convened, on short notice, for prayer and conference. The members of the church also met weekly, in convenient sec- tions, for prayer, and commonly on the evenings selected for the meetings of the anxious. From these various meetings, the peo- ple were accustomed to retire directly, and with little communica- tion together, to their respective homes. They were disposed to be much alone, and were spontaneously led to take the word of God for their guide. The Bible was preferred to all other books, and was searched daily and with eager inquiry.

Mr. Nettleton continued with us, except during a few short in- tervals, till about the middle of April. To his labors, so far as human instrumentality was directly concerned, the progress of the revival must chiefly be ascribed. The topics on which he principally dwelt, were the unchangeable obligations of the divine law, the deceitful and entirely depraved character of the natural heart, the free and indiscriminate offers of the gospel; the reasonableness and necessity of immediate repentance; the variety of those refuges and excuses to which awakened sinners are accustomed to resort; and the manner, guilt and danger of slighting, resisting and opposing the operations of the Holy Spirit. His addresses were not formal discussions, first of one and then of another of these subjects, but a free declaration of the truth of God concerning them all, just as they lie in the course of spiritual experience, and would best subserve the particular end which he was laboring at the time to gain. They were too plain to be misunderstood, too fervent to be unheeded, and too searching and convincing to be treated with indifference.

It was a favorable circumstance that among the first subjects of the work, there was a large proportion of the more wealthy and intelligent class. A considerable number of youths, belonging chiefly to this class, had just finished a course of biblical instruction, for which I had met them weekly for more than a year. These, with scarcely an exception, at the very commencement of the revival, embraced the gospel which they had learned; and by their experience of its power, commended it to the families where they belonged. Within about three months, I suppose there were two hundred and fifty members of the congregation, who supposed that they had passed from death unto life. On the first sabbath in June, a hundred and fourteen were added to the church; and at subsequent periods, a hundred and twenty besides. Of these a few have since been rejected, and others have declined from their first love. But I have not perceived that a greater proportion of hopeful conversions in this revival, than in others, previous or subsequent to it, have proved unsound. Many have died, and many have removed from our immediate connexion, but those who remain, now constitute the chief strength of the church.

In the winter of 1823, there was a revival in two contiguous school districts of this town. Insulated in their situation, they alone shared in the blessing, except a few individuals who attended the meetings there. It commenced in the revived piety of a few members of the church, whom God honored as instruments of his grace to others. Generally, when a revival has occurred among us, God has prepared some of his servants for the work, and their reward has been a permanent increase of their piety and spiritual enjoyment. By this revival, ten were joined to the church in the summer following.

In the summer of 1826, three young females of this congregation, then residing in Hartford, were made partakers of a gracious effusion in the school of which they were members. The first information of this was communicated to some of their companions in the academy in this town, with an earnest persuasion immediately to seek their salvation, and on the evening of the same day, their parents were assembled for prayer, and exhorted to be faithful to them. In these measures the teachers of the academy took a ready part, and immediately a revival commenced, which continued till the end of the term; and in which almost the whole school received deep impressions of divine truth. Exclusively of a number belonging to other congregations, who were hopefully converted, and including a few youths, who, though not at that time members of the school, shared in the blessing, twenty-five, in consequence, were admitted to the church, in the spring and summer of the following year. These were chiefly females from twelve to sixteen years old. It was on account of their tender age that their admission to the church was so long delayed. Some, in the mean time, declined a public profession of their faith; but of those who joined in that profession, no one has given serious occasion of distrusting the sincerity of it.

In the fall of 1828, a revival which had commenced in a neighboring congregation, extended to the eastern district of this town, and continued there with signal power through the winter, and a number of individuals in other parts of the town also were converted. There, religious meetings were more frequent, and the excitement was stronger, than in any other revival in which I have been personally concerned. As fruits of it thirty-seven were added to the church. Several others came to the enjoyment of hope, some of whom have appeared to be constant followers of Christ, while the goodness of others has been as the morning cloud.

Early in the last year, and more immediately in consequence of a surprising instance of conversion in the neighborhood, a number

APPENDIX.75

of the members of the church were stirred up to a new spirit of repentance and prayer, which was gradually extended to others in almost all parts of the town. In the month of April we had a protracted meeting of four days. The assemblies were full, and impressions of the truth seemed to be extensively felt; and on the last day thirty or forty persons came to an avowed purpose of earnestly attending to the concerns of their salvation. Yet the impression on the minds of the people at large was not such as long remained, amidst the cares of the opening spring. A number, however, will forever remember the grace of God which crowned the solemnity. We have since admitted forty to the communion of the church, about two-thirds of whom date their conversion from the revival last spring.

It thus appears that, by these gracious visitations, during a period of thirty-seven years, four hundred and sixty persons have been added to this church. Within the same period, the whole number added beside, only a little exceeds three hundred, and of these more than one hundred have come from other churches. Of the other two hundred, how many have dated their conversion from seasons of revival, it is impossible for me to say; but that a very large proportion of them, have either reckoned their conversion from these seasons, or then received their first permanent impressions of divine truth, I have no doubt. In these few short seasons, God has done far more for us, than during all the protracted months and years that have intervened; and, indeed, it has seemed to be chiefly in these that the church has so far renewed her strength, as to hold forth her testimony with any degree of success in the intervals. But for revivals, as it seems to us, the church would well nigh have ceased to exist, or have lost her distinctive character, in the spirit of the world.

No agency was ever more decisively manifested by its effects, than has been the agency of the Holy Spirit, in these revivals. The observer who should have watched them with the minutest care; who should have brought together the greatest number of facts; who should have become the best acquainted with the previous character, education and circumstances of the subjects of the work, and compared them with those of their connexions, who have had no similar experience, would have the strongest conviction. I cannot hesitate to say, that according to all correct reasoning on other subjects, no adequate cause can be assigned for these effects, but that which the Apostle Peter named, when, on the day of Pentecost, he said to the doubting multitude, " This Jesus being at the right hand of God exalted, and having received of the Father the promise of the Holy Ghost, hath shed forth that which ye do see and hear." Still, in the moral, as in the natural world, God performs his work by wisely appointed means. Among these means, not the least important has been found the union of Christians, in distinctly and obediently seeking the blessing, confiding in the promises of God. Our want of this, I have been led to consider a principal reason why the partial revivals which we have had, have not been more extensive. Individual Christians there have been, who have come up to the help of the Lord ; but often we have not had that common sympathy—that coming together to the work, which ought always, and more especially at such seasons, to characterize a church. Meetings appointed especially for persons in an anxious state have also been found important, not merely on account of the opportunity which they afford for appropriate instruction, but as means of assisting the struggling and wavering mind, by a consideration of the question concerning an attendance on them.

That much depends on the character of preaching in revivals, cannot be doubted ; and in this perhaps nothing is more important than a scriptural and skilful application of the doctrines of dependence on the one hand, and of obligation on the other. I have sometimes painfully apprehended, that but for my own indiscretion in this respect, our experience during the twenty tedious years that followed the revival in 1799, more than two-thirds of which were subsequent to my ordination, might have been different. Those doctrines which exhibit God as the sovereign cause,—decrees, election, &c., had, for a series of years, been leading topics of preaching in this town ; and by means of them, many self-dependent hopes had been destroyed, many hearts of enmity against God unveiled, and many souls converted and saved. But many also remained unconverted ; and the time at length arrived, when this kind of preaching had produced its full effect upon them. They either would not listen to it, or they made it a pretext for abandoning all serious attention to their salvation. Now, Dear Sir, never for a moment have I doubted the importance of an undisguised declaration of the whole counsel of God, and particularly of those doctrines which exhibit the dependence of fallen man on the sovereign grace of God; but if experience and observation have taught me any thing, it is, that there is a way of discussing these subjects most logically in the pulpit, which does little good; that there are theories sometimes connected with them, which are productive of great evil; and that even when preached as they lie in the sacred volume, if the hearers are not also taught their relations to God, as accountable subjects of his government, and capable heirs of salvation, and if the obligations and encouragements which belong to these relations, are not carried home to their hearts, a a general recklessness as to the concerns of salvation may be expected to prevail. If they are not, in fact, made to feel that they are their own destroyers, that fallen, dependent and lost as they are, salvation is most freely and sincerely offered to them, and that if they perish, the blame must forever rest upon themselves; no wonder if hard thoughts of God, and a heartless, discouraged and obdurate spirit of self-justification be the general result. That preaching no doubt is the best, which is most conformed to the example of Him who was not disobedient unto the heavenly vision, but showed first to them at Damascus, and at Jerusalem, and throughout all the coasts of Judea, and then to the Gentiles, that men should repent and turn to God, and do works meet for repentance.

I am, Dear Sir, most affectionately,

Your fellow servant

In the gospel of Christ,

N. PORTER.

REV. W. B. SPRAGUE, D. D.

LETTER IX.*

FROM THE LATE REVEREND EDWARD PAYSON, D. D.

Pastor of a Congregational church in Portland, Maine.

Portland, May 29, 1821.

DEAR BROTHER,

I have just received the " Narrative, &c.,"† which you were so
kind as to send me, and for which I return you many thanks. It
was indeed highly acceptable, and I wish it was in my power to
write something which would be equally acceptable to you. But
I am just recovering from a long and severe illness, and am still
too feeble to make much use of a pen; and were I in usual health
I could write nothing which would be of any service to you. I
will, however, in compliance with your request, state a few facts
relative to my ministry.

I have been connected with this society about thirteen years.
We have had no general revival, but there has been some religious
attention during the whole period of my ministry. The smallest
number which has been added to the church in any one year, is
eighteen; the largest, eighty-four; annual average, about forty.
I established inquiring (or, as they are called in the Narrative,
anxious) meetings soon after I came here, and have continued
them without interruption, (except on account of ill health for a
few weeks,) unto the present time. We conduct them precisely
as they are conducted with you, and have found them exceedingly
useful. The number of inquirers has often been small, but we
have always had some, and the number has increased or diminished, as the church has been more or less engaged in prayer. We
have found no means so much blessed to keep religion alive in the
church as fasting and prayer. Ever since my settlement, the
church has set apart one day quarterly for this purpose. On
these occasions, our first great object is to obtain just views of our
sins. With this view, the several beings with whom we are

---

* This letter was obligingly furnished me by an esteemed clerical brother, to whom it was
addressed.

† Narrative of the extensive revival of religion which occurred about this time within the
limits of the Albany Presbytery.

connected are mentioned; the duties we owe to each are pointed out, and the inquiry, "how far have you performed these duties during the last three months," is pressed upon the consciences of all present. Every other means which we can devise to set our sins fully before us, and to excite deep repentance is also employed. Then, as the Jewish high priest was directed to lay his hand on the head of the scape goat, and confess over it all the iniquities of the children of Israel, so we attempt, in the exercise of faith, to bring all our sins to Christ, and confess them as at the foot of the cross, pleading that pardon may be granted and sealed to us afresh for his sake. We then proceed to a solemn renewal of our covenant with God, after which, in a number of prayers, we plead for all the blessings of the covenant. Days thus spent have been exceedingly profitable. But my weakness forbids me to say more. Indeed, I have written thus far rather to shew my readiness to comply with your request, than with a hope that any thing which I can write will be profitable. I rejoice in God's goodness to you, and should my life be spared shall be glad to hear from you often.

That God may continue to bless your labors, and make you far more faithful than I have been, is the prayer of

Your friend and brother,

EDWARD PAYSON.

LETTER X.

From the REVEREND ALEXANDER PROUDFIT, D. D.

Pastor of an Associate Reformed church in Salem, New-York.

Salem, April 4, 1832.

My Esteemed Friend,

I received your letter, and agreeably to your request, venture to communicate my views on the nature of revivals of religion—a subject which so deeply involves the peace and prosperity of the American churches.

This is the thirty-eighth year of my ministerial labors in Salem. We have uniformly been in the habit of dispensing the ordinance of the Supper four times in the year, and so far as I recollect, have never had a sacramental occasion without some accession to our numbers. But during this long period we have enjoyed, at different intervals, what would now be pronounced "a revival of religion." The refreshing influences of divine grace descended silently and softly upon the heritage of the Lord, like the showers of spring after the dreariness and barrenness of winter. A genial warmth appeared to pervade the whole church, to the joy of the generation of the righteous, and at the same time, multitudes were added to the Lord by an external profession of his name. One of these occasions occurred in the year 1796, when a very unusual influence apparently accompanied the outward dispensation of the word, sealing it upon the souls both of sinners and saints. A similar season occurred about six years afterwards; and another and still more memorable visitation of the Spirit was enjoyed in the year 1815. During all these seasons of enlargement to myself, and of spiritual joy to the children of adoption, under my immediate care, and of the "espousals of others to Jesus as their husband," no extra efforts were used; no brethren from other towns were called in to our aid, but the work advanced silently and regularly, promoted exclusively under the divine blessing by the ordinary administration of ordinances, private and public. Yet, during the whole course of my ministry, I have never been favored with seasons more delightful in their recollection; none the results of which I anticipate with more joy in that day when the final account of my stewardship will be required. Contemplated in a moral or spiritual light, the work on those occasions might be compared to that gradual yet perceptible reanimation, which pervades the vegetable world amidst the vernal showers, and the refreshing influences of the returning sun, when the face of nature is clothed with fresh verdure, and the trees which had stood barren, are adorned with blossoms and fruit. These might emphatically be called "times of refreshing from the presence of the Lord;" and yet I know of no particular cause, except on the last occasion, the revival of the Lord's work appeared to come as an answer to extraordinary importunity in prayer. Few churches during this period, perhaps, have been more honored for raising up young men to adorn the ministerial office;—men full of the "Holy Ghost and of faith," who now appear as "burning and shining lights" in various parts of our country. On one occasion in the autumn of 1815, six youths took their seats together at the sacramental table, who are now exercising the ministry of reconciliation, and some of them with more than ordinary success. These facts I feel constrained particularly to notice, for the purpose of correcting that novel and prevailing opinion, that religion cannot flourish without some special and unusual effort.

In the year 1824, a revival of a different character from those I have already mentioned, appeared. Several persons residing in different parts of our town, were suddenly and almost simultaneously struck with deep convictions of sin. This arrested the attention of the friends of religion; meetings for prayer and conference were held almost every day in the week, and generally crowded to overflowing. These meetings were usually attended by the Rev. Mr. Tomb or myself, with private members of the church, who assisted in the religious services: ministers and private Christians from other towns were called in, and afforded their aid. So far as I recollect, there was rarely any instance of disorder, although I have seen multitudes melted in tears, and during the year great numbers were added to the fellowship of the two churches.

In May 1831, during my absence, a protracted meeting, as it is generally termed, was held in Mr. Tomb's society, which was attended by a variety of ministers from different parts of the country. A great excitement was produced in almost every part of the town, which has resulted in the addition of a large number to our churches.

With respect to the fruits of these revivals, on which you desire information, I have almost uniformly remarked that where the subjects had been early and competently instructed, the impressions have been permanent: those of this character who assumed the profession of religion have been enabled to persevere; but in other instances the excitement has too often been transient as " the morning cloud and the early dew :" the latter class, like those in the parable of the sower, I have frequently seen receive the word with joy, but not having root in themselves, endured for a time, and afterwards returned to the world. From these facts, founded on long observation, I have been particularly impressed with the importance of early instruction. I feel more strongly attached to *the good old way* trodden by the venerable fathers of the Reformation in Scotland, and Holland, and England, and afterwards by our Pilgrim fathers, who brought the " light of immortality and life" to our western wilderness. With them the instruction of youth in the elementary doctrines of religion, by catechising and family visitation, constituted an important part of ministerial labor. It cannot be uninteresting to your readers, nor foreign from the nature of your publication, to incorporate the sentiments of the revered Flavel, in a sermon which he preached to the Puritans after their restoration in 1688. " Prudence," he remarks, " will direct us to lay a good foundation among our people by catechising, and instructing them in the principles of Christianity, without which we labor in vain. Unless we have a knowing people, we are not like to have a gracious people. All our excellent sermons will be dashed on the rock of their ignorance. You can never fall on a better way for securing success to your labors, than the fruitful way of catechising. What age of the church has produced more lively and steadfast professors than the first ages ; and then this duty most eminently flourished in the church. Clemens, Optatus, Austin, Ambrose and Basil, were catechists." Such were the sentiments of this distinguished servant of Christ, delivered on a most memorable occasion, and before an assembly of divines little inferior to any that ever adorned our world. With these observations of Flavel in *Old*, let us compare those of Doctor Mather, a character equally eminent in *New*, England—" That catechising is an ordinance of God few will doubt, when they consider that apostles thus laid the foundation of religion by feeding babes with milk, teaching them in this manner the first principles of the oracles of God. This hath therefore been a constant practice in the church, and in the first ages of Christianity they had a particular person appropriated to this exercise. All well governed churches have still maintained this practice, knowing the necessity of it for youth, to inform them in the principles of that religion into which they were baptized, and for the establishment of the more aged." With these sentiments of the Puritans in the *old* and *new* world, correspond the following remarks of the Presbyterians in Scotland, as expressed in a preface to the Shorter Catechism : " It has been acknowledged in all ages that the catechetical way of instruction is the most speedy and successful method of conveying the knowledge of divine things: the truths of God are thus made level to the weakest capacity, being separately proposed with plain and distinct answers to each."

We cannot appreciate too highly the establishment of sabbath schools and bible classes. They may be considered as constituting some of the brightest features of our distinguished age, and forming a new era in the religious world. Through the instrumentality of the former, many have been raised from the lowest degradation, mental and moral, who are now ornaments to the church ; and by means of the latter the seed has been sown in ten thousand youthful hearts, which will spring up to life eternal : yet in connexion with these I wish to see revived that system of catechetical instruction, which prevailed so extensively among your ancestors in England, and mine in Scotland. I wish to see means every where in operation which shall secure to the juvenile mind *profound* instruction in the doctrines of religion. No period since the Apostolic has been adorned with a generation of professors more intelligent and stedfast, than during the administrations of Owen, and Flavel, and Baxter, and Boston, and the Erskines; and at that time, catechising in the week was considered scarcely less essential to the " fulfilment of the ministry," than preaching on the sabbath.

A comparison of those who composed the ranks of the spiritual soldiery in their day, with those who compose them in the present, would certainly, in many respects, be much to our disadvantage. Nevertheless, there are many of our modern converts doubting even the piety of some of those illustrious men, although during their lives they shed around them the lustre of every Christian grace, and died in the triumphs of faith, and some of them martyrs to the truth. With mingled emotions of surprise and sorrow, I have heard some in the ministry who claim to be distinguished for zeal and spirituality, affecting to represent as lifeless and even graceless, many of the clergy of that age, who occupied their talents in the illustration of divine truth, and " preached the gospel with the Holy Ghost sent down from Heaven," and clad in the panoply of God, drove the enemy from the field. I do not pretend that these men were perfect, or that the progress of things in coming ages might not require that with their studious habits there should be joined an increased degree of active enterprize ; but I do say that if those who regard them so lightly would consent to stand up with them in a comparison as it respects solid attainments in literature and theology, and holy heroism in their Master's cause, it would be like bringing the shrub beside the cedar, or the infant beside the full grown man.

With respect to *extra* or *protracted* meetings, which are becoming so common in our country, I entertain no doubt that they have been blessed for the conversion of souls to the Saviour. Many, I believe, are sealed on these occasions to the day of redemption, and as gems will adorn forever the Mediatorial crown of our Master; yet I think, considering the extent to which they are now multiplied, there are connected with them serious and obvious disadvantages. They serve too often to derange the regular order of the church ; to cherish a gossipping disposition on the part of professors, and render them dissatisfied with the ordinances of grace, unless dispensed in an extraordinary manner. They interfere with those duties which ministers owe to their immediate charge ; they leave them little time for digesting their discourses in private, that they may afterwards give to every man a portion of meat in due season ;—little leisure for the improvement of their ministerial gifts, by reading and reflection, and conversation; and whatever diverts the attention of the spiritual steward from a course of study, although it may promise immediate advantage, must, in the issue, militate essentially against the interests of religion. There is no injunction of the great Apostle more imperative than the following :—" Give attendance to reading; neglect not the gift that is in thee; give thyself wholly to them, that thy profiting may appear unto all." Without suitable preparation in the week, no uninspired man ever did, or can preach the gospel for any considerable time to the same people, either with acceptance or success; and he cannot make this preparation without suitable opportunity. Did he possess the intellectual resources of an angel, they must be exhausted by continual expenditure, unless they are replenished by painful and laborious application to study. The present, perhaps, more than almost any preceding age, calls for active exertion on the part of the clergy. Our Tract, and Missionary, and Bible and other kindred societies are probably the means by which the gospel is universally to be diffused, and the nations converted to the Saviour; and in the support of these and every other benevolent enterprize, the ministers of religion ought always to appear prominent. It is, however, incumbent upon us to persevere, as much as possible, in habits of study, and thus improve those spiritual gifts which are requisite for the profitable discharge of our ministry.

But the great, shall I say the fatal error in the management of revivals, is the hasty admission of the subjects to the privileges of the church. Convictions, we have reason to apprehend, are often mistaken for conversion ;—a momentary impulse for " the renewing of the Holy Ghost," without which no man can see the Lord. Under the influence of this excitement, application is made for the seals of the covenant; and when an unregenerate man obtains a name in the visible church, his condition may be considered as almost desperate : he feels entrenched in his profession, and without a moral miracle, is invulnerable : there is more hope of reaching with the arrow of conviction, the conscience of the " harlot or the publican," than the conscience of the formal professor. There is an analogy in all the works of Jehovah, and the *incorruptible* seed, like the *natural*, requires time to vegetate in the soil, before it can be expected to spring up, and present " the blade and the ear."

Having taken this deliberate survey of the subject presented for consideration, and noted some points of difference between the past and the present, I am constrained to express my conviction, that however much we have to be grateful for in the present state of the church, there is much that needs to be corrected; and that even *pure* revivals of religion would be far more prevalent, if we were willing, in some respects at least, to walk more closely in the footsteps of our revered fathers. Let the true doctrines of the gospel be held up with great prominence; and let the minds of the young, by catechetical instruction and private visitation, be imbued with the knowledge of God's word; and our spiritual heritage, under the dews of divine grace, would appear " fair as Eden," and the trees of righteousness would present in due season their fragrant blossoms and ripening fruits. But when I see the wanton, visionary speculations indulged by some, to the neglect of a religion founded on the Bible, and the open dereliction and even renunciation of their standards by others, who had solemnly subscribed and sworn to defend them; when I see these appalling facts, I cannot help trembling for the Ark. May the God of our fathers disappoint our fears, and purify our American Zion, and fill the earth with his glory.

Yours in the Saviour's love,

ALEXANDER PROUDFIT.

Rev. W. B. Sprague, D. D.

LETTER XI.

FROM THE REVEREND CHARLES P. McILVAINE,

Rector of St. Anne's church, Brooklyn, New-York.

Brooklyn, April 6, 1832.

REVEREND AND DEAR SIR,

I was much pleased to hear of your intention to publish on the subject of the Revivals of religion in this country; believing that there is not another on which a well digested, discreet, intelligent and spiritually-minded work is, at this period, so much needed. We need it at home—it is earnestly desired abroad. When I was in London, about eighteen months since, among sundry earnest inquiries, as well from ministers of the established church, as those of dissenting denominations, requesting direction as to some publication to inform them accurately in respect to the nature, means and fruits of revivals of religion among us; I recollect a conversation with the Rev. Josiah Pratt, (well known as author of the Memoir, and editor of the works of the excellent Cecil,) in which, after expressing a strong desire that Christians in England should know more on this subject, he twice, and with much solemnity of manner, enjoined it upon me that I should endeavor to prepare a work in regard to it, and send it to England for publication. I rejoice that the undertaking has fallen into hands so much more qualified, in every sense, to do it justice. I pray, and doubtless you have made it a matter of much prayer, that all you write may be according to the mind of Christ, and under the sanctification of the Holy Spirit, so as to be " profitable for doctrine, reproof, correction and instruction in righteousness."

I understand you as requesting of me a brief expression of such hints in relation to revivals, as my experience in them may have suggested, and my time will permit me to write. This I will attempt most cheerfully ; but must perform it with the strictest confinement of my pen to the mere giving of *hints*.

My experience of revivals has not been so extensive as that of many others ; but it has been, more than that of many others, among *young men of education and force of character*. It has been my lot to witness the power of the Spirit in circumstances peculiarly unpropitious; overcoming obstacles of the most formidable kind, and effecting, in spite of them, conversions of a nature specially distinguished by the decision, force and consistency of Christian character which they have since exhibited. But I have not time for preliminaries.

As to what a revival of religion is, and what its great objects ought to be—I would suggest that the public mind (I mean of Christians,) is in danger of overlooking, or only slightly regarding one out of the two great constituents and blessings of a genuine revival. One of these is the *conversion of sinners.* But it is not the only object; though too much treated as if it were. The other is *the quickening of the people of God to a spirit and walk becoming the Gospel.* Where this is not sought and obtained, the revival is more than suspicious. But I fear that, where it is sought, it is sometimes desired much more as a necessary *means* to the accomplishment of the other, than as a most important end in itself, which alone is unspeakably precious, and must be productive of all good fruits. If the quickening of the souls of God's people to liveliness of life be regarded rather as a means to the bringing about of a resurrection among the dead in sins, than as a great end in itself; the consequence will be, as experience proves, that their increase of life will be confined very much to those efforts which bring them before the view, and into direct operation on the feelings of the impenitent, such as the leading and attending of public and other meetings for prayer and exhortation, instead of being, first and last, an improvement of their hearts in all the inward things of the Spirit of God, elevating, purifying, adorning, invigorating the whole Christian character.

As to the means of obtaining a revival of religion in a congregation—I need not say that the faithful, plain, direct preaching of the truth is *one* of these means. But is there not danger of putting reliance on this or that *mode* of saying things ; this or that selection of topics or management of an address, because in some places, or in the hands of some men they are supposed to have been very successful, when at best they may be peculiarly suitable only in peculiar cases, or when used by peculiar persons ? Is there not danger of our getting to rely on a Paul or Apollos, and supposing that a revival can hardly take place and flourish unless they, or some persons very much like them, in manner, are at the head of the effort? Would not such a reliance be altogether inconsistent with a simple dependence upon the sword of the Spirit, and the demonstration of the Spirit, as placed at the disposal of every minister of the word who will know nothing among men but Jesus Christ and him crucified? Do we not need to think and feel much more of *this truth*, that the power of preaching is not to be improved so much by seeking out new and more striking modes and expressions, as by combining our discourses with more prayer in their preparation, and more faith in the power of God while delivering them?

I need not urge that *combined and earnest prayer* is another of the means of obtaining a revival. But it is needful to urge that there is a tendency to make this too exclusively a matter of the prayer-*meeting*, and that in the prayer-meeting, there is a proneness to pray *an address to the people*, more than to God, seeking more to produce an effect than to obtain an answer. The chief power of prayer for a revival of the work of God must be sought where *effect* cannot tempt, and where genuine revivals always begin,—*in the closet.* Let people be *assembled* for prayer; but let the chief concert be the daily union of hearts, each in secret, wrestling with God.

But there is another important means of having religion revived. *Some legitimate, sober effort to create a general disposition to attend to the word,* is very important. One great reason why the word is not more blessed lies in the fact that it is so little heard— not only among those who do not assemble where it is preached, but those also, even professors of religion, who sit beneath its sound. We need something to open the ears of those who come to hear, and to congregate those who are too indifferent to come. Much depends on this. But here is where experience utters its most serious cautions. It is in the council of the Sons of God, upon such measures, that Satan puts on the dress of light, and too often gets himself appointed on "the committee of ways and means." There are means to be used, in awakening a disposition to come and see and hear, which truth and soberness, scripture and good sense fully warrant. These I doubt not you have discussed.

But how easily may zeal, having a little more excitement than discretion and conscience, overstep the bounds of sobriety and truth, and not only revive intemperance instead of piety, but bring back the old contrivances of "*pious frauds.*" I think there is hardly any matter connected with revivals that needs more guarding than this. Great scandal has been raised by indiscretion, and what I cannot call by any lighter name than *fraud* on the part of some seekers of a revival. The agency of the Holy Spirit as the beginning and ending has been almost or entirely set aside. A revival has been represented and sought for as an article of manufacture for which you have only to set the machinery and raise the steam of excitement, caring little with what fuel, and converts will be made to hand. Artifices to catch attention ; devices to entrap the careless; representations to create impression; an exaggerated style of preaching to produce alarm ; to shake suspicious hopes and raise a state of general excitement, no matter of what kind, so that it brings people to hear, have in some cases been put into requisition, over which truth, and reverence, and humility, and faith must weep, and which have done more to injure revivals in certain places, than all the direct opposition of coldness and unbelief. When the world and slumbering Christians see these things, it is not strange that they should speak against revivals. Blessed be God, these things are not characteristic of revivals of religion, but only of some minds associated with the name. In the great majority of what have been called by this name, they have not appeared, or have been only very partial exceptions to the general rule. But in proportion as a revival-spirit shall spread in the churches, will the danger of these mischiefs increase. The very excellence of the cause will be its exposure to the abuse of unbalanced zeal and to the devices of Satan. There was a great work in Samaria, under the preaching of Philip. Simon Magus was a spurious convert of that revival. He turned in with the heart of a sorcerer, under the face of a Christian, and wanted to help the work by imitating the wonders of the Apostles. But he thought the gift of God could be purchased with money. He wanted to *bewitch* the people, instead of enlightening them. He supposed the Apostles had some magic secret in communicating the Holy Ghost, which perhaps they might be induced to reveal, so as to enable him to go about and do great things as well as they. Is this character never seen among genuine revivals of the present day? I fear Satan still finds those who give themselves out to be *some great ones;* and who, passing by the great truth that it is the Spirit who is to convince of sin and of righteousness and of judgment, attempt the work of a revival as if there were a magic secret in certain modes and artifices, and expect to change stubborn hearts by bewitching weak heads. No. The Apostles had no device but that of plain truth, and strong faith, and humble boldness, and fervent love. Let us be content with these. Let it be written of us as of them—*" We believe, and therefore speak."* Our weapons will be " mighty through God," only in proportion as they are " *not carnal but spiritual.*" Let us get the ear of sinners by the zeal of truth and soberness, and then fill it with Jesus Christ and him crucified.

And now supposing a general revival is in progress, and much interest prevails in the community, and inquirers come in and some profess to have obtained the hope of faith—let me suggest that it is not sufficiently remembered that *a time of great blessing is also a time of great exposure.* When an individual Christian is on the mount, we think him specially in need of caution, lest he be lifted up above measure. Paul needed a thorn to keep him humble, after his abundant manifestations. Thus a church revived, and rejoicing, and full of zeal, must take especial heed, lest the sails be too much for the ballast, and while the hands are all ahead delighting their eyes with the power of her advance, the spirit of evil should get up behind and take the helm, and secretly substitute another needle than that of the truth as it is in Jesus.

A time of revival is necessarily to some extent, a time of excitement. But excitement is of two kinds. One is that of the soul receiving nourishment from the meat of the word, which quickens its affections, strengthens its desires after holiness, and promotes a healthy state of spiritual life. This is the genuine excitement of a revival of religion. But there is another resembling it very deceitfully in colour and temporary sensation, but differing from it very widely in permanent consequences. It is *the fever of the mind,* to which human nature is exceedingly prone. Some of it is probably unavoidable in revivals, because revivals have to do with a diseased nature ; as powerful medicines, while working together for the good of the body, produce a feverish excitement, not by their own fault, but the morbid condition of the patient. But how unwisely would a physician act, should he mistake the hectic of the fever for the glow of health, and endeavor to increase it because accompanied with warmth and apparent strength ! Delirium and prostration would ensue. This is precisely the mistake not unfrequently made by friends of revivals. It is extremely dangerous. They mistake disease for health. They seek excitement. It is well. The dead heart must be excited. But let them be cautious. There is an excitement which, like that of electricity upon a corpse, will open the eyes, but they will not see ; stir the heart, but it will not love ; throw the whole body into violent action, only to remain when the machinery is withdrawn, a more melancholy spectacle of death than before. Excitement that does not proceed from the influence of truth on the heart, and lead towards the obedience of truth in the life, is the fever of a diseased soul, and not the evidence of increasing life. To stimulate this is as much to hinder grace, as if you should attempt to make a dying man well, by filling him with alcohol. The fever may look and act exceedingly like healthy religion— but it will either mount at last to wild derangement, or pass off and leave the subjects more perfectly prostrate and helpless than ever. I conceive that clear conceptions of the nature and genuine means of real, spiritual excitement, as distinguished from every counterfeit, are much needed, in order that revivals may be protected against the weakness of the flesh, and the forgeries of Satan.

Now let me again suppose a revival in progress. In consequence of the ignorance, inexperience, sinfulness, indiscretion of the promiscuous mass of minds and hearts concerned in it, we must expect more or less of diseased excitement, though the work be full of holy fruits. The labor of the minister is to protect the good work, as much as possible, from abuses to which it is liable from this cause. Let me therefore suggest that a season of revival is one in which special care should be had in the *regular keeping up of all the rules of the church*. Old modes of doing things are apt to seem worn out, and decrepid, and dry, to minds under new excitement. A sudden flood in the river not unfrequently opens

new channels, but never without desolation. Let the springs of
the river of life be revived and swollen with the rains of heaven ;
but that the streams thereof may make glad the city of God, let
them be kept within the banks which the ordinances of the gospel
have established, and the wisdom of all ages has been content with.
Let the novelty consist in newness of life, in an unwonted spirit of
prayer, and faith, and love, rather than in new devices and novel
modes.

How far should meetings be multiplied during a revival?—This
question must be answered according to circumstances, but requires much wisdom. The appetite of excitement is for meetings.
The tendency of an animated minister is to feed it with meetings.
How far may he go? Not beyond his own strength in their vigi-
lant superintendence. He must have meetings enough to be able
to meet and feed the people with as much bread as they can profitably receive ; but the dangers to be guarded against are in the
idea that the love of meetings is religion ; that the chief element
and nutriment of religion in the heart is the influence of meetings ;
that the frequent renewal of their excitements may be substituted
for habitual watchfulness and diligence ; that secret devotion and
the study of the word are of comparatively little importance ; that
when circumstances require an abridgment of the number of the
meetings, the revival is done, a season of coldness *must* ensue, and
the people may be content to wait in sloth and exhaustion till the
next season of the outpouring of the Spirit. Whoever has seen
much of man and of revivals, must know that on these points,
much wisdom and much firmness are required.

Who shall officiate in the meetings?—Some seem to imagine
that any body with a warm heart will do to speak and pray in public during a season of revival. On the contrary, it is just the time
when the work of exhortation and leading in meetings for prayer
should be confined to the steadiest heads. A raw hand may steer
the ship with a gentle, fair breeze, in open sea ; but when the
wind is high, and the channel narrow, and false lights abound, and
new lights are ever appearing, let experience alone be entrusted
with the helm. Many of the abuses of revivals have arisen from
a multiplication of meetings beyond the ability of the minister and
his most experienced assistants to superintend them ; so as to call

up persons having more zeal than knowledge to the lead, sometimes to the misguiding of the young, and the indiscreet offending
of many.

How should inquirers be treated?—With light as well as heat;
with instruction as to the way; its cost; its temptations, &c., as
well as exhortation to walk therein.   Bunyan put the wicket gate
too far off, and made a Slough of Despond too directly in the road.
Many do worse, saying nothing of any difficulties to be avoided,
and leaving out the entire dependence of the sinner on the Spirit
of God to be able to reach the straight gate.

Let care be used *as to who shall be put to the work of conversing
with inquirers.*   Every Christian is not fit for this work in a time
of excitement.   Especially new converts are not fit.   They have
not learned sufficiently to separate the wheat from the chaff.
They often confound feelings with affections; fears with desires;
and require an experience like their own, rather than like the rule
of the word.   They are apt to " compare themselves among themselves," and encourage too soon, or expect too much; so that
sometimes they break the bruised reed and quench the smoking
flax.

Inquiry meetings have, I believe, been much perverted from
their original object.   The great use of an inquiry meeting is to
enable the minister to converse with those whom it would be better to see more privately, but who are too numerous to allow his
seeing all of them often enough at their separate houses.   It
should be strictly an opportunity for him to inquire of them, and
they of him.   But this important object is often nullified, and the
meeting rendered an entire misnomer, in consequence of *numbers.*
It is so large that to make any real inquiry into each case is impossible, unless many agents are employed, and then a painful and
deleterious publicity is given to the inquiry and the answer.   An
inquiry meeting should be a retired meeting, involving as little
exposure to others beside the conductor, and as little profession of
religion as the object may allow; if the number desiring to attend
be greater than can be profitably and individually conversed with,
there should be more meetings than one.   The object should be
to get as much as possible of the individuality of a quiet conference from house to house, and yet effect an important saving of

time and strength. I much fear that instead of this, there have been meetings under this name, in which *inquiry* was a very secondary matter on the part of the conductors, and the fanning of excitement and the inducing of those who felt a little, to *commit themselves*, in other words, to make some *profession*, were the engrossing objects.

I have dreaded much from perceiving an inordinate disposition in some friends of revivals to get inquirers to " *entertain a hope*," as if hope were always the offspring of a living faith. New minds very naturally acquire the idea that if they can only get comfort they shall do well. They thirst for hope more than holiness. The work seems done when consolation begins. By and by when tribulation ariseth, they are offended. The phraseology of revivals needs reform. The tendency of much of it at present is to set the sinner to seeking hope and joy rather than faith and love. Deliberation with hearts which by nature are " deceitful above all things," is of great moment at all times, and especially in a season when, however good the work, Satan finds so many means of producing hurry, and confusion, and presumptuous hope.

Is there not much evil to be apprehended from the plan of having a meeting restricted to those " *who have obtained a hope*"—another for inquirers merely, so that as soon as one of the latter expresses a hope that he has found peace, he is passed into the company of the former, and is thenceforth numbered with those who profess to be in Christ ? Does not the commonest acquaintance with human nature ; the well known infirmity of the infant state of a new convert, and all experience warn us that by such measures we are tempting the weakness of incipient seriousness to seek a hope for other motives, and cherish it on other grounds, than those of the Spirit of God? The inquiry meeting is very naturally regarded as the lowest degree—the other a second and more honorable. *A hope* will elevate the candidate from the noviitiate to the grade of the initiated. Vanity and love of distinction are not dead in the hearts of inquirers. How insidiously and easily may they animate the candidate to think well of his evidences and blind his eyes to their suspicious aspects, that he may be said to entertain a hope, and may be introduced among those who are rejoiced over as converts rejoicing in Christ. That hope is often helped exceedingly by this address to human weakness, there is great reason to fear. But let it be considered that when an inquirer is thus passed into the company of those who profess a hope of salvation; or when he is induced to stand up in a more promiscuous assembly, as having found peace through faith, it is on his part a *public profession of religion;* those who encourage him to do so are regarded as having *set their seal to his evidences and pronounced them good.* It is nothing to say that he has not yet approached the Lord's supper. There is more than one way of making a public profession of religion. Christians and the world consider the individual described as having openly called himself a Christian. But is it not too soon for such a profession? Has he had sufficient time; has he obtained sufficient knowledge to search and try his heart? Is not the consideration that he is regarded as having publicly professed a hope, a dangerous motive *to go on in hope* without that cautious self-examination which the newness of his spiritual state demands? Is it not thus that too many, after having crossed the line of profession, and feeling themselves committed to the entertaining of hope, continue crying *peace, peace,* after every thing but the form of godliness, and the melancholy features of spiritual pride, has passed away? But do we not bring the cause of religion and the character of revivals into great disrepute by such measures? When a number of newly awakened persons rise up in a public assembly, or appear in a special meeting as professing a hope of being in Christ, they are noted as professors of religion by the world. We can neither correct the view taken by worldly people of this public appearance, nor find fault with it. But can it be expected that some of these, so new, so untried, will not fall back? Are we prepared to set them out before the world as converts to whose stedfastness we challenge the attention of the ungodly? On the contrary, we expect that some, by and by, will be offended and go back, before they shall have come to a meetness for the supper of the Lord. But when this takes place, it is necessarily regarded as the backsliding, not of inquirers—not of persons merely under serious impressions; (we cannot expect the world to distinguish carefully between a profession of serious concern about religion and of religion itself) but as the backsliding of persons who have once called themselves

Christians, and on whom the judgment of experienced Christians did once set the seal of deliberate approbation. Thus " it is impossible but that offences come." *But let us take heed by whom or how they come.* Some publicity to the fact that an inquirer has been enabled to hope in Christ is unavoidable; when judiciously managed, it is useful; but the *individual* should not be the instrument of making his spiritual state a matter of publicity, and should have his mind as free as possible from the idea that he is in any sense before the community, until he has had time to get somewhat beyond the extreme delicacy of a babe in Christ. Religion, in a sinner's heart, is like a tropical plant amidst the snows of Siberia. Great protection and tenderness, and a cautious attention to cherishing temperature are of the last importance, till it is acclimated. It may remain, but not grow. It may shoot out a sudden growth of half formed leaves, while dying at the root.

These remarks apply with more force to the dangerous practice (I hope very limited in extent) of encouraging those who profess conversion, to come forward, almost immediately, to the table of the Lord. The ambition of numbering the people; the desire of an exciting spectacle may adopt this plan. Shallow views of religion and of human nature may approve of it. Satan will subscribe to its wisdom in the signature of an angel of light. The winnowing of the last day will show that a large portion of such ingatherings was fit only to be cast into the fire, to be burned.

I have already written so much more than I anticipated, when I began, that I have no room to dwell upon two points of great interest in themselves, and rendered specially so by the present times. One is *the measure of prominence and work that may safely and usefully be given to new converts.* The other is *the necessity of seeing to them vigilantly, " reproving, rebuking, exhorting them,"* while as yet they are new, inexperienced and self-ignorant. As to the first, wisdom is greatly needed. We ought not to take a green sapling and set it up for a pillar in the church. The weight would bend it down and make its branches grow into the earth. We ought not to take a new recruit, untried, undisciplined, however zealous and brave, and set him to drill a company, or lead the advance, when skill and coolness, as well as enthusiasm and courage, are the order of the day. By such measures we may engender much boldness with great indiscretion, and show an undaunted front with a flank exposed to all the fiery darts of the wicked. How to give the new convert enough exercise for his own health and growth without taking him too much from himself, laying too much upon his weakness and exposing him too much to the snares of vanity, spiritual pride and censoriousness, is a question which I hope your book will well determine.

I must now conclude. The dangers and cautions I have suggested, arise out of the power and eminent value of the spirit of genuine revivals. I owe too much of what I hope for as a Christian, and what I have been blessed with as a Minister of the Gospel, not to think most highly of the eminent importance of promoting this spirit, and consequently of guarding it against all abuses. Whatever I possess of religion began in a revival. The most precious, stedfast and vigorous fruits of my ministry have been the fruits of revivals. I believe that the spirit of revivals, in the true sense, was the simple spirit of the religion of Apostolic times, and will be, more and more, the characteristic of these times, as the day of the Lord draws near. May the Lord bless us with it more abundantly and purely, and use your work eminently in its promotion.

I remain, very truly and affectionately,

Yours, &c.,

CHARLES P. McILVAINE

REV. W. B. SPRAGUE, D. D.

LETTER XII.

FROM THE REVEREND WILLIAM NEILL, D. D.

Late President of Dickinson college, Carlisle, Pennsylvania.

Germantown, April 6, 1832.

MY DEAR SIR,

I am pleased to find that you are about to publish a course of lectures on Revivals of religion. The subject, always interesting to Christians, has become peculiarly so, of late, by reason of the frequency and power of those precious refreshings from the Lord ; and, also, because of the extraordinary means employed, in some instances, to promote and perpetuate them. The views of some of the clerical brethren, of several denominations, which you are endeavoring to collect, may form a useful appendix to your work. In contributing an expression of good will towards this latter object, my words shall be few ; and it is my prayer, that they may be well ordered, and in keeping with the law and the testimony.

A revival of true religion is a blessing of no ordinary import ; and, if every good and perfect gift cometh down from the Father of lights, then, clearly, a genuine revival is from the same divine source. "Paul plants and Apollos waters ; but God gives the increase." "Sanctify them through thy truth ; thy word is truth," saith the Redeemer. From these two passages of Holy Writ, not to mention others, we may say—nay, I must believe we are bound to acknowledge, that, of every true revival, God is the efficient cause ; and his revealed will, with his instituted ordinances, the chosen instruments. I know, indeed, that men are under obligation immediately to repent and turn to God ; and I also know, that when God works in the soul, disposing it to will and to do his good pleasure, he calls its faculties into vigorous action ; so that the divine influence, in no respect, infringes man's moral agency. To attend to the truth—to believe the gospel—to repent after a godly sort— to love God, and obey his commands, and lay hold on eternal life, are duties incumbent on every man ; and, when performed, are acts or exercises of his own mind : but it is the Spirit of God, in view of the word of precept and promise, that moves and enables him to put forth these mental efforts, in a spiritual and acceptable manner.

When I say that the word and instituted ordinances of the gospel, are the instruments designed of God to be used in producing and promoting revivals, I mean to be understood as disapproving of all means and measures, intended to advance the cause of religion, which are not sanctioned by the example of Christ and the Apostles, or which are not warranted by the discipline of God's house, as laid down in his Holy Bible. In judging thus, I do not impugn the motives, or undervalue the zeal and labors of those brethren in the ministry, who employ expedients in their efforts to bring sinners to Christ, which I deem unwarrantable. When we are reminded of the effects produced in connexion with the use of some such means, as are alluded to above, the question arises— whether results equally good, and extensive, and permanent, would not have been experienced, without the use of any questionable means? The means of salvation which God has prescribed in his word, are the best; and it is a reflection on his wisdom and goodness, to suppose that they need any additions or modifications of ours. Human devices, however ingenious and well-meant, and however they may have the effect of producing strong excitement, for a time, will, in the long run, be found fraught with mischief to the truth; and to that decency and order which Christ has established in his kingdom.

Allow me, here, to mention a few particulars, connected with some of the revivals, of which we have read in the religious papers, that I cannot but regard as evils, or, at least, of evil tendency.

1. That style of preaching, which, while it aims to make the impenitent sinner feel his blame-worthiness, tends, indirectly, to cherish the idea that it is an easy thing to become a Christian, and that he can give his heart to God whenever he sees fit so to do, independently of a divine influence. Let him take up this idea, and he will feel easy, and be very apt to postpone repentance, till he shall have enjoyed the pleasures of sin for a season.

2. The use of anxious seats, and putting the people to the test of a public vote, under the influence of strong feeling. Have mi-

nisters a right to propose this measure? Is it not embarrassing to the humble? Does it not foster forwardness and self-confidence in those who have not yet learned what spirit they are of?

3. Public confession of sins, in the face of promiscuous assemblies. This practice, in my view, is based on a misinterpretation or wrong use of a scriptural precept—" Confess your faults one to another"—that is, in private, or in the presence of a few, select Christian friends. When done in public, it looks like aiming at effect; gives occasion of reproach to the enemies of religion, &c. We should avoid all appearance of evil.

4. Calling upon zealous but unauthorised persons to perform the appropriate duties of ordained ministers. This is calculated to bring the ministry into contempt, and to inflict upon the church a host of self-commissioned and unqualified teachers.

5. Hasty admissions to the communion, of very young persons, or of those who have given but little proof of their knowledge of the gospel, or of their having experienced a gracious change of heart. The good seed often falls on stony ground, where there is not much depth of earth. A reasonable time of probation seems expedient, if not demanded, by a proper regard for the persons admitted, and for the peace and purity of the church.

6. A neglect of ministers of the gospel, who are not considered thorough-going revival men. I honor an intelligent and zealous preacher, whose services God has honored, in promoting revivals; but I also hold in reputation the man, whose ministrations are serious, and of an evangelical strain, though they may never have been strongly marked, by what are commonly called revivals. There is a diversity of gifts, under the guidance and hallowing influence of the same Spirit. In some revivals, I fear, a minister, not distinguished *as a revival man, and an advocate of strong, decisive measures*, would hardly be invited to preach, lest he should come with an extinguisher in his doctrine or manner. In my humble judgment, these things ought not so to be.

How far the foregoing remarks will meet your views, Dear Brother, I know not. They have been made freely; but without any unkind or uncharitable feelings towards those who differ from me in opinion. They are submitted to your disposal; with my best wishes and earnest prayers, that your forth-coming work may prove a blessing to the cause of revivals, and be owned of God in advancing the kingdom and glory of our dear Redeemer.

Your fellow servant in the Gospel,

WILLIAM NEILL.

Rev. W. B. Sprague, D. D.

LETTER XIII.

From the REVEREND PHILIP MILLEDOLER, D. D.
President of Rutgers' college, New-Brunswick, New-Jersey.

New-Brunswick, April 3, 1832.

REVEREND AND DEAR SIR,

Your esteemed favor of March 12th has been duly received. The application made in it needs no apology. It involves a subject of deep interest to the whole church of God. Viewing it in this light, I feel no reluctance in attempting to comply with your request.

The phrase "Revival of religion" has respect to two sorts of persons:—1. To those who are awakened from a state of spiritual death to a state of spiritual life: and, 2. To those who being thus awakened, are reanimated after seasons of depression, by a renewed and divine unction or impulse. Both these operations are recognised in the sacred scriptures; and both are attributed to the Holy Spirit. Hence those who are born again are said to be born of the Spirit; and times of reviving or refreshing are every where attributed to him as their undoubted author.

This influence of the Spirit is exhibited under various symbols or emblems: For example, under the emblem of the *rain*. Hence it is predicted of Messiah, that "he should come down as rain upon the mown grass, as showers that water the earth."* Under the emblem of *fire*—"He shall baptize you with the Holy Ghost and with fire."† Also under the emblem of the *wind*—"The wind bloweth where it listeth, and thou hearest the sound thereof, but canst not tell whence it cometh, and whither it goeth: so is every one that is born of the Spirit."‡ The movements of this element are, as we know, exceedingly diversified. It sometimes gently breathes upon, and at others moves with tremendous and resistless power over the face of the earth. In both cases, it is unseen: in neither case, unfelt. Its operations are, indeed, every where perceptible, whilst the laws by which it is governed are, in

---

* Ps. lxxii. 6.   † Luke iii. 10.   ‡ John iii. 8.

many respects, deeply mysterious.   The prophet, in his vision of
the valley of dry bones, was commanded to prophesy to the wind.
He did so, and the wonderful result was not merely the symbol of
a political, but also of a spiritual, and even of a physical resurrection at the last day.*

That human experience accords with this scriptural account
of the works of the Spirit, there can be no doubt.   For, 1. We
have almost numberless instances of a resurrection from a death of
sin to a life of righteousness.   2.   There are many examples recorded in scripture of the ebbing and flowing of the tide of spiritual influence : or, in other words, of the communication and comparative
withdrawment of that influence both from individuals and from
churches.   The alternations of hope and fear thereby produced
are strikingly exhibited in the experience of David, of Job, of the
Apostle Paul, of the Asiatic churches, and of many churches both
of Europe and America in our own day.   And are we not authorized to infer that the changes experienced in this respect by individuals, may occur on a larger scale ; that is, in families, churches,
districts of country, and whole nations ?

Now if this view be correct, it is strange that the reality of revivals should be called in question, and especially by those who
read the Bible, are acquainted with church history, or have any
knowledge whatever of the ordinary or extraordinary operations of
the Spirit of God upon the soul.

I have witnessed two revivals during my own ministry.   The
first occurred between the years 1800 and 1805, whilst I was officiating as pastor of the Pine-street church, Philadelphia.   The
second between the years 1807 and 1812, whilst officiating as
pastor of the Rutgers-street church, New-York.   The former
continued more than eighteen months ; the latter three years.
Both occurred under the regular administration of the Word and
Sacraments.   Large additions were made during their continuance to the communion of those churches.   The church in Rutgers-street grew in a few years from somewhere about eighty to
upwards of seven hundred communicating members.   This work
was connected with no extra means, except an additional weekly

* Ezekiel xxxvii.

lecture or prayer meeting. It was attended with no extravagant demonstrations of any description whatever; but with much apparent humility, with Christian affection, and there is reason to believe, also, with much searching of heart, and of the Holy Scriptures. Of those admitted to full communion at that time, few, if any, are known to have apostatized. I do not myself recollect a single instance of apostacy. That which was witnessed in the cases above mentioned, has occurred in various parts of our country.

That revivals of religion are extraordinary operations, is admitted on all hands. That as such they must endure the ordeal of God and man is inevitable. If so, it appears to be desirable that there should be some criterion by which we may form a proper estimate of their character. The only safe rule that has occurred to me in forming such an estimate is the following, viz: That if the means used to obtain them are scriptural, and their fruits wholesome and permanent, we are authorized to conclude that they are of heavenly origin, or, in other words, that they are not the work of man, but of God.

If revivals of religion then, may, and do occur, and are so exceedingly important to the church, is it to be wondered at, if the enemy of God and man should assume the disguise of an angel of light, and should audaciously mimic or counterfeit God's glorious work to answer his own evil purposes?

I can easily conceive of at least four objects to be answered by him in making the attempt, viz:

1. To draw off the attention of Christians from a work in which he is very actively engaged, at the present day—that of suppressing God's truth, or of sowing the tares of false doctrine among the wheat in the churches.

2. To induce a presumptuous reliance on a self-determining will and power to be all, and to do all, that God requires; thus leading men to question their dependence on the Holy Spirit—to usurp his office—eventually to deny his work and influence—and what will inevitably follow, his eternal Godhead.

3. To seduce into all manner of extravagance, that the whole work of revivals may thereby be brought into disrepute. And as

men are prone to vibrate from one extreme to another, the enemy may design also,

4. To open a door for the introduction of all manner of scepticism, or at least, for what is called rational religion, or cold-blooded Socinianism.

From a careful examination of certain views and measures recently adopted in relation to revivals, I am induced to apprehend,

1. That a mere excitement of animal passions, or at most an indefinite conviction of sin, is, in many instances, mistaken for conversion.

2. That the subjects of these exercises are not unfrequently hurried into the communion of the church, before they have had time to acquire, either a competent knowledge of themselves, or of the person, offices and benefits of Christ.

I am aware that apostolical example is offered as a plea for this hurried operation. But it appears to me that the two cases are extremely dissimilar. To mention no other point of difference—the persons who embraced Christianity at that period, did so, in opposition to all their former prejudices and habits, and at the sacrifice of all their worldly comforts and prospects. It is not so at the present day. Unless ministers and ruling elders therefore will run the risk of filling the church with mere nominal professors, at the expense of diminishing its actual strength and purity, they ought to take time to know their converts, or at least to give the converts time to know something of themselves, and of God's truth. In addition to these remarks, I am constrained to add,

3. That some fruits of modern revivals are not precisely such as could be desired. The Apostle asserts in the fifth chapter of his epistle to the Galatians, that " the fruit of the Spirit is love, joy, peace, long suffering, gentleness, goodness, faith, &c." And we know that the marks of Christ's flock are humility, sacred regard to the truth, and a wise and heavenly charity. If then, instead of these fruits, we find in many instances, conceit, self-confidence, presumption, pride, rash judging, and lack of Christian sincerity, is it not requiring too much of us to believe that these fruits grew upon the tree of life? Do they not appear more like the grapes of Sodom and the clusters of Gomorrah? Is it to be wondered at, Reverend Sir, that the cause of revivals, under these circumstan-

ces, should be deeply injured ? I have heard individuals of sound mind, and of undoubted piety, assert, and that recently, that they could no longer read with the same degree of pleasure they once did, the accounts of revivals in our public journals. And why ? Not because they question the reality of revivals in the abstract—nor because they do not consider them as precious—nor because they have ceased to feel a deep interest in them ; but because they are dissatisfied and disgusted with the human machinery employed in them ; and because their confidence in the correctness of these accounts has, for various reasons, been exceedingly diminished.

That the publication of your Lectures on this momentous subject, may do much to maintain and advance the glorious cause of revivals in its purity on the one hand, and to expose and repel a most lamentable abuse of it on the other, is the prayer,

Reverend Sir, of your friend and

Brother in the Lord,

PHILIP MILLEDOLER.

Rev. W. B. Sprague, D. D.

LETTER XIV.

FROM THE REVEREND HENRY DAVIS, D. D.

President of Hamilton college, Clinton, New-York.

Clinton, March 29, 1822.

REVEREND AND DEAR SIR,

I have learned with much pleasure that you have lately preached a course of Lectures on Revivals of religion ; and that the people
of your charge, and many others in your city, have expressed a
desire that they may be presented to the public through the press.

Several gentlemen in this region, whose piety and judgment entitle them to great confidence, had an opportunity of listening to
some of those sermons. From the opinion which they have expressed, I am led to believe that the publication of them would be
highly seasonable, and tend much to subserve the interests of vital
godliness ; and permit me to say that I am fully of the opinion that
they ought not to be withheld from the public.

The design of these discourses, I understand, has been, on the
one hand, to defend revivals against the cavils of their open opposers ; and on the other, to rescue them from the abuses of their
professed, but injudicious friends, and to point out the dangers to
which we are exposed, from the very constitution of our nature,
in seasons of high religious excitement. The subject is always
important—immensely so at a time like this. We are favored
with the unspeakable privilege of witnessing a day of God's power.
The friends of Zion have great cause for humiliation and gratitude :
yet the signs of the times, in some respects, cannot be contemplated
without gloomy forebodings.

We live in an age of peculiar character—marked by a restless
spirit of bold and daring enterprize, and an eagerness for discovery
and invention which is reckless of consequences. There is a prevailing and strong propensity to adopt what is new, because it is
new ; to stop our ears to the voice of experience and the dictates
of common sense, and to turn aside from the *good old paths* in
which our fathers have walked. This spirit affects all our most
important concerns. Even religion itself is not exempt from its

influence. Indeed no one of our interests is so much endangered by it. Never is the adversary more busy than during a high general excitement on the subject of religion. Never are ministers and private Christians more in danger of overlooking the plain and unerring declarations of God's word ; and in their zeal for the salvation of the soul, of acting on the principle that " *If it is only saved, it is no matter by what means it is saved;*" and without resorting to the law and the testimony, of regarding the success of their measures as unquestionable proof of the divine approbation. In this way they cause their good to be evil spoken of, and bring reproach upon the blessed work they are striving to promote.

It is easy to show to a *sober man* the fallacy of such feeling and such reasoning. They will justify the wildest disorder and extravagance—even falsehood and fraud ; and actions which God expressly forbids as crimes of the deepest malignity. They tend directly to destroy the distinction between virtue and vice, truth and error. For they will prove that systems of faith and modes of practice, directly opposed to each other, are all right ; and by implication that they are all wrong. They will condemn the best men that ever lived. Prophets and Apostles are not exempted— for they were not *always* successful. Nay, Christ himself ; for he says, " Who hath believed our report ?"

The history of the great excitement in the time of Davenport, and the state of religion in New-England for the next subsequent half century at least—as well as his own confession, and the heart-rending misgivings of his most zealous associates—are full of warning to the churches in a season like the present. They show us how liable even great and good men are, at such a time, to mistake the wild and ungovernable emotions of the animal nature, for the operation of the Holy Spirit, and to substitute for the commandments of God the inventions of men. We have on record a still higher example for our admonition. " Ye know not what manner of spirit ye are of," said Christ to some of his Apostles, when in their great zeal for doing God service, they were ready to call down fire from heaven for the destruction of his enemies.

That you may be guided by wisdom from above, and experience the blessing of God in all your labors for the advancement of his glory, is the fervent prayer of,

Your friend and brother,

HENRY DAVIS.

Rev. W. B. Sprague, D. D.

LETTER XV.

From the REVEREND NATHAN LORD, D. D.

President of Dartmouth college, Hanover, New-Hampshire.

Dartmouth College, March 12, 1832.

Reverend and Dear Sir,

I have been obliged by ill health to defer my answer to your
favor of the 20th of January last, almost to the very limit which
you set.

You have undertaken a work which I regard as of the highest
importance in reference to the religious interests of our country.
Many are in the habit of representing these interests as being in a
state of unexampled prosperity. I cannot so regard them. The
religious excitement is, indeed, well nigh universal; but I am not
satisfied that it is all safe, and much of it which has been called
the work of God, will not, I fear, long bear that designation.
The sober theology which once was the instrument of salvation,
seems to have given place, in many instances, to a questionable
philosophy; human conceits and systems of measures have been
in higher regard than the simple truths and ordinances of the gospel; large masses of the people have been hurried into excesses of
fanatical delusion; and busy infidelity has taken its advantage to
mislead the simple, and inflame the more grossly wicked against
every form and exhibition of Christianity. Much as I believe that
the spirit of religious freedom, to the rapid increase of which these
evils may be ascribed, will ultimately be regulated and controlled
by the knowledge to which it will give birth, and subserve the
cause of Christian piety to an extent that the world has never yet
known, I still fear that these evils will become yet more prevalent,
and for a time obscure the glory of our Zion. And I have ardently desired that some judicious pen might describe our dangers,
and assert and vindicate the nature, and claims, and evidences of
vital Christianity, the work of the Holy Spirit upon the human
soul, against the mistakes of friends, and the assaults of enemies.

You ask for an account of revivals of religion in this college.
The first President Wheelock, in his " Narratives," writes of fre-

quent instances of general seriousness, and numerous conversions among the students, during his administration. I have not been able, however, to obtain much information in respect to that remote period.

The memory of our present neighbors extends back no farther than 1805, on this subject. Then, apparently in connexion with the accession of a new Professor of Theology, Mr. Shurtliff, and a more direct influence of religious instruction than had been previously used, the minds of the students generally became religiously affected, and about twenty gave evidence of conversion. From that time till 1815, the college was not without more or less apparent divine influence. In that year a scene of wonderful interest occurred. While the college was beginning to be agitated by difficulties between the President and the Trustees, which led to the memorable "question" in the courts, at once, and without a premonition, the Spirit of God evidently descended, and saved the great body of the students. A general and almost instantaneous solemnity prevailed. Almost before Christians became aware of God's presence, and increased their supplications, the impenitent were deeply convicted of sin, and besought instruction of their officers. The chapel, the recitation room, every place of meeting became a scene of weeping, and presently of rejoicing; so that in a few weeks about sixty students were supposed to have become regenerate. A revival of such rapidity and power has been rarely known, and perhaps never one of such unquestionable fruits. Not one of the number of apparent converts, at that time, is known to have forfeited a Christian standing. Most of them are ministers of the gospel, a few are missionaries, and all are using their influence for Christ.

Revivals afterwards occurred in 1819, 1821 and 1826, the latter perhaps more extensive than any other, but not so perfect in its character and results as that of 1815. Within the last eighteen months, also, the college has received divine blessing, and about twenty of our young men have united with the church.

The work of the Holy Spirit in a college is immediately perceptible. A company of young men now moved only by ambition, or the love of pleasure, and presently by convictions of religious truth, present aspects wholly different, and opposite, impossible to be overlooked or mistaken. I have myself seen them, and have been filled with wonder at the great power of God. I would that the unbeliever might witness these different phases, minds ardent, excitable, impatient of dictation and control, beguiled by maxims of false honor, and governed only by the force of laws; and the same minds, the next month, or week, subdued, quiet, obedient, benevolent, yielding to the force of moral obligation, and governed by the simplest intimations of right. Existence itself, it has seemed to me, is not more unquestionable, than the reality of divine influence in such cases.

In regard to these revivals of religion in our college, I think it important to remark, that in every instance they seemed the product of the Spirit's influence, silently affecting different minds with the same truths, and multiplying the trophies of divine mercy. They were an effect, and not a cause of divine interposition; and except as occasionally blemished through human weakness and sinfulness, bore the characteristics of the wisdom that is from above. We have known here nothing, except by report, of the "new measures" for building up the kingdom of Christ. We have no machinery for making converts; and we could allow none to be introduced. We should be afraid to make, or suffer an impression upon the young men under our care, many of whom will be ministers of Jesus Christ, that the gospel can be helped, or the work of the Holy Ghost facilitated by human devices. And I think we shall hold, on this subject, to our general principles, too long settled by the experience of ages, and confirmed by the blessing of God attending the application of them, to be now thrown away in the ardor of questionable excitements, or for the love of innovation, or even to escape the imputation of being the enemies of revivals. When shall the ministers and churches of the Redeemer know effectually their proneness to mar the beautiful simplicity of the gospel, to add something of their own inventions to its sufficient ordinances, to lead instead of following the divine Providence, and to mistake their own dreaming for a heavenly impulse, to inflame the sacrifice with unhallowed fire, and to arrogate that power and that glory which belong to God only? I cannot tell you how much I sometimes fear, when I look abroad upon our country, that Christianity will degenerate in our keeping.

Yet let us hold to the old foundations. There are many yet to maintain the right, and the recovering spirit, we are assured, will accomplish the purposes of divine mercy, will correct and convert the world.

I may add that the past year has been distinguished by revivals of religion throughout New-Hampshire, generally in connexion with protracted meetings, and of a highly interesting character. A great amount of professional influence has been brought into the churches. In a few instances, I suppose, the meetings have not been under the most judicious management, but generally our ministers have been wise. An important convention of ministers has been recently holden at Windsor, for the discussion of protracted meetings, and the discussion will prove immensely advantageous.

With my best wishes in behalf of your undertaking,

I am, Dear Sir, yours sincerely,

N. LORD.

REV. W. B. SPRAGUE, D. D.

LETTER XVI.

FROM THE REVEREND HEMAN HUMPHREY, D. D.

President of the College at Amherst, Massachusetts.

Amherst College, April 10, 1832.

MY DEAR BROTHER,

I am glad to learn that you have consented to the publication of your sermons on the all-important subject of *Revivals;* and in compliance with your request, I send you such brief sketches of what I have myself witnessed, in "times of refreshing from the presence of the Lord," as the extreme pressure of other duties will permit. Although my experience, in this regard, falls far below that of some of my brethren, I desire always to retain a grateful remembrance of what "my eyes have seen and my ears have heard."

While I confine my remarks, chiefly, to the character and fruits of the revivals which have taken place in this college, since I became connected with it, in 1823, I cannot persuade myself wholly to pass over the memorable summer of 1821, in the church of Pittsfield, Mass. which was then under my pastoral care. There had been large additions to the church, in the preceding year, under the blessed effusions of the Holy Spirit; and I did not, I am ashamed to say, expect to " see greater things than these," so soon after the cloud seemed to have passed away. But early in the spring, Mr. Nettleton came, " to rest a while," in my family; which, however, the importunities of the people did not permit him to do: and so far as means were concerned, I have always ascribed it, chiefly, to his earnest and pungent preaching, that the attention of many was soon called up, and that in the course of a few weeks, we were all constrained to exclaim, " What hath God wrought!" It was, indeed, a " year of the right hand of the Most High." Never were such tokens of the presence and power of God seen before in that community. And yet there was very little animal excitement, even at the height of the revival. The sinner would often turn pale and tremble, under the awakening and searching truths of the gospel: but there were no outcries,

either in our public, or more private meetings—no attempts to enlist the passions. The object was, to make the impenitent feel
that they were under a righteous condemnation—that they had
destroyed themselves—that their hearts were entirely alienated
from God—that in this alienation lay their guilt and not their excuse—that, of course, they were bound to repent and become reconciled to God without a moment's delay—that, nevertheless, so
desperate was the depravity of their hearts, that nothing short of
the power of the Holy Ghost would ever subdue it; and that God
was under no obligation to exert that power.

So far as could be known at the time, and so far as the "fruits"
enable us to determine, these and other kindred truths were "the
power of God unto salvation," to multitudes that were ready to
perish. The design was, to exalt God and bring the sinner in
guilty at every step—not to terrify, even the vilest transgressor,
so as to render him incapable of reasoning and reflection; but to
induce him, under the strong convictions of an enlightened conscience, "to flee from the wrath to come, and lay hold on eternal
life." I cannot enter into particulars at all. I wish I could.
Many of them would be highly interesting to every pious mind.
By those who witnessed and felt them, the scenes of that summer
will never be forgotten,

> While life and thought and being last,
> Or immortality endures.

But I hasten to the more immediate object of this communication. It was near the close of the spring term, in 1827, that God
poured out his Spirit for the second time upon Amherst college.
The revival began in the church, as is most commonly the case.
For several weeks there was a manifest increase of concern for
those "who were ready to perish," till there came to be mighty
wrestlings with the Angel of the covenant—such as I believe always prevail. The "noise and shaking among the dry bones"
was sudden, and the work was rapid in its progress. The word of
God was quick and powerful! In many cases, convictions of sin
were extremely pungent. In some, they may be said to have
been overwhelming. But in most instances, they were short.
When the student became convinced that the wrath of God was
justly abiding upon him, he shut himself up with his Bible, and

his stricken heart, under the full persuasion that the crisis of his eternal destiny had come. " Once he was alive without the law," but now "the commandment came, sin revived, and the young pharisee, as well as the publican, died." In a few days about thirty, and among them several who had been very far from the kingdom, and leaders in the broad way, were raised up, as we trust, and made to sit together in heavenly places in Christ Jesus. It was a glorious change—a most delightful spectacle. "These, where had they been?" We saw the rock from whence they were hewn, and the hole of the pit from which they were digged. It was the Lord's doing, and it was marvellous in our eyes.

The next year, 1828, God poured out his Spirit again upon the college, and to a considerable number of the students, "the gospel," as we believe, was "the power of God unto salvation." This work was not so decisively marked in all respects as the former; nor were so many "brought out of darkness into marvellous light," as in the preceding revival. All the leading characteristics, however, were the same. "The fruits of the Spirit were, in both cases, love, joy, peace, long-suffering, gentleness, goodness, faith, meekness, temperance;" and the effects upon the institution were visible and happy.

In the spring of 1831, the divine Saviour once more came to our unworthy seminary, "upon the chariot of salvation." The church had been for some time in a low state, and among the first favorable indications of returning life, there were those deep searchings of heart, which generally precede a powerful work of the Spirit, in the conversion of sinners. Soon the great inquiry was made, by one and another, "What must I do to be saved?" As had been the case in 1827, the work was rapid, and very marked in all its leading features. Fear of punishment there undoubtedly was, in many cases, perhaps in all. But we heard little of this in our most intimate conversations with the awakened. The burden of their complaint was, a hard and stupid heart. They had sinned against a holy God, and in this they were utterly inexcusable. The sentence had gone out against them, and it was just. It was their *immediate* duty to submit themselves to God, and believe on the Lord Jesus Christ. There was extreme guilt and infinite hazard in every moment's delay. All this they would in general ad-

mit, and when they really *felt* it all, they were in most instances
soon brought to the great decision.   Indeed, from a careful observation of some hundreds of cases since I entered the ministry, I
have been led to think, that a sinner rarely remains but a short
period under genuine conviction before he either submits to the
terms of the gospel, or begins to lose his impressions.   A person
may be thoughtful for weeks, and even months.   He may feel a
great deal of distress at times ; he may think, and his friends may
think, that his convictions of sin have been deep and searching for
a long while, when, in fact, he has never seen himself in the
blazing light of God's holy law, and of course has never been prepared to lay hold on the hope set before him in the gospel.

The number of apparent conversions in the revival of which I
am now speaking, was about the same as in 1827 ; and in this,
as well as that, some were almost literally plucked as brands from
the burning.   Such and such young men, we had been ready to
say, will hold out against every threatening and every invitation.
But where was our faith ? " A new song was put into their
mouths, even praise to our God."

I need not tell you, that these "times of refreshing" have been
of inestimable advantage to the college, by raising the standard of
morals, and diffusing a strong religious influence throughout our
whole youthful community.   During the ten years that the institution has now existed, there has been a decided average majority
of professed Christians in the four classes.   In some years more
than two-thirds have been professors. *Two hundred and seventy*
have graduated—*sixty* of them at the last commencement—more
than two hundred of whom are hopefully pious; and about one
half the number of students who have entered college without
piety, since it was established, have, as we trust, found "the pearl
of great price," before completing their academical course.   " It
is the Lord's doing, and marvellous in our eyes."   I ought to
add, in this place, that there was a powerful revival in this seminary, under the presidency of Dr. Moore, and that within a few
months past, several individuals have expressed " hope in Christ,"
though nothing like general inquiry has prevailed.

If you ask me, what means and measures have been most eminently blessed, in the revivals which have fallen under my own

personal observation, in college and elsewhere, I answer,—substantially the same as were "mighty through God, to the pulling down of strong holds" in the Apostolic age—the same as were employed by Edwards, and Bellamy, and Brainard, almost a century ago—the same that have been so remarkably owned of God, under the labors of our beloved brother, now in a foreign land— the same that have been generally adopted by the most successful preachers in New-England, during the last thirty years. "The sword of the Spirit," I need not say, has been the great weapon— nor that "there is none like it." The style of preaching has been direct, earnest and uncompromising. The law has been held up in all its strictness and spirituality. The sinner has been driven from his last refuge, and stripped of all his vain excuses. The entire depravity of his heart, and the utter impossibility of his being saved, without the "washing of regeneration, and renewing of the Holy Ghost," have been clearly pointed out and earnestly insisted on; but in such a way, as to show the rebel, that if he persists in his rebellion and perishes, he is literally a self-destroyer. I might greatly enlarge on this general topic, did my time permit, and were it at all necessary. But the style of revival preaching, in this part of the country, is too well known to need a more particular description.

Meetings for personal conversation, commonly called *inquiry meetings*, have been held weekly, or oftener, and with great spiritual advantage, in all the revivals which have fallen under my notice. The duty of prayer, both secret and social, has been earnestly and daily urged upon Christians; but late meetings have generally been discouraged, as interfering with the religious order of families, and tending, in a short time, to exhaust the physical and mental energies of God's people, as well as to mingle strange fire with that which is kindled from the skies. When met for social prayer, neither ministers nor laymen have indulged themselves in loud and boisterous vociferations, in audible groans, or in smiting the hands together in token of their sincerity and earnestness. They have observed, that the most noisy waters are seldom deepest; and have laid more stress upon "fervency of spirit," than upon strength of lungs, or muscular contortions. With us it has never been customary, either in our larger or smaller religious circles, to pray for sinners, who may happen to be present, by name, or to indulge in equivalent personalities. The general tendency of such a practice, it is thought, would be detrimental to the cause of piety, however different the effect might be in solitary instances. Females have kept silence in all the meetings, except such as were composed exclusively of their own sex.

Calling anxious sinners into the aisles, to be addressed and prayed for, has not been practised, within the circle of my observation; nor have they been requested, before the great congregation, to come forward from every part of the house, and occupy seats vacated for that purpose; and wherever such measures have been adopted, within my knowledge, I believe the cause of revivals has lost more than it has gained by them. It is unsafe to argue from the present effect of any new system, that it is better than the old. It may accomplish more in a week, but not so much in a year. It may bring a greater number of persons into the visible kingdom of Christ, but not so many into his spiritual kingdom. This all will admit is possible.

For myself, every new revival of religion which I am permitted to witness, serves to confirm me in the opinion, that it is safest to walk in "the old paths," and to employ those means and measures which long experience has sanctioned, and in the use of which the churches in this part of the land, have been so greatly enlarged and edified.

With the warmest Christian salutations, I subscribe myself
Your Brother in the Gospel,
H. HUMPHREY.
Rev. W. B. Sprague, D. D.

LETTER XVII.

From the REVEREND JEREMIAH DAY, D. D.

President of Yale college, New-Haven, Connecticut.

Yale College, March 2, 1832.

Reverend and Dear Sir,

An answer to your letter of January 15th, requesting some general account of the religious revivals with which this college has been favored, has been, from time to time, postponed, on account of unforeseen and pressing engagements.

The special presence and influence of the Spirit of God, have been repeatedly manifested in the institution. The means which have been used, in these seasons of deep and solemn interest, the views and feelings which have been expressed, and the results which have followed, correspond so nearly with what has frequently been related of other congregations in New-England, that a very summary account of what has been witnessed here, will probably be deemed sufficient.

The college church was constituted in June 1757. Since that time, there have been several seasons of earnest attention to the great interests of religion, on the part of the students; three of which, at least, were during the administration of President Dwight. The two which were the most general and powerful, were in 1802 and 1831. I find, by consulting the records of the church, that the numbers added to it by profession, from among the undergraduates, were, in 1783, 20; 1802, 58; 1808, 20; 1815, 25; 1821, 31; 1831, 69.

Though these additions to the college church, may give a *comparative* view of the numbers of those who, in different years, professed to devote themselves to the service of Christ; yet they are far from expressing the *whole amount* of converts from among the students. Many have preferred to become connected with churches in places where their parents resided. Others have united with churches of different denominations in New-Haven. The present number of communicants, among the undergraduates, including those who belong to other denominations, is 190.

The *means* which have been used here, in seasons of unusual religious attention, are such as are suggested by a deep conviction of the practical bearing of two essential principles; one, that the conversion of sinners is effected through the instrumentality of *truth*, scriptural truth: the other, that no exhibition of the truth will be effectual, without the special agency of the Holy Spirit. The former of these principles has excited Christians to make earnest and persevering efforts to gain the attention of sinners to the great truths, on a belief of which their salvation depends; such as the depravity of their hearts and lives, the extent and purity of the divine law, the righteous condemnation of those who remain under its curse, the all-sufficient sacrifice of Christ, the freeness of the offers of salvation in his name, the obligation of all immediately to repent, and believe, and obey. These, and other kindred truths, have been presented, not as subjects of speculation, but as affecting realities, involving the eternal welfare or ruin of the soul. They have been pressed on the conscience, in the stated ministrations of the sabbath, in occasional sermons and addresses, in circles composed of those who were deeply solemn, and in affectionate private conversation. The aim has been, by embracing every favorable opportunity of exhibiting and enforcing the truth, to keep the conviction of guilt and of danger, together with the only way of deliverance, so steadily before the mind, that the sinner could find no rest, but in yielding to the claims of the gospel. He has been taught that continuance in unbelief is wholly without excuse, and that no reliance is to be placed upon purposes of future repentance.

While Ministers and Christians have been thus earnest in their exhortations and entreaties, their conviction that all would be in vain, without the influence of the Spirit, has led them to engage in united and fervent supplications for renewing and sanctifying grace. Meetings for this purpose have been multiplied; the church sometimes assembling " with one accord in one place," and at other times meeting in smaller circles, in different parts of the college buildings.

Though meetings for religious instruction, as well as for prayer, have been frequent, yet care has been taken to have them so arranged, as to interfere, as little as possible, with the established order of the institution. The stated literary exercises have rarely been suspended; though the minds of individuals have occasionally been so deeply agitated, as to render it proper, that for a short time, some indulgence should be granted them, with respect to the appointed course of study.

The *fruits* of these revivals have been seen, in the turning of numbers from the dominion of sin, to a life devoted to the service of God. Some who had been open and bold in iniquity, have forsaken their vicious courses with abhorrence, and have joyfully, and with full purpose of heart, consecrated themselves to the interests of the Redeemer's kingdom. Much the greater portion, however, were the sons of pious parents, had received a religious education, and had been accustomed to regard the doctrines and institutions of Christianity with respect. Of those who have here made a public profession of religion, few have been known openly to dishonor the cause to which they engaged to devote their hearts and lives. Numbers have gone forth to bless the churches and our public councils, with their labors and influence; to give instruction to the tribes of the wilderness; and to carry the light of salvation to the isles of the sea, and the idolatrous nations of Asia. Many, and among them the lamented Evarts and Cornelius, have already finished their course with joy, and have gone to receive their reward. It will be left to the disclosures of the future world, to make known to us all the good which has been done, or is yet to be done, by those who have been brought into the kingdom of Christ, by the revivals in this college.

With great regard,
Your friend and servant,
JEREMIAH DAY.

Rev. W. B. Sprague. D. D.

LETTER XVIII.

From the REVEREND ASHBEL GREEN, D. D.
Late President of the College of New-Jersey, Princeton.

Philadelphia, April 10, 1832.

Reverend and Dear Sir,

It was my intention, as I have heretofore informed you, to take a somewhat extended view of the state of religion in our country, in time past, especially with reference to revivals of religion. But this I now find impracticable, in as much as your contemplated publication is, it appears, already in its passage through the press; and the state of my health, and some unavoidable engagements, permit me to devote but a small portion of time to this important service.

Leaving then to yourself, or to your other correspondents, the proper notice of the religious revivals which have occurred in our land at large, I shall confine myself to four points. 1. Revivals of which I have had some personal knowledge. 2. More especially those which have taken place in the college of New-Jersey. 3. Remarks on the best method of conducting revivals, so that under the blessing of God they may be productive of the greatest amount of good. 4. The errors and abuses which are too often witnessed in a time of great and general excitement on the subject of religion—On each of these points I shall endeavor to be brief.

On the first, I must say something negatively—In the second presbyterian church of Philadelphia, to which I sustained the pastoral relation for something more than five and twenty years, there has never been what is usually understood by the phrase "a general revival of religion;" that is, a period when nearly the whole congregation, or a large majority of those who have composed it, have been in a state of serious and deep anxiety in regard to their eternal interests; and this resulting in a large number of hopeful conversions, and great additions to the communicating members of the church. The congregation I served, was originally composed, almost exclusively, of the friends and followers of the celebrated Mr. Whitfield; and the church was, at first, constituted, I think wholly, of converts made under his ministry, and that of his coadjutors, the Tennents, Blairs, and Dr. Finley, afterwards president of the college at Princeton, New-Jersey. The first pastor of this church was the Rev. Gilbert Tennent, whose wonderful success, in a preaching tour which he made through New-England, in the close of the year 1740 and the beginning of 1741, is still pretty correctly known by tradition.* Yet there was never any special revival of religion in the congregation to which he ministered in this city ; and he was its pastor for more than twenty years. He had, first and last, a good many seals of his ministry, but they never appeared in clusters. The immediate successor of Mr. Tennent was the well known Mr. John Murray, who after he fled from Philadelphia, was settled at Newburyport. Under his ministry, as I have been informed, there was, for a short time, something like a partial revival of religion—Probably more were awakened, and more added to the church, in the short period of his ministry, than in any one year of Mr. Tennent's labors in this congregation. To him succeeded my venerable and beloved colleague, the Rev. Dr. James Sproat. His faithful ministrations were blessed to a goodly number, during the five and twenty years of his pastoral relation to this people ; but still, there was no special or general revival of religion. During my incumbency—for about half the time in a collegiate connexion with the Rev. Dr. Janeway—there were some periods, as there were under the ministrations of our predecessors, in which there was a much more lively attention to religion than at others, and in which much larger additions than usual were made to the church. There was one period, extending from the latter part of 1802, to the former part of 1804, when both my colleague and myself had a degree of raised expectation, that we were about to witness a day of God's power, in a general turning to the Lord of the beloved people of our pastoral charge. But in this we were not gra-

---

* In the early part of my ministry in this city, there were still living several members of the church who had belonged to it in the time of Mr. Tennent. One of these, a very pious and intelligent old lady, told me that she once asked Mr. Tennent what was the manner of his preaching which was so singularly and generally successful, in his journey through New-England. She said his answer was—"Madam, there was nothing peculiar in my manner of preaching, in that journey. I was constantly travelling, and had scarcely any time to study or meditate. But I went into the pulpit and preached as well as I could, and God taught the people. I had very little to do with it."

tified ; although a considerable number of hopeful conversions did then take place. The most numerous addition to the communion of the church, in any one year of my ministry, did not I think exceed fifty. Yet there was no year without some additions.

I have witnessed two or three revivals of religion in the place of my nativity—Hanover, Morris county, New-Jersey. The most remarkable one, and the only one I shall particularly notice, was in the year 1790. It commenced and attained its height under the ministry of my father, and he died in the midst of it. My mother wrote to me, to hasten me to my father's death bed; but although I made as much speed as I could, he was dead and buried before I could reach his residence. The state of the congregation was deeply interesting and affecting. About thirty individuals—the gleanings of the harvest—came to converse with me on the state of their souls, in one day. Some of them greatly lamented that they had permitted their pastor to die, without letting him know their anxious feelings, and receiving his counsel—They were kept back by fear and shame. On one occasion, at this time, when I was preaching in the pulpit vacated by the recent death of my father, and making a particular address to the youth of the congregation, recognizing them as my coevals and some of them as my school fellows, they rose, by a kind of sudden and simultaneous impulse, and stood up in every part of the house. This was not a matter of any preconcert, for the occurrence was, I believe, entirely singular, and they certainly did not know that I intended to address them, for my intention was known to no one but myself. Having mentioned this fact, it seems peculiarly proper to observe, that this revival was conducted with a remarkable freedom from ostentation and noise. A minister only nine miles distant, told me, that till he went to attend my father's funeral, he did not know that there was any particular attention to religion in the place. The people had been unusually well indoctrinated and grounded in religious truth ; and hence, when the special influences of the Holy Spirit descended on them, they were not overwhelmed with the confusion and agitation, which the ignorant and uninstructed often manifest when their eyes are first effectually opened on their guilty and undone condition—I find I am running into too much length, and will therefore not add any thing farther under this head, but proceed—

2. To give some account of the revivals of religion which have taken place in the college of New-Jersey. A more extended and particular narrative than I can now give, may be seen in my history of the college, appended to the Baccalaureate discourses, which I published twelve years ago—You are aware, I suppose, that Nassau Hall was founded by the friends and advocates of the great and general revival of religion in the time of Whitfield; and that the favorite object of its founders was, to provide a nursery for the church, or for the education of youth for the gospel ministry. In less than the first twenty years of its existence, it lost by death five presidents—Dickinson, Burr, Edwards, Davies and Finley—all of them ardent friends of revivals. Many of the first students of this institution, being educated professedly for the gospel ministry, were hopefully pious when they entered college; and to cherish and promote practical piety, was ever an object of care and solicitude with the eminently holy men whose names I have mentioned. Nor were their hopes disappointed, or their labors without a rich reward. The first location of the college was at Newark, where it remained for ten years, under the presidency of Mr. Burr, who sustained at the same time the pastoral relation to the presbyterian congregation in that town. During this period, I have not heard of any thing that could be called a religious revival among the students—a large part of them were probably pious when they entered the institution. In 1757 the college was removed to Princeton; the buildings there having been previously prepared for its reception. The following extract of a letter from Dr. Finley, to Mr. Davies then in Virginia, and who had given the Doctor some " good news" of his success in preaching the gospel, both to the white population and the negroes—will give the best account now obtainable, of the first general revival in the college—
" April 16th, 1757—I greatly rejoice that our Lord Jesus has put it in my power to make you a large compensation, for the good news you sent me. God has done great things for us. Our glorious Redeemer poured out his Holy Spirit upon the students of

our college,* not one of all who were present neglected; and they were in number sixty. The whole house, say my correspondents, was a Bochim. Mr. William Tennent, who was on the spot, says, 'He never saw any in that case, who had more clear views of God, themselves and their defects, their impotence and misery, than they had in general; that there never was he believes in any house, more genuine sorrow for sin, and longing after Jesus : that this glorious work was gradual, and spread like the increasing light of the morning; that it was not begun by the ordinary means of preaching, nor promoted by alarming methods; yet so great was their distress, that he judged it improper to use any arguments of terror in public, lest some should sink under the weight : that what makes the gracious visitation more remarkable was, that a little before, some of the youth had given a greater loose to their corruptions, than was ordinary among them ; a spirit of pride and contention prevailing, to the great grief, and even discouragement of the worthy president; [Mr. Burr] that there were no public outcries, but a decorous, silent solemnity; that before he came away, several had received something like the spirit of adoption ; being tenderly affected with the sense of redeeming love, and thereby disposed and determined to endeavor after universal holiness. Mr. Treat and Mr. Gilbert Tennent tell me in theirs, that the concern appeared rational, solid and scriptural; and that in a remarkable degree."

The next account of a general revival of religion in Nassau Hall, I had in a letter addressed to me personally, while I was writing the history of the college, by the late Rev. Dr. John Woodhull, in answer to certain inquiries I had sent to him, in regard to the state of the institution in the time of Dr. Finley. He says—" As to revivals of religion, there were some partial ones in college, [the foregoing account shows, that one at least was more than *partial*] before Dr. Finley's time; but in his time there was something general. It began in 1762 in the Freshman class, to which I then belonged. It was a pretty large class, containing between twenty-five and thirty members. Almost as soon as the session

---

* Both Dr. Finley and Mr. Davies were eventually presidents of the college, but before either of them was so, as was the case when this letter was written, they called the institution " our college." It was so in fact; they and their friends both founded it, and sustained it.

commenced, this class met, once in the week, for prayer. One of the members became deeply impressed; and this affected the whole class—The other classes and the whole college soon became much impressed. Every class became a praying society. Societies were also held by the students, in the town and in the country. I suppose there was not one that belonged to the college, but was affected more or less. There were two members of the senior class who were considered as opposers of the work at first. Yet both of these persons were afterwards preachers of the gospel. The work continued about one year. Fifteen, or about half of my class, was supposed to be pious; and in the college about fifty, or nearly one half of the whole number of students."

Dr. Witherspoon was the successor of Dr. Finley, and entered on his office in August 1768. There was a remarkable revival of religion in the college under his administration; but I am not able to determine accurately the time of its commencement, nor that of its termination. From a collation of some facts and circumstances, I believe that it began in 1770, and that its effects were felt in the college till 1773; but of this revival no printed or written account has ever been seen by me. I have heard much of it; and while I was a professor in the college, before my settlement in Philadelphia, one of the subjects of it, Lewis Fuilleteau Wilson, then a practising physician in Princeton, but afterwards a minister of the gospel of much reputation and esteem in North Carolina, gave me something like a connected narrative of this display of divine power and mercy; although his own case was chiefly the subject of his communication. He was an Englishman by birth, and had his grammar training in the celebrated Westminster school, but was sent to Princeton to complete his education under Doctor Witherspoon. He graduated in 1773; and his statement was in substance this—A very serious attention to religion, he said, began in the college while he was a student, and increased till a large proportion, perhaps a considerable majority, of all the inhabitants of the house, became deeply affected with a concern for their eternal well being. The work, however, had at first some opposers; and among these, my informant represented himself as the most decided and active of all. When he discovered that a meeting for prayer and religious conference was held in a particu-

lar apartment, as was often done, he said that he used to go into
an adjoining room and play on his flute, that he might interrupt
the exercises: and when some of his fellow students endeavored
to talk with him, seriously and tenderly, he not only repelled their
advances, but went and entered a complaint against them to Dr.
Witherspoon. He told the Doctor that he, Wilson, was an Englishman, and an Episcopalian; and that no one had a right to in-
termeddle with him, or with his religion. The Doctor said something to quiet him, and sent him to his room. Shortly after this
occurrence, the Rev. Dr. Spencer, a trustee of the college, delivered a sermon in the prayer hall of the edifice, which Wilson
attended of course; and an impression was now made on his conscience, which he was never able to shake off. After some time of
sore conflict, he obtained a comfortable hope of his reconciliation
with God through Jesus Christ; and when he gave ·me this account, I thought him an eminently humble and fervent Christian.
This individual was one of the dearest and most valued friends of
my early life; and hence I have indulged my feelings in repeating his
statement so particularly. But it serves to shew, better than any
thing else I could say, the nature and extent of the revival which
is now under consideration. I could name a number of men, afterwards of great distinction in our country, who were at this time
very deeply impressed with religious truth; and who for years
were considered as practically pious; and yet, eventually, lost all
serious sense of religion, and probably became infidels in principle.
On the other hand, however, a number—and I believe a larger
number—retained and adorned their religious profession through
their subsequent lives—I have understood that several eminent ministers of the gospel, besides him whom I have particularly mentioned, dated their change of heart and life, from whàt they experienced in the college at this time.

For the long period of full forty years, after what I have just
stated, there was nothing in Nassau Hall that had the appearance, or
the name, of a religious revival. The military spirit that pervaded
our whole land, shortly after what took place as narrated above,
was exceedingly unfriendly to vital piety, among all descriptions
of our citizens. Before the colleges of our country were broken
up, as the most, if not all of them were, in the course of our revo-

lutionary war, military enthusiasm had seized the minds of the students, to such a degree that they could think of little else than warlike operations. The gentleman whose case I have mentioned, was, for a few months, a tutor in the college at Princeton; and he told me that the students formed themselves into a military company, chose their officers, furnished themselves with muskets, learned the manual exercise, and could not be kept from practising their evolutions, even during the hours of study, and in the college edifice. He said that they in fact drove him out of the house; that is, they rendered his situation so unpleasant that he abruptly resigned his tutorship, and went to the study of medicine in Philadelphia. The exercises of the college at Princeton were totally suspended, for more than three years; and the edifice was a barrack, in turn for both the British and American troops; and the interior of it was completely defaced, exhibiting nothing but filth and dilapidation. In the spring of 1782, when I became a member of the institution, about two years after the recommencement of its exercises, the walls of the building were still perforated in a number of places, the effect of the cannon balls which had passed through them, from the artillery of the American army in the battle of Princeton—with a view to drive out of the edifice a British corps that had taken shelter there; and only two of the entries were in a habitable state. While I was a member of college, there were but two professors of religion among the students, and not more than five or six, who scrupled the use of profane language in common conversation, and sometimes it was of a very shocking kind. To the influence of the American war succeeded that of the French revolution, still more pernicious, and I think more general. The open and avowed infidelity of Paine, and of other writers of the same character, produced incalculable injury to religion and morals throughout our whole country; and its effect on the minds of young men who valued themselves on their genius, and were fond of novel speculations, was the greatest of all. Dr. Smith, the president of the college at that time, used to complain grievously and justly, of the mischievous and fatal effects which the prevalent infidelity had on the minds of his pupils. He told me, that one man, who sent his son to the college, stated explicitly in a letter, that not a word was ever to be said to him on the subject of religion—The youth was refused admittance. During Dr. Smith's incumbency, there were perhaps some instances, not known to me, although a trustee of the institution, of young men who became pious while they were students of the college; and there were always a number of religious students on the charitable funds, appropriated by the donors to the education of poor and pious youth for the gospel ministry; and some also who had become pious before they went to college, who there supported themselves on their own funds. But there certainly was nothing that so much as approximated to a revival of religion; and Dr. Smith's infirm state of health, in the latter part of his time as president, disqualified him for all vigorous action, in sustaining the government of the college; and this favored that tendency to dissipation and dissolute morals, which had long prevailed; and which, aided by some other concurring causes, had risen to a most fearful height, when I was called to the presidency in the autumn of 1812.

If ever a man entered on an office with fear and trembling I did so; but yet it was with a firm purpose, that by the help and blessing of God, on which I most sensibly felt my dependence, I would either work a reformation or sink under the attempt; and for a time it seemed very doubtful, which of these events would be realized. In looking over the first address that I made to the students, I find that I concluded it with these sentences—" Could you be engaged to seek effectually the favor of God, and to live habitually in his fear, you would be a law to yourselves; and all our business would be instruction, and all our labor a delight. Then your pursuits would be rightly directed, and while your prospects in this world would be cheering, those beyond it would be rapturous. Earnestly seek, therefore, the knowledge of the true God, and Jesus Christ whom he hath sent, whom to know aright is life eternal. The time has been, when scarcely an individual in this house was inattentive to the concerns of his soul's salvation—It may be so again—Gracious God! let me but behold it, and thy servant will depart in peace, having seen thy salvation."
——Yes, and through the undeserved and boundless goodness of God, I did at last "behold it;" but it was not till after a two years' struggle, and with such difficulties and discouragements as

no worldly recompense would induce me to think for a moment of again encountering ; but for all of which I was infinitely overpaid, when it became literally true, that " scarcely an individual in that house was inattentive to the concerns of his soul's salvation." My first measure, in attempting reformation, was the organizing of a system of religious instruction for the whole institution. It was summarily this—Every student was required to commit accurately to memory, and to recite to his teacher, the catechism of the church or denomination, to which his parents belonged. The Junior class studied and recited Paley's Natural Theology—The Senior class, Paley's Evidences of the Christian Religion : and the whole of the students, indiscriminately, prepared five chapters of the Bible, which were previously pointed out to them, for examination and recitation on the afternoon of the Sabbath. The recitations on Paley's Evidences and on the Bible, were always taken by myself— the other officers of the college heard those on the Catechisms and Natural Theology. This arrangement made it necessary that every student should possess a Bible ; and I was surprized to find that scarcely a student, except the professors of religion, owned a copy. The deficiency was so great, that the stores in the town could not fully supply it, till they obtained a number from the cities. An account of this great and glorious work of divine grace was laid before the trustees of the institution, in a semi-annual report on the state of the college, which I was then in the habit of making. A part of this I shall transcribe, as affording the best statement of facts which I can give—The account, contrary to my expectation, was ordered by the trustees to be made public—" For nearly a year past, (says the report) a very large proportion of the students have attended on all the religious exercises of the college with more than ordinary seriousness. There was nothing more apparent, however, for six weeks after the commencement of the present session, in November 1814, than an increase of their serious attention to the religious duties of college ; an increase both of the degree of seriousness, and of the number of those in whom it was visible. Every religious service, both on secular days and on the Sabbath, was attended with a solemnity that was very impressive. In the second week of January, however, without any unusual occurrence in providence ;—without any alarming event,

without any extraordinary preaching, without any special instruction, or other means that might be supposed peculiarly adapted to
interest the mind, the effect became more apparent; and in about
four weeks there were very few individuals in the college who
were not deeply impressed with a sense of the importance of spiritual and eternal things.   There was scarcely a room—perhaps
not one—which was not a place of earnest secret devotion.   For
a time it seemed as if the whole of our charge was pressing into
the kingdom of God.   This state of things has continued without
much variation to the present time.   Some indeed have become
confirmed in the hopes and habits of evangelical piety; while
others are serious, thoughtful and devout, though perhaps not in
so great a degree as once they had been; and some are losing the
impressions they lately felt.   The result is, that of one hundred
and five students, there are somewhat more than forty, in regard
to whom, so far as the time will permit us to judge, favorable
hopes may be entertained that they are the subjects of renewing
grace.   There are twelve or fifteen more, who still retain such
promising impressions of religion, as to authorize a hope that the
issue may be favorable: and nearly the whole of the remainder
show a great readiness to attend on the social exercises of religion;
not only on those which are stated and customary, but on those
which are occasional, and the attendance on which is entirely voluntary."   Such was the general statement then made.   The
means which had been employed and blessed of God in producing
the revival, were stated to be—" First and chiefly, the study of
the Holy Scriptures, accompanied with comments on the portion
read, and a practical application of the leading truths contained in
it.   God has remarkably honored and blessed his own word——
it has qualified them to hear preaching with advantage, and at
length the revealed truth has, we trust, been powerfully and effectually applied to their consciences, by the Holy Spirit, its author.
* * * * 2. Appropriate addresses have frequently been made;
and the [public] services have been conducted with a special
view to their advantage and religious edification. * * * * 3.
The discipline of the college vigorously and vigilantly maintained,
has preserved the youth generally from those vicious practices and
indulgences, which counteract and destroy all serious impressions.

* * * * 4. The few youths who were previously pious, had, for more than a year, been earnestly engaged in prayer for this event. When they perceived the general and increasing seriousness which has been noticed, several of them made an agreement to speak, privately and tenderly, to their particular friends and acquaintance, on the subject of religion: and what they said was in almost every instance, not only well received, but those with whom they conversed became earnestly engaged in those exercises which, it is hoped, have issued in genuine piety. To promote and cherish this spirit, a short address on the subject of religion was made after prayer on every Saturday evening. In preaching on the Lord's day morning, subjects were selected suited to the existing state of the college; a weekly lecture, intended for the students exclusively, was given by myself, on every Tuesday evening; a prayer meeting was held every Friday evening, at which one of the Theological professors commonly made an address; a prayer meeting was, every evening, held among themselves, at which a large proportion of the whole college attended; smaller and more select associations for prayer were also formed; the individuals whose minds were anxious were, as often as they requested it, carefully conversed and prayed with in private; writings of approved character, on doctrinal and practical religion were recommended; and a short system of questions and counsel* was drawn up by myself, for the use of those who appeared to have entered on a life of practical piety."

Such, my dear Sir, is a summary account of the great revival of religion with which it pleased a gracious and sovereign God to bless the college of New-Jersey, while I presided over it—For a more particular and extended account, if any desire to see it, reference may be had to the pamphlet published by the order of the trustees. I know not by whom this pamphlet was sent to the editor of the Christian Observer in Britain; but nearly the whole of it was republished in that periodical for the month of October 1815, with some remarks of a laudatory kind, and some of a different character. Whether this revival was more general and extensive than some that preceded it, I am not able to determine.

---

* This has since been published as a tract, and widely distributed. When written, I had no expectation that it would go beyond the walls of the college, except as a student might choose to keep a copy for his own use in future.

First and last, but a single individual, as I had good reason to believe, remained without serious impressions of greater or less pungency : but there was one, and he a diligent and orderly student, who declared, as I was well informed, that through the whole he felt no seriousness, or emotion of a religious kind at all. The fruits of this revival were happy and lasting. For although a number lost their impressions, some speedily and some very gradually, yet there are a goodly number now in public life, who are bringing forth the fruits of that renovated nature, which was imparted to them by the gracious Spirit of God, in this revival. I once counted the number of ministers of the gospel whose conversion was believed to have taken place at this time. I forget what the number was, but I remember I thought it greater, than that produced on any similar occasion in Nassau Hall. There were two other periods, during my presidency, at which hopes were excited, that we were on the eve of another general revival. But the favorable appearances passed away, without realizing this hope ; yet not without leaving several monuments of divine grace ; some of them very remarkable. Mr. Ramsey, who has recently gone on a mission to the East Indies, in the employ of the A. B. C. F. Missions, narrated to me, shortly before he left this city, the circumstances of his conversion, at one of the two periods to which I have referred. There have also been favorable appearances, and some instances, apparently of a real change of heart and life, since I left the college. But of these you can obtain better information than I can give, from the present president of the college—There has not, however, been any thing like a general revival. May a gracious God soon grant it !—to an institution consecrated by its founders to the promotion of science in union with piety ; and in behalf of which many fervent prayers, both of the living and the dead, have ascended to the throne of his mercy.

3. My remarks on the best method of conducting revivals, so that under the blessing of God they may be productive of the greatest amount of good, are now to be offered. Of what you may have said in your forthcoming discourses, on this topic, I am not apprized ; but I suppose it probable that either incidentally or directly it has received your attention ; and the statement I have just made in regard to what took place under my presidency in

Nassau Hall, indicates my general views in relation to the conducting of revivals; for what was then done I approved, and nothing that I wished done was omitted; nor has any thing since occurred to change the opinions that I at that time entertained—I then say briefly that in a time of revival, so far am I from thinking that the preaching employed should be merely hortatory, and principally addressed to the feelings, that I am persuaded it ought to be eminently doctrinal. Lively, and tender, and close, and full of application it certainly should be; but the great and fundamental doctrines of the gospel should be brought out clearly—be lucidly explained, and much insisted on. There ought to be a good many of what I would call *discriminating* discourses—in which true religion should be distinguished from every counterfeit, and the danger of embracing and resting on a false hope be fully exhibited. Of what may be denominated, by way of eminence, gospel preaching, there ought to be no lack; that is, the all-sufficiency of the Lord Jesus Christ to save even the chief of sinners, and his readiness to receive them, when they come to him in the exercise of faith and a contrite spirit—his readiness to cleanse them in his atoning blood, to clothe them with his perfect righteousness, to justify them freely, to sanctify them by his Spirit, to adopt them into his family, and to crown them with eternal glory, should be set forth in the most clear and persuasive manner. The true nature of regeneration—of evangelical faith, genuine repentance, and new obedience, should be carefully explained and illustrated—The danger of grieving away the Spirit of grace, by those with whom he is striving, and the danger of all *delay* in accepting the gospel offer, should be often brought into view. The peril to the unawakened and the careless, when others are anxious and pressing into the kingdom of God—the awful peril of passing a season of revival without sharing in its blessed effects, should often be pressed home, on those who remain at ease in their sins—There may be an excess of public or social exercises; for neither an inquiring sinner nor a young convert, should spend so much of his time at public meetings, or more privately with Christian friends, as to leave him very little for serious meditation and prayer by himself. Yet certainly there ought to be many meetings, not only for preaching, but for conference and prayer—some in which

experienced and established Christians should meet with inquirers ;
some in which inquirers and young converts should meet by themselves, or with their pastor and an elder or two of the church, or
other judicious Christians; and some, I think, in which the people of God should come together, chiefly by themselves, to pray
for the continuance and increase of the heavenly influence that has
been shed down around and upon them, and that it may eventuate
in a large ingathering of souls to the fold of Christ—Much, very
much, it should be recollected, is to be hoped for from fervent,
effectual and persevering prayer ; and very little to be expected, if
this be wanting, let other means that are used be whatever they
may.   I am decidedly in favor of protracted meetings, if not *un-
duly* protracted.   I think that we have scriptural examples of
them, in the holy convocations of the old testament, and in the
lengthened attendance of multitudes on the ministry of our blessed
Saviour, as recorded in the Evangelists.   But great care should
be taken to prevent all abuse of these meetings, and to see that
they are conducted with entire sobriety of behavior, and if possible with a pervading and deeply felt solemnity, from the beginning
of them to their termination.   Their happy effect, under the blessing of God, seems to result from their being adapted to keep the
solemn truths of the gospel, and the realities of eternity, before
the view of the mind, long enough to make a deep and lasting impression—an impression not so easily effaced as that which is often made and lost, by the single-day exercises of the sabbath.
They are in fact, only a modification of the protracted sacramental
solemnities, well known in Scotland, and in some parts of our
country and church.   To *anxious seats*, (a strange appellation) in
a promiscuous congregation, on which the awakened and alarmed
are placed by themselves, to be addressed and prayed for separately, and to be gazed at by the whole assembly, I confess I am
not friendly.   I do not deny that they may have been used without injury, perhaps with some advantage, in certain places, and on
particular occasions.   But as a general measure they seem to me
unnecessary, and seriously objectionable.   That the anxious
should be specially addressed and prayed for, I not only admit,
but consider as highly important.   But this can surely be done,
and I think to much greater advantage, after the promiscuous au-

dience has retired, or in what I think still better, a meeting specially appointed for the purpose—Such a meeting I held weekly,
for the students of the college at Princeton, in the revival there of
which I have spoken. But anxious seats in a promiscuous assembly, seem to me far less calculated to ascertain the number and
the individuals who are truly and deeply impressed, than a meeting
to which there is no motive to go, but a deeply felt anxiety of
soul, and desire of relief—There is an ostentation about anxious
seats, in an indiscriminate assemblage, which I am persuaded keeps
some back, who are really laboring in spirit, and brings others
there who feel very little; and the use of these seats has I think
been, in some places, the first step to ulterior proceedings of a very
exceptionable character—There ought to be as much private, individual conversation, between a pastor and those of his charge who
are deeply convinced of their lost estate, and inquiring what they
must do to be saved—as much of this, as his time will admit;
and here in particular he should call the elders of his church to his
aid, and add to it the assistance of some other discreet and judicious Christians. But the conversation of awakened sinners with
persons wanting prudence and experience, although perhaps not
destitute of piety, has often done much harm, and should be guarded against as far as practicable—Books, as well as conversation,
ought to be used, by those whose minds are laboring in spiritual
things—especially when they have reached a state in which they
have hope mingled with fear, in relation to the momentous inquiry whether they have passed from death to life, or not. My
"Questions and Counsel," heretofore mentioned, were prepared
for my pupils at Princeton, when they were conceiving hopes
that they had become new creatures in Christ Jesus. Great care
should be taken to deal faithfully, tenderly and discreetly, with all
who are in this situation. Besides the Bible, the daily and prayerful reading of which should be enjoined on all who are endeavoring to ascertain their religious state, the works of our standard
writers on the subjects of doctrinal and experimental religion,
should be recommended, and as circumstances favor, diligently
perused. I might add other remarks, but I have already exceeded proper bounds, under this particular. I cannot however omit
to say, that during the whole of a revival, the solemn truth, that

true conversion is a work of God, and not of men, ought to be made prominent, in all discourses, both public and private.

4. I am to mention some of the errors and abuses which are too often witnessed, in a time of great and general excitement on the subject of religion. It may seem mysterious, that God should permit a work of his own holy and blessed Spirit to be accompanied, marred and perverted, by errors and abuses. But so it has been from the beginning. It appears from the 14th chapter of the first epistle to the Corinthians, that in the time of the Apostle Paul, there was such an abuse, even of the miraculous gifts of the Holy Ghost, that there was danger that at least the " ignorant and unbelievers" would draw the conclusion—and the Apostle intimates that it would not be an unnatural conclusion—that those who acted in the disorderly and extravagant manner which he describes, were " mad." Alas ! how often, since the time of the Apostles, have religious excitements been permitted to run into wild excesses, even greater and more pernicious than those which he rebuked. Such, it is well known, were witnessed in some parts of our country, in the great revival in the time of Whitfield, though always discountenanced by him, and by all the discreet, pious, and distinguished ministers of the gospel, who co-operated with him. I have before me while I write, a pamphlet on this subject, written and published by the Rev. Jonathan Dickinson, the first president of the college of New-Jersey. The title of the pamphlet is too long for me to insert, but it is headed with the words " A display of God's special grace, in a familiar dialogue." The copy I have, was from a second edition, printed in this city, in 1743, and the whole design of the publication avowedly is, to maintain that what then appeared was " a display of God's special grace ;" and at the same time, to bear a most pointed testimony against all the extravagances and errors by which it was attended ; and they were very much the same, in the substance of them, as have since appeared in our country, and are, at this time, exhibited in certain places. There is a recommendation of this work, called " A prefatory attestation," subscribed in Boston, under the date of August 10th, 1742, by Benjamin Colman, Joseph Sewall, Thomas Prince, John Webb, William Cooper, Thomas Foxcroft, and Joshua Gee. A similar attestation, accompanied the second

edition, and is dated " Philadelphia, June 1st, 1743," and sub-scribed by Gilbert Tennent, William Tennent, Samuel Blair, Richard Treat, Samuel Finley and John Blair. By this publica-tion, the fathers of the Congregational and Presbyterian churches, whose names are attached to it, "being dead yet speak;" and they speak as decidedly against some of the *new measures* now in vogue, as if it had been their immediate object to condemn them. At the time when the excesses, which were witnessed in Kentucky, about thirty years ago began to appear, and which terminated most disastrously to the interests of vital piety, I advised the re-publication and transmission to that region, of numerous copies of Mr. Dickinson's pamphlet. But this was not done ; and indeed before it could be done, those who needed it most, had gone be-yond the reach of all reason or argument. They regarded them-selves as the only truly enlightened men, and the exclusive friends of revivals of religion, and they looked with pity or con-tempt, on all who endeavored to counteract their fanaticism, and regarded and denounced them as cold hearted formalists and wretched hypocrites. You are aware, I presume, of the result of this great religious excitement. There were a considerable num-ber, doubtless, who became truly pious. But Cumberland pres-byterianism, Shakerism, Socinianism and Deism, reaped a large part of the harvest that grew up from the seed which was sown by the exclusive revival men at that time. Kentucky has not yet fully recovered from the injury which was done to her reli-gious interests, at this memorable period. It was followed by an open avowal and general prevalence of infidel principles, with all their mournful consequences, beyond any thing that had previous-ly appeared.

I cannot pretend to enumerate all, nor the half, of the errors broached, and the abuses committed, in the times of religious ex-citement which have occurred in our country. The distinguishing doctrines, and the ecclesiastical order of our church, have, at such periods, always suffered. The doctrines of God's sovereignty, original sin, the entire dependence of the sinner on the special in-fluence of the Holy Spirit in the work of regeneration and con-version, and justification solely by the righteousness of Christ im-puted to the believing penitent, and received by faith alone, have

almost invariably been either denied, or perverted and misrepresent-
ed, in a manner that was equivalent to a denial. The order of our
church has been disregarded—All who chose have become exhorters and leaders in social worship—not, in some places and on
some occasions, to the exclusion of women, even in promiscuous
assemblies. The eldership of the churches, and indeed all church
discipline, and all church judicatures have been disregarded, if they
attempted to restrain or censure the intemperate zeal of those who
considered themselves as more enlightened, and more endowed
with spiritual gifts and graces, than men, however long might have
been their standing in the church, and eminent their piety, previously to the period of excitement. It has even happened that a
minister who has led others into extravagance, has at length found
himself left behind them, and been considered and treated as a
mere formalist, for whose conversion prayer needed to be made,
and has been made accordingly, in the social meetings of his former disciples. I have neither time nor inclination to specify the
almost innumerable acts, of imprudence in speech and action—the
harsh language addressed to individuals, privately and publicly, the
disregard of decorum, and the introduction of novel and ostentatious practices, in the sanctuary itself—which have characterized
the advocates and leaders of new measures, in times of great religious excitement in our country. But there is one measure which
seems to be pre-eminently *new*—for I have not heard of its ever
having been adopted in our church, till very recently—of which
I must take a little particular notice—It is the measure of admitting to the full communion of the church, persons whose supposed conversion has happened but a day or two ; or perhaps but
a few hours, before their admission—persons, too, who had previously manifested no serious regard to religion, and who in some
instances, had been even dissolute and profane. I can scarcely
conceive of a practice more evidently calculated than this, eventually to bring dishonor on religion, by filling the church with unsound professors, who will ultimately become open apostates, or
at best demonstrate that they have never possessed a spark of
vital piety. Who that has ever seen a general awakening of a
congregation to the concerns of the soul, but has had to lament,
that numbers whose exercises, for a time, seemed to be as hopeful,

perhaps even more hopeful, than those of almost any others, eventually lost all their religious impressions, and became as careless as they ever had been, and often far more hard and unimpressible, than in their former unsanctified state ? Now, these individuals who thus lost their impressions, would assuredly have been taken into the communion of the church, if the new measure under consideration had been in use, in the places where these instances have occurred. And what reason have we to believe that sudden and hopeful impressions, and the appearance and profession of having experienced a change of heart, which now occur, will prove more solid and lasting than those of former times? It is admitted, that there may be, and will be, some false professors, after all the care and pains that can be taken to keep them out of the church. But they will be multiplied to an awful and reproachful extent, if some period of probation, and a good deal of sifting and close examination, be not employed to prevent the evil. The plea that is made, in favor of the mischievous practice in question, derived from what was done by the Apostles on the day of Pentecost, is, in my apprehension, of no avail. The cases supposed to be similar, are very unlike. A profession of Christianity, at that time, could not be made, but at the imminent risk of all earthly possessions, and of life itself. Besides, there was, among other extraordinary bestowments at that time, the gift of " discerning of spirits," and I have not heard that the new measure men have, as yet, pretended to this gift. Indeed the whole dispensation of the Holy Spirit, at that period, was extraordinary and miraculous ; and to draw a parallel between the occurrences then, and those which now take place—a parallel extending to all the circumstances of the two cases—seems to me utterly unwarrantable and exceedingly presumptuous.

Numerous are the lamentable consequences of the errors and abuses which arise in times of religious revival—They stop the progress of revivals, as well as prevent the blessed results which might otherwise appear ; they bring revivals themselves into suspicion and reproach. Many think, that if they begin to yield to any serious impressions which they may feel when a revival begins, they will be carried away into all the excesses and delusions of which they have heard so much, and they shake off their seriousness, and harden their hearts against all warnings and exhortations. One of the worst consequences of the errors and abuses contemplated is, that they lead unsanctified men, especially worldly wise men, to think that all vital piety is delusive ; and that some decent regard to religious institutions and observances, with moral conduct, is religion enough, and indeed all the religion which is worthy of the name—Of this consequence of these errors and abuses the examples are multitudinous and most deplorable. New measure men, reproach us with being enemies to revivals, but they are themselves the greatest real enemies to those displays of God's special mercy, that they ever have. Those who openly oppose and blaspheme them are recognised at once as enemies, treated as such, and injure but few beside themselves. But these indiscreet and mistaken men, who claim to be, and are believed to be, the warmest friends to revivals of religion, are *in the camp,* are identified with the cause, and all that they advise and do is considered as belonging to the cause ; and they make it the subject of reproach and aversion to the world at large. Now, if the world is to be converted to God by revivals of religion—which I fully believe, and think must be evident to reflecting minds—those who abuse and pervert revivals, whatever may be their pretensions or intentions, are really opposing the plan and purposes of God. They are therefore to be withstood, with decision and firmness, yet with meekness and prudence. Now and then, an individual of them, like Davenport in the time of Whitfield, and Marshall in Kentucky may come out, and confess and bemoan their errors publicly—as every truly pious man who has been deluded, as they were, ought to do—but the instances of this frank and public acknowledgment of error, are rare ; and if they were not rare, the mischief done, is done irreparably, before those who renounce their error, are brought to bewail and repent of the share which they have had in producing it. We must oppose them, therefore, openly, and without fear or hesitation, and the sooner it is done after their operations have commenced, the better ; for after the delusion has proceeded to a certain length, it becomes like a resistless torrent, which nothing can stop, till it has spent its force. You have therefore, in my judgment, done well, in preaching and publishing discourses intended to have an effect in correcting the errors and abuses to which I have referred ; and on the evening of my ministerial life, I willingly bear my solemn testimony against them, and am glad of an opportunity to record it, as here I do— May the Lord assist and bless you, in all your endeavors to plead his precious cause, and extend his blessed kingdom. So prays your friend and brother in the gospel of our dear and adored Redeemer.

ASHBEL GREEN.

REV. W. B. SPRAGUE. D. D.

LETTER XIX.

From the REVEREND MOSES WADDEL.

Late President of Franklin College, Athens, Georgia.

Willington, South-Carolina, Feb. 25, 1832.

REVEREND AND DEAR SIR,

Your letter of 26th ult. is received, in which you request me to communicate to you some general account of the revivals of religion which have occurred under my observation, or within the sphere of my labors; and also my opinion on some other subjects connected with them.

Shortly after the Revolutionary war ended, during the year 1784, there was a very solemn attention to religion excited in the minds of many persons in the congregation of Concord, where I was born, and in the adjacent churches of Bethany and Fourth-Creek; which were then under the pastoral care of that zealous, indefatigable and faithful Minister of the Gospel, the late Rev. James Hall, D. D. He then resided in Iredell county, North-Carolina, where he also died a few years ago. This revival was brought about by no other means apparently than the divine blessing which attended the evangelical, experimental and practical preaching of the pastor, together with his untiring attention to public catechising and family visitation of the churches under his care. In these two last mentioned duties, he was *in labors more abundant* than any pastor I have ever known. This period was marked with no noise or sensible disorder; but a visible solemnity seemed to pervade the congregations, and a number were added to those churches of such as, I trust, have been and shall be saved. Sacramental occasions, I think, were attended with more reverential solemnity than any I have ever witnessed.

During the years 1788 and 1789, there was a considerable attention to religion in the (then) upper parts of Georgia, including the present counties of Wilkes, Elbert, Oglethorpe, Taliaferro, Hancock and Greene, in which last I then resided. The Baptist churches partook largely of it, by the ministry of the Rev. Silas Mercer and Abraham Marshall. The Methodist churches were much increased by the ministry of the Rev. Hope Hull and others. The Presbyterian churches at that time in Georgia were "few and far between;" yet by the missionary labors of the Rev. Daniel Thatcher, and the occasional and most refreshing visits of the Rev. John Springer, a considerable number was added to the Presbyterian church, and several congregations were organized. In these eventful and important changes, seasons of public worship in our congregations were altogether noiseless, but deeply marked with grave solemnity.

In the year 1802, what has been often called the *great* or *old revival*, commenced in this State, and continued in some degree to appear at some places of public worship until in 1805. This was distinguished from all others I have ever seen in our church, in many respects. It was said to have commenced in Kentucky, and gradually passed on through Tennessee and North-Carolina, into this State. The first time I attended a meeting of this kind was in July 1802, in one of our congregations called Nazareth. This meeting lasted four or five days, and was followed by the appointment of several others in different congregations within the bounds of our Presbytery, all of our ministers being then present. At that meeting many things occurred which I never had before witnessed; such as, persons falling to the ground as suddenly as if they had been pierced through the heart by a bullet or a sword, while a sermon or exhortation was being delivered, which had nothing unusually animated or appropriate in it either as to matter or manner. Some, when falling, would utter a shriek, and lie during hours, still and silent; others would weep and moan mournfully. The numbers who attended this meeting at Nazareth were variously computed by different persons, from five to eight thousand. I inclined to believe the latter more correct. I never have seen so many people collected at a place of worship before or since. This was a *camp-meeting*, and the first I ever saw, although I have witnessed a number since. Some of the following meetings of that kind, though not quite so numerously attended, yet exhibited more instances of persons falling than were exhibited there. I have never dared to say, that the operations of God's Spirit did not produce those, or many of those wonderful effects which were witnessed there and elsewhere on such occasions ; nor would I presume to say that none of those " *bodily exercises*," as they were often called, did ultimately terminate in the saving conversion of the souls of those who were so wonderfully affected ; but I must say, with regret, that a number of those within the bounds of my personal acquaintance, who were prostrate on the ground for several silent hours, did not afterwards give satisfactory evidence of their heart's having been savingly changed.

The revival of religion which came more immediately and fully under my view, was that which took place in the town of Athens and state of Georgia, in the year 1826, at which time I was president of Franklin college. During five years preceding, a few professors of our small church, which had been organized there in 1820, had attended a weekly prayer meeting, and united in imploring the King of Zion to grant us an effusion of his Holy Spirit, and a season of refreshing from his presence. Two young men who had finished their academical studies in the college not long before, sickened and were cut off by death, within one month. As one died in the town and the other in the neighboring part of the country, they were both visited by a number of their fellow students, most of whose minds were deeply affected by the sufferings and the sayings of their dying friends. A more solemn attention to the ministration of the word and ordinances soon became visible, and the solemn concern of many in the college for the salvation of their souls could no longer be concealed. Seriousness became almost universal in the members of the institution, and inhabitants of the town. It commenced in August. In September and October twenty-seven students professed to have obtained a hope of the pardon of their sins, and about the same number of persons who resided in Athens and its vicinity ; all of whom I think attached themselves to some church. The succeeding year continued to be visited with cheering tokens of the Divine presence and blessing, not only in the college and Athens, where the revival commenced, but the attention to religion diffused itself, if I may so speak, to and through all the adjacent counties, and many more remote parts of the State. Its effects were soon felt in the different congregations of which Hopewell Presbytery consists, as well as those in the Baptist and Methodist denominations. During this revival there was no disorder or unusual noise in any of our religious meetings, notwithstanding numbers were known to be under pungent convictions and deep distress of mind.

To genuine revivals of religion every true minister and faithful follower of Jesus Christ must be a friend. The most proper and promising means that man can use to produce and promote a revival, I conceive to be frequent and fervent prayer on the part of ministers, elders and professors in their closets, in the sanctuary, and in social meetings, consisting of smaller numbers of professing Christians. Ministers should insist often and earnestly on the nature and necessity of regeneration founded on the entire depravity of human nature—the absolute necessity of an interest in Christ's righteousness by an humble, appropriating faith, and of the quickening, enlightening and sanctifying operations of the Holy Spirit to work in the soul, both to will and to do, of God's good pleasure. To insist upon and urge these topics upon the attention of his hearers, should be the evangelist's great employment in the pulpit; and afterwards to be undeniably importunate in imploring the blessing of *Him who alone can give the increase,* upon his labors. This blessing should be sought daily in his closet. To converse privately with his hearers on experimental religion is a duty, to the neglect of which the want of ministerial usefulness and success is often attributable. Those pastors who have been most attentive to this duty, as far as my observation has extended, have been the most wise in winning souls to Christ : and what is a revival of religion but a season of gathering souls into the Ark of safety ?

Family visitation is also another most important duty of a minister whose heart's desire is to see the pleasure of the Lord prosper in his hand. On such occasions, personal interviews with the individuals composing the household, I have generally thought to be most useful. A general exhortation to the family, concluding always with social prayer in their behalf, is indispensable. Such visits endear the pastor, and inspire confidence in his ministrations and concern for their spiritual interest.

Prayer for God's blessing on his word and ordinances, and frequent conversation on the experimental exercises of their souls in matters of religion with the members of the congregation and others, when opportunity is afforded, together with such cautions and counsel as may appear necessary, are also duties incumbent on ruling elders who desire to see religion revive among them, and *the pleasure of the Lord to prosper in their hands.*

With respect to the manner of conducting a religious revival after it has pleased God to commence one, I have witnessed various methods, some of a more public, others of a more private nature; but I have observed when I visited and conversed with persons privately who were anxious for their souls, they appeared more unreserved in the statement of the exercises of their minds than when surrounded by a number of others, besides the elders of the church. I have thought that some persons whom I have seen attaching themselves to the church had been too easily and hastily admitted.

May the blissful period speedily arrive, when " the knowledge of the Lord shall cover the earth as the waters fill and cover the sea"—" when the righteousness of Zion shall go forth as brightness, and her salvation as a lamp that burneth," is the prayer, I doubt not, of yourself, and of

Your friend and

Fellow laborer in the Gospel,

MOSES WADDEL.

Rev. W. B. Sprague, D. D.

LETTER XX.

FROM THE REVEREND EDWARD D. GRIFFIN, D. D.

President of Williams College, Williamstown, Massachusetts.

Williams College, Jan. 20, 1832.

REVEREND AND DEAR SIR,

You ask me for some account of the early American revivals in the modern series, particularly those in which I was permitted to take a part, and those which have occurred in this college; together with my views of the proper means of conducting them and of guarding against the dangers incident to their abuse.

Long before the death of Whitefield in 1770, extensive revivals in America had ceased. And except one in Stockbridge and some other parts of Berkshire county, Mas. about the year 1772; and one in the North Quarter of Lyme, Conn. about the year 1780; and one in several towns of Litchfield county, Conn. about the year 1783; I know of none which occurred afterwards till the time of which I am to speak.

About the year 1792 commenced three series of events of sufficient importance to constitute a new era. That year the blood began to flow in Europe, in that contest which, with short intervals, was destined to destroy the "man of sin" and to introduce a happier form of society and the glorious state of the Church. That year was established at Kettering in England, the first in the continuous series of societies which have covered the whole face of the Protestant world and introduced the age of missions and of active benevolence. And that year or the year before began the unbroken series of American revivals. There was a revival in North Yarmouth, Me. in 1791. In the summer of 1792 one appeared in Lee, in the county of Berkshire. The following November, the first that I had the privilege of witnessing showed itself on the borders of East Haddam and Lyme, Conn. which apparently brought to Christ about a hundred souls. Since that time revivals have never ceased. I saw a continued succession of heavenly sprinklings at New Salem, Farmington, Middlebury, and New Hartford, (all in Connecticut,) until, in 1799, I could stand at my door in New

Hartford, Litchfield county, and number fifty or sixty contiguous congregations laid down in one field of divine wonders, and as many more in different parts of New England. By 1802 revivals had spread themselves through most of the western and southern States; and since that time they have been familiar to the whole American people.

I preached my first sermon at New Hartford Oct. 26, 1794. In the fall of 1795 a revival commenced, which in the course of the winter apparently brought about fifty to the knowledge of the truth. The neighbouring towns were not then visited: but in October 1798 a great revival began at West Simsbury on the east, and soon extended to Torringford on the west, and we were left like a parched island in the midst of surrounding floods. The agonies of that hour can never be told. First one, and then two, and afterwards more met me in my study for prayer, and the wrestlings were such as I had never witnessed in a meeting before. On the 4th of November I went to the house of God, saying as I went, " My soul, wait thou only, only, *only* upon God, for my expectation is from him." During the morning service I scarcely looked at the audience, and cared not whether they were asleep or awake, feeling that the question of a revival did not lie between me and them, but was to be settled in heaven. In the afternoon, in alluding to the fact that Jesus of Nazareth was passing by, and we were left, and could hardly hope for another visit so soon, and to the awful prospects of sinners in the middle of life if another revival should not come in twelve or fifteen years, I seemed to take an eternal leave of heads of families out of Christ; I came near falling; I thought I should be obliged to stop; but I was carried through. The next day it was apparent that a revival had commenced; a dozen heads of families of the most respectable class were under conviction; and in the course of the winter and the following year a hundred were hopefully added to the Lord. The last time that I heard that 4th of November referred to at New Hartford, I was told that between forty and fifty of those who had been received to the church, dated back their convictions to that day.

In October 1800 the health of my family and the peremptory advice of physicians compelled me to leave New Hartford. I spent the winter in Orange, New Jersey. A time of refreshment from the presence of the Lord was afforded us, and about fifty were added to the church. In October 1801 I was installed at Newark. A revival commenced the following winter, which continued through 1802 and extended into 1803. In my journal, under date of Feb. 16, 1803, I find a hope expressed that the number of converts amounted to a hundred. The neighbouring ministers were revived, and in the spirit of prayer went forth two and two to visit the congregations, spending a day and holding two meetings in a place, and continuing out six days. These means began to be blest as early as January 1803, and that year about twenty contiguous congregations experienced the mighty power of God.

In the spring of 1807 some seriousness appeared in Newark and a very few obtained hopes; but the impression past off. In the summer some half a dozen Christians were much exercised for a revival, and, as it appeared afterwards, several sinners were nightly carried in their dreams to the judgment seat, who threw off their impressions by day. In the latter part of August a great revival broke out at Elizabethtown on the south and at Orange on the west. The Friday before the first sabbath in September, (which was our communion sabbath,) was observed by the church in Newark as a day of fasting and prayer. On sabbath morning a meeting was held expressly to pray for a blessing on the word that day. Some went with little impression, who found themselves and their brethren lost in that desire, and returned with a strong hope that such a blessing would follow. The next day I found several Christians saying that they never had had such a sense of the truths brought out on the sabbath before. At a meeting in the evening I saw and felt such tokens of the divine presence, that I had no longer a doubt that a revival had begun. It *had* begun with mighty power. In all such seasons, if any feeling had been more prominent than the rest, it was a deep sense of absolute dependance: but never had I had so deep a sense of this before. I could not keep at home; I was constantly going from house to house; and yet I felt that I was doing nothing but holding a torch to the tinder which God had prepared. The work extended to about the same number of congregations as before, and by the same means, the ministers going out two and two as in the former case. In Newark ninety eight joined the church at one time, and about two hundred in all. By this time it was understood why a greater sense of dependance had been granted : the work was to be greater than I had ever seen before.

The first of June 1809, I was removed by the providence of God and by the advice of my brethren, to the Theological Seminary at Andover, and to a connexion with the infant church in Parkstreet, Boston, as a stated preacher. The house in Parkstreet not being finished, and the Rev. Mr. French of Andover dying that summer, I took the pulpit and supplied it till winter for the benefit of the family. It pleased God to pour out his Spirit. A revival of very considerable extent ensued, calculated to fit that atmosphere to be breathed by the sons of the prophets. One of the subjects of the work, an only child, went out afterwards a missionary's wife to India, and the affectionate parents, I have been informed, were heard to say, they never were so happy in their lives.

The church in Parkstreet having become discouraged by several unsuccessful applications for a pastor, I thought it my duty, in the spring of 1811, to devote myself wholly to them. For four years we had a continual sprinkling, but things were not ripe for a heavenly shower. The congregation in Newark having amicably divided, and the second congregation being vacant, they solicited me in the spring of 1815 to return to them. There were circumstances which led me to believe that such was the will of God. I went about the first of June. In December 1816 a powerful revival began in the two congregations, and about the same time in some neighbouring towns, which continued through most of the following year. I have no document to show the numbers that were added to the churches.

In September 1821 I was appointed President of this college ; and the indications of the divine will were so clear that I durst not refuse.

Thus, my dear Sir, I have wandered over the first part of the ground which your partial friendship assigned me, and will now confine myself to the more important history of God's dealings with this institution.

It was from Litchfield county that the spirit of the new era gradually crept upon this college. For near seven years after the charter was obtained, the professors in all the classes amounted only to five; until, in February 1800, two of the members professed religion in Litchfield county, where they had been subjects of one of the revivals of 1799. At the next commencement one of them graduated and another from the same revivals entered. These two were the only professors in the classes, until joined by four more from the revivals of the same county the following spring, which made an important change in the religious character of the college. The next class that entered were nearly half professors, who in their senior year took part in the first revival.

The earliest revival known to this town commenced in the spring of 1805 and continued between two and three years. It soon extended to the college, where five began to hope. In the spring of 1806 a new impulse was given to the work. That spring was made memorable to the college by the admission to its bosom of those distinguished youth, Samuel John Mills and Gordon Hall. Mills had been prepared by the revival at Torringford, Litchfield county, in 1798, 9, and he joined a class which contained such men as James Richards and Robert Chauncey Robbins. He entered into the revival with all his heart; and in the course of the summer eight or ten of that class became subjects of the work, and one or two others, among whom was Gordon Hall, who joined the church in Williamstown that same year. The work seems to have continued beyond the summer; for one account says, "Thirteen were added to the church, of whom nine became ministers of the Gospel. Ten others were supposed to be subjects of the revival." Another account, drawn up in 1827, says, "Besides those who became church members from the classes that graduated in 1805, 6, 7, 8, 9, about seventeen have since become professors of religion."

Mills had devoted himself to the cause of missions from the commencement of his new existence, and by the influence of that revival he was enabled to diffuse his spirit through a choice circle who raised this college to the distinction of being the birth place of American missions. In the spring of 1808 they formed a secret society, to extend their influence to other colleges and to distinguished individuals in different parts of the country. One of them first roused the missionary energies of Pliny Fisk, who afterwards died in Palestine. In the autumn of that year, in a beautiful meadow on the banks of the Hoosack, these young Elijahs prayed into exis-

tence the embryo of American missions.   In the fall of 1809, Mills
and Richards and Robbins carried this society to Andover, where
it roused the first missionary band that went out to India in 1812,
and where it is still exerting a mighty influence on the interests
of the world.   In that band were Gordon Hall and Luther Rice
of this college.   Richards soon followed and laid his bones in India.   Mills and his coadjutors were the means of forming the American Board of Commissioners for Foreign Missions, the American
Bible Society, the United Foreign Missionary Society, and the Af-
rican School under the care of the Synod of New York and New
Jersey; besides all the impetus given to domestic missions, to the
Colonization Society, and to the general cause of benevolence in
both hemispheres.   Such were the fruits of the revivals in Litchfield county and of the first revival in this college.

In January 1812 another revival commenced in town under the
preaching of Samuel Nott, one of the first five missionaries who
went out that year to India.   In April and May it extended to the
college, chiefly to the three lower classes.   Twenty four were hopefully converted then and a number afterwards.   Another account
says, " Twenty one were added to the church, of whom thirteen
have become ministers of the Gospel.   Several others felt the power of this revival, and their lives have since proved that the effects
were not transient."

In June 1815 the first President left the college.   His parting
sermon had a great effect on the students.   A third revival followed.   Fifteen were hopefully renewed in the course of the summer.
Another account says, " Twelve were added to the church, of
whom nine became ministers of the Gospel.   Several others received very salutary impressions, whose lives have since shown
the value of this revival to them."

About the first of March 1824 a fourth revival appeared to commence in the person of William Hervey, now a missionary in India.   Twelve or fourteen used to attend the inquiry meetings.   Several obtained hopes who endured but for a time.   Hervey alone
persevered.   Of the others that were impressed, one obtained a hope
in the summer of 1825, and is now a minister of the Gospel; another joined the church after he graduated, and is now a professor
in the institution.

When college came together in October 1825, the arrows of the Almighty stuck in several hearts. Some old hopes were scattered to the winds. A fifth revival ensued. During the latter part of the term the power was astonishingly great, affecting almost the whole college. Of eighty five students, full seventy thought themselves Christians. The impression was kept up through the spring term, but there it ended. In this revival thirty five experienced hopes, some of which were soon renounced. For aught I know, from twenty five to twenty seven are hoping still, and another who relapsed has apparently been recovered. Twelve or thirteen are in the ministry or looking forward to it. Of these, Hollis Reed went with Hervey to India; two belong to a company of ministers who, in the spirit of missions, have located themselves for life in the new settlements beyond the Mississippi; and two or three others have been pondering on a missionary life.

The sixth revival began about the first of March 1827, and continued till vacation. It spent its chief force on the two lower classes, from which six professed religion.

In October 1828 some seriousness appeared, which continued through that and the next term. Nine visited me under some impressions. Inquiry meetings were set up. One obtained a hope which was soon renounced. Not an individual held out. Three of them however have since given evidence of a saving change.

A seventh revival appeared to commence in November 1829. That month two gave evidence of piety who still continue. High hopes were entertained and a determination was taken to pray till the blessing came. Meetings for prayer, accompanied with considerable excitement, were kept up through the term, and through the long winter vacation, and through the spring term. I attended till broken off by sickness in April 1830. In the course of the winter two more expressed hopes, one at least of which proved doubtful.

On the evening of January 6th, 1831, I was sent for to visit Troy, where the first in the series of protracted meetings in this region had lately been held, and where a great revival had begun. I went on the 8th and returned on the 19th. Something hopeful had begun to appear in town before I left home, and on Friday evening the 21st I went to a meeting to tell the people what I had seen. One of the students, hearing that a statement was to be made, went, and was awakened. The next week we had a four days meeting, beginning with a fast and ending with the communion sabbath. This was the second protracted meeting in the series, and was attended with an evident blessing. A revival began in town. During vacation two of the students obtained hopes here, and two more in Troy. When college came together the 10th of February, it was a time of great solemnity. The month of March was full of power. By the second of April twenty, including those already mentioned, were apparently rejoicing in the truth. Of these, four soon renounced their hope; the other sixteen, for aught I know, still endure, and the greater part appear like devoted Christians.

These are the eight revivals which the pity of heaven has granted to this college in twenty six years, five of which, including two of less extent, have appeared in seven years.*

The means employed in these revivals have been but two,—the clear presentation of divine truth and prayer : nothing to work upon the passions but sober, solemn truth, presented, as far as possible, in its most interesting attitudes, and closely applied to the conscience. The meetings have been still and orderly, with no other signs of emotion in the hearers than the solemn look and the silent tear. We have been anxiously studious to guard against delusive hopes and to expose the windings of a deceitful heart, forbearing all encouragement except what the converts themselves could derive from Christ and the promises, knowing that any reliance on our opinion was drawing comfort from us and not from the Saviour. We have not accustomed them to the bold and unqualified language that such a one *is* converted, but have used a dialect calculated to keep alive a sense of the danger of deception. For a similar

---

* April 18, 1832. There is at the present moment the ninth revival going on in college. On the 18th of January we had a fast in town to pray for such a blessing in the college and congregation. After that I recommended it to the students who staid in vacation, to hold meetings for prayer. The third which they held was on the 1st of February, and I was invited to attend. I found the meeting uncommonly interesting and encouraging. I was then labouring under the commencement of a disease which confined me till near the middle of March. In that interval a protracted meeting was held in town and a revival commenced there, and the spirit of prayer was greatly increased in college and a spirit of inquiry began among the impenitent. The first hopeful conversion in college took place on the 16th of March, two days before I renewed my public labours in the house of God. There are now seven students who venture to hope that they have "passed from death unto life." Every thing is conducted with perfect stillness and decorum.

reason we have kept them back from a profession about three months.

Sinners have been constantly urged to immediate repentance, and every excuse has been taken away. At the same time we have not denied or concealed their dependance for the sake of convincing them of their obligations. On the contrary, we have esteemed it vital to urge that dependance in order to drive them from all reliance on their own strength, and to make them *die* to every hope from themselves. All that you can possibly gain by flattering their independence, is to extort a confession of their *obligations;* for as to matter of fact, they *will not* submit until they are made willing in the day of God's power. And if you can fasten upon them their obligations without that falsehood which robs God of his glory, pray let it be done. This we have found it possible to do. We have shown them that their obligations rest on their faculties, and are as reasonable and as complete as though the thing required was merely to walk across the floor; that their faculties constitute a natural ability, that is, *a full power to love and serve God* IF *their hearts were well disposed,* leaving nothing in the way but a bad heart, for which they are wholly to blame if there is any blame in the universe; that sin can rest no where but in the heart, and that if you drive it beyond the heart you drive it out of existence; that *they alone* create the necessity for God to conquer them, and to decide whether he will conquer them or not; that it is an everlasting blot on creation that God has to speak a second time to induce creatures to love him, much more that he has to constrain them by his conquering power; and yet after all his provisions and invitations,—after he has sent his Son and his Spirit to save them, —after he has opened the door wide and stands with open arms to receive them,—they will still break their way to perdition if his almighty power do not prevent; that by their own fatal obstinacy they are cast entirely upon his will; that they are wholly in his hands,—that if he frown they die, if he smile they live forever. This is the grandest of all means to press them out of themselves, to cast them dead and helpless upon God, to make them *die* that they may be made alive. Conceal their dependance in order to make them feel their obligations! The maddest purpose that ever was conceived, unless the thing required is to be done in their own strength. And then why do you *pray* for the Spirit? " In all thy ways *acknowledge him,* and he shall direct thy paths." But in this greatest of all his works he is chiefly jealous for his honour. He will not hear your prayers for a revival, if, when you go out from his presence, you tell sinners that he has nothing to do in the business but to convict,—that the god which regenerates is light. If there is any truth sweeter than all the rest, it is this, that we are absolutely, totally, and eternally dependant on his sanctifying grace and that he will have all the glory ;—if any view of God more supporting and encouraging than all the rest, it is that which the Christian takes when he feelingly says, " My soul, wait thou only upon God, for my expectation is from him." Take any thing else away, but take not away my God. This is the last truth that I will give up till I yield my reason and my immortal hopes. If there is any truth in defence of which I would go on a crusade,—or, better still, in support of which I would go to the stake,—it is this. If you see this denial shut up heaven, and then, instead of the Holy Ghost, you see revivals carried on by human devices operating on the passions, there is more cause to mourn than to rejoice.

I do not object to all measures to arrest attention, to move moderately the imagination and passions, and to put the whole man into action towards God and his revealed truths. I am no advocate for addressing men as intellectual statues. But there is always some danger in working on this part of the human constitution by other means than truth set in its most affecting light and pressed home upon the conscience, and at no period of existence is the danger so great as at the crisis referred to. The imagination and passions are useful handmaids ; but when they assume dominion, they make a religion of bad proportions if not altogether delusive. This the history of religious enthusiasm shows on every page.

All this is known to the educated in our country ; and if any of them have adopted measures calculated to give undue preponderance to imagination and passion, it has been, for the most part, to answer other purposes of religious policy. Much has been done of late to lead awakened sinners to *commit themselves,* in order to get them over that indecision and fear of man which have kept them back, and to render it impossible for them to return with consistency. For this purpose they are called upon to request public prayers by rising, to come out into the aisle in token of their determination to be for God, to take particular seats, called, in bad English, anxious seats, to come forward and kneel in order to be prayed for, and in very many instances, to *promise* to give themselves to religion at once. For much the same purpose converts are called upon to take particular seats, and thus virtually to make a profession in a day, and are hurried into the church in a few weeks. These measures, while they are intended to commit the actors, are meant also to awaken the attention of others, and to serve as means of general impression. I would not make a man an offender for a word; but when these measures are reduced to a system and constantly repeated,—when, instead of the former dignity of a Christian assembly, it is daily thrown into a rambling state by these well meant maneuvers,—it becomes a solemn question whether they do not give a disproportionate action to imagination and passion, and lead to a reliance on other means than truth and prayer, and on other power than that of God. I have seen enough to convince me that sinners are very apt to place a self righteous dependance on this act of commitment. " I have taken one step, and now I hope God will do something for me," is language which I have heard more than once. Against any *promises*, express or implied, I utterly protest. If they are promises to do any thing short of real submission, they will bring up a feeling that more the sinner is not bound to do: if they are promises to submit, they are made in the sinner's own strength and are presumptuous. The will, which forms resolutions and utters promises, cannot control the heart. Sinners are bound to love God at once, but they are not bound to promise beforehand to do it and rely on their own will to change their heart. This is self-dependance. They are bound to go forth to their work at once, but they are not bound to go alone: it is their privilege and duty to cast themselves instantly on the Holy Ghost and not to take a single step in their own strength. In these extorted promises there is another evil,—the substitution of human authority for the divine. It is right for Christians to urge upon sinners the obligation of immediate submission, and they cannot enforce this too much by the authority of God; but to stand over them and say, "Come, now promise; promise this moment; *do* promise; you *must* promise; promise and I will pray for you, —if you dont I wont;" is overpowering them with human authority and putting it in the room of the divine.

Sometimes these new measures are plainly intended to work on the imagination and passions.   When, in addition to all the rest, a whole assembly are called upon to kneel, what is this but a measure intended merely for *effect*?   No new *truth* is thereby conveyed to the mind.   Truth has to do with reason and conscience, but these tactics with imagination and passion first, and afterwards with a stupid reliance on forms, as the whole history of the Church attests.   Is there no danger that we may again "be corrupted from the simplicity that is in Christ"?   The frequent repetition of these imposing ceremonies will destroy their effect, and leave us with forms instead of feelings.   It was in this way that the primitive Church sunk into all the dead formalities of the church of Rome. The ceremonies were first adopted because they were thought to be impressive.   In time they ceased to impress, and then the magnificent and garnished body of worship was accepted for the soul. This is the certain course of fallen nature.   It is dangerous to work in human inventions upon the forms of our worship.   He who made and united the body and soul, best knows what forms are adapted to our nature.   The more simple they are the less they draw the mind off from God and truth.

God forbid that I should speak against protracted meetings, but I will speak against their abuse.   In this imperfect world it is almost impossible that such a stimulating institution should not be abused.   It is so much easier to enter into the excitements of a protracted meeting than to "tug at the oar of prayer" in secret, or even to exercise a holy heart; it is so much easier to move the people by these impassioned forms than to bring down the Holy Ghost by the struggles of faith; that there is the utmost danger that these meetings will be put in the room of secret prayer and of the Holy Ghost and even of personal religion.   When I see them relied on to produce revivals without previous prayer, and a boast made that Christians were stupid when they began; when I see a revival of ten days produce its hundred converts, and the people, who were stupid before, relapse into the same stupidity at the end of the protracted meeting; I cannot but say, How different are these from the revivals of the last forty years, which were preceded by long agonies of desire and prayer, and which transmitted their spirit to many succeeding months.

There is another difference, I fear, in many cases. In those revivals unwearied pains were taken to lay open the divine character in all its benevolence, holiness, and justice; to present the divine government in all its righteousness and purity, in all its sovereignty and covenant faithfulness, in all its reasonableness and benignity and awful terrour; to lay open the carnal heart, festering with every evil passion, and the horrid nature of sin, with its infinite demerits; to explain the great provision of the atonement and the terms of acceptance with God; to bring out the mercy which melts in the Gospel and to press home the invitation; to show the reasonableness and sincerity of God in all his treatment of sinners, and the unreasonableness of their obstinacy in rejecting the Gospel. All these and many other topics furnished matter always new and always affecting to the conscience. It was all regarded as an exhibition of *God*, in his character, government, and relations to men; and if we could make a clear manifestation of God, we felt a confidence in leaving the issue in the hands of that Spirit whose office work it is to take of the things of God and show them to men. But now I fear that in many instances there is so much reliance on these newly invented means of impression, that the truths of God are but very imperfectly brought out or even studied; dependance being placed on a few topics of exhortation, without the *reasons* which the truths of the universe furnish. The consequence must be that the people will be left in ignorance, with a high susceptibility of irregular excitement, and exactly fitted, should more sober habits return, to fill the ranks of the most extravagant sectaries,—the same that happened in New England some eighty years ago.

I have no fellowship with harsh or violent measures; such as abruptly telling a professor that she has no religion and is going directly to hell, (merely because she is cold;) and when she is horror struck and begs you to pray for her, tearing yourself away and saying, I *wont* pray for you, and breaking out of the room, leaving her in agonies on the floor; all to shake her off from dependance on you, but really endangering her reason and life.

Nor have I any more complacency in public personalities; such as calling people by name in prayer or preaching; holding up certain neighbourhoods as subjects of public prayer on account of their special wickedness or neglects; and worse than all, deliberately labouring to make sinners angry, in order to show them how they hate God and his people and his truth; thus doing evil that good may come.

" Let your women keep silence in the churches," says Paul; " for it is not permitted unto them to speak.—*And if they will learn any thing, let them ask their husbands at home;* for it is a shame for women to speak in the church."* They may not even make public inquiries after truth. " Let the women learn in silence with all subjection; but I suffer not a woman to teach nor to usurp authority over the man, but to be in silence."† The contexts will show that the church referred to was not a judicatory, but a common Christian assembly for instruction and worship; and the reasons assigned for the prohibition apply as much to public *prayers* as to public teaching, and certainly as much as to public *inquiries after truth.* And prayers are public in any assembly of men and women collected for devotion. It is not necessary, to make it public, that the assembly should be in the sanctuary or on the sabbath. The primitive Christians had no sanctuary, and often held those assemblies of which Paul speaks on other days of the week. Wherever the sexes are mixed up in an assembly for social prayer, there the prohibition applies. Nor is this against our mothers and wives and sisters and daughters. They will gain more respect and influence by keeping in the place which nature and nature's God assigned them, than by breaking forth as Amazons into the department of men.

From these excesses two special evils are sure to follow; one among the ignorant, the other among the learned and refined. That among the ignorant is gross, palpable *disorder.* It is impossible that the local scenes of the last six years should have been enacted, and that the events of the last year should have given currency so wide to some of them, without producing among the ignorant outbreaking disorder somewhere. These fruits, I hope, have not yet extensively appeared; but a late scene which has been descri-

---

* I Cor. 14. 34, 35.   † I Tim. 2. 11, 12.

bed to me as "a perfect revel of fanaticism," may serve as an example. Among other excesses, when the awakened were called out into the aisle, some women found themselves converted, and in the midst of a crowded assembly, and with a loud voice, began to pray for their husbands. And this was taken, by men hitherto deemed sober,—perhaps *too* sober,—as proof of the extraordinary descent of the Holy Spirit. Such disorders, and worse than these, will infallibly spread themselves all abroad, if ministers and distinguished members of the Church do not combine in earnest to check present measures. Human nature must cease to be human nature if this is not the result. The other evil referred to is, that these excesses, (I speak not of the *disorders*,) prejudice men of learning and taste against revivals, and arm the influence of society against them. And thus while they throw discredit on the most precious of God's works and obscure his glory where it was chiefly to be shown, they lay stumbling blocks before the blind over which millions will fall into hell. Let the attention of the world be aroused by every hallowed means; let the imagination and passions be wrought upon as far as the most sweet and solemn and awful truths of God can move them; let every knee be pressed to the earth in prayer, and every authorized tongue be strained with entreaties to dying men; let the whole operation be as impressive, as irresistible, as love and truth and eloquence can make it: but O, for the honour of Christ and his Spirit, and in pity to the cultivated millions of our race, let revivals be conducted with order and taste, and shun every thing by which our brethren may be offended or made to fall.

I am, Dear Sir,

With every sentiment of affection,

Your friend and brother.

E. D. GRIFFIN.

Rev. W. B. Sprague, D. D.